This is Our Song

This is Our Song

Women's Hymn-Writing

Janet Wootton

✛ EPWORTH

British Library Cataloguing in Publication data

A catalogue record for this book is available
from the British Library

978 0 7162 0655 2

First published in 2010
by Epworth Press
Methodist Church House
25 Marylebone Road
London NW1 5JR

Typeset by Regent Typesetting, London
Printed and bound in Great Britain by
Lightning Source

Contents

Introduction

I have been involved in singing hymns all my life. As a little child, I objected to singing about 'my small corner'! Later, attending churches without Sunday schools, I learned to love the great wealth of hymnody. It seemed grand, splendid and complete. These were the hymns of the Church, and we sang them.

Then everything changed. The folk revival brought new songs and a new kind of music – not grand, but realistic, challenging. The Fisher-folk visited, and blew our minds again. The Roman Catholic Church exploded with *Celebration Hymnal*. And we sang and sang, in a delirium of variety.

Soon after ordination, I became involved in the compilation of a new hymnbook, the Methodist *Hymns & Psalms*, which at the time had ambitions to be ecumenical. A few years, and a couple of hymnbooks later, Stainer & Bell asked if I would be interested in editing a worship journal, and *Worship Live* was born. I have been editing this, with a wonderful editorial committee, for the last 15 years, and had the privilege of working with established writers, and encouraging new ones.

So this has been a hugely moving book to write. It has been amazing to hold in my hand an eighteenth-century book of Anna Laetitia Barbauld's hymns, with her own manuscript notes on the pages,[1] or a flier relating to a Sunday School Anniversary and Pageant from Manchester in the nineteenth century. I have felt that I have been in the company of the women who wrote the hymns – such a tremendous variety, speaking with so many voices.

I have talked to and corresponded with living writers, who have been my heroes during my own journey of faith. Some of their stories are in this book, as a counterpoint to the last chapter. They are women whom I have admired, some have been friends, others simply names in books until they came to life in conversation.

Others have been at conferences and meetings I have attended, and which have taken on more significance because I have been involved in this enterprise. So it was a pleasure to meet Gracia Grindal and Mary

Louise Bringle at the joint meeting of the Hymn Societies in Poland, just as the book was coming to its conclusion; and to chat to Cynthia Bacon, who edited the new Congregational hymnbook in the USA.

I have been thrilled with the women who agreed to tell their stories in this book. I interviewed Betty Pulkingham over the phone. Her involvement in the leadership of the Fisherfolk in the 1970s brought a fresh style of music and fresh voices to worship. Many of the writers were women, and the music was dramatic and often playful. Shirley Erena Murray, Ruth Duck and Kathy Galloway represent traditions that have explored inclusivity with great joy, and awoken other women's voices.

I enjoyed singing songs from the folk revival by Marian Collihole and Susan Tuck (now Gilmurray) and found their hymn-writing stories fascinating – very different from each other. Sue Gilmurray has recently become a contributor to *Worship Live*, to my delight. Another contributor, but with similarly long experience as a writer, is Cecily Taylor, whose journey of faith and life is reflected in her songs.

Many, of course, have become friends over the years. I have worked with June Boyce-Tillman on a number of projects, and Marjorie Dobson has been a valued member of the *Worship Live* editorial committee almost since its beginning. I was honoured to be asked to write the foreword to Elizabeth Cosnett's collection of hymns – a pleasure, since I have admired her intelligent and creative work for a long time.

I am aware that some voices are missing. There is no Roman Catholic writer. A few years ago, I interviewed Estelle White, a lively and challenging voice in post-Vatican II Catholicism. But despite my efforts, no other writer from this prolific field was forthcoming. All the writers are white, and none was born later than the 1950s. I think that this is a feature of the book's subject matter. Maybe it means that hymns are a white, middle-aged pursuit. But the material itself is varied, lively and fresh, and the writers are amazing, wonderful women in a long tradition of tremendous historical characters.

And yet, over and over again, the story is tragic. Women's writing has been ignored and overlooked for centuries. F. J. E. Raby, whose *Oxford Book of Medieval Latin Verse* contains what he calls 'this vast body of Latin verse . . . which was the product of a thousand years of assiduous composition',[2] missed Hildegard altogether! He and his compilers thought her writing was prose – but then their commentary on the writing of women is generally dismissive. It is only recently, in the work of historians such as Peter Dronke and hymn-writers such as June Boyce-Tillman, that her extraordinarily rich and creative voice has been heard again.

Women have also been torn apart by their sense of a calling to write, when society and the Church have inculturated them with self-loathing, because they are women. Many of the medieval women writers experienced this, and women through the eighteenth and nineteenth centuries have had to find ways of justifying this authoritative and active pursuit.

Ann Douglas poignantly records her own experience in researching the subject matter for her book *The Feminization of American Culture*:

> As I researched and wrote this book, I experienced a confusion which perhaps other women scholars have felt in recent years. I expected to find my fathers and my mothers; instead I discovered my fathers and my sisters. The best of the men had access to solutions, and occasionally inspiring ones, which I appropriate only with the anxiety and effort that attend genuine aspiration. The problems of the women correspond to mine with a frightening accuracy that seems to set us outside the process of history.[3]

I respond to this. I had embarked on a book of women hymn-writers, thinking that it would be a cheering subject. After all, the hymnbooks are full of women – aren't they? Well, nineteenth-century hymnbooks are. This is something that Richard Watson notes in his study on *The English Hymn*. But some kind of an axe falls in the 1950s. Following a period, in the first half of the twentieth century, of almost no new writing by men or women, the men find a new voice, but the women are excluded.

My own moment of realization came as I trawled through the books of the 'hymn explosion' of the 1960s to 1980s. At first I was merely counting texts by living writers. Then it occurred to me that the living writers were mostly male – no, pretty well without exception male. I began to calculate percentages, and to look, in vain, for women writers of the hymn explosion. From between a quarter and, sometimes, a third of texts by women in the nineteenth century, the level of new writing by women dropped to less than 10 per cent, and sometimes less than 1 per cent in the books of the hymn explosion.

For a while I could not bear to open another 1970s hymnbook supplement. Then I began to set my own experience and that of my friends who were hymn-writers in this context. Many of the women writers from the same traditions (liberal or radical) as the hymn explosion writers began to write texts that challenged the patriarchy of worship.

They were finding publication, not in the hymn supplements that were in the hands of those attending worship but in resources arising from women's worship groups or consciously inclusive communities.

This would be another interesting study. I, and one or two of the story-writers in this book, have tried to offer some reasons for the exclusion of women from the hymn explosion. But there is a possibility that ghettoizing women writers encouraged the development of a feminist hymnody. Hymnody on the margins of the Church has always interacted with other social concerns, and it would be interesting to see how far this is the case here.

Women have challenged social mores through the ages. Hildegard suffered mightily because of her battle with her own sense of unworthiness, but dared to confront the church authorities of her day. Vittoria Colonna was energetically involved in the literary and political debates of the sixteenth century. Harriet Martineau was pleased that her family had 'failed' financially, so that she would not have to bow to the requirements of respectability and write in secret.

Martineau and others in the nineteenth century began a more systematic dialogue with the culture of respectability, which confined women to the domestic sphere. They came to see that women could have a public voice, without the need to justify or apologize for the fact. Hymn-writers wrote protest songs and campaigning songs in the causes of emancipation for women. Indeed, for a while, the dual causes of freedom for slaves and the emancipation of women worked together, in a great vision of a free and equal world.

At the same time, women were engaged in trying to save the world by bringing people to Jesus through song. As Europe pursued expansionist policies, bringing vast swathes of the world under colonization or dominion, the churches poured their energies into mission. Many popular hymns were translated into language after language as they took their message into distant lands. Charlotte Elliott's 'Just as I am' had immense influence as it leapt from language to language.

During the writing of this book, I gave a talk on the impact of English-origin hymnody on the development of world Christianity: 'Singing the land strange with the Lord's song'. Because mission was seen as 'civilizing' as well as 'saving', indigenous music and musical instruments were dismissed or condemned as barbaric. This is a fascinating study of its own. It is only now, and only tentatively, that world Christian music is beginning to find its own variety of voices.

At home, women took up the cause of mission, writing some breathtakingly racist and triumphalist hymns! The very youngest children were taught what an inestimable privilege it was to be English and Christian. But there was also some wonderfully inspiring writing in this area.

Children, of course, were also seen as a mission field in their own right. Again, the development of hymns for children is fascinating. Hymn-writers have bullied children, frightened them, blamed them for problems in their families, laid on them the burden of saving the world, and catechized them. Each generation of writers castigates its predecessors for their attitudes to the young. And yet children's hymns, perhaps because of their associations with happy times, are among the best loved.

The influence of hymns and hymn-singing on British, American and, through mission, global culture is only just now being recognized. Because hymnody is popular, rather than classical, literature, it has not been widely studied as a cultural influence. And yet, for two hundred years or so, everyone sang hymns all through their lives.

From the mid-eighteenth to the mid-twentieth century, people would learn hymns in their infancy, grow up with them and sing them at services two or three times a week throughout their lives. It is well known that people with dementia, if they are of a hymn-singing generation, respond to well-loved hymns emotionally and with understanding when other forms of communication have become impossible. The hymns, and the experience of singing them, are deeply embedded in people's minds.

This means that the theology and language of hymns is of incalculable importance. Their concentration on some images of God and parts of Scripture over others creates biases that are very hard to counteract. I have argued elsewhere that hymn-writing has unthinkingly continued the bias of the early creeds against the humanity of Jesus and in favour of his divinity and sovereignty; against the dynamic, prophetic message of Scripture and in favour of a static, unchanging God.

Brian Wren has called this 'KINGAFAP' (King, God, Almighty Father, Protector),[4] and he finds it a dominant voice in the hymns he studies. It has been exciting to discover alternatives to this set of images, to rediscover and sing about other voices in Scripture, and explore female language for God: exciting, but also dangerous. I have been amazed at the violence of some people's responses to singing of God in the feminine, even when the language is drawn from Scripture.

So where does this story go next? Richard Watson gives a very sober estimate of the future of hymn-singing as a form of worship and cultural expression. Music for worship is moving away from congregational singing and towards performance. Publication is no longer in books, with their static contents, but on websites and as downloadable recordings. A suicide bombing or tsunami appears in a hymn text emailed to a group of friends for use within days or hours.

And yet hymn collections are getting bigger and bigger. The first years of the new millennium have seen the publication of 'Complete' and 'Combined' resources, gathering up the mass of material produced in the second half of the twentieth century in something like the way the denomination resources produced in the last part of the nineteenth century did.

Above all, I wonder what will happen to inclusive and feminist hymnody. Most of the big books are from traditions that have no interest in inclusivity of theology of hymnody. Iona, some American resources and the New Zealand Hymn Book Trust, on the other hand, have carried a considered and multi-faceted inclusivity into the mainstream. Maybe this is part of the future too.

Notes

1 John Aikin, *Hymns for Public Worship: selected from various authors and intended as a supplement to Dr. Watts's Psalms*, Warrington, 1772. The copy with MS notes by Barbauld is at the British Library, 1220 f. 39.

2 F. J. E. Raby (ed.), *Oxford Book of Medieval Latin Verse*, Oxford: Clarendon Press, 1959, p. x.

3 Ann Douglas, *The Feminization of American Culture*, New York: Alfred A. Knopf, 1977, 1992 edn, p. 11.

4 Brian Wren, *What Language Shall I Borrow? God-talk in Worship: A Male Response to Feminist Theology*, London: SCM Press, 1989, p. 119.

Part One

Virgins, Visionaries and Heretics

It is quite amazing that the entire corpus of Greek and Latin classical literature (with the exception of the poems of Sappho) is male in authorship. Given its overwhelming and formative influence on Western culture throughout the ages and, through colonization and evangelism, on the rest of the world, this is a shocking and painful fact. When I studied classics (Greats) at a women's college in Oxford in the early 1970s, this imbalance was not mentioned at all. Neither was Sappho studied, or even mentioned, except with a knowing smirk at lesbianism.

This, in turn, is exacerbated by the patriarchal nature of Scripture, the other major influence, which interacts with classical literature so that each strengthens the innate misogyny of the other, and together they prevent the emergence of women's voices in society and literature.

Very little writing of any kind by women survives from the first millennium of the common era. What does, has survived through the agency of male collaborators or hagiographers. Indeed, in such an overwhelmingly male milieu, when women were regarded as carriers of human frailty and evil, having no independent authority or voice, and deprived of access to education, it is amazing that any writing survives at all.

One poignant early text is a diary of the days following her conviction for failing to offer sacrifice to the emperor because of her Christian beliefs and leading up to the point of martyrdom, by a young woman, known to us as Perpetua, martyred in 203 CE in Carthage. It describes her steadfastness in the face of her father's pleading, and the need to care for her infant son. The short diary survives within a hagiography of the martyr by a male author, who assures the reader that he has transmitted it faithfully: 'sicut conscriptum manu sua' ('just as it was written by her own hand').[1]

Other women's names come down to us through their association with male theologians and writers of the so-called 'patristic' age. The post-classical, early Christian era did allow women, particularly wealthy women, some new freedoms. Emperor Constantine made extensive changes to the unpopular Augustan marriage law, which had penalized celibacy and reduced women's control over their lives. Under Constantine, a woman's consent to marriage was, at least technically, required, and unmarried women over the age of 25 had control over their own person and property. This gave women the opportunity to aspire to a consecrated life, both as a way of avoiding the treadmill of marriage and motherhood and as a means of achieving virginity or chastity as a religious ideal.

They were freed to engage in intellectual as well as spiritual pursuits, and they took up the opportunities with enthusiasm, earning the name of 'mad' or 'virile' (that is, manly) souls. Their stories bubble under the surface of patristic literature. Macrina (c. 330–79), the sister of Basil and Gregory of Nyssa, over whom she exercised a considerable influence, remained unmarried and founded a convent and monastery. Gregory wrote her biography, and a dialogue based on her ideas.[2] Marcellina (c. 330–98), the sister of Ambrose, shared in his work and set an example of asceticism and purity.

Jerome worked with and respected women. Paula (347–404), a consecrated widow of noble birth, and her daughter Eustochium (c. 368–419) learned Hebrew so that they could assist with his translation of the Bible. Paula was influenced by Marcella (325–410) who held regular seminars or symposia at her house, and was entrusted with exegetical correspondence in Jerome's name.[3] A work by Methodius, the *Symposium*, describes a meeting between ten virgins, who gathered to discuss the philosophy of virginity, and may well be modelled on the seminars and discussions held by influential consecrated women. Their names are known, but, as Jo Ann McNamara reminds us, 'There were, however, thousands of less spectacular women who lived in their circles and who can only be seen dimly within the community.'[4]

These partnerships between women, who had secured their freedom from married life through consecration, and male clerics were to prove a pattern for the next ten centuries. Even within the freedom of a consecrated life, women were not autonomous. They depended on male sponsorship for their means of living, but, more importantly, had no independent authority to write or teach.

Powerful and talented women had to gain male authorization for the exercise of their abilities. There was no emotional or spiritual framework of independent action for women, though it has recently been recognized that women were not infrequently equal or senior partners in the relationship.

The other factor relevant to this study is that women's involvement in writing often takes the form of poetry, drama or hymnody. Carolyn

Muessig writes: 'Since medieval women were often silenced at the pulpit, perhaps it is from the choir that we will hear the distant echoes of the intelligence and eloquence of women's voices.'[5]

Remember, in comparison with the vast theological outpourings of the major patristic writers, what we have here is a few very tentative forays into publication, a flickering light that struggles to catch our attention in the glare of male authorship.

One such glimmer of light emerges from the friendship of Radegunde (518–87), Agnes (d. 588) and Venantius Fortunatus at Poitiers. Radegunde's early life was caught up in the intrigues of Merovingian court life and royal marriage. She was the daughter of the King of Thuringia (now in central Germany) and was married against her will to Chlothar, a man of extreme violence who had murdered her brother. Like many others, she took refuge in a life of chastity. She founded the double monastery of the Holy Cross at Poitiers, where she became Abbess, and for which she acquired a relic purported to be a fragment of the True Cross.

Her successor as Abbess was her protégée, Agnes, and the two women became friends with Venantius Fortunatus, who moved to be near them in Poitiers. They exchanged written communications in the form of poetry, of which only Fortunatus' side survives. His devotion to the two women is shown in the texts addressed to them, but also in his devotion to the holy cross under their inspiration. An amazing acrostic 35–character word square venerates the cross, and includes the line, 'Crux pia devotas Agnen tege cum Radegunda' ('Sacred cross protect the devoted Agnes and Radegunda') as part of the cross itself, picked out in the middle of the square.[6]

The holy cross also inspired Fortunatus' hymn text, '*Pange, lingua, gloriosi proelium certamini*', in which the influence of Radegunda's devotion to the cross can be seen. The hymn was translated by John Mason Neale as, 'Sing, my tongue, the glorious battle' as part of the revival of Latin and medieval hymns in the nineteenth century. The penultimate verse is pure devotion to the cross itself:

Faithful Cross, above all other,
One and only noble tree,
None in foliage, none in blossom,
None in fruit compares with thee:
Sweet the wood and sweet the iron,
And thy load, how sweet is he.[7]

A collected edition of Fortunatus' writings was produced in the convent soon after his death. Some minor verse by Radegunde is preserved, but not the 'carmina magna' to which the poet refers. Peter Dronke comments: 'It would seem that the two women were self-deprecating and did not think their own efforts worth preserving.'[8]

Removed from the heartlands of European Christian culture, though soon to be embroiled in a struggle between that culture and the Celtic Christianity of northern Britain, the Abbey of Streonæshalch, or Whitby, was under the leadership of Abbess Hild. One of the best-known stories of the Abbey is that of Caedmon, an illiterate herdsman who miraculously sings Christian songs with the power to move and even convert their hearers.

The story is told by Bede, through whom we know of Hild as a nurturer of learning, presiding over a 'nursery' of bishops. But Bede barely mentions Hild in the tale of Caedmon, even though she is, as Clare Lees and Gillian Overing have it,

> the abbess in charge of Caedmon's monastery, the woman who acts as the ultimate arbiter for the veracity of Caedmon's miracle, the woman responsible for advising Caedmon to take monastic vows and for facilitating his continued work as a Christian poet by ordering him to be instructed in the events of sacred history.[9]

This is important, because of Caedmon's place at the beginning of English vernacular poetry. Lees and Overing again:

> There is no better example of the implicitly gendered stance of originary narratives than Bede's silence about Hild. She is granted the status of supporting role in his account, giving centre stage to Caedmon, but contemporary critics have been reluctant to grant her even that. Women have no place at the beginning of English poetry, it would seem.[10]

But there is something else going on here as well. Caedmon's gift is, at the beginning, oral song. As an illiterate, whose voice is miraculously lifted in effective song, he foreshadows many later women singers and poets. What happens to him is that he is co-opted by the establishment. By assisting his development as a poet, Hild implicitly removes him from the spontaneous, oral tradition.

This is a peculiar mirror image of the collaboration between women mystics and poets, and male clerics, in the Middle Ages. Caedmon is the innocent; Hild is the one who authenticates his gift and brings it into the institution. The dynamic between oral and written, and male and female, cuts across later European patterns. By drawing Caedmon into the monastery, Hild makes his poetry available to future generations, but perhaps she also subjects his inspiration to the patriarchal institution.

So far, we have writing and debate by learned women, and hymn texts by male writers, in association with women. No hymns by women survive. However, in the early second millennium, there is a fascinating possibility that the hymn 'Dulcis Jesu Memoria', long attributed to Bernard of Clairvaux, is actually by a woman writer. One manuscript calls it 'Meditatio cuiusdam sanctae Virginis de amore Christi' ('A meditation on the love of Christ by a certain holy virgin'), and it has been accepted since the 1940s that it is of twelfth-century Cistercian origin.[11]

Raby comments that, while the sentiment is very much that of Bernard, his authentic verse is 'of such mediocre quality that it is impossible to conceive of him as being the author of these beautiful verses'.[12] Indeed the text is a passionate and sophisticated poem in praise of Jesus. It was translated by Edward Caswall as 'Jesus, the very thought of thee' and 'O Jesus, King most wonderful', but the English translation misses some of the finer points of the original.

By splitting the end of verse 3, between his verses 3 and 4, Caswall achieves a certain drama:

> Oh hope of every contrite heart,
> Oh joy of all the meek,
> To those who fall how kind thou art!
> How good to those who seek!
>
> But what to those who find? Ah this
> Nor tongue nor pen can show;
> The love of Jesus, what it is,
> None but his loved ones know.

But this destroys the climactic nature of the original verse 3:

> *Jesus spes poenitentibus,*
> *Quam pius es petentibus,*
> *Quam bonus te quaerentibus!*
> *Sed quid invenientibus!*

The verse ends in two exclamations, not a question: 'How good to those who seek you! But what to those who find!'

Caswall also changes the 'direction' of the love expressed later in the verse (translated from a later verse in the Latin). In his text, the love of Jesus is known only by those who experience Jesus' love for them. In *Hymns & Psalms*, this was changed to 'none but his lovers know',[13] trading on the ambiguity of the words 'the love of Jesus', which can mean his love for the singer or the singer's love for him.

In fact it is the latter that the original writer intends. The verse reads:

Nec lingua valet dicere,
Nec littera exprimere:
Expertus potest credere
Quid sit Jesum diligere.[14]

Only by experience can one learn what it is to devote oneself to, or love, Jesus – this is what 'nor tongue nor pen can show'.

What a tragedy that, as far as we know, we have no further verse by this anonymous holy virgin who was such a brilliant poet and hymn-writer!

Heloise and Abelard

Perhaps the most famous male/female collaboration of this period is that of Heloise (1101–64) with Abelard. Initially lovers, they created a powerful intellectual partnership, which benefited from Heloise's breadth of learning and intellectual rigour. Counter to the prevailing view of the time, Abelard clearly had an exceptionally high appreciation of women. He responded to Heloise's requests for a rule for her convent of the Paraclete, and for hymns that would reflect the living faith of her time.

Abelard's prefaces to the three hymnals (Book I, *The Daily Round*; Book II, *Hymns for Feast Days, Proper of Seasons*; Book III, *Hymns for Saints' Days*) give the rationale behind the composition of the new texts. The main impetus is the inadequacy of existing hymns to the liturgical and pastoral needs of the Christian community. It is clear that the difficulties to which the prefaces respond were raised by Heloise in her requests to him.

Although we do not have Heloise's request, her other letters, particularly letter VI, asking for a rule for her convent, adapted to the needs of women, demonstrate a detailed pastoral concern for her own congregation, wide knowledge and reading, a passion for authenticity and integrity, and keen intelligence. Abelard's prefaces respond to precisely the kinds of issues that Heloise is likely to have raised. Indeed the preface to Book I refers explicitly to arguments put forward by her.

They show a very modern-seeming concern for accuracy and authenticity: for example, they complain that the texts of the Psalms do not follow the best translation of the Bible, and their authorship is often uncertain. The texts themselves are confused and unpoetical: 'the inequality of the syllables is frequently so great that they scarcely fit the melody of the song'.[15]

Neither were they fitted to their liturgical or pastoral setting. Some of them require the singers to 'lie, at least about the time of day, as when they sing night hymns during the day or day hymns at night'.[16] This is exacerbated in parish settings, where night prayers are not offered, because of the working patterns of lay people. Other lies are perpetrated in hymns through excessive or bad writing:

> the authors of certain hymns have in some things so exceeded due measure, either through proclaiming absurdities by some compunction of spirit, or through an incautious desire to extol the saints in pious zeal, that we often proclaim some things in these hymns that are against our conscience, being quite foreign, as it were, to the truth.[17]

He quotes, as examples of these, lines such as:

> In weeping prayer and contrite song
> We ask thine intercession, Lord.

Or, of the saints:

> Oft to thy holy tomb they turn for healing
> Lighten the burden of the weak and crippled.

Lastly, there were gaps in the provision of hymns, for example for the feasts of the Innocents, the Evangelists or holy women who were not virgins or martyrs.

It is in the provision for the last of these that Abelard's extraordinarily high view of women shines out. In an age that regarded women as the gateway to hell, he drew on Scripture and tradition to accord them great honour and authority. In his initial response to Heloise's request for a rule for the Convent of the Paraclete, he accords them the status of apostles:

> [Christ] appeared first of all to Mary Magdalene and said to her: 'Go to my brethren and say to them: I ascend unto my father.' From this we infer that these holy women were constituted as if they were female apostles superior to the male ones, since they were sent to the male apostles either by the Lord himself or by angels. These women announced the highest joy of the resurrection, which everybody awaited, so that the male apostles might first learn through women what they should preach thereafter to the whole world.[18]

He draws similar conclusions from the Hebrew Scriptures, the early Church and later tradition. This is borne out in his hymns *in commune sanctarum mulierum* and *in commune virginum* (common, or general hymns relating to holy women/virgins) in the last of the four books. Although he begins from the conventional view that women's sex is lower in nature than men's, and therefore was raised by greater grace,[19] he goes on to make quite extravagant claims:

> *Paradisi*
>   *primus Adam incola*
> *Extra factus,*
>   *fuit intus femina,*
> *Ut et locus*
>   *ipse sit indicio,*
> *Quam excellens*
>   *harum sit creatio,*
>   *Quae de costa*
>   *viri conditae*
>   *Fortes essent*
>   *velut osseae.*
>
> *Haec in multis*
>   *fortitudo irruit,*
> *Cum virorum*
>   *virtus exaruerit,*
> *In exemplo*
>   *perstat iudex Debora*

Et, quae stravit
  Holofernem, vidua
    Sollemnemque
        missam merita
    Septem fratrum
        mater inclita.

Paradise's first inhabitant was man;
He outside and Eve within when life began.
Thus the place itself gives her the primacy,
Marking her creation blest especially.
  What is built from Adam's rib and side
  Has the strength his bone and flesh provide.

Women's strength in many things has greater force
When the bravery of men has run its course.
Deborah as judge held fast in Israel;
Holofernes by a widow's courage fell.
  Seven sons who with their mother died
  Earned for her the church's honest pride.[20]

Heloise also had a reputation as a poet and musician in her own right. In the letter of Peter the Venerable written to her after Abelard's death, in the middle of a long simile comparing her application of secular learning to the gospel, with the flight of the Israelites, bearing the treasures of Egypt, he writes:

> With Miriam you sang a hymn of praise as Pharaoh sank beneath the waves, like her in days of old, you took up the tambourine of blessed mortification, so that your skill with it sent the strain of new harmonies to the very ears of God.[21]

David Wulstan quotes from the twelfth-century writer Hugh Metel, who refers to her 'refurbishing of familiar words in fresh combinations', in a letter written to her. Wulstan expresses his view that 'These were not formal plaudits, but genuine recognition of her learning and her originality as poet and musician.'[22] As with Radegunde, we can only lament that little of that learned and original poetry survives.

Hildegard

Of course, the giant of medieval women's hymn-writing is Hildegard of Bingen (1078–1179). Her extensive corpus of work has been widely rediscovered and translated in recent years, and forms an incredibly important contribution to the writing of this period.

As well as hymns, she wrote sermons and practical treatises, and had enormous influence on the Church of her time. She developed a distinctive voice, which comes partly from a highly original and visionary theology, and partly from her position as a female writer in an overwhelmingly male world.

The internal conflict caused by acting so counter-culturally cannot be overestimated, and can be seen in many women writers of these centuries. They have no cultural authority to publish their works, and urgently need their gift to be accepted under male authority. And they do not have the education to write down their words. While they may not be completely illiterate, they are not fluent in the written Latin that they need for publication, and need to make a partnership with a trusted male writer. This makes them doubly dependent on men.

For Hildegard, this was a long and agonizing journey. She had experienced dramatic visions, but did not feel that she had the authority to write them down and make them public. She describes the devastating effect this repression of her gift had on her personally.

Though she had experienced visions from childhood, Hildegard did not begin to make them public until she heard a divine voice commanding her to 'tell and write' what she saw. By this time, she was abbess of the community in which she had lived since taking the veil in her teens. She describes the devastating effect this repression of her gift had on her personally. Her first reaction was to retreat from the call, and she became very ill. She confided in a sister nun, Richardis von Stade, and in the provost of her convent, Volmar.

> I [Hildegard] was driven by the great burden of my sorrows to manifest openly what I had seen and heard. But I was very afraid and embarrassed to make known what I had hidden for so long ... I intimated these [mysteries] to a certain monk [Volmar] who was my teacher. He was a person of good observance and sincere intention and averse to prying into others' conduct the way many do. Hence, he listened willingly to these miraculous happenings. He was astounded, and he enjoined me to write them down secretly until he could ascertain what and whence they were. Once he understood that they were

from God, he informed his abbot and with great desire he worked on these things with me.[23]

The conjunction of illness, or weakness, and visions is important in women's writing of this kind. Having no inherent authority, women can only operate as direct vessels for God's word. So Hildegard describes the experience of receiving the visions in very dramatic terms. They are accompanied by a divine voice, which dictated the words that she published. She would write the words on wax tablets, which Volmar transcribed, correcting the Latin where appropriate but changing nothing of the substance of the texts.

Barbara Newman describes the illnesses to which Hildegard was prey as 'brought on by the acute conflict between the divine voice and the limitations imposed by her gender and her own anxiety'.[24] Elizabeth Petroff sets this in the general context of female sainthood or power. The basic paradox was that the requirements of womanly virtue and the requirements for sainthood were mutually exclusive. As the 'devil's gateway', women were required to be obedient, submissive and humble. But, in addition to moral goodness, sainthood required 'exceptional heroic powers to transform the world'.[25] She goes on:

> Society told these women that they were not to become spiritual leaders, but divine voices told the women that they must become leaders. And so they did. But it was not easy for them: there is evidence in most saints' lives that women were internally conflicted over their new roles, and that the church was often suspicious of or hostile toward their efforts.[26]

It is impossible to overstate the destructive force of being overwhelmingly called to do and be something that is existentially impossible.

Given this, it is quite extraordinary that Hildegard not only produced such a large corpus of her own writing, but developed a musical style and theological language that was completely unique. Peter Dronke compares it with more conventional Latin Christian verse: 'She establishes in the music a pattern of echo and modification which is beautifully reflected in the thematic development of the poetry: in each pair of versicles, the images and meaning of the second both mirror and carry forward those of the first.'[27] He recognizes some of her work as Sequences, but without the convention of using the same metrical pattern across the length of the Sequence.

I find her poetic style oddly timeless. I have translated some Latin hymns,[28] and the dual discipline of conveying the sense, together with maintaining the metre and rhyme scheme of the original, can feel very restricting. It is hard to do all this and produce poetry that reads well in English. But Hildegard's style is far more instinctive. It follows the range of the meaning in what reads like modern blank verse. It lacks some of the sophistication and skill that gives conventional metric Latin verse its 'clever' feel. But she uses language and imagery with breathtaking creativity.[29]

This vivid use of language and imagery is matched to a quite startling theology, in which many modern authors see a range of parallels with feminist liturgy and theology in our own time. As with modern (or postmodern) feminism, this can be seen as a means of validating or supporting her own experience as a woman writer in a patriarchal society. In the twentieth and twenty-first centuries, women writers have delighted in rediscovering female language for God in the Bible, and remaking connections with women in biblical narratives.[30]

Hildegard does this in two ways, familiar to feminist writers still. She highlights female aspects of divinity: Sapientia, or Wisdom, and Caritas, divine love, as the third person of the Trinity. Both are involved in creating and sustaining the richness of the natural world, which she describes in holistic terms, quite at odds with the dualistic views of her time.

Her Antiphon for Caritas sees this powerful cosmic presence as the divine consort of the High King, offering him the kiss of peace. The short hymn carries one continuous movement through the whole of creation, culminating in the kiss:

Karitas
habundat in omnia,
de imis excellentissima
super sidera
atque amantissima
in omnia,
quia summo regi osculum pacis
dedit.[31]

Love
reaches out in abundance to all things,
most wonderful, from the abyss
beyond the stars
and most loving
towards all things,

because she has given to the High King
the kiss of peace.[32]

Similarly, Sapientia encompasses the whole of creation, in this surreal
and exhilarating verse:

O virtus Sapientie,
que circuiens circuisti,
comprehendendo omnia
in una via que habet vitam,
tres alas habens,
quarum una in altum volat
et altera de terra sudat
et tercia undique volat.
Laus tibi sit, sicut te decet,
o Sapientia.[33]

O power of Wisdom,
which circles and circles,
encompassing all things
in one way which holds life,
having three wings,
of which one soars to the heights,
one brings moisture to the earth
and the third flies through all things.
Praise to you, as is your due,
O Wisdom.

It is clear from these two short verses that not only is Hildegard using
female images for God, but her view of the created universe is holistic,
not dualistic. The power and love of God permeate the whole universe,
from the depths to the heights, and including the moist, living earth.
The green world is not separate or apart from God, but embraced and
swept by divine being.

Greenness or freshness, *viriditas*, is right at the heart of her writing.
No other writer uses the word in quite this way. It describes the lush-
ness of the living world, but also the quality of Paradise, the garden. Sin
is not giving in to the delights of this world (except for sexual delights,
which she does regard as sinful) but spoiling its freshness, corrupting
God's creation.

The hymns to Mary frequently contrast the redemption won through her with the sin of Eve, seen, as in tradition, as the one who brought catastrophe to the world.

> *O splendidissima gemma*
> *et serenum decus solis*
> *qui tibi infusus est,*
> *fons saliens*
> *de corde Patris,*
> *quod est unicum Verbum suum,*
> *per quod creavit*
> *mundi primam materiam,*
> *quam Eva turbavit.*[34]

> O most splendid jewel
> and serene glory of the sun
> which is poured into your being,
> a spring leaping
> from the heart of the Father,
> which is his unique Word,
> through which he created
> the primordial matter of the world,
> which Eve threw into chaos.

Eve's sin was to corrupt or destroy the whole fabric of creation. In contrast, Mary is as interwoven with the cosmos and creation as are the divine figures of Sapientia and Caritas. She is *viridissima virga*, the greenest branch, from which blossom and fragrant flowers burst forth. The birth of the Saviour is described as re-creation of Paradise:

> *Nam in te floruit pulcher flos*
> *qui odorem dedit*
> *omnibus aromatibus*
> *qui arida erant.*

> *Et illa apparuerant omnia*
> *in viriditate plena.*

> *Unde celi dederunt rorem super gramen*
> *et omnis terra leta facta est,*
> *quoniam viscera ipsius frumentum protulerunt*
> *et quoniam volucres celi*
> *nidos in ipsa habuerunt.*[35]

For in you the beautiful flower blossomed,
which gave fragrance
to all the spices
which had become dry.

And they all appeared
in lush greenness.

So the sky gave dew to the grass,
and all the earth was filled with delight,
because your womb brought forth wheat
and because the birds of the air
made their nests in it.

Fragrance, fruitfulness and greenness return to the dry, barren earth through the fecund womb of the Virgin Mary.

This sense of the earth's joy and delight is often expressed in terms of music. In a beautiful song put into the mouth of the Virgin, she praises her divine Son:

O Fili dilectissime,
quem genui in visceribus meis
de vi circueuntis rote
sancte divinitatis,
que me creavit
et omnia membra mea ordinavit
et in visceribus meis
omne genus musicorum
in omnibus floribus tonorum
constituit.[36]

O most prized Son
whom I bore in my womb
by the force of the circling wheel
of holy divinity,
which created me
and set all the parts of my body in order
and laid in my womb
every kind of music
in all flowering of tone.

The story of the silencing of Hildegard's music is well known. Towards the end of her long career, she allowed the burial of a former excommunicate in the cemetery of her convent. She was ordered to exhume the body for burial in unconsecrated ground, but refused. The punishment was to prevent her and her sisters from singing – a very harsh punishment indeed.

In her letter to the Mainz prelates, protesting at her treatment, she works out a philosophy of music. Drawing from the experience of reading the divine office instead of singing, she meditates on Psalm 150 with its reference to musical praise. She refers this to the music that Adam knew before the fall. Although this music was lost on the expulsion from Paradise, prophets and musicians have grasped at its memory with song and instrumental music.

Music has the capacity to transform and shape the inner being, as the words of the songs help to shape the mind (*convertere et informare*). She calls the soul 'symphonic' (*symphonialis*), so that it naturally responds to the complexities and delights of music.

Satan is therefore implacably inimical to human praise in music, which has the power to remind the singers of the joys of Paradise, and bring about transformation ('*homo ex inspiratione dei cantare cepisset, et per hoc ad recolendam suavitatem canticorum celestis patrie mutaretur*'). The prelates should beware any move to silence the praises of God![37]

Just before she died, the Archbishop of Mainz lifted the ban on music in the convent, and Hildegard and her sisters were free to lift their voices again in the rich and vivid hymns of their founder.

Experiments in spirituality

The twelfth and thirteenth centuries saw a rise in experiments in spirituality, as lay people and clerics sought to live sanctified lives. For women in Northern Europe, the movement took the shape of free communities or beguinages. At first (as with earlier women's religious movements), this was unorganized and spontaneous. Individual women would commit themselves to a life of chastity and holiness. Towards the end of the thirteenth century, they began to gather into communities, with a recognized leadership.

Jacques de Vitry, an influential preacher, and other male clerics recognized the integrity of the women and supported them in their own writing. De Vitry specifically associates the purity of virginity with the divine gift of song:

Virgines enim cantant canticum quod nullus alius cantare potest: hoc est singulare gaudium de conformitate quam habunt cum Christo. [38]

For virgins sing a song that no one else can sing: this is the unique joy they have through their conformity with Christ.

Et cantare canticum novum quod nullus aliter cantare potest, quod est incomparabile gaudium cordis de similitudine expressa quam habunt cum Christo et Matre eius, et insuper cum angelis sanctis. [39]

And they can sing a new song that no one can otherwise sing, which is the incomparable heartfelt joy, through the likeness they have with Christ and his Mother, and above with the holy angels.

He published a life of Marie d'Oignies (d. 1213), who sang spontaneous verse of great biblical and theological depth in her native French. Carolyn Muessig writes:

Jacques suggests that she sang about refined theories, such as how angels receive their understanding, the glorified body of the Virgin, and issues related to the resurrection of the human body. Although Jacques makes it clear that Marie did not preach, he portrays her without hesitation as singing aloud about the Trinity, the humanity of Christ, and other theological issues. [40]

Another ecstatic singer, Christina of Saint Trond (d. 1224), sang without words, but in an ecstatic voice that came from somewhere deep in her chest. It was so inspiring that her sisters, when they heard it, burst out in singing the Te Deum Laudamus. Lutgard of Aywières (d. 1246) describes her own experience of ecstatic singing as Christ placing his mouth over hers and sucking the music out of her. [41]

Elizabeth Petroff suggests that the male scribes and biographers of these women recognized a genuine spiritual movement, and that they 'investigated this new movement, and carefully summarized it in traditional terms which emphasize the importance of visionary activity'. [42] There was certainly what Peter Dronke calls 'an astounding proliferation of writings by religious women', [43] in the 120 years following Hildegard's death.

However, there is also a danger that the biographers collude with the writers themselves in denying the inner authority of women to write, by highlighting visionary experience. They identify the writing as out of the ordinary, justified only by the overpowering inspiration of God. This is exemplified in the life of the Beguine, Mechthild of Magdeburg (c. 1207–c. 1282). She claims a divine call to write, confirmed by her Dominican confessor, who authorized her visions and revelations and told her to write:

> Then he instructed me to do what often gives me cause to weep for shame, for I am acutely aware of my own unworthiness, that is he ordered a pitiful woman to write this book out of the heart and mouth of God. Thus this book has come lovingly from God and is not drawn from human senses.[44]

So authorized, Mechthild wrote her 'book', which is how she refers to it, a collection of writings called *Das fliessende Licht der Gottheit* (*The Flowing Light of the Godhead*). She refers continually to her unworthiness and lack of education, but, as with other women writers, it is her lack of formal qualifications that opens her directly to the inspiration of God. She reports God's words to her:

> it is a great honour to me and strengthens holy Christianity considerably that the untutored mouth, inspired by the Holy Spirit, instructs the learned tongue.[45]

Book II of *The Flowing Light of the Godhead* is filled with songs of love, and a continuing dialogue between God and the soul, in a constant interplay between prose and poetry. One exchange consists of 'A song of the Soul to God about five things', to which God's response is to sing 'of five things to the soul'.

> You light up my soul
> As the sun does gold.
> When I rest in you, Lord,
> This is many-splendoured delight.
> You wear my soul like a garment,
> And you are like the clothes next to her skin.
> That parting must come –
> Ah – there can be no greater heartache for me.
> If you were to love me more
> Then I would certainly leave here
> To find the place
> Where I could love you with all my heart.

I have sung to you,
But I have not reached there yet.
If you sing to me
Then I would reach that point.

God responds:

When I shine, you must light up.
When I pour out, you must be filled.
When you sigh, you breath my divine heart into yourself.
When you weep for me, I take you into my arms.
But when you love, we two are one.
And when we two are one, there is no more parting,
But a delightful anticipation
Between us.

And the soul returns the song with a passionate image of absorption and unity:

Lord, I anticipate, with hunger and thirst,
With the zest of the hunt, and with desire,
That moment of joy
When from your divine mouth
The choice words pour out,
Which can be heard by none
But only the soul
That takes off the clothing of the earth,
Puts her ear close to your mouth,
And, yes! – discovers love.[46]

Towards the end of her life, Mechthild left the beguinage and entered the convent at Helfta. This may have been due to the vulnerability of Beguine communities and growing hostility against them, or simply that her health was failing with advancing age, and she sought a more secure and supportive environment.

The biography of Umiltà of Faenza (d. 1310), a preacher and hymn-writer, was written about twenty years after her death. Her biographer also justifies her public preaching and writing by reference to the vision-ary nature of her inspiration. Petroff comments:

What we can see in her, and what her contemporaries obviously intuited, is exactly what her biographer wishes to avoid seeing: a strong woman who had independent ideas, who broke rules and violated taboos, who took responsibility for herself and others very effectively.[47]

This, of course, echoes Umiltà's self-awareness. Like other women writers of her time, she has internalized the Church's hostility to woman, and so she writes:

> I am amazed and fearful and ashamed [*Miror & timeo atque rubesco*] concerning these things, which I dare to write and dictate, for I have not read them in other books, nor have I ever applied myself to learning human knowledge; but only the Spirit of God has spoken in me, who fills my mouth with the words that I ought to speak . . . Beware therefore lest you receive in emptiness these words which my tongue brings forth, moved by the Holy Spirit . . . I go to the Lord, that he may order me to do this work; and at once the spirit of my Lord Jesus teaches me. Then and always I am secure in all things, that I do not speak as one ignorant: but I understand whatever I see, and I am fully instructed concerning that which I think.[48]

She claims nothing on her own authority, but on the basis of her divine inspiration she makes a very powerful claim on her listeners, that they attend to her words as the words of Jesus himself, revealed under the inspiration of the Holy Spirit.

This is true not only of her sermons, but also of her hymns in praise of the Virgin Mary, composed after the Virgin appeared to her in a vision and commanded her to wrap the infant Jesus in a three-coloured robe, interwoven with gems. When the saint protested that she did not have the materials to do this, the Virgin said that the garment should be woven from spiritual riches, such as, 'the expansion of the heart, the humility of spirit, the burning love in the soul, the inexpressible sweetness of adoration . . .'.[49]

The resulting hymns of praise were published in a tractate, and sung by the nuns of Saint Salvio, and by other visitors to the monastery, where they are said to have worked miracles of healing and restoration.

Umiltà describes the method of their transmission:

> these hymns are not taken from any book, nor received from any human doctrine. The masters supervising the writing of them were

Jesus Christ and the Virgin Mary . . . A certain woman dictated them, and another woman wrote them down, and the Holy Spirit inspired them in a certain sinner.[50]

Like Hildegard and others, Umiltà dictated her sermons and hymns to scribes, using, in this instance, two of her sister nuns, Donnina and Margarita. All-female partnerships of this kind were unusual, but not unknown. Hildegard had dictated to her protégé, Elisabeth of Schönau, as well as to Volmar. Kimberley Benedict suggests that women working with female scribes was a pattern that did not sit well with medieval ways of thinking, and these partnerships were often short-lived. 'The subject of women loving one another in Christ, living together and writing together may have proved too difficult for medieval narrators to render in conventional terms.'[51]

Around this time, we begin to hear a different kind of voice, from groups condemned as heretical by the Church. These are women who challenge the establishment not from divine inspiration that overrides the disability of their gender, but on the authority of their own experience of God. Dronke draws the comparison with Hildegard, who spoke 'with the prophet's impunity', while these thirteenth-century women 'speak in their own name. They are not prophets, but passionate, often anguished, minds.'[52] While the Church could tolerate and even interact with women who spoke out of humility, it could not bear the direct challenge of women who claimed the authority to criticize in their own right.

Dronke describes Grazida Lizier, on the margins of the Cathar movement, and Marguerite Porete, both persecuted for their writing. He comments:

Grazida Lizier's testimony and Marguerite Porete's are two of the most moving expressions of love by medieval women that have come down to us. At the beginning of the fourteenth century, they caused Grazida to be imprisoned, and Marguerite to be put to death, by the men – Christian at least in name – who ruled the official Church of the day.[53]

Marguerite Porete (d. 1310) was burned at the stake in Paris for her challenge to the ecclesiastical authorities, whom she saw as 'La Sainte Eglise La Petite' – the 'Little Church'. She spoke of God's love and the experience of it in sometimes provocative language, claiming to speak in the name of the 'simple souls' or 'free souls' who belonged to the Great Church.

Dronke calls her 'the most neglected of the great writers of the thirteenth century'.[54] After her execution, all copies of her book, the *Mirouer (or Miroir) des simples ames (Mirror of simple souls)* were called in for destruction. Only one manuscript is known to have escaped, but translations into Latin, Italian and English bear witness to the enduring popularity of the work.

Her lyrical poetry forms an integral part of her writing: Dronke says that 'She floats into lyrical moments and out of them again, back into prose dialogue, which then, gaining fresh intensity and with it fresh symmetry, hovers once more on the brink of lyricism.' [55]

The *Miroir*'s lyrical texts are intense and erotic, often deliberately shocking. Some are polemical, challenging the theologians and clerics, and even the Beguines, directly and by name:

Amis, que diront beguines   *et gens de religions*
quant ilz orront l'excellence   *de vostre divine chanson?*
Beguines dient que j'erre,   *prestres clers et prescheurs,*
Augustins et Carmes,   *et les Freres Mineurs . . .*

Beloved, what will beguines say,   and the pious throng,
when they hear the excellence   of your divine song?
Beguines say that I am wrong,   priest and clerk and preacher,
Austins and Carmelites   and the Friars Minor . . . [56]

The book concludes with a simple and moving description of divine love.

J'ay dit que je l'aymeray.
Je mens – ce ne suis je mie.
C'est il seul qui ayme moy –
il est, et je ne suis mie,
et plus ne me fault
que ce qu'il vault
et qu'il vault.
Il est plain
et de ce suis plaine:
c'est le divin noyaulx
et amour loyaulx.

I've said that I will love him –
I lie, it is not I:

it's he alone who loves me –
he is, and I am naught.
And I need nothing
save what he wills
and that he prevails.
He is fullness
and with this I am filled:
this is the divine kernel
and loyal love.[57]

Perhaps Marguerite's fate throws into sharper relief the success of those women writers whose sometimes similar challenges to church authorities won them acceptance and even honour in their own time. The Church at no time accepted the independent authority of women writers. Petroff notes: 'There is little doubt that the church in the thirteenth century would have maintained its traditional attitude toward women if it had been possible: the persecution of witches and heretics offers abundant evidence of that.'[58]

Women writers had to battle against their own sense of unfitness for the task to which they felt that God had called them. We have seen that this led to deep anxiety and anguish as they began to accept the public nature of their calling. They could only justify their activities by claiming intense visionary experiences, which meant that they were acting as mouthpieces for God, not writing or speaking on their own authority.

They were often admired and supported by male biographers and scribes, who, however, colluded in promulgating the perception of women as having no authoritative authentic voice, by describing their work as ecstatic and visionary.

For nearly a thousand years, many of these writers have been hidden. Publishers of collections such as Raby's *Oxford Book of Medieval Latin Verse* either ignored them or belittled them. It is not until recently, under the influence of feminist scholarship, that their voices have been heard again.

Kimberley Benedict applauds the work of Dronke, for example, as 'a groundbreaking study of medieval women writers that helped introduce Hildegard to English-speaking audiences'.[59] It is scandalous that such a major writer should have been silent for so long, and it is the task of this generation to make her, and other medieval women writers, heard again.

Notes

1 Migne, *Patrologiae Cursus Completus, Latina*, 3, 17A, 7, *Passio SS Perpetuae et Felicitas*. The diary itself is in Migne, *Patrologiae Cursus Completus, Latina* 3, 18A–45A. There is a translation in Peter Dronke, *Women Writers of the Middle Ages: A Critical Study of Texts from Perpetua († 203) to Marguerite Porete († 1310)*, Cambridge: Cambridge University Press, 1984, pp. 2–4. It is likely, judging by the plain and lively style of the Latin, in contrast to the surrounding hagiography, that the author is transcribing Perpetua's own words as he claims.

2 See Anna M. Silvas, *Macrina the Younger, Philosopher of God*, Turnhout, Belgium: Brepols Publishers, 2008.

3 Jerome, *Epistola* 127.7, PL22:1091, cited in Jo Ann McNamara, 'Muffled Voices: The Lives of Consecrated Women in the Fourth Century', in Thomas Shank (ed.), *Of Medieval Religious Women*, vol. 1, *Distant Echoes*, vol. 1, Cistercian Study Series no. 71, Kalamazoo MI: Cistercian Publications, pp. 11–29, p. 18.

4 McNamara, 'Muffled Voices', p. 18.

5 Carolyn Muessig, 'Prophecy and Song: Teaching and Preaching by Medieval Women', in Beverly Mayne Kienzle and Pamela J. Walker (eds), *Women Preachers and Prophets through Two Millennia of Christianity*, Berkeley: University of California Press, 1998, pp. 146–58, p. 153.

6 F. Leo (ed.), *Venanti Honori Clementiani Fortunati Presbyteri Italici Opera Poetica Monumenta Germaniae Historica, Auctorum Antiquissimorum*, 1881, IV. I, p. 30. See also http://www.hs-augsburg.de/~harsch/Chronologia/Lsposto6/ Venantius/ven_cao2.html, accessed 28 August 2009.

7 'Pange lingua gloriosi proelium certaminis', ll. 22–4, John Mason Neale (1818–66), 'Sing my tongue the glorious battle', v. 8.

8 Dronke, *Women Writers of the Middle Ages*, p. 28.

9 Clare Lees and Gillian Overing, *Double Agents: Women and Clerical Culture in Anglo-Saxon England*, Pennsylvania: University of Pennsylvania Press, 2001, p. 21.

10 Lees and Overing, *Double Agents*, pp. 28–9.

11 André Wilmart, *Le 'Jubilus' sur le nom de Jésus dit de Saint Bernard* [the text of the poem, with a commentary by A. Wilmart], *Ephemerides liturgicae*. anno. 57, p. 285. Città del Vaticano, 1943, cited in Dr F. J. E. Raby, *Christian Latin Poetry from the Beginnings to the Close of the Middle Ages*, Oxford: Clarendon Press, 2nd edn 1953, p. 329.

12 Raby, *Christian Latin Poetry*, p. 329.

13 Edward Caswall (1814–78), 'Jesus the very thought of thee', *Hymns & Psalms*, London: Methodist Publishing House, 1983, no. 265.

14 Attributed to Bernard of Clairvaux, *Jubilus Rhythmicus, De Nomine Jesu* in Migne, *PL*, 184, 1517, 898, Caswall, 'Jesus the very thought of thee', vv. 3–4.

15 Peter Abelard, *The Paraclete Hymnal*, Preface to Book I (The Daily Round), cited in Constant J. Mews, 'Liturgy and Identity at the Paraclete: Heloise, Abelard and the Evolution of Cistercian Reform', in Marc Stewart and David Wulstan (eds), *The Poetic and Musical Legacy of Heloise and Abelard: An Anthology of Essays by Various Authors*, Ottawa, Canada: The Institute of Mediaeval Music,

Westhumble, Surrey: The Plainsong and Mediaeval Music Society, 2003, pp. 19–33, p. 31.

16 *The Paraclete Hymnal*, Preface to Book 1, in Mews, 'Liturgy and Identity at the Paraclete', p. 31.

17 *The Paraclete Hymnal*, Preface to Book 1, in Mews, 'Liturgy and Identity at the Paraclete', p. 32.

18 Letter 7, Abelard to Heloise, in Betty Radice, revised M. T. Clanchy, *The Letters of Abelard and Heloise*, London: Penguin Books, 2003, p. 115.

19 No. 124 Joseph Szövérffy, *Peter Abelard's Hymnarius Paraclitensis: An Annotated Edition with Introduction: Part II The Hymnarius Paraclitensis Text and Notes*, Albany NY: Classical Folia Editions, 1975, pp. 256–7, Feasts of Holy Women, Matins, first nocturn, v. 2, ll. 1, 4, tr. Sister Jane Patricia, *The Hymns of Abelard in English Verse*, New York: University Press of America, 1986, p. 132.

20 No. 125 Szövérffy, *Peter Abelard's Hymnarius Paraclitensis: Part II*, pp. 256–7, Feasts of Holy Women, Matins, second nocturn, vv. 1 and 2, tr. Sister Jane Patricia, *The Hymns of Abelard in English Verse*, p. 132. Note that the translation reduces the inclusivity of the original by translating 'Adam' as 'man'.

21 Peter the Venerable, Letter (115) to Heloise, in Radice, revised Clanchy, *The Letters of Abelard and Heloise*, p, 218.

22 David Wulstan, 'Heloise at Argenteuil and the Paraclete', in Stewart and Wulstan (eds), *The Poetic and Musical Legacy of Heloise and Abelard*, pp. 67–90, p. 67.

23 Gottfried of Disibodenberg and Theodoric of Echternach, *The Life of the Saintly Hildegard*, tr. Hugh Feiss, Toronto: Peregrina Publishing, 1996, p. 45, cited in Kimberley M. Benedict, *Empowering Collaborations: Writing Partnerships between Women and Scribes in the Middle Ages*, London: Routledge, 2004, p. 32.

24 Hildegard of Bingen, *Symphonia*, with introduction, translation and commentary by Barbara Newman Ithaca: Cornell University Press, 2nd edn, 1998, p. 3.

25 Elizabeth Petroff, *Consolation of the Blessed*, New York: Alta Gaia Society, 1979, p. 3.

26 Petroff, *Consolation of the Blessed*, p. 3.

27 Peter Dronke, *Poetic Individuality in the Middle Ages: New Departures in Poetry, 1000–1150*, London: Westfield College, University of London Committee for Medieval Studies, 2nd edn, 1986, p. 158.

28 See Janet Wootton, *Eagles' Wings and Lesser Things*, London: Stainer & Bell, 2007, nos. 42, 44, 70.

29 See Barbara Newman, *Sister of Wisdom: St Hildegard's Theology of the Feminine*, Berkeley: University of California Press, 1987; Newman also comments on the 'modern' feel of the poetry: 'Her unrhymed, unmetrical songs, wholly unpredictable as to line division, length, and stanzaic pattern, follow the rhythms of thought alone. Their content belongs to the twelfth century, but their form anticipates the twentieth.' *Sister of Wisdom*, p. 25.

30 See Chapter 5.

31 Hildegard of Bingen, *Symphonia*, no. 25. All the references to *Symphonia* are to the Newman edition – see note 24 above.

32 All translations of Hildegard's texts in this section are mine.

33 Hildegard of Bingen, *Symphonia*, no. 2. See Newman's note on the hymn, where she speaks as the gem or crystal as 'one of the many devices, beloved of medieval poets, used as analogies for the Virgin Birth'. Hildegard of Bingen, *Symphonia*, p. 272.

34 Hildegard of Bingen, *Symphonia*, no. 10, ll. 1–9.

35 Hildegard of Bingen, *Symphonia*, no. 19, vv. 2–5.

36 Hildegard of Bingen, *Symphonia*, p. 260, ll. 1–10.

37 Migne, *Patrologiae Cursus Completus, Latina* 197, 218C–221D, cited in Dronke, *Women Writers of the Middle Ages*, pp. 197–8.

38 *Sermo s. Cecilie*, Douai, Bibliothéque municipale 503, ff. 158v-160v, cited in Muessig, 'Prophecy and Song', pp. 149 and 157, n. 30, my translation.

39 *Sermo de virginibus*, Douai, Bibliothéque municipale 503, ff. 217v–220r, cited in Muessig, 'Prophecy and Song', pp. 149 and 157, n. 31, my translation.

40 Muessig, 'Prophecy and Song', p. 151.

41 Muessig, 'Prophecy and Song', p. 153.

42 Petroff, *Consolation of the Blessed*, p. 4.

43 Dronke, *Women Writers of the Middle Ages*, p. 202.

44 IV, 2 (p. 73), cited in Elizabeth A. Andersen, *Mechthild of Magdeburg: Selections, The Flowing Light of the Godhead*, Cambridge: D. S. Brewer, 2003, pp. 13–14.

45 II, 26 (p. 48), cited in Andersen, *Mechthild of Magdeburg*, p. 14.

46 II, 6, cited in Andersen, *Mechthild of Magdeburg*, pp. 42–3, translation mine.

47 Petroff, *Consolation of the Blessed*, p. 9.

48 Petroff, *Consolation of the Blessed*, pp. 9–10, citing AASS (*Acta Sanctorum*) 22 Maii, *Humilitas, Analecta de virtutibus, scriptus, translationibus & miraculis*, ch. 1, para. 1.

49 *Analecta*, ch. 2, para. 10, in Petroff, *Consolation of the Blessed*, p. 146.

50 *Analecta*, ch. 2, para. 11, in Petroff, *Consolation of the Blessed*, p. 147.

51 Benedict, *Empowering Collaborations*, p. 80.

52 Dronke, *Women Writers of the Middle Ages*, p. 203.

53 Dronke, *Women Writers of the Middle Ages*, p. 228.

54 Dronke, *Women Writers of the Middle Ages*, p. 202.

55 Dronke, *Women Writers of the Middle Ages*, p. 218.

56 Marguerite Porete, *Miroir des simples ames* 103v; R. Guarnieri (ed.), 'Il "Miroir des simples ames" di Margherita Porete', *Archivo italiano per la storia della pieta* IV 1965, pp. 501–635, cited in Dronke, *Women Writers of the Middle Ages*, p. 227, translation by Dronke, p. 227.

57 Porete, *Miroir des simples ames* 104r, tr. Dronke, in *Women Writers of the Middle Ages*, p. 227.

58 Petroff, *Consolation of the Blessed*, p. 14.

59 Benedict, *Empowering Collaborations*, p. 87, referring to Dronke, *Women Writers of the Middle Ages*.

2

Reforms in Theology and Technology

Two huge revolutionary movements brought about seismic changes in the late Middle Ages and into Early Modern times. One was the Reformation, foreshadowed in the reforming movements of the later Middle Ages and also, arguably, by developments among women and communities of women such as the Beguines. The Reformation brought education to some women, and some communities moved radically towards equality between women and men; some, indeed, gathered around prominent women leaders. But the orthodox position did not alter. Women were still, by and large, silent; the object, rather than the subject of scholarship and writing.

The other major revolution was technical. It interacts with the rapid spread of Reformation thought, since the invention of printing with moveable type enabled new ideas to be promulgated far more widely and rapidly than did the spoken word or manuscript.

It is disheartening but unsurprising that it is only recently that the impact of printing on women's writing has been much studied. Diana Maury Robin, in a study called *Publishing Women*, notes that she is crossing a threefold boundary between the academic disciplines of women's literary history, history of the book and Counter-Reformation studies, and that, in particular, the isolation of women's literary history from the history of the book has served to marginalize women's writing even further.[1]

Robin begins her story 'on a small island off the coast of Naples', Ischia, where, in the divided Italy of the mid-sixteenth century, 'a group of elite women worked at forging cultural hegemony on two fronts: they played leading roles in the new literary academies and salons in Italy as well as in the religious reform movement that swept the peninsula'.[2] The women were from the wealthy and influential d'Avalos-Colonna family, and used their connections and resources to foster radical religious ideas as well as providing gathering places for poets and thinkers. They maintained contact with male editors and printers, who published their work. Most notably, Vittoria Colonna's (1490–1547) poetry was included in an anthology of poems by 53 women writers, published by Lodovico Domenichi is 1559. This was at the height of the Inquisition and represented an act of great courage by the compiler. It was also the first collection of all-women poets ever to be published in Europe.

Mirjam de Baar makes the same point in her biographical study of Antoinette Bourignon (1616–80), who bought her own printing press, and maintained tight control over the publication and distribution of her considerable publishing output. Like Robin, de Baar recognizes the originality in linking gender history and cultural history with the history of books.[3]

While the invention of printing undoubtedly opened up the dissemination of women's writing, they found it far more difficult than male writers to gain access to the new medium. With no publishing houses, as we know them now, publication depended on patronage. Bourignon poured her own fortune into making her writing available, as did many other women. That limited access to publishing to a few elite, wealthy women.

Besides this, most women still lacked access to the kind of education that would lead them to consider putting their words into print. And when they did, they were still operating against the massive dead weight of tradition, which was deeply disapproving and suspicious of women using words, breaking the silence which it was believed that Scripture enjoined upon them. For every publication by a woman, there were countless publications *about* women, reinforcing misogynist views and binding them to silence.

This point is illustrated powerfully in Axel Erdmann's beautiful book of facsimiles of the title pages of books about women and books by women. He gives a very rough estimate that the former outnumber the latter by 100 to one.[4]

Where women did overcome this powerful set of cultural barriers, they often demonstrated that they had still internalized the prevailing cultural attitudes by either justifying their enterprise or regretting their gender. Where they gained approval, it was often couched in terms that denied their gender. Scholarly women would be commended for having overcome their sex and become masculine. In these respects, little had changed from the Middle Ages.

The circle of Vittoria Colonna

When Vittoria Colonna's *Rime* (collection of poetry) was published in Parma in 1538, it was the first such book to be published by a woman under her own name. Women generally, if they published at all, did so anonymously, or using pseudonyms. To publish openly, using her own name, showed great confidence both in her writing and in her reputation. During her life, she established salons in Ischia, Rome, Naples, where she became involved in the Valdensian movement, Ferrara, through which she made contact with Queen Marguerite of Navarre, and Viterbo where she became a key figure in the circle surrounding Cardinal Reginald Pole.

Like other members of her family, she was free of dependence on marriage or male relatives. She was widowed in 1525, and could move freely from city to city, engaging in literary and intellectual life in her own right. Although historians have often depicted her as a passive figure, drawn to the orbit of great male intellectuals and radicals, closer inspection reveals her to have been an active and passionate participant in the dissemination of texts and ideas.

Her poetry shows the influence of reformed theology. It is Christo-centric and evangelical, in that she aims to illustrate the life of the *spirituali*, as followers of reform in Italy were known, whose religious life was based on inner illumination.

She sent two collections of her verse to two influential people: Michel-angelo, and Queen Marguerite of Navarre (1492–1549) in 1540 or 1541. The collections are different, and the selection of items is interesting. They reveal a different person from the pious widow living in mourning for her husband, which was the way she was portrayed both during her life and after her death.

It is in her gift to Queen Marguerite and the correspondence between them that she reveals most of herself. Marguerite had been trying to acquire a copy of Vittoria's poems through intermediaries. Vittoria contacted her through her (Marguerite's) cousin, the Duchess of Ferrara, a place in which she had lived for a while.

The two women had a great deal in common. They had been widowed in the same battle, Pavia, in 1525, though their husbands had been fighting on opposite sides. Like Vittoria, Marguerite was a courageous and passionate supporter of the reform movement, then nascent in France as *évangélisme*. Though they wrote of their longing to meet in their letters, they never met – the times were too troubled. But their relationship was one of mutual admiration and support.

Their admiration for each other is expressed in their correspondence and poetry. Vittoria initially approached Marguerite as a spiritual mother. She wrote of herself as a daughter, whose difficult birth and upbringing would give the Queen satisfaction in achievement.

The gift manuscript opens with a sonnet to the Virgin Mary, which calls upon the Virgin to act as mother to the poet in her desire to attain transformation, building on the Virgin's manifold relation to Jesus.

> *Immortal dio nascosto in human velo*
> *L'adorasti signor, figlio 'l nodristi,*
> *L'amasti sposo, e L'onorasti padre;*
> > *Priega lui dunque che i miei giorni tristi*
> *Ritornin lieti, e tu, donna del cielo,*
> *Vogli in questo desio mostrarti madre.*

> Immortal God hidden in human veil,
> You worshipped him as Lord, nurtured him as son,
> Loved him as husband and honoured him as father;
> > Therefore pray to him now that my sad days
> May be transformed to joy, and may you, lady of heaven,
> Act as mother to me in this my desire.[5]

Marguerite responds in her correspondence by praising Vittoria's writing as a source for her own spiritual enlightenment. A sonnet attributed to her also hints at a comparison with the Virgin:

> *Voi Donna, che domate i fieri mostri*
> *Che la terra produce, e 'l gran serpente,*
> *Sopra voi stessa alzata con la mente*
> *Pura salite à gli superni chiostri.*

> Oh lady, you who tame the fierce beasts
> of the earth, and the great snake,
> raising your mind beyond your mortal being,
> pure, you rise to the celestial cloisters.[6]

The reference to taming the serpent paints the Virgin as the second Eve, recalling an image often found in medieval and early modern art.

The two women are using imagery and language with great delicacy. It reads like flattery, but there is a genuine affection between them – and more: Brundin describes 'a mutual process of self-assertion, subtly

demonstrating their aptitude as models for imitation by other women
. . . couched in suitable socially acceptable terms that do not exceed the
bounds of acceptable behaviour for aristocratic females'.[7]

Through Marguerite, Vittoria Colonna's influence spread more
widely. The Queen gave refuge to reformers in her court, and encouraged the education of a number of women, including the sisters Mary
and Anne Boleyn. Mary was a future mistress of Henry VIII of England,
and Anne, besides being one of the executed wives, was a woman of
great learning, whose Reformation theology was persuasive in Henry's
eyes, and thus influenced the development of the Church in England. Her
daughter Queen Elizabeth I translated Queen Marguerite's poetry.

Two French mystics

Half a century later, in Lille, the daughter of a Roman Catholic mer-
chant family. Antoinette Bourignon (1616–80), recognized, like her
medieval foremothers, that she had to choose between the respectable
marriage her parents had arranged for her and the fulfilment of her
vocation. At the age of 20, she ran away from home and began an
extraordinary spiritual journey, which would affect many lives. Mirjam
de Baar calls her 'unquestionably one of the most fascinating personali-
ties of the seventeenth century'.[8] She argues that, while most accounts
of Bourignon's life see her as an isolated phenomenon and describe
her as an hysteric and a zealot, in fact she engaged enthusiastically and
controversially with the religious communities of her day, developing
her thought 'on the crossroads of and in dialogue with the most diverse
churches and religious movements'.[9]

Following a period running a home for poor girls, she moved
first to Mechelen and then to Amsterdam. There, she found a multi-
confessional community, with freedom from censorship, and she began
to enter debate, and to write. She was immensely prolific, producing
two autobiographies, treatises, letters, poems, rules for Christian life
and exegeses.

As has been noted, the printing press was an important piece of tech-
nology, which Bourignon used skilfully and to her own advantage. Her
works were already influential during her lifetime, and were collected
and published by one of her followers, Pierre Poiret, soon after her
death.

Her theology was eschatological and her call was to 'true Christianity', which emphasized the inner spiritual life. She offered herself as

spiritual mother to true Christians. This gave her a maternal authority which could be accepted by hierarchical leaders without doing violence to their position, and was attractive to people disaffected with the Church. She drew them into a family, but did not seek to sever their links with their own religious communities.

Although she spent her last years moving from place to place in north-western Germany, suspected by Lutheran ministers of the intention of forming a sect, this was not her aim. Rather, she aimed to offer people teaching and spiritual care so that they could live as 'true Christians' in their own place.

Madame Guyon (1648–1717) was born into an aristocratic family, daughter of Claude Bouvières, Seigneur de la Mothe Vergonville. After 12 years of marriage, and following the death of her husband, she travelled in France, Switzerland and Italy, and developed a following for her teaching, which emphasized the interior life, experiential rather than rational faith.

Her book *Le Moyen Court et très facile de faire oraison* (*A Short and Easy Method of Prayer*) was very influential. Like Bourignon, she published a wide range and large corpus of work, including exegesis, spiritual direction, poetry and letters. Her works were published, in about 40 volumes, over the last decade and more of her life, and immediately after her death.

Guyon spans the end of the age of mysticism and the rise of radical Protestantism. Patricia Ward describes her as occupying 'an ambiguous space between the old and the new, the institutional and the non-institutional, the rational and the intuited, the mystical, or the unconscious,' and goes on to say, 'She is part of a transformation of paradigms that opens the way to a new psychology of religious experience, and experimental theology.'[10] Both Bourignon and Guyon had great influence during their lives and after their death, though both experienced persecution. Bourignon spent the last period of her life moving from place to place, harried by the Lutheran establishment; her books were placed on the Index by the Inquisition, and proscribed by the Church of Scotland! Guyon faced imprisonment on more than one occasion for her beliefs.

However, Bourignon's works were translated into a number of European languages, running into some 164 separate publications, and widely read, alongside major devotional writers such as John of the Cross.[11] She was read by John Wesley, and her text 'Venez, Jésus, mon salutaire' appears in a translation attributed to him: 'Come, Saviour Jesus, from above', in the *Methodist Hymn Book* of 1933, and then in books of the Evangelical tradition – *Redemption Hymnal* (1951) and *New Redemption Hymnal* (1986), and the 1953 and 1986 *Salvation Army Song Books*.[12]

The text was written in 1640, and appears in the second volume of her autobiography *La Vie Continuée* at the point when she has renounced her marriage, divested herself of all her jewellery and fine clothes, and sought the love of God alone. Her earlier poems describe terrifying encounters with the devil, who attempts to prevent her abandoning the world she knows, and intense internal struggles to dedicate herself to God. Now, having turned away from everything the world has to tempt her with, she utters a poem of divine love, and ends with a note: '*Il seroit ridicule de chercher dans ces verses autre chose que l'Amour de Dieu & la pieté*' ('It would be stupid to seek in these verses for anything thing other than the Love of God and devotion').[13]

Richard Watson comments: 'Wesley found enough in her writings to edit them for his followers, but in so doing he toned down Bourignon's distinctive doctrines.'[14] Nevertheless, John Wesley's translation of this intense text is full and faithful to the original. He translates each of her eight-line verses with two of four lines. His 8888 verse form is not as taut as her 8484D, with very short alternate lines. But Wesley does not shy away from the expressions of love, or the address to Jesus as 'Spouse'.

Que mon coeur à plus rien n'aspire
    Sinon qu'à Vous.
Qu'icy plus rien il ne desire,
    Mon cher Epous.
Que jamais rien ne préne place
    Dedans ce coeur
Sinon vôtre Divine grace,
    Mon doux Sauveur.

To Thee my Earnest Soul aspires,
To Thee I offer all my Vows,
Keep me from false and vain Desires,
My God, my Saviour, and my Spouse.

Henceforth may no profane Delight
Divide this consecrated Soul;
Possess it Thou, who hast the Right,
As Lord and Master of the whole.

The language of 'Lord and Master' is more patriarchal than Guyon's gentle words of grace and salvation. But Wesley captures the sophistication of her final verse very accurately:

Je ne veux plus ni Ciel, ni terre,
    Mon doux JESUS.
Votre pur Amour solitaire
    Qu'il soit tout nud!
Ne vous aimant ni pour vos graces,
    Ni vos faveurs:
Vous rendant tout pour faire place
    Au seul Donneur.

Nor Heav'n nor Earth do I desire
But Thy pure Love within my Breast,
This, this I always will require,
And freely give up all the rest.

Thy Gifts, if called for, I resign,
Pleas'd to receive, pleas'd to restore;
Gifts are Thy Work; it shall be mine
The Giver only to adore.[15]

Madame Guyon's autobiography and other works were widely read in Herrnhut among the Moravian community there, and her *Moyen Court et très facile de faire oraison* became a favourite of Teersteegen. Teersteegen translated her *Les états différents de l'amour sacré et profane* (*The different conditions of sacred and profane love*) into German as *Die Heilige Liebe Gottes und die Unheilige Naturliche* and it was reprinted in Pennsylvania in 1828, thus bringing her influence to the Lutheran communities of the New World.

A collection of her poems appears in translation by William Cowper, in a volume edited by William Bull, to which the latter writes a rather grudging foreword. He notes that he had encouraged the poet, who had become his friend, to translate her works, for his own amusement. Cowper did so, in some spare time, but did not revise them nor intend them for publication. They were published in the end, as often happened, or was claimed, only in order to produce an authorized version, as the popular verses were finding their way into the public domain.

Damningly, Bull writes:

To infer that the peculiarities of Madam Guion's theological sentiments, were adopted either by Mr. C. [*sic*] or by the Editor, would be almost as absurd as to suppose the inimitable Translator of Homer to be a pagan. He reverenced her piety, admired her genius and judged that several of her poems would be read with pleasure and edification by serious and candid persons.[16]

Just as John Wesley eventually repudiated the French mystics,[17] so it seems these two Christian gentlemen were embarrassed to be seen publicly endorsing them!

His translation of 'Amour que mon ame est contente', appears, starting at the second verse, as 'All scenes alike engaging prove', in a similar range of books to those in which the Bourignon text appears. Like Bourignon's 'Venez, Jésus, mon salutaire', this is a text of intense Christian devotion. The writer expresses her complete reliance on God's presence to overcome exile, loneliness and persecution. 'All scenes' are alike because God is in them, and she goes on:

> *Tout est mon païs, ma retraite:*
> *Il n'est pour moi païs, ni tems, ni lieu:*
> *L'ame est contente & satisfaite;*
> *Tous les lieux lui deviennent Dieu.*
>
> . . .
>
> *Seigneur, toi seul es ma patrie;*
> *Je n'en reconnois point d'autre que toi,*
> *Mon centre, mon bien et ma vie,*
> *Mon amour, mon unique loi.*

Cowper translates:

> To me remains nor place nor time;
> My country is in ev'ry clime;
> I can be calm and free from care
> On any shore, since God is there.
>
> . . .
>
> My country, Lord, art thou alone;
> Nor other can I claim or own;
> The point where all my wishes meet:
> My law, my love; life's only sweet.[18]

Marian devotion is no longer the focus of the personal relationship between the singer and her God. Guyon sees herself as the beloved of God who is her husband. A very beautiful text, also translated by Cowper, employs the language of passion to express the intimacy between the true Christian and God – entitled, 'Aspiration de l'ame languissante d'amour' ('Aspiration of a soul languishing in love'):

> Adorable Epoux de mon ame,
> Toi qui possédes tout mon cœur,
> Qui connois bien quelle est ma flame,
> Tu peux croître encore son ardeur.
> . . .
> Mes sens, mon esprit se consomme.
> Victime de ton pur amour:
> . . .
> Je me voi reduite au silence;
> Et c'est tout ce qui m'est permis.

Cowper translates:

> My Spouse! in whose presence I live,
> Sole object of all my desires,
> Who know'st what a flame I conceive,
> And canst easily double its fires;
> . . .
> My spirit and faculties fail;
> Oh, finish what thou hast begun!
> . . .
> I can only be silent and gaze;
> 'Tis all that is left to me now.[19]

German-speaking Spirit-filled communities

A new Protestant hymnbook, *Evangelisches Gesangbuch*, was published in 1995. Elisabeth Schneider-Böklen, in a study of the publication, laments the lack of women writers and asks, '*gab es in den Jahrhunderten christlicher Liederdichtung keine Frauen?*' ('in the centuries of Christian hymn-writing, were there no women?').[20] She notices what I have argued elsewhere,[21] that the middle of the twentieth century represents a nadir even in the sparse representation of women writers. There were 12 women writers in the 1912 *Württemburgisches Gesangbuch*, but only 3 in the 1953 *Evangelisches Gesangbuch*! The 1995 book redresses the balance somewhat with 17.

However, the tradition from which the women come, whose biographies Schneider-Böklen goes on to present, was the first to encourage women's writing enthusiastically alongside that of men. This took place against the background of a resurgence of hymn-singing and an emphasis on congregational or community participation. Luther wrote hymns and encouraged congregations to sing (while Calvin, as we shall see later,[22] whose influence was greater in England and Scotland, tended to favour the singing of psalms, taken as being of divine authorship, rather than hymns written by human hand).

The influence of hymn-writing and -singing, from the earliest years of the Reformation, cannot be overestimated. Hymns brought the radical theology of the academics and clerics within the reach of lay people, who were fired by the new ideas. As we have seen, the printing press made it possible for new ideas to be rapidly and effectively disseminated. The translation of the Bible into vernacular languages, and the emphasis on the authority of Scripture, gave an evangelical purpose to hymn-writing and the publication of hymnals.

Robin Leaver, in a lecture on Elisabeth Creutziger and the Magdeburg *Enchiridion*, notes that 'the hymnal, small enough to be carried in a pocket, assumed a particular importance for shaping and sustaining the faith of ordinary people'.[23] This was a deliberate policy on the part of Luther, who actively encouraged the writing of hymns. Leaver quotes from a letter from Luther to Georg Spatulin:

Following the example of the prophets and fathers of the church, I intend to make vernacular psalms for the people, that is, spiritual songs so that the Word of God even by means of song may live among the people.[24]

The writer at the heart of Leaver's lecture was the first Protestant woman hymn-writer in print. Elisabeth Creutziger or Cruciger (1504–35) was born into a Roman Catholic family in East Pomerania, which is now in North East Germany and Poland. She entered a convent but renounced her vows on conversion to an evangelical faith, and married Caspar Creutziger, who was at the time a student at Wittenberg. He began his ministry in Magdeburg, moving back to Wittenberg where he later became a professor at the university.

Elisabeth wrote the hymn 'Herr Christ, der einge Gottes Sohn' ('Lord Christ, the only Son of God') during the winter of 1523–24. Leaver ascribes a fundamental importance to this text, which was the first of a new kind of hymn, the *Jesuslied* or hymn expressing the new

Christology of the Reformation. He writes: 'Since the heart of Reformation theology involved what was then a "new" understanding of the person and work of Christ, the importance of this first Lutheran Christological hymn can hardly be overestimated.'[25]

The hymn has several other features which developed as distinctive of hymns in the Lutheran tradition. It begins as an interpretation of an older text, 'Corde natus ex parentis',[26] but, rather than rendering the text in the metre of the original, the author sets it to a popular folk tune. Beginning from the incarnational theology of the Latin text,

> *Herr Christ, der einge Gottes Sohn,*
> *Vaters in ewigkeit,*
> *aus seinem herz'n entsprossen:*
> *gleichwie geschreiben steht:*
> *Er ist der Morgensterne,*
> *sein'n glanz;*
> *strekt er so ferne*
> *für andern sternen klar.*

it moves on to a statement of the basic Reformation doctrine of atonement in the next verse, with a passionate response on the part of the singer in the rest of the text.

> *Für uns ein mensch gebohren*
> *im lezten theil der zeit;*
> *der mutter unverlohren*
> *ihr jungfräulich keuscheit:*
> *den tod für uns zerbrochen*
> *den himmel ausgeschlossen*
> *das leben wiederbracht.*

The singer's response is expressed partly in eucharistic language (see Winkworth, below):

> *dass wir hier mögen schmeken*
> *dein' süssigkeit in herzen,*
> *und dürsten stets nach dir.*[27]

All these are markers of Reformation hymnody. They bear testimony to the evangelistic aim of the hymn, to use congregational song to embed the new Christology into people's hearts and lives.

Leaver notes that the hymn quickly entered the repertory of German chorales. The text appeared in the *Herrnhuter Gesangbuch* (see below) at no. 29,[28] and was partly translated by Catherine Winkworth, not in her *Lyra Germanica* but in the later compilation by William Sterner Bennett, *The Chorale Book for England*. Winkworth translates verses 1, 3 and 4 of the five-verse text, thus concentrating on its incarnational rather that its atonement theology.

> O Thou, of God the Father
> The true Eternal Son,
> Of whom 'tis surely written
> That Thou with Him art one;
> Thou art the bright and Morning Star,
> Beyond all other radiance
> Thy glory streams afar.
>
> O let us in Thy knowledge
> And in Thy love increase,
> That we in faith be steadfast
> And serve Thee here in peace;
> That so Thy sweetness may be known
> To these cold hearts, and teach them
> To thirst for Thee alone.
>
> Maker of all! who showest
> The Father's love and might,
> In heaven and earth Thou reignest
> Of Thine own power and might;
> So rule our hearts and minds, that we
> Be wholly Thine, and never
> May turn aside from Thee.[29]

A more recent version by Carl Daw translates the first two verses, homing in on the text's doctrinal content rather than the worshipper's response.[30]

> Joined with our human nature,
> born as time was waning,
> hope for sinners who ponder
> God in glory reigning:
> death's power was shattered for us,
> heaven's gate unlocked before us,
> life restored and made new.

In Strasbourg, another major female figure in the Reformation also recognized the centrality of hymns. Katharina Schütz Zell (1498–1562) was not a hymn-writer herself, but she published an annotated edition of the first German-language hymnal of the *Unitas Fratrum* or Bohemian Brethren. This reforming movement was based on the teachings of John Hus, who had himself given voice to an indigenous rebellion against clergy corruption in Moravia and Bohemia. The *Unitas Fratrum* was formed in 1464, intended as a movement within the Roman Catholic Church, but broke away from Rome within three years.[31]

Katharina Schütz was converted in her twenties from the Roman Catholicism in which she had grown up, and became enthusiastically involved in the fast-moving era of Reformation. McKee comments on the importance of her story, which 'gives access to the perspective of a lay person and a woman of the ordinary citizenry'.[32] Elsie Anne McKee calls Schütz Zell 'a remarkable participant in an exciting and turbulent age and spiritual movement . . . early modern Europe and its religious reform'. She was never a nun, nor was she from an aristocratic family. Her father was an artisan, and she received what McKee calls, 'a good vernacular education'.[33] She married Matthew Zell in 1523, one of the first marriages of a priest, following Luther's teaching on the matter. They founded their relationship on the principle of equality of vocation and service. Katharina called herself *Kirchenmutter* – 'mother of the church', which she regarded as an office with duties and responsibilities. She developed her theology in correspondence with the leaders of the Reformation. Her published pamphlets and open letters derive from conflicts or arise out of pastoral concern. She is independent, courageous and practical.

In the late 1520s, Schütz Zell perceived the need for vernacular hymns to replace the old Roman Catholic repertoire. She turned to the hymn-book of the *Unitas Fratrum* as a source of biblical hymns with reformed doctrine, making it more accessible by dividing the hymnal into four pamphlets, which were easier to carry, and afford. She also inserted her own preface, which is reprinted in the second volume of McKee's substantial study, and annotated the hymns, aiming, as McKee describes it, 'to help singers use the book as a guide to prayer, praise and doctrine, a kind of teach-yourself-catechism or lay sermon book'.[34]

Kirsi Stjerna comments that 'The hymnbook more than any other work, perhaps, shows the many dimensions of Katharina's contributions as a reformer, as a theologian, as a catechetical teacher, as a pastoral caregiver, and as an empowerer of the laity.'[35] She comments on the last term, that the hymnbook 'gave people a concrete tool to reform and deepen their spiritualities, to learn, and to have a voice – through hymns'.[36]

The edition was a response to a real need. The laity felt somewhat confused and bereft as what was considered idolatrous was swept away and liturgical life was purified. McKee quotes from the preface, the complaints of the people: '"Do you want us never to sing? Must we become wooden blocks and stones?"'[37] The publication of the hymnal provided a new source of congregational songs, with biblical basis and reformed theology.

There were other women who saw the publication of hymnbooks and the writing of hymns as part of their service to their people. Louisa Henrietta, Electress of Brandenburg (1627–67), published a hymnbook in 1653, which included four of her own texts, in the context of wide-ranging social provision, including the establishment of schools and the introduction of innovations in agriculture. Emilia Juliana (1637–1706), Countess of Schwarzburg-Rudolstadt (now in central Germany), wrote 587 hymns, and her sister-in-law Countess Ludaemilia Elisabeth (1640–72) wrote 207, despite her early death.

Many other women joined the Herrnhut community, either permanently or for a period of time, and wrote hymns under the encouragement of its leader Nicholas von Zinzendorf. In the early 1700s, von Zinzendorf, a Lutheran nobleman, gave refuge to survivors of the *Unitas Fratrum*,[38] whose members had been expelled from Bohemia and their property confiscated in 1620. Some 36,000 families left, and were scattered throughout neighbouring countries.[39]

Zinzendorf took some of these onto his estate in Saxony. They were joined by other religious refugees, and, on 13 August 1727, the new community, called 'Herrnhut' (the Lord's Watch), experienced a new Pentecost and the birth of the renewed Moravian Church.

Hymns and hymn-singing played a great part in the Herrnhut community. Johansen notes regular occasions when hymns were sung:

At eight o'clock every morning and evening, Herrnhut resounded with happy song. Each Sunday night, the young men made a complete circuit of Bethelsdorf and Herrnhut, singing hymns old and new ... [Zinzendorf] gradually developed a unique kind of service called the '*Singstunde*', which became in time his favourite form of worship.[40]

Peter Vogt mentions another way in which this creativity was encouraged: *Poeten-Liebesmahle* (poets' love feasts), which were 'sociable competitions in which the participants, brothers and sisters alike, individually composed hymns to a common theme, which were afterward sung and discussed'.[41]

At the same time, a unique form of community organization gave women access to high levels of authority, albeit in the women's section of the community. The members were organized into choirs, or bands, consisting of people of the same age, gender and marital status. The young men's choir would have conducted the Sunday circuit of the community. Women's bands or choirs were run by women elders. Although these were not admitted to the decision-making council, they were otherwise equal in authority to the men and were equally encouraged to compose and write hymns.

The third person of the Trinity was very important in the Herrnhut community, and particularly within the freedom of the bands and choirs.

> The Holy Spirit was present in the bands and choirs, sharing, in fact creating, the intimacy and love experienced there. The motherly office of the Holy Spirit both reflected that activity of women within the community and also justified it.[42]

Zinzendorf himself openly used feminine imagery for the Holy Spirit, whom he referred to as 'Mother'. Gary Kinkel notes that this first happened in a hymn in 1736, in a hymn whose first verse begins, 'Mother! While the ungrateful hearts/Of your gentiles are still sought with so many sorrows/You are delighted that people still in these days desire to risk body and life.'[43] The reference is brief and unexplained, and Kinkel suggests,

> This could mean that the bands and choirs had already begun to refer to the Spirit as Mother under the direction of Zinzendorf and were familiar with it. Or it could mean that Zinzendorf was experimenting with the image and wanted to see how it worked.[44]

Given this encouragement and theological model, it is not surprising that women flourished in the Herrnhut community and diaspora, and that they contributed to its hymnody. The *Herrnhuter Gesangbuch*, published in 1735, with a total of 12 appendices published up to 1747, included hymns by 35 women writers – about 11 per cent of a total of 312 authors.[45]

The *Gesangbuch* was reprinted in 1981, with an index of authors, giving brief biographical notes.[46] The women are fascinating. Many came to Herrnhut with their families and took serving or leading roles in the community. Others travelled carrying the mission of the Moravian Church throughout Europe and beyond. Among the less well known are Anna Maria Benzin, born in Herrnhut in 1724, who later lived in London's Fetter Lane. In 1754, she moved to America, where she worked in the Brüdergemeinen in Bethlehem, Pennsylvania, until she died in 1783. Esther Grünbeck née Naverholl (1717–96) was the daughter of a converted Jew, and went on, with her husband, to work with Jews in Poland and Lithuania.

Better known was Henrietta Louisa von Hayn (1724–82) who went to live at Herrnhut at the age of 20, seemingly against the wishes of her family. She quickly took on responsibility in the community, as a teacher, and later with the unmarried sisters. She wrote about 40 hymns, but the one for which she is best known, 'Weil ich Jesu Schäflein bin', was written for her schoolchildren. Kübler writes that the hymn 'may be called the most favourite children's hymn in Germany, for nearly all Protestant German children have learned it and love it; and it is, in pious households especially, the common prayer, which children daily repeat.'[47] Winkworth translates it as 'Seeing I am Jesus' Lamb'.[48]

The three major women writers of the *Gesangbuch* were all closely connected to Zinzendorf: his first wife Dorothea Erdmuth von Zinzendorf (1700–56), with 62 hymns, plus verses in two others; his second wife, married on the death of Dorothea, Anna Nitschmann (1715–60), with 51 hymns (some doubtful); and Anna's co-founder of the Single Sisters' Choir in 1730, Anna Dober (1713–39), with 30 hymns (some doubtful).

Not many of these have come down to English-language singers of the twentieth century and beyond. Two of Nitschmann's texts appear in translations by John Wesley in evangelical and Methodist books. 'Mein König, deine Liebe',[49] attributed to her, together with Count Nicholas von Zinzendorf and Johann Nitschmann, appears in *Redemption Hymnal* and *New Redemption Hymnal, Christian Hymns, Making Melody* and the *Salvation Army Songbooks* of 1956 and 1983, in John Wesley's translation, 'I thirst, thou wounded Lamb of God'. *Hymns & Psalms* includes a portion of Wesley's translation of 'Ach mein verwunder Fürste',[50] also attributed to the three Herrnhut writers, starting 'O Lord, enlarge our scanty thought'.

The impact of Moravian spirituality on the Wesleys is well known and well documented. John Wesley learnt German so that he could talk and correspond with German writers, and visited Herrnhut himself in

1738. Through the Moravian *Gesangbuchs*, the Wesleys would have been introduced to the hymns of earlier German writers as well as the prolific output of the Herrnhut community.[51]

English hymns

The German hymns were far more intense and varied than those being written by contemporary English writers, who generally maintained a restraint in language and were restricted in their use of metre and style. Hymn-writing in the British Isles had followed a very different course from what was happening in continental Europe. The Reformation here was influenced by Calvin rather than by Luther, and there was a generally suspicious approach to the singing of any words other than those of Scripture.

Most of the hymns available for worship were rather indifferent versifications of the psalms, usually in four-line verses in short, common or long metre. Thomas Sternhold and John Hopkins' English versions were contained in what came to be known as the 'Old Version', published in 1559. After establishment, the Church of England controlled Anglican publication of hymns through the Stationers' Company, which licensed the *New Version of the Psalms of David* by Tate and Brady in 1696, with a supplement in 1703.[52]

More poetic and singable versions did exist. A century or more before, Mary Herbert (1561–1621), Countess of Pembroke and sister of Sir Philip Sidney, had collaborated with her brother to produce *The Psalmes of David, Translated into Divers and Sundry Kinds of Verse*, in which she seems to have been responsible for all but the first 43 psalms.

Her version of the lovely psalm of creation, Psalm 104, for instance, begins:

Make, O my soule, the subject of thy songe,
Th'eternall Lord: O Lord, O God of might,
To thee, to thee, all roiall pompes belonge,
Clothed art thou in state and glory bright:
For what is else this eye-delighting light;
But unto thee a garment wide and long?
The vaunted heaven but a curtaine right,
A canopy, thou over thee hast hunge?

The complex rhyme scheme is maintained with deftness throughout, and there are some wonderful turns of phrase that echo the delight in creation which characterizes the psalm:

> The freeborne fowles, which through the empty way
> Of yielding aire wafted with winged speed,
> To art-like notes of nature-tuned lay
> Make earelesse bushes give attentive heed.
>
> . . .
>
> Soe highest hills rock-loving goats sustayne;
> And have their heads with clyming traces worne:
> That safe in rocks the conyes may remaine,
> To yield them caves, their rocky ribbs are torne.[53]

Percy Dearmer comments on this oddity:

> the work of providing metrical versions of the Psalms was all-important; and this was given by the authorities not, as it happened, to poets like Sir Philip Sidney and his sister, Lady Pembroke, but to men who were not poets.[54]

Outside the Established Church, the same debate was taking place. The development of an indigenous hymnody would have a slow beginning, from early tentative Christianizing of the psalms to the writing of original hymns, still generally in the same small range of metres, in the hands of the 'father of hymnody', Isaac Watts. Watts and Doddridge dominate all discussion of this period of English hymn-writing, to the exclusion of others, and particularly of women, whose writing was popular and influential at the time.

Benson's classic *The Hymnody of the Christian Church* comments:

> Watts founded a 'school' of writers . . . Dr Doddridge was head scholar and Anne Steele a good second. Indeed her truly feminine emotionalism for a time *deceived the elect* into believing she was founding a school of her own.[55]

Madeleine Forrell Marshall and Janet Todd mention no women writers at all (except for a passing reference to Madam Guyon as an influence on William Cowper) in their 1982 survey of *English Congregational Hymns*. But then, they introduce the period by describing the kind of person who would be likely to break the Calvinist deadlock:

Ideally the champion of hymns would belong to a denomination unbound by church hierarchy . . . he would be a man of irreproachable piety . . . the father of the English hymn ought probably to be a clergyman or preacher.[56]

Even as recently as 1993, Donald Davie's treatment of the same period gives Anne Steele only a dismissive mention, in one sentence in a paragraph comparing Doddridge with Watts.[57]

Anne Steele and Ann Dutton

In fact, the hymns of Anne Steele (1717–78) were widely known and well loved during her lifetime and for a century or more after her death. She brought out her first collection in two volumes in 1760, under the pen name of Theodosia (God's gift), to the delight of her father William Steele, also a hymn-writer, whose diary for 27 November records his prayer to God to 'make it useful and keep her humble'![58]

Sixty-two of her hymns were included in the *Bristol Baptist Collection of Hymns* 1769, compiled by John Ash and Caleb Evans, which made them available outside her own community. Evans, who was the Principal of the Bristol Baptist Academy, went on to publish a collection of her hymns and poems in 1780, with his own preface, which was widely used in America, and was reprinted in 1808. At the end of the nineteenth century, Julian is citing 75 of her hymns as still in current use.[59]

Her family's acquaintance with Ash and Evans marks their place as at the liberal forefront of thinking within the Particular Baptist movement at the time. Ash, who was a relative of the family by marriage, published a book, *Sentiments on Education*, in 1777,[60] which included an essay on 'Female Accomplishments', in favour of women's education, while Evans was opposed to slavery and a supporter of America's liberation in the War of Independence.

Ann Steele was by no means a passive participant in these circles. Although she had little in the way of formal education, she was well read. Her father bequeathed an impressive range of books to her on his death. Her early education was at a school in Trowbridge, quite possibly the girls' school attached to the Trowbridge Particular Baptist Academy, which was a Dissenting Academy, training young men for the ministry and offering them the education from which they were otherwise barred, since Nonconformists could not attend Oxford or

Cambridge Universities. In fact Dissenting Academies offered an excellent education, pioneering learning methods that came to form the basis of much modern education.[61]

It is also clear from her correspondence and verse that she took a keen interest in the matters of the day. She was aware of the flow of national events, and wrote hymns for use at times of national crisis such as the two public fasts called in February of 1756 and 1757. These occasional hymns were for use in the congregation in Broughton, where she worshipped and her father preached. They are not triumphalist at all, but speak very specifically of the nature of the crisis,[62] and rather generally of the sin and need for repentance that had brought Britain to this point.

As a member of a Nonconformist congregation, Anne Steele would have known and sung Isaac Watts' hymns. His influence on her own writing can be seen, and is considerable. On his death, as on the deaths of many of her friends, she celebrated his life in verse.

Like Watts', her writing is steeped in Scripture. Many hymns are directly based on Scripture passages, which she interprets with a sure hand, in the context of lived spiritual experience. The parable of the prodigal son becomes an impassioned invitation to the gospel feast:

> In him [Jesus] the Father reconcil'd
> Invites your souls to come;
> The rebel shall be called a child,
> And kindly welcomed home.

The hymn ends with a resounding call to faith:

> And yet ten thousand thousand more,
> Are welcome still to come:
> Ye longing souls, the grace adore;
> Approach, there yet is room.[63]

The influence of Watts is even more clearly seen in a text such as 'Great King of kings, eternal God', entitled 'Humble Worship', in which she echoes Watts' 'Eternal Power, whose high abode', in comparing the insufficiency of human worship with the humility of the heavenly powers. Compare Steele's

> The brightest Seraph veils his face;
> And low before thy dazzling throne,
> With prostrate homage all confess
> Thou art the infinite unknown,[64]

with Watts':

> Thee while the great archangel sings,
> He hides his face beneath his wings,
> And throngs of shining thrones around
> Fall worshipping and spread the ground.

Even the phrase, 'infinite unknown' appears in Watts' 'God is a name my soul adores', where the capitalization of 'Infinite' renders the phrase clearer and more sophisticated than in Steele's hymn.[65] But where Watts follows the objective thought of 'Eternal power' to silence,

> God is in heaven, and Men below,
> Be short our tunes, our words be few;
> A sacred reverence checks our songs
> And praise sits silent on our tongues,[66]

Steele gives the theme a christological twist. Into the darkness of the night where 'Man' is wrapt, comes 'the bright, the morning star!', which brings 'Sweet promise of immortal day!' and the hymn ends with the possibility of praise restored through him:

> To him our longing eyes we raise,
> Our guide to thee, the great unknown,
> Through him, O may our humble praise
> Accepted rise before thy throne.[67]

While writers of the twentieth century may ignore or dismiss Steele, she is more equably treated in more recent literature. J. R. Broome compares her favourably to Watts, considering that Watts far excelled in his ability to raise worshippers' eyes to the majesty and ineffability of God, but in engaging with people's own spiritual experience Broome considered them equal: 'Her hymns carry a vein of experience [sometimes wrongly called introspection].'[68]

Certainly, Anne Steele took her own writing seriously. She had confidence in producing texts for her own congregation to sing, even though she published under a pen name. She did not marry. There is a romantic story of her fiancé being drowned on the eve of their marriage, but this does not seem to be supported by evidence. In fact, she writes to her half-sister Molly that, though she has received at least one proposal, she does not see much benefit in married life and prefers to remain single.[69] Broome suggests that she rejected marriage for the sake of her writing.

Another educated, authentic female voice raised in the debates of the time was Ann Dutton (1698–1765), also from a Baptist background, and a vigorous correspondent with both Whitefield and Wesley, disagreeing with the latter.[70]

She published her autobiography to great acclaim in 1743 and, enlarged, in three volumes in 1750.[71] The later version returned to a theme familiar in the writings of women, in a letter about 'the Lawfulness of Printing Any Thing Written by a Woman'. Much of her work was published anonymously or under the initials A. D., but her books were widely read and influential on both sides of the Atlantic in the early days of what became known as the First Great Awakening.[72]

The preface to her book of hymns and poems describes the reluctance with which she allowed her work to be published. Her verses flow from her own deep inner faith and her relationship with Jesus, which she describes in a rich allusion to bridal imagery: 'when my Beloved had took me by the Hand, and led me to take some Turns with himself in the vast Field of boundless Grace, he there shew'd me a Variety of Wonders'.[73] This led her further into the writing of verses, which she initially intended for her own private devotion, but shared with some intimate friends. As the verses began to find their way into the public domain, she writes, she was compelled to publish a correct version, to counter the errors that were appearing in the texts.

This is how she faces the age-old dilemma of women writers: how to hold together her evangelical conviction that women should remain in the private sphere with the public acclaim with which her writing was greeted. D. Bruce Hindmarsh sees her attitude as characteristic of her time: 'She did so precisely by reflecting on the boundaries between public and private spheres, boundaries that were shifting in significant ways in the wider society during her lifetime.'[74]

Hindmarsh is commenting on Dutton in a study of conversion narratives. During this period of Awakening, on both sides of the Atlantic, a powerful common narrative was disseminated through personal accounts of overwhelming conversion. The stories were told in major autobiographies such as that of Ann Dutton, but also in a number of evangelical periodicals that sprang up in the 1740s.

These engendered an apocalyptic fervour, in lively expectation that the seeming conversion of the whole world, and avalanche of Pentecostal fervour, presaged the imminent second coming of Christ. They also enabled people to experience and enter into the common narrative when revival came to their own community. They longed for the movement of the Spirit and their own awakening, and recognized it when it came, in terms that they had read of in the lives of others.

Ann Dutton interpreted her own life in the same terms, and so writes about her own experience in ways that others could identify with. Her collection of hymns and verses is published as a narrative of her own experience of God's grace, called *A Narration of the Wonders of Grace in Verse*. Hindmarsh comments:

> Dutton had learned not only to read her life like a text, but to use it like a text to preach a gospel message. She entered the rhetoric of conversion as a child, owned it and experienced it for herself, and then she offered it up as an exemplary life for others. Conversion was the axis upon which her life turned not only from sin to grace, but also from private experience to public expression and indeed public advocacy.[75]

The relentless message from the hymns is the fact of the incarnation, crucifixion and resurrection, by which human beings are saved and in which we have our hope. Our life of faith is imperfect here, but we look towards perfection in eternity, a perfection that we see in Christ.

This evangelical gospel is proclaimed in hymn after hymn, sometimes rather didactically, always with a wealth of biblical references, which are noted in the margins beside the text, and occasionally with images of originality and freshness. Hymn VIII, based on the Song of Songs 6.10, is about the beauty of Christ's spouse, the believer. The theme running through the text is that of light – the light of the morning sun, which is Jesus. In comparison:

> Our Beauty now is like the Moon,
> That shineth with a borrow'd Light;
> Increasing, waning, changing soon,
> And full of Spots, though she is bright.

In Christ, however, we appear to God in full light:

> But we, as Christ the Sun, are clear,
> Compleatly, like our glorious Head;
> As we in him to God appear,
> Our Beauty is most perfect made.

But this beauty is not perfect in us. We long for the day when the Bride of the Lamb will enter into her own true beauty:

> But, O! when shall the Lamb's dear Bride,
> That now is cloath'd with Christ the Sun,
> Be openly plac'd at his Side,
> And put her royal Garments on.

The marginal references to the Bible almost cease during the verse on the moon, since here Dutton is drawing on a long tradition of comparing the female character to that changeable body. The bright masculine Sun, identified with the male Saviour, Jesus, provides the source of light which the moon can only reflect imperfectly. The reference to the female menses is perhaps unconscious in the context of bridal hopes. But Dutton uses the bridal imagery with doctrinal confidence. The female is not obliterated or subsumed in the male in the moment of transformation. She remains a bride, and her glory comes when she puts on her own garments and shares the kingdom with Christ.

> The Glory that the Bride will wear;
> When in Christ's Throne she shall sit down,
> And with him in the Kingdom share,
> While God shall be her Glory-Crown![76]

Notes

1 Diana Maury Robin, *Publishing Women: Salons, the Presses, and the Counter-Reformation in Sixteenth-century Italy*, Chicago: University of Chicago Press, 2007, p. xx.

2 Robin, *Publishing Women*, p. 1.

3 Mirjam de Baar, '*Ik moet spreken: Het spiritueel leiderschap van Antoinette Bourignon (1616–1680)* Utrecht: Walburg, 2004, English summary, p. 181.

4 Axel Erdmann, *My Gracious Silence: Women in the Mirror of Sixteenth-Century Printing*, Lucerne, Switzerland: Gilhofer & Ranschburg GmbH, 1999, p. xxi.

5 Colonna, *Sonnets for Michelangelo*, p. 333, cited in Abigail Brundin, *Vittoria Colonna and the Spiritual Poetics of the Italian Reformation*, Aldershot: Ashgate, 2008, p 111, her translation in n. 29, p. 111.

6 *Libro Quarto delle rime di diversi eccellentiss. autori nella lingua volgare. Nuovamente raccolte*, Bologna: Anselmo Giaccarello, 1551, p. 13, cited in Brundin, *Vittoria Colonna*, p 113, her translation in n. 35.

7 Brundin, *Vittoria Colonna*, p. 104.

8 De Baar, *Ik moet spreken*, p. 809.

9 De Baar, *Ik moet spreken*, p. 809.

10 Patricia A. Ward, 'Madame Guyon (1648–1717)', in Carter Lindberg (ed.), *The Pietist Theologians*, Oxford: Blackwell, 2005, pp. 161–73, pp. 172–3.

11 De Baar, *Ik moet spreken*, p. 811.

12 *Methodist Hymn Book*, London: Methodist Publishing House, 1933, no. 546; *Redemption Hymnal*, Wendover: Rickfords Publishing, 1951, no. 599; *New Redemption Hymnal*, Bletchley: Word (UK) Ltd., 1986, no. 778; *Song Book of the Salvation Army*, London: Salvationist Publishing and Supplies, 1953, no. 433; *Song Book of the Salvation Army*, London: Salvationist Publishing and Supplies, 1986, no. 480.

13 Antoinette Bourignon, *Toutes les Oeuvres de Mlle Bourignon*, Amsterdam, 1686, vol. II, p. 67.

14 Richard Watson, *The English Hymn*, Oxford: Oxford University Press, 1997, p. 213.

15 Antoinette Bourignon 'Venés Jesus, mon salutaire', Bourignon, *Oeuvres*, vol. II, pp. 65–7, vv. 3, 5; John Wesley (1703–91), 'Come, Saviour Jesus, from above', John and Charles Wesley, *Hymns and Sacred Poems*, London, 1739, pp. 123–4, vv. 5–6, 9–10.

16 William Bull, 'Preface', in William Bull (ed.), *Poems Translated from the French of Madame de la Mothe Guion by the late William Cowper to which are added some original poems not inserted in his works*, Newport Pagnel, 1801, pp. v–viii, pp. vii–viii.

17 David Hempston, 'John Wesley (1703–1791)', in Lindberg (ed.), *The Pietist Theologians*, pp. 256–71, p. 257.

18 J. M. B. de la Mothe Guion, 'Amour que mon ame est contente', *Poesies & Cantiques Spirituels sure divers Sujets qui regardent la Vie Interieure ou l'Esprit du Vrai Christianisme*, Cologne, 1722, vol. 2, cantique CVIII, vv. 3, 6, William Cowper, 'O thou, by experience tried', *Poems Translated from the French of Madame de la Mothe Guion*, pp. 33, 34, vv. 3, 6. See p. 86 for this text's use in a missionary context.

19 Guion, 'Adorable Epoux de mon ame', *Poesies & Cantiques Spirituels*, vol. 2, cantique XCV, vv. 1, 5 (ll. 1–2), 6 (ll. 3–4); Cowper, 'My Spouse! in whose presence I live', *Poems Translated from the French of Madame de la Mothe Guion*, pp. 23–4. This metre, 8888, anapaestic with an iambic foot opening each line, was used by Charles Wesley for his most mystical writing: see Richard Watson and Kenneth Trickett (eds), *Companion to Hymns & Psalms*, London: Methodist Publishing House, 1988, p. 427.

20 Elisabeth Schneider-Böklen, *Der Herr hat Grosses mir getan: Frauen im Gesangbuch*, Stuttgart: Quell Verlag, 1995, p. 7.

21 Janet Wootton, 'Hymn-writing, the Lost Generation', *Hymn Society Bulletin* 257, vol. 19, no. 1, January 2009, pp. 91–6.

22 See below, p. 46.

23 Robin Leaver, *Elisabeth Creutziger: The Magdeburg Enchiridion 1536 and Reformation Theology*, The Kessler Reformation Lecture, 18 October 1994, Occasional Publications of the Pitts Theological Library, 1995, p. 4.

24 Liturgy and Hymns, vol. 53 of *Luther's Works*, ed. Ulrich S. Leopold, Philadelphia: Fortress Press, 1965, p. 512, cited in Leaver, *Elisabeth Creutziger*, p. 4.

25 Leaver, *Elisabeth Creutziger*, p. 9.

26 A Latin office hymn of Prudentius, translated as 'Of the Father's love begotten' by John Mason Neale (1818–66).

27 *Nicolaus Ludwig Graf von Zinzendorf Herrnhuter Gesangbuch: christliches Gesang-Buch der Evangelischen Bru der-Gemeinen von 1735, mit einem Vorwort von Erich Beyreuther und Gerhard Meyer un einer Einleitung, 'Zinzendorf und seine Gesangbücher als Ausdruck barocken Lebensgefühls' von Gerhard Meyer,* Hildesheim: Ols, 1981, no. 29, p. 32, vv. 1, 2, 3 (ll. 5–7).

28 See *Nicolaus Ludwig Graf von Zinzendorf Herrnhuter Gesangbuch*.

29 Catherine Winkworth, *The Chorale Book for England*, London: Longman, Green, Longman, Roberts and Green, 1863, no. 155.

30 'From God alone begotten', in Carl Daw, *A Year of Grace*, Carol Spring: Hope Publishing Company, 1990, no. 37, v. 2.

31 See John Johansen, *Moravian Hymnody*, Moravian Music Foundation Publications, no. 9, Winston-Salem: The Moravian Music Foundation, 1980.

32 Elsie Anne McKee, *Katharina Schütz Zell*, vol. 1, 'The Life and Thought of a Sixteenth-Century Reformer', Leiden: Brill, 1999, p. xi.

33 McKee, *Katharina Schütz Zell*, vol. 1, p. xxii.

34 McKee, *Katharina Schütz Zell*, vol. 2, 'The Writings: A Critical Edition' Leiden: Brill, 1999, p. 56.

35 Kirsi Stjerna, *Women and the Reformation*, Oxford: Blackwell Publishing, 2008, p. 121.

36 Stjerna, *Women and the Reformation*, p. 123.

37 McKee, *Katharina Schütz Zell*, vol. 2, p. 56.

38 See above, p. 42.

39 For a fuller history and list of hymn books, see Johansen, *Moravian Hymnody*.

40 Johansen, *Moravian Hymnody*, p. 14.

41 Peter Vogt, 'A Voice for Themselves: Women as Participants in Congregational Discourse in the Eighteenth-Century Moravian Movement', in Beverly Mayne Kienzle and Pamela J. Walker (eds), *Women Preachers and Prophets through Two Millennia of Christianity*, Berkeley: University of California Press, 1998, pp. 227–47, p. 237.

42 Gary Steven Kinkel, *Our Dear Mother the Spirit: An Investigation of Count Zinzendorf's Theology and Praxis*, Lanham MD: University Press of America, 1990, p. 221.

43 Kinkel, *Our Dear Mother the Spirit*, p. 73.

44 Kinkel, *Our Dear Mother the Spirit*, p. 73.

45 Vogt, 'A Voice for Themselves', p. 237.

46 Zinzendorf, *Herrnhuter Gesangbuch*.

47 Theodore Kübler, *Historical Notes to the Lyra Germanica*, London: Longman, Green, Longman, Roberts and Green, 1865, p. 224.

48 *Bruder-Gesangbuch*, (1778), no. 1179; tr. in *Lyra Germanica: Second Series, The Christian Life*, London: Longman, Brown, Green, Longman and Roberts, 1858, p. 90.

49 Zinzendorf, *Herrnhuter Gesangbuch*, no. 1233; John Wesley, 'I thirst, Thou wounded Lamb of God', *Redemption Hymnal*, no. 590; *New Redemption Hymnal*, no. 772; *Christian Hymns*, Bridgend: Evangelical Movement of Wales,

1977, no. 597; *Making Melody*, Nottingham: Assemblies of God Publishing House/Reflections Distribution, 1983, no. 566; *Song Book of the Salvation Army*, no. 367; *Song Book of the Salvation Army*, no. 424.

50 Zinzendorf, *Herrnhuter Gesangbuch*, no. 1197; *Hymns & Psalms*, Peterborough: Methodist Publishing House, 1983, no. 568.

51 See Madeleine Forell Marshall and Janet Todd, *English Congregational Hymns in the Eighteenth Century*, Kentucky: University Press of Kentucky, 1982, pp. 19–26.

52 N. Tate and N. Brady, *A New Version of the Psalms of David: Fitted to the Tunes used in Churches*, London, 1696.

53 *The Psalmes of David, Translated into Divers and Sundry Kindes of Verse, more rare and excellent for the Method and Variety than ever yet hath beeing done in English. Begun by the noble and learned Gent, Sir Philip Sidney, Knt., and finished by the Right Honorable The Countess of Pembroek, his sister*, Hereford: John Davies, 1823, Psalm CIV, pp. 193–7, vv. 1, 5 (ll. 5–8), 8 (ll. 5–8).

54 p. xii. I imagine that his use of the word 'men' here is instinctive rather than ironic.

55 Louis Fitzgerald Benson, *The Hymnody of the Christian Church*, Philadelphia: Westminster Press, 1927, p. 114, my emphasis.

56 Marshall and Todd, *English Congregational Hymns*, p. 28.

57 Donald Davie, *The Eighteenth-Century Hymn in England*, Cambridge: Cambridge University Press, 1993, p. 5.

58 Cited in 'Memoir' by John Sheppard, in Anne Steele, *Hymns, Psalms and Poems*, London: Daniel Sedgwick, 1863, p. xii.

59 John Julian, *A Dictionary of Hymnology: setting forth the origin and history of Christian hymns of all ages and nations*, rev. edn with new Supplement, London: John Murray, 1925, pp. 1089–90.

60 John Ash, *Sentiments on Education, collected from the best writers; properly methodised, and interspersed with occasional observations*, Dublin: W. Whitestone, 1777.

61 J. W. Ashley Smith, *The Birth of Modern Education: The Contribution of the Dissenting Academies, 1660–1800*, London: Independent Press, 1954.

62 The hymn for 1756, 'See gracious God, before thy throne', mentions 'Tremendous judgments' (v. 2, l. 1) that display God's power but spare Britain. A footnote in the 1808 edition of the hymns refers to the 'Earthquake at Lisbon, &c.', *The Works of Anne Steele*, Boston: Munroe, Francis and Parker, 1808, vol. 1, p. 225.

63 Anne Steele, 'Ye wretched, starving, hungry poor', *The Works of Anne Steele*, vol. 1, pp. 38–9, vv. 4, 6.

64 Anne Steele, 'Great King of kings, eternal God', *The Works of Anne Steele*, vol. 1, p. 55, v. 2.

65 Isaac Watts, 'God is a name my soul adores', Isaac Watts, *Horae Lyricae: Poems, Chiefly of the Lyric Kind*, corrected edn, London, 1731, pp. 13–14, v. 1 (l. 4).

66 Isaac Watts, 'Eternal Power whose high abode', *Horae Lyricae*, pp. 141–2, vv. 3–6. Verse 3 originally read, 'Thy dazling Beauties whilst he sings/He hides his face beneath his Wings;/And ranks of shining Thrones around/Fall worshipping and spread the Ground'. The 'he' is Gabriel, who is mentioned in the usually

omitted second verse. The hymn is titled 'Conclusion' and ends the first book of poems *To Devotion and Piety*.

67 Anne Steele, 'Great King of kings', v. 5.

68 J. R. Broome, *A Bruised Reed: The Life and Times of Anne Steele*, Harpenden, Gospel Standard Trust Publications, 2007, p. 165.

69 Broome, *A Bruised Reed: The Life and Times of Anne Steele*, pp. 112–13.

70 Ann Dutton, 'A Letter to the Rev. Mr. J. Wesley. In vindication of the Doctrines of Absolute Election, Particular Redemption, Special Vocation, and Final Perseverance. Occasioned chiefly by some things in his Dialogue between a Predestinarian and his friend; and in his Hymns on God's Everlasting Love', London: S. Mason, 1742.

71 Ann Dutton, *A Brief Account of the Gracious Dealings of God, with a Poor, Sinful, Unworthy Creature*, London, 1743, and in three volumes, with an appendix and letter (prefixed) on the lawfulness of a woman's appearing in print, London, 1750.

72 But see Thomas Kidd, who argues that the divisions into the 'First' and 'Second' Great Awakenings belie the continuity of the evangelical movement: 'The long First Great Awakening started before Jonathan Edwards's 1734–35 Northampton revival and lasted roughly through the end of the American Revolution, when disestablishment, theological change, and a new round of growth started the (even more imprecise) "Second" Great Awakening.' Thomas Kidd, *The Great Awakening: the Roots of Evangelical Christianity in Colonial America*, New Haven CT: Yale University Press, 2007, p. xix.

73 Ann Dutton, *A Narration of the Wonders of Grace in Verse*, London, 1734, p. v. The margin gives a reference to the Song of Songs 7.11.

74 D. Bruce Hindmarsh, *The Evangelical Conversion Narrative, Spiritual Autobiography in Early Modern England*, Oxford: Oxford University Press, 2005, p. 300.

75 Hindmarsh, *The Evangelical Conversion Narrative*, p. 297.

76 Ann Dutton, 'As Morning-Light the Saints look forth', *A Narration of the Wonders of Grace in Verse*, Hymn VIII, vv. 4, 6, 7, 9.

3

The Nineteenth Century:
Evangelical and Evangelistic

Commenting on the publication of *Hymns Ancient and Modern* in 1861,[1] Richard Watson mentions four existing traditions of nineteenth-century hymn-writing that were drawn into the new book. Two of the four relate to women writers. The first is 'the important new source of German hymnody, translated by Frances E. Cox, Catherine Winkworth and others'.[2] By far the majority of hymns translated from German writers which have continued in use are by women writers, mostly Catherine Winkworth, who, as we shall see, was captivated by the intense spiritual nature of their texts.

The other was simply 'the emergence of the woman writer'. While women's hymn-writing was not unknown in earlier centuries, as we have seen, Watson goes on, 'In the nineteenth century, women hymn-writers became much more important, contributing what came to be regarded as a particular ministry to the writing of hymns.'[3]

Two things are important here. First, that hymn-writing by women became far more prevalent and widespread in the nineteenth century, and second that women were perceived as providing what Watson refers to as a 'particular ministry'. In fact, it was a number of particular ministries, whose particularity arose at least partially from the need to justify the prominence of women as writers, speakers and even leaders in nineteenth-century religious movements.

The mental anguish caused by women's internalizing the patriarchal norms of their times has given way to a justification of women's writing as somehow distinct from men's, as innately feminine, gentle, born out of suffering, or aimed at specific audiences, such as the lost, or children.

This has been documented most closely in studies of nineteenth-century American Protestantism, beginning with Ann Douglas' classical text, *The Feminization of American Culture*, in which she describes an alliance between clergy and women, forged, or perhaps forced, in response to the bifurcation of society with the rise of industrial and commercial interests, leading to the privatization of religion.

She does not document this without passion, as we shall see in these chapters. She describes the feminized alliance thus:

> The minister and the lady were appointed by their society as the champions of sensibility. They were in the position of contestants in a fixed fight: they had agreed to put on a convincing show, and to lose. The fakery involved was finally crippling for all concerned.[4]

Sandra Sizer concentrates specifically on the surge of hymn-writing in America in the 1850s, with a great increase in the proportion of women's writing, amounting to nearly a third of the post-1820 texts in Sankey's *Gospel Hymns*.[5] Following Douglas, she also attributes the rise of a feminine spirituality and increase in women's hymn-writing to the privatization of religion. Religious life became the function of the domestic sphere, the home, with its connotations of safety, nurture and purity, the domain of the wife and mother, while the industrialized public sphere was increasingly perceived as dangerous, corrupting and (of course) masculine. Evangelical spirituality constantly called the sinner 'home' from the lost exterior world, to where the static feminine offered God's salvation.

In Britain as well as in America, there was a flood of hymn-writing by women, which flowed from this desire to call the sinner home, whether the sinner was the young man, too tempted by the world, the child, who needed a thorough grounding in the moral certainties, or the African or Hindu, bereft of the 'civilizing influence' of the Christian Church.

Women were tirelessly active, then, in a range of evangelistic and social concerns. The world, from which all these people needed saving, was awash with the temptations of alcohol, sexual licence and moral turpitude. Women were at the forefront of temperance movements and work among the poor, as well as home and overseas missions.

However, while these activities provided a platform for women's speaking and writing, they also exercised powerful limiting factors. By identifying with these causes, Nancy Cott notes, women became confined to them. Their writing is by and large passionate, emotional, rather than intellectual, evangelistic rather than doctrinal, filled with challenge and call to the human person rather than worship of God.

The other limiting factor was the failure of these writers to develop beyond the sentimentality of their genres. Douglas comments: 'America lost its male-dominated theological tradition without gaining a comprehensive feminism or an adequately modernized religious sensibility.'[6] It is a shame that the hymns that continue in use are, by and large, from the evangelistic traditions, rather than the more radical traditions of women's writing, which did exist, and were openly critical of intellectual vacuity or sentimentality. These are the subject of the next chapter.

This chapter explores the enormous wealth of women's hymn-writing in the nineteenth century, continuing the story of the great evangelical awakenings that swept through America and Britain, and gave rise to mission movements at home and abroad.

Early revival in Wales

In Britain, the story of revival continues with the voice of an amazing woman, daughter and wife of tenant farmers, who lived all her life in the same farmhouse in Wales. Ann Griffiths (1776–1805) produced hymns of great theological sophistication and beauty. I say 'produced', since the texts come to us in the writing of her maid/companion's husband. Ann used to sing the hymns as the expression of her own relationship with God. Her maid, who was illiterate, remembered them, and sang them to her husband, who wrote them down.

The hymns have been regarded as pretty well miraculous. An untutored woman, living in a remote part of Wales, producing hymns of such depth and magnificence is a miracle in itself, and their transmission makes them even more unlikely.

Quite rightly, A. M. Allchin punctures the romance of this Anglo-centric view. Rural Wales is remote only from an urban English perspective, and revival generally tended to reverse society's perspectives and reveal the talents of people on its margins.

In fact, the voice of Ann Griffiths is enriched by the traditions and culture of the Wales of her time. Allchin points to the strong oral poetic and musical traditions that existed in Wales, and that reached back through the Royal Bards to ancient times. Allchin writes: 'Ann belongs to that one Celtic nation which in the origins of its language and its literature was deeply touched by the order and discipline of the Roman Empire.'[7]

A famous Eisteddfod had been held in Bala in 1789 when Ann was 13 years old. She would have taken part in *plygain* carol singing, which brought together a strong Protestant theology and an ancient musical form. She would also have sung the hymns of Watts and Wesley, and the great evangelical hymn-writer William Williams, *Pantycelyn*.[8]

Besides this, she would have come into regular contact with the *Book of Common Prayer* during her time as an Anglican worshipper, and then, quite likely, with the Welsh translation of Richard Baxter's *The Saint's Everlasting Rest*.[9] Once part of the evangelical revival, she would have heard preachers like Thomas Charles of Bala and Thomas Jones of Denbigh. Thus, though remote from more mainstream channels of learning and influence, Ann was steeped in a rich poetic tradition and surrounded by deep thinkers in the theology of the evangelical reformation.

This is the theology that runs with passion through her hymns. She is fascinated by the notion of the Trinity, and the dual nature of Christ, and expresses her longing not just to understand these as doctrines, but to experience them as divine reality. She maintains her focus on her relationship with Christ, but manipulates a wide range of Old Testament imagery with breathtaking dexterity.

A hymn that begins in the tent of meeting with the blood sacrifice providing 'the sinner's nesting place'[10] ('I bechadur wneyd ei nyth'), ends with this tour de force of imagery, passion and doctrine:

O am ddyfod o'r Anialwch
I fynu fel Colofnau mŵg,
Yn uniawn gyrchiol at ei orsedd,
Mae yno'n eistedd heb ei wg;
Amen diddechreu a diddiwedd,
Tyst ffyddlon yw, a'i air yn un,
Amlygu y mae ogoniant trindod
Yn achubiaeth Damniol ddyn.[11]

O, to come like smoke in columns
rising from this wilderness,
straight toward his throne to see him
seated with unfrowning face;
without end, without beginning,
witness to the one in three,
making known the threefold glory,
True Amen, who sets us free.[12]

She often expresses her devotion to Jesus in language drawn from the Song of Songs, in which she, the singer, is the bride. Sometimes, this is interwoven with the Bible's female imagery for Zion.

There are some one-verse hymns of intense, occasionally erotic emotion.

Nag Edryched neb i gloffi
Arnaf, am fy mod yn ddu;
Haul, a Gwres ei belederau
Yn tywynu'n danbaid arnaf sŷ;
Mae a'm cuddia, &c
Cysgod lleni Solomon.[13]

Do not stare with hesitation:
I am black, but though the sun
pours its scorching heat upon me
fiery splendour blazing down,
I am sheltered
by the veils of Solomon.[14]

Her letters describe her inner struggle. Again, she brings what is evidently an able and questioning mind to bear on her faith. Allchin says,

> without question, she was a thinker. She longed to penetrate into the mysteries of faith and she used her powers of reflection constantly to go further, to go beyond the formulations and the words she employed to the reality which lies beyond them.[15]

We can see this, and enter into the fruits of her impassioned reflections, through her letters, but above all through her hymns.

Anglican evangelicalism

Around the turn of the eighteenth/nineteenth century, an influential group of evangelical Anglicans came together in the then village of Clapham, worshipping at the Parish Church of the Holy Trinity. The group engaged in some of the great moral and social debates of the time, including the abolition of slavery, working with William Wilberforce and others, and the evangelization of working-class children. One of the major voices was the campaigner and writer Hannah More (1745–1843).[16] At its heart was a profound evangelical faith, influenced by the revivals of Whitefield and the Wesleys, but remaining within the Church of England.

Charlotte Elliott (1789–1871) was born in Clapham, into a family that was at the centre of the Clapham Sect. She was a frequent invalid, and her writing draws from that experience, and is offered to similar sufferers. Her opening poem 'To the Reader', in her book *Hours of Sorrow*, addresses the collection to sufferers:

Not for the gay and thoughtless do I weave
These plaintive strains; they have not learnt to grieve:

Instead, she speaks to people in all kinds of distress, specifically from her own experience:

To tell them where another heart found rest,
Once like their own, disquieted, unblest;
And where, though sought in vain on earthly ground,
A balm of sovereign virtue may be found.[17]

She came to faith herself under the ministry of evangelist Cesar Malan of Geneva, in 1822, after a bout of serious illness the year before. Her sister's memoir relates that Charlotte asked Malan how she should come to God, to which he replied, 'Come just as you are'. The hymn inspired by those words was not written for another 12 years, when, still an invalid, she was living with her brother, who was an Anglican priest. Too ill to accompany the family to a charity sale of work, she sat down to write from the experience of the moment.[18]

In fact, the hymn, 'Just as I am', became instantly popular. In James King's survey of Anglican hymnody in 1885, Elliott was the only woman author with more than one hymn in the 'first rank' (that is, hymns that appear in more than 30 books. Her two are 'My God, my Father, while I stray' (44 books) and 'Just as I am' (35 books)).[19] Of the latter, King notes that it has been 'translated into almost every language of Europe as well as into Arabic'.[20]

This is echoed in a fulsome tribute paid by the incumbent at Emmanuel Church, Brighton, Octavius Winslow, in a sermon preached on the Sunday following her interment. He proclaims, 'It is sung in the jungles of Hindoostan, on the burning sands of Africa, amid the eternal snows of Greenland . . .', and much more in the same vein: 'In short, its music has gone out through all the earth, its words unto the end of the world.'[21] Her brother commented, 'In the course of a long ministry I hope I have been permitted to see some fruit of my labours; but I feel far more has been done by a single hymn of my sister's.'[22]

King's survey has a section on hymns which are 'rapidly finding their way into modern Hymnals, and in future they will probably take rank as "standard hymns"'.[23] Among these 'hymns for the future' are three by Cecil Frances Alexander (1818–95),[24] and Frances Ridley Havergal's (1836–79) 'Thou art coming, O my Saviour', which appears in five of the surveyed books. James King was right to 'spot' Havergal. Her hymns, especially 'Take my life and let it be', gained enormous popularity.

Frances Ridley Havergal was the youngest child of William Henry Havergal, Rector of Astley, musician and composer. She wrote poetry from an early age, and earned money from a few publications early on. She was very involved, with the rest of her family, in parish life, and in the work of missionary societies, and packed an immense amount of activity into a short life.

She was very close to her father, sharing his musical ability. After his death, she was approached by the Revd C. B. Snepp, originally for permission to publish her father's tunes as a companion to his own compilation of evangelical texts. This proved difficult at first, because her stepmother was possessive towards his compositions.

Eventually, Frances was able to compile her father's tunes in *Havergal's Psalmody*, and even (with some persuasion) added some of her own in an appendix. She also wrote some texts for Snepp's hymnbook, and then worked with him in compiling a full music edition of Snepp's book, *Songs of Grace and Glory*,[25] with tunes by her father and herself. As they worked on the publication, Frances developed a firm friendship with the Revd and Mrs Snepp and their family.

Like Snepp, Frances was a convinced and polemical evangelical. She revelled in her middle name, given for her godfather, but to her a link with the martyred Bishop Ridley. In a poem on her name, she writes:

But what the R doth represent,
I value and revere;
A diamond clasp it seems to be
On golden chains enlinking me
In loyal love to England's hope,
Bulwark 'gainst infidel and Pope,
the Church I love so dear.[26]

She was adamantly against the new *Hymns Ancient and Modern*, which she regarded as 'the thin edge of the wedge of Popery'.[27]

The positive side of this was a fervour for evangelical mission. She was energetically involved in missions in Bewdley and Liverpool, where her contribution was 'the ministry of song'. She trained choirs – with the aim that their leadership of music should itself be evangelical –

played the organ, and occasionally spoke and led prayers, though it was her sister Maria that seems to have had a vocation for preaching, nursing, as she did, a dream of preaching in St Paul's Cathedral.[28]

Frances Ridley Havergal herself found blessing at Advent in 1873. It was a completely sudden, overwhelming experience, which she described in a conversation recorded by her sister Maria:

> I first saw clearly the blessedness of true consecration. I saw it as a flash of electric light, and what you *see* you can never *un*see . . . I just utterly yielded myself to Him, and utterly trusted Him to keep me.[29]

The story surrounding her most famous hymn, 'Take my life and let it be', demonstrates the interweaving of evangelism and song. The author tells it in her own words:

> There were ten persons in the house, some unconverted and long prayed for, some converted but not rejoicing Christians. He gave me the prayer, 'Lord, give me ALL in this house.' And he just did. Before I left the house every one had got a blessing. . . I was too happy to sleep, and spent most of the night in praise and renewal of my own consecration, and these little couplets formed themselves and chimed in my heart, one after another, till they finished with, *Ever*, ONLY, ALL for Thee![30]

As well as for her poetry and hymns, Frances was much in demand as a writer for evangelical publications, as a speaker for the YWCA and several other organizations, and she devoted time to the Mildmay Institution, founded by the Revd and Mrs Pennefather for training women in mission, and modelled on Lutheran Deaconess Institutions. The output of her short life was tremendous. As Routley notes, 'This is not the introverted evangelicalism of Christina Rossetti but a supremely unself-conscious and extroverted frame of mind.'[31] More than that, her outward-looking evangelicalism was lived out in a passion for the conversion and betterment of others.

Her 1874 book, *The Ministry of Song*, begins (after a poetic prelude) with a poem of that title. There she urges those with that ministry to sing in a whole variety of circumstances: to children, by cottage bedsides, where grand organs play in city churches, and 'where the village voices/Fall harshly on your ear'![32] The purpose of the song is to inspire, convert, comfort, teach and, above all, to praise.

Sanctification and holiness

This was a time when the energy from the Second Great Awakening was sweeping back across the Atlantic from the United States. In 1873, the American evangelist Robert Pearsall Smith came to Britain. He found evangelicalism in a bitter and divided state, emphasizing martyrdom and suffering, and mired in moral gloom. He and his wife Hannah proclaimed a different kind of evangelical spirituality, called the 'Higher Christian Life', which promised a sense of joyous peace to be found through total reliance on Jesus.

Through a series of encounters, this visit led to the establishment of the Keswick Convention in 1875, and a whole series of conventions and missions.

Havergal's hymns were taken up and sung at Keswick and published in the various editions of the Keswick hymnbook, *Hymns of Consecration and Faith*.[33] This brought Frances into contact with the great American evangelical hymn-writers. In 1874, Sankey and Moody toured the British Isles, sparking revival and fanning existing enthusiasm. Mr and Mrs Moody visited Frances during the tour. Fanny Crosby corresponded with Frances, and the two women admired each other's work, though they never met.

The Keswick Conventions were modelled, at least in part, on the American tradition of camp meetings. These were great outdoor campaigns, which had their roots in the outdoor preaching of the Wesleys and Whitefield, but took on a life of their own and flourished through the nineteenth century and into the twentieth.

In the nineteenth century, Methodists in Britain and the United States laid an emphasis on the attainment of sanctification, following personal conversion. This was a state of complete holiness, the conquest of sin, not only by redemption but as an active state of existence. Phoebe Palmer (1807–74) was among those who claimed to have attained complete sanctification, and she is considered to be one of the founders of the Holiness Movement in America.

The Movement can trace its roots to the spirituality of the German Pietists and those of mystics such as Madame Guyon.[34] There was a revival of interest in their writings, and in the theology of the Wesleys. Phoebe Palmer published a treatise in favour of the ministry of women, *Promise of the Father*,[35] which greatly influenced Catherine Booth (1829–90).

When William and Catherine Booth founded the Salvation Army in 1878, they saw it very much as a joint enterprise, and encouraged women as well as men to take up positions of leadership. Women were often as visible as men, preaching in mission halls and on street corners, many of them young women, facing hostile crowds to share the gospel message.

Part of the popular appeal of the Army was its music. The band, playing on the street corner, and the songsters with their timbrels, became something of a caricature in later days, but, as with other evangelistic movements, the musical tradition developed as a democratic, participative element of worship.

As it emerged from Methodism, and into an era of revivalism, Salvation Army worship drew on existing evangelistic hymns and songs, but when the soldiers and officers went out into the mission field, they began to write their own songs, at first published in magazines like the *Young Soldier*, or in small collections.

William and Catherine's daughters were prolific writers. The eldest, Catherine Booth-Clibborn (1858–1955), became a travelling evangelist at the age of 17. In 1881, she headed a group that travelled to France to establish the movement there. She earned the name of 'La Maréchal'. She also pioneered work in Switzerland, where she spent time in prison, and later travelled as a missionary through the Low Countries and to Canada, the USA, Australia and New Zealand.

Her hymns express a longing for the state of sinless holiness, or sanctification:

O spotless Lamb, I come to thee,
From thee no longer can I stray;
Break every chain, now set me free,
Take all my sins away.
Take all my sins away.
Take all my sins away.
O spotless Lamb, I come to thee,
Take all my sins away.

. . .

Weary I am of inbred sin,
O wilt thou not my soul release?
Enter and speak me pure within,
Give me thy perfect peace.
Chorus.[36]

Catherine encouraged members of her family in song-writing, and published a collection of their songs, *Wings of Praise*, in 1930.[37]

Three other of William and Catherine's daughters produced songs, alongside very active lives in mission. Two served in India: Emma Moss Booth-Tucker (1860–1903), and Lucy Milward Booth-Helberg (1868–1953). Their seventh child, Evangeline Cory Booth (1865–1950), oversaw Cellar, Gutter and Garrett work in Britain, when she was only 18. She served as the fourth General of the Salvation Army from 1934 to 1939. Evangeline published her own hymns in 1927 and in an enlarged edition in 1937 as *Songs of the Evangel*.[38]

Their hymns were among those collected in the two Songbooks produced by the Salvation Army in 1953 and 1986, and in the Supplement, *Keep Singing*, published in 1976. One or two have come down into the Assemblies of God book, *Making Melody*.

American revival

In America, the revival movement took the momentum and leadership away from the religious elite in Boston, and thrust it into the hands of ordinary people. It caught up vast numbers of ordinary people, and inspired them to preach, teach and write. Kidd describes the social impact:

> Radical evangelicals ordained untutored, and occasionally nonwhite, men as pastors. They sometimes allowed women and nonwhites to serve as deacons or even elders. They led crowds of the poor, children, and nonwhites singing through the streets. They permitted Native Americans, African Americans, and women to exhort in mixed congregations, and they commended their words as worthy of white male attention . . . In the revivals, the world seemed to turn upside down as those with the very least agency in eighteenth-century America felt the power of God surge in their bodies.[39]

One movement on the far radical fringe was the Shakers, a movement that emerged from the Quakers in England in the eighteenth century, moved to America and, to a certain extent, interacted with the spirit of revivalism.

Mother Ann Lee had left Britain under persecution in 1774, and migrated with a small group of followers to America. The movement referred to itself as the 'United Society of Believers in Christ's Second Appearing', and formed communities, segregated by gender, which aimed to live simple lives in communion with God, who was considered to be both male and female.

Ann Lee's designation of herself as 'Mother' reflected the Shaker view that women and men were equal in ministry, and in their reflection of God. That is not to say that gender was a matter of indifference, but that the gifts of men and women were equally godly and valuable. This was evidenced in the leadership of Ann Lee as spiritual mother, through whom the 'children' were reborn in Christ.

Her leadership did not mark her out as an exception, or a masculine woman, but rather demonstrated a pattern of equality in the human community that made up the Church, reflecting the male and female nature of God. In a collection of Shaker writings, Robley Whitson notes: 'The lived experience of equality together with the personal impact of Mother Ann as "spiritual mother in Christ" laid the foundation for the emergence of the doctrine of God as Father and Mother'.[40] There is a sense, in the writings that Whitson has gathered, of discovery, rather than doctrine. The experience of living in communities led by women and men, in which women and men contribute fully, leads to an exploration of something new and mysterious about God.

There were attempts to express this radical exploration in hymns written to convey Shaker tenets to the Kentucky revival. 'The Testimony of Eternal Truth' is a rather didactic text attributed to Richard MacNemar, who wrote an account of the revival from a Shaker perspective.[41]

The text centres on the duality of the Godhead, Power and Wisdom. There is a polemic against the Trinity, 'The monstrous beast, and bloody whore', the 'mysterious three-fold God', which is 'He'. There remained the 'righteous persecuted few', who 'ador'd the everlasting two'.

The second verse describes the act of creation:

The Father's high eternal throne
Was never fill'd by one alone:
There Wisdom holds the Mother's seat,
And is the Father's helper-meet.
This vast creation was not made
Without the fruitful Mother's aid;
For by the works of god we know
The fountain-head from which they flow.

The fall is attributed to 'man', which is used ambiguously in the text as a male or an inclusive word. Eve, the vicious temptress and type of the vileness of woman, is nowhere to be seen. Instead, the 'helper-meet' is the human counterpart to Wisdom. The last verse deals with the incarnation of God in a Mother:

The Holy Ghost at length did bear
Th'anointed one, the second heir,
A virgin soul, a holy child,
A Mother pure and undefiled:
In her the heirship is complete,
In her the types and figures meet,
And God's last building stands upon
The sacred truth of two in one.[42]

This text is unusual among Shaker hymns in having been composed in written form, and designed to convey a complex doctrinal position. There was at first no formal or written worship, for fear that this would quench the Spirit. In the introduction to a collection of Shaker songs, Christian Goodwillie writes:

> Music was a democratic mode of spiritual expression, a blank canvas onto which all Believers were welcome to project the feelings and ideas that the Shaker religion had manifested in their hearts The earliest of these songs was just that, pure wordless feeling. Mother Ann is said to have won over many a convert with her wordless songs.[43]

Music was often accompanied by ecstatic dancing, or turning. Mother Ann also used movement to express the intensity of her feeling. Robley Whitson cited a Sister Jemima, speaking of Mother Ann:

> She seemed to possess within herself an inexhaustible fountain of that power which she would often communicate to a whole assembly by singing, not in a loud voice, and gently motioning her hands or by speaking a few words.[44]

One of Ann's songs is transcribed at the beginning of the Song Book:

> Bow low, low, low and cry to God,
> Dear children, with your Mother.
> For I do weep, Yea weep and mourn,
> I weep for my dear children.[45]

The single verse song is typical of the songs in the book. It is purely emotional, not doctrinal; there is a strong sense of connection between the Mother and the singers, who are seen as her children; the song refers to movement ('Bow low'), which would have been accompanied by dance; and the words are simple and repetitive.

During the Kentucky revival of 1800, Shaker missionaries met with Methodists and Baptists, and began to write down and collect their songs. They had developed a form of musical shorthand which enabled tunes, sung and composed spontaneously, to be written down quickly. Some were sent back to the eastern United States, where they appeared in the first Shaker collection, *Millennial Praise*, in 1812.[46]

Songs were often communicated directly or through mediums from Mother Ann or her successor, Mother Lucy, after their deaths. For example, the song 'Angel of love' was recorded as sent by Mother Ann to Eliza Ann Taylor, accompanied by a picture, sent by Mother Lucy through medium Polly Jane Reed in 1849.[47] Eliza Ann Taylor (1811–91) later (1869) became First Eldress, the highest female rank in the Shaker church.

The 1840s were a period of particular intensity, known as the 'Era of Manifestations'. During this time, the song 'A call for love' was sent to Joanna Kitchell (1796–1878), a deaconess at the New Lebanon Shaker Community, by Mother Ann. The song has long notes with the rubric, 'Shout', and begins, 'O brethren and sisters rejoice O rejoice for I have love, yea Mother's heavenly love for you.'[48]

The songs retain their sense of spontaneity, with rubrics allowing for ecstatic shouting or singing. They are often hard to attribute, as Goodwillie notes, because they were sung under the inspiration of the Spirit, and written down by other worshippers or hearers before being passed on, edited and collected. Goodwillie regards this as a rich heritage, 'wellsprings of remarkable creativity', largely untapped.[49]

Camp meetings

The same kind of fervour and spontaneity marked the development of music at the Camp meetings of the revival era. Camp meetings and their songs were intended to be readily accessible to the crowds of people attending. They were typically chorus-based and personal, rather than doctrinal, designed to be easily picked up and sung. As in earlier community movements, such as Herrnhut, new verses or entire new hymns would sometimes arise spontaneously during the meeting, to be written down and published afterwards. Very often, individual couplets would find their way into different compilations of verses, 'whenever conditions were right – that is, whenever the vocal voltage was high enough and the rhythmic gait of the song under way fitted their pattern',[50] with the massed congregation lustily joining in the chorus.

One such text is 'Let Jesus come into your heart' by Lelia Naylor Morris (1862–1929). Mrs C. H. Morris (as her attribution often appears) was the wife of the revivalist Charles H. Morris and a prolific writer. She toured the camp meetings with her husband, and introduced her popular hymns, many of which have endured in evangelical hymnody. The 1951 *Redemption Hymnal* and 1986 *New Redemption Hymnal*, as well as the 1983 hymnbook *Making Melody*, published by the Assemblies of God in Nottingham, contain around twenty of her hymns and tunes. One or two have found their way into the Salvation Army songbooks, and a number into the American *Christian Life Hymnal*, published in 2006.

George Sanville tells the story of the text,[51] which is supposed to have originated at an altar call, when penitents came to the front of the meeting to seek redemption. Mrs Morris is said to have gone to the side of a troubled young woman, and prayed with her. She urged her, 'Just now your doubtings give o'er', to which the meeting's song leader responded, 'Just now reject him no more', with the preacher adding, 'Just now throw open the door', and Mrs Morris supplied the last line of what became the song's chorus: 'Let Jesus come into your heart.'

Before the end of the meeting, Mrs Morris had supplied the verses and tune. The pattern of the text is absolutely typical of the camp meeting song. The verses consist of two lines, each followed by 'Let Jesus come into your heart', and each verse is followed by the four-line chorus. Each set of two lines stands alone: for instance, the first verse is

If you are tired of the load of your sin,
Let Jesus come into your heart:
If you desire a new life to begin,
Let Jesus come into your heart:
Just now your doubtings give o'er;
Just now reject him no more;
Just now throw open the door;
Let Jesus come into your heart.

The only sense of movement is that the song ends in heaven: the symbolism of the home as the place of safety and rest comes to its fulfilment in the heavenly home, the final place of rest.

If you would join the glad songs of the blest,
Let Jesus come into your heart:
If you would enter the mansions of rest,
Let Jesus come into your heart.[52]

The camp meetings were evangelistic in their focus and aim, and, indeed, saw huge numbers of conversions. But as the movement spread and settled down, it gave rise to a number of outdoor Christian meetings which were aimed at specific elements of Christian life. For example, Mary D. James (1810–83) who wrote 'All for Jesus!'[53] was instrumental in organizing a Women's Gospel Temperance Camp Meeting in New Jersey in 1877, where 'Great crowds gathered to hear a powerful battery of women speakers which included the first president of the Women's Christian Temperance Union, Mrs Annie Wittenmyer.'[54] Wittenmyer (1827–1900) was also a hymn-writer, whose text 'All glory to Jesus be given' was published in Sankey's *Sacred Songs and Solos* and in the 1953 and 1986 editions of the *Songbook of the Salvation Army*.[55]

In the same decade, a prominent Methodist layman, Lewis Miller, was working on the idea of a national institute to provide serious education for Sunday school leaders and teachers. He floated the idea of adopting the camp meeting style to this end at the 1872 session of the Ohio camp meeting, where one of the women attending suggested the Fair Point Camp Ground at Chautauqua. The camp ground gave its name to the Chautauqua Institute, and by 1904 there were more than 150 'Chautauquas' around the USA, and the movement eventually recruited around 1 million participants worldwide.

The 'laureate'[56] of Chautauqua was Mary Artemesia Lathbury (1841–1913). Two of her hymns, 'Day is dying in the west' and 'Break thou the bread of life', demonstrate the influence of the camp setting on her writing, and the way in which she interwove the living experience of worshippers with biblical narrative. Edward Ninde is very much taken with Lathbury's hymns, and quotes Gareth Horder to the effect that 'Day is dying in the west', 'deserves to rank with "Lead kindly light" of Cardinal Newman, for its picturesqueness and allusionness'.[57]

The hymn was written as a vesper, to be sung outdoors at the camp. It draws on its setting, in the verses, with intense, descriptive language. The chorus, meanwhile, quotes the song of the seraphim at the call of Isaiah, itself an intense and colourful passage of Scripture. June Haddon Hobbs notes how the writer 'casts the singers in the roles of angels adoring God and allows her to assume the role of Isaiah, watching the scene unfolding in her mind'.[58]

It is worth citing the whole text to show how this develops through the hymn.

Day is dying in the west,
heaven is touching earth with rest;

wait and worship while the night
sets her evening lamps alight
through all the sky.
Holy, holy, holy, Lord God of hosts:
heaven and earth are full of Thee,
heaven and earth are praising Thee,
O Lord most high.

Lord of life, beneath the dome
of the universe Thy home,
gather us, who seek Thy face,
to the fold of Thy embrace;
for Thou art nigh.
Chorus

While the deepening shadows fall
heart of love enfolding all,
through the glory and the grace
of the stars that veil Thy face,
our hearts ascend.
Chorus

When for ever from our sight
pass the stars, the day, the night,
Lord of angels, on our eyes
let eternal morn arise,
and shadows end.
Chorus[59]

Typically of hymns of this era, the last verse is eschatological, linking the coming of morning with the dawn of eternity.

Her other well-known text, 'Break thou the bread of life',[60] uses the feeding of the five thousand to describe the hunger of the worshipper for the Word of God: 'My spirit longs for thee, the living Word.' Here the writer cast herself as someone in the crowd, perhaps even one of the numberless women and children. Hobbs again:

As a person identified with those too insignificant to be counted in the scriptural narrative, Lathbury demands spiritual recognition . . . her hymn asserts that subjective spiritual identity comes from a relationship with the divine, which cannot be denied by social status or precisely prescribed by organized religion.[61]

The symbol of bread which satisfies hunger subverts control over the Word by the powerful and literate. You would expect the Word to be found on the pages of the Bible, but this Living Word is found 'beyond the sacred page' and is the 'Lord' sought by the singer in the form of a direct, personal experience open to anyone.

Fanny Crosby and gospel hymns

Of course, the greatest and best known of the American evangelical women writers is Fanny Crosby, or Frances van Allstyne, writer of around 9,000 hymns[62] under a number of pseudonyms as well as her own name. Famously, she was blind from childhood, a fact that added a romanticism to her fame.

Crosby's hymns were certainly sung at camp meetings, but they fall into a related genre of gospel hymns or songs. The gospel hymn, like the camp meeting song, draws on experience rather than doctrine, and aims to be accessible to its singers. Its setting is in the public hall or church, and it derives from religion as 'now the means of developing both a personal religious commitment and social virtues – temperance, domesticity, and social responsibility – among young workers and a bulwark against the temptations of the city'.[63] The aim is not conversion so much as confirmation and support in Christian life.

A great many of them appear in Sankey's *Sacred Songs and Solos* and they have formed the backbone of revivalist and evangelical singing, with great favourites like 'Blessed Assurance' and 'To God be the glory', both found in major hymnbooks right up to *Church Hymnary* (fourth edition), published in 2005.[64] Others, such as 'All the way my Saviour leads me', 'I am thine, O Lord, I have heard Thy voice', and even 'Rescue the perishing', are instantly characteristic of an era, and are still in print in books in the evangelical tradition, up to *Christian Life Hymnal* of 2006.[65]

Although these hymns use choruses, the verses are more complex and more likely to develop through the hymn. Fanny Crosby's 'Blessed assurance', from the chorus of which the title of this book is taken, is typical. The verses are made up of rhyming couplets, like the camp meeting song, but formed into four-line stanzas, with the chorus following. There is a sense of movement through the hymn from the 'Blessed assurance' which resides in a concise statement of the gospel of redemption:

Heir of salvation, purchase of God;
Born of his Spirit, washed in his blood.

The response of the singer is 'perfect submission, perfect delight',[66] which is resolved in the last verse into a posture of rest, stillness and anticipation of the glory divine, which is promised in the first verse. This hymn retains its power and is still sung with great intensity. Crosby both states the gospel simply and draws out a response of great comfort in the singers.

Unusually, the composer of the tune 'Assurance' was also a woman. In her autobiography, Crosby describes the circumstances of writing of many of her texts. Only two women are mentioned, but the stories of these compositions are particularly intimate. She had long collaborations with male writers such as Ira D. Sankey. But her hymn 'Only a little while'[67] arose from her weeping together with a woman friend, whom she had known for many years, over the death of a mutual friend. She says, 'we sat down and wept together, and [the] words flowed from my heart . . . When I repeated the hymn to Mrs. Currier, she immediately sang it to the music coming from her heart as the words did from mine.'[68] She continued to provide hymns for Mrs Currier, who was a gospel singer.

In the case of 'Blessed assurance', as was usual, the melody came first. Crosby relates that Phoebe Palmer Knapp (1839–1908), the daughter of Phoebe Palmer,[69] and a prolific composer, had already composed the tune, and played it over to her. The words came to her, as often, when she heard the tune, and she writes: 'The hymn thus written seemed to express the experience of both Mrs. Knapp and myself.'[70]

Because of her enormous output, Fanny Crosby typifies many characteristics of women writers of this time and genre. Hobbs comments on two more of her texts.

In 'Jesus is tenderly calling thee home', once again, the woman is in the home, static, but reaching out to the sinner who is lost out in the world. Here, the singer is identified with Jesus, calling on his behalf. The implication is 'that a woman's position in the home identifies her with God. Thus, she transcends her confinement by becoming like God, who can move at will through influence.'[71]

Another text, 'Safe in the arms of Jesus', creates a close loving relationship between the singer and Jesus. The quatrain,

Safe in the arms of Jesus
Safe on His gentle breast,
There by His love o'er-shaded,
Sweetly my soul shall rest[72]

forms the first verse and then the chorus. Later in the hymn, Jesus becomes the 'Rock of Ages', but here the image is like a mother holding a child, or, as Hobbs suggests, a relationship between two women, not sexual, but loving nonetheless: 'an embrace appropriate for a woman and her "bosom companion"'.[73] She quotes Mary de Jong to the effect that the relationship with Jesus for evangelicals here parallels the kind of female love available to Roman Catholics in the figure of Mary.[74]

There is a strong vein of erotic imagery and language in hymns by both men and women. Often, as in Ann Griffiths, this draws on the Song of Solomon, but often it is simply the expression of the love relation in sexual terms.

June Haddon Hobbs recalls a game which she and her contemporaries used to play with hymn words, by adding 'between the sheets', for example, 'O why not tonight' (between the sheets). She says that, 'It seemed very funny and very naughty to add sexual innuendos to hymns, but the hymns themselves suggested the possibility because erotic references in gospel hymns are very common.'[75]

But then she finds that her grandmother had been doing something of the same kind, when she read through her hymnbook and found handwritten notes, changing the name of Jesus to 'Rob', as in ''Tis so sweet to trust in [Rob]'.[76] She says that this suggests that hymns have a playful element to them, as opposed to the more serious elements of the liturgy, but it certainly suggests that they play into the erotic feelings of young women.

This erotic strain works in two ways. The Bible describes the relationship between God and the people of God in sexual terms, often violent or repressive, but also often extremely tender.[77] The human partner is always depicted as the woman, not the man, in the partnership, so the imagery plays into women's sexuality and challenges men's.

So, for example, Annie Sherwood Hawks' 'I need thee every hour' is static, moving within need rather than on from need. It ends in total possession by the lover:

I need thee every hour, Most Holy One,
O make me Thine indeed, Thou blessed Son.[78]

And Sarah Addison Pollard's (1862–1934) 'Have thine own way' reaches the same conclusion:

Have Thine own way, Lord, Have Thine own way;
Hold o'er my being Absolute sway.

Fill with Thy Spirit till all shall see
Christ only, always Living in me.[79]

Hobbs compares these with the male writer C. Austin Miles' 'I come
to the garden alone', which is just as intimate in the verses and the
chorus:

And he walks with me and he talks with me
And he tells me I am his own
And the joy we share as we tarry there
None other has ever known.

That last line of the chorus is extraordinary – claiming a unique experience of intimacy with the God who walks in the garden. The reference
is to the second chapter of Genesis, in which God walks in the Garden
of Eden with the man and the woman at the beginning of creation.
However, the garden is also an erotic theme in the Song of Songs (for
example 5.1) and throughout art, music and literature. The middle
verse contains an image familiar from love songs, as the birds fall silent
at the voice of the beloved.

Hobbs notes that this hymn ends with a reluctant return to the masculine world, leaving the delights of the garden, whereas the hymns by
female writers remain in the close intimate relationship:

I'd stay in the garden with Him
Though the night around me be falling,
But He bids me go; through the voice of woe
His voice to me is calling.[80]

The other subtheme of erotic writing is submission. Salvation is often
seen in terms of 'perfect submission', which (in Crosby's words) is
'perfect delight', leading to 'visions of rapture'.[81] This of course runs
through the texts cited, in which Jesus is invited to have his own way,
or to respond to an existential need: Hobbs notes that Hawks' 'I need
thee every hour' enacts her spiritual development as a matter of coming into relationship: it articulates her sense that her identity somehow
cannot sustain itself alone.[82]

This is by no means confined to women's writing either. There can
scarcely be a more sexually expressed song of submission than Judson
W. van der Venter's 'All to Jesus I surrender', with the lines 'Take me,
Jesus, take me now', 'Make me, Saviour, wholly Thine', 'Fill me with
Thy love and power'.[83] 'Between the sheets', indeed!

Hobbs suggests that the masculine backlash, when it came, was at least partly a reaction against this language of sexual submission. Singing (and writing) these hymns brought men into the same relation as women to the only symbolically male figure, God. In God's presence, all were women, all subsumed in the image of the Bride. But, because the image was female, the hymns subtly gave women's sexuality a normative and powerful position.

But it was not healthy imagery for women either, and, sadly, the backlash removed only men from its influence. Women were left with submission – not only to God, but now to male human beings as well. The domestic, submissive, safe world of the home had always been the domain of woman. While for a time it held a kind of moral authority over the male, risky outside world, it was also her prison.

Men were never quite (despite their fervent songs) morally contained in the domestic sphere. And when the men escaped, they left women trapped inside, with neither authority nor voice. It took several generations for women to 'come out' as well.

This can be seen from the male dominance of the Christian music business. Many of the hymn-writers may have been women, but the composers (who held the copyrights) and, most significantly, the publishing houses, that controlled the flow of gospel music, were male. And the publication of gospel songs was soon very big business.

As Sandra Sizer points out, the American evangelical revival attracted 'white, aspiring middle-class, evangelical Protestant Northerners' who were almost by definition 'Republican . . . sound-money advocates'.[84] Seeing the opportunity to spread gospel songs even more widely, and seeing no conflict between financial enterprise and the gospel the songs proclaimed, a number of entrepreneurs set up publishing firms, each with its own stable of writers.

Donald Hustad offers a list of these, with their composers and writers.[85] Composers were almost all male, as we have noted. Writers were generally male, but there are some exceptions. John J. Hood Co. contracted only two authors, and both were women: Lelia Morris[86] and Eliza E. Hewitt (1851–1920, writer of 'More about Jesus I would know', 'Onward still and upward').

William B. Bradbury engaged Fanny Crosby, contracting her to write three songs a week. He sold the business to The Biglow and Main Company, who kept her on and became the biggest publisher of gospel songs in the nineteenth century. They also had on their books Anna Bartlett Warner (1827–1915, writer of 'Jesus loves me, this I know'), Annie Sherwood Hawks (1835–1918, writer of 'I need thee every hour'),

Elizabeth Prentiss (1818–78), Lydia Baxter (1809–74) and Phoebe Palmer Knapp, the only woman among composers.

However, the income generated by these large business enterprises did not flow into the pockets of the writers. Hobbs comments wryly on the preface written by Billy Sunday for *Great Revival Hymns*, which 'claims that Rodeheaver and Ackley have "spared no expense" to advance "the work of bringing the unsaved to Christ." One wonders exactly what expenses were not spared. The female hymnists – including Fanny Crosby – who provided many of the texts for their book probably received nothing at all.'[87]

As in popular music of the time, lyricists were undervalued in comparison with composers. But even so, some of the publisher's dealings seem to border on sharp practice. It seems that Biglow and Main were so dependent on Crosby that they asked her to write under a series of pseudonyms, so that the extent of her contribution would be concealed. And yet, when she published her *Life Story* at 83, she placed an advert in the front of the book encouraging sales, 'that she may be enabled to have a home of her own, in which to pass the remainder of her days'.[88]

Hobbs, who relates this, remarks that 'Crosby's career as a hymnist is a sad and probably representative tale of the exploitation of female hymn writers.'[89] In the nineteenth century, it was by no means only hymn-writers, or even only women, who were being exploited, but the fact that such a prolific and well-loved hymn-writer should end her life genteelly begging must call into question the ethics of the publishers who made such capital out of her writing.

These gospel hymns performed a very specific function in the late nineteenth century. They grew out of the evangelical tradition as it responded to the intellectual challenge of the Enlightenment. The experience of earlier women writers, that their creative output flowed directly from God's Spirit, now worked in a new way. Formerly, this had been seen as a justification for a woman claiming the authority to write. Now it served to justify the authority of inspired words to speak truth.

Crosby writes in her autobiography,

That some of my hymns have been dictated by the blessed Holy Spirit I have no doubt; and that others have been the result of deep meditation I know to be true . . . I have sometimes felt that there was a deep and clear well of inspiration from which one may draw the sparkling draughts that are so essential to good poetry.[90]

Stories were told – and treasured – about the miracles worked by the singing of the hymns. Crosby told the story of someone who was converted simply by hearing 'Saved by grace', and who said, 'It seemed that God had spoken to me through the voice of that song.'[91]

Undoubtedly, the songs influenced a whole generation of singers. Donald Hustad writes: 'It is difficult to overestimate the grip these simple experience songs, written by theological and musical amateurs, had on the general public.'[92] John Ogasapian goes even further: 'In a very real sense, the religious ferment of the Second Great Awakening during the early nineteenth century defined the nature of place of religion in the United States.'[93]

Saving the world

Parallel to the Great Awakenings that swept across Britain and America was a vast overseas missionary enterprise, following European discovery and colonialization into the whole world.

From the earliest years of European expansion into the rest of the world, the churches seized the opportunity to carry the gospel to new lands. This was rationalized as a response to the Great Commission of Matthew 28.18–20, where the risen Jesus commands his disciples to go and make disciples of all nations. Now, at last, it was possible to do this, and to envisage a time when the whole world would be evangelized.

A huge fervour for overseas mission grew up. The major British denominations formed missionary societies at the end of the eighteenth century,[94] and hymn-writers responded in an outpouring of missionary hymns. For Isaac Watts, the British Isles had become the location of God's chosen race, from which the gospel would resound throughout the world:

> Sing to the Lord with joyful voice,
> Let every land his name adore;
> The British Isles shall send the noise
> Across the ocean to the shore.[95]

The missionaries became heroes. Their travels were dangerous and often deadly. When they returned on furlough, they brought back tales of mysterious places and people whose ways of life seemed exotic and strange to members of British churches, who conversely congratulated themselves on being born in a temperate and civilized land.

While both men and women travelled in mission, wives often taking over leadership when their husbands died, long before women could exercise such leadership at home, it was the women at home who organized themselves into mission 'auxiliaries', energetically promoting the work and raising funds.

Women also entered wholeheartedly into the writing of hymns in celebration and support of overseas mission. Many of these seem to us triumphalist and racist, much in the vein of Watts, seeing Britain as a privileged land, dispenser of divine favour to savages and heathens. There is little or no recognition of the sophistication or richness of cultures other than their own.

This is most blatant in the simplistic language used in many nineteenth-century children's hymns. Ann (later Gilbert, 1782–1866) and Jane (1783–1824) Taylor wrote specifically to combat the perceived failures in Isaac Watts' hymns for children, and to provide texts more suitable for young minds.[96] Their *Hymns for Infant Minds* launches straight in with 'A Child's Hymn of Praise':

> I thank the goodness and the grace
> Which on my birth have smiled,
> And made me, in these Christian days,
> A happy English child.[97]

Subsequent verses begin: 'I was not born . . .', and list the fates of other children, who are born as pagans, slaves or gypsies.

Later editions contained hymns on overseas mission, including one, 'Are we better than the heathen?' The answer is 'Yes, for a little space', but the privilege brings responsibility, which weighs heavy even on the infant who sings this hymn. The heathen will rise in judgement against them if they do not preach the gospel. And if they despise their own privileged position and fail to repent of their own sin, astonishingly,

> . . . better had it been for thee,
> Thou never hadst been born.[98]

Cecil Frances Alexander's (1818–95) *Hymns for Little Children* approaches the second commandment with a hymn that begins:

> There are strange countries far away,
> Where GOD's Name is unknown,
> Where children live, who say their prayers
> To gods of wood and stone.
>
> But Christian children go to church . . .[99]

The hymn goes on to warn against idolatry in more domestic guises.

Like revival and camp meeting music, overseas mission eventually proved fertile ground for women's writing for all ages. The earliest collections were pamphlets for specific occasions or types of occasions such as weeknight meetings. Many of the early books were frustratingly imprecise in their attributions of material, and a certain amount of detective work is necessary to get a feel for the outflowing of women's hymns represented in them.

The London Missionary Society published a collection of *Missionary Hymns* in 1801, not long after its foundation. This was a short collection of 29 hymns, unattributed, but many by Watts.[100] Subsequent revised and enlarged editions appeared throughout the first half of the nineteenth century, the 1840 edition having 150 items.

The language of these hymns is that of the conquering army, the sounding trumpet, the heathen gloriously joining the paean of Christian praise. The occasional hymn by a female author carries the same message. For example, 'Soon may the last glad song arise' is attributed to 'Mrs Stokes' in the later *Centenary* book (see below), and rings with eschatological triumphalism, ending,

> Oh that the anthem now might swell,
> And host to host the triumph tell—
> That not one rebel heart remains,
> But over all the Saviour reigns![101]

At the end of the century, the society brought out the *Centenary Mission Hymnal*, compiled and edited by the Revd Stanley Rogers. Of the 161 items, 32 can be identified as being by women, with a further eight to ten with attributions suggestive of women's authorship (for example 'Women's Baptist Missionary Society of the West'[102]). That is nearly a quarter of the collection.

The Preface notes that the book contains, as well as some familiar hymns, and some that are more recent but in general currency, 'the rest . . . entirely new, having been composed for the Hymnal'.[103] This is borne out in the contents. Some authors are drawn from evangelical hymnody: Frances Ridley Havergal, for example, with three hymns; but many familiar names are missing. It is clear that a number of the less familiar authors are writing specifically for the mission field, or even more specifically to address women's auxiliary committees involved in raising support and fundraising, a unique element of which in the London Missionary Society, was the 'Ship'.

The Ship was a brilliant piece of promotion and fund-raising. I can remember saving 'Ship halfpennies' in the 1950s and 1960s (the halfpenny at that time had a ship on the reverse), and listening to romantic stories about the *John Williams*. John Williams and his wife were missionaries in the South Pacific from 1817 till he was killed in 1839. The first ship named in his honour was launched in 1844, and it and its successors carried missionaries to the Pacific Islands well into the twentieth century.

Mary J. Willcox (1835–1919), an American writer, picks up the romance of the voyage to distant lands, and the imagery of Isaiah 42.4, which Isaac Watts had used to such effect, in her hymn 'O Mission Ship! Dear Mission Ship!' Here is the end of the first verse and beginning of the second:

From isle to isle thy white wings fly
To bear a message from on high,
Telling on earth's remotest shore,
The sweet old story o'er and o'er.

Where distant islands wait to see
God's law of love and liberty.

The Ship carries with it the ideals of the homeland, which are the familiar feminized ideals of domesticity and peace – in verse 2:

Make 'home, sweet home,' where hate has been,
And bring to every troubled soul,
God's peace that maketh pure and whole.

The singers are contained within the home, because they are the children who have been collecting whatever the equivalent of ship halfpennies was, and will continue to offer money and prayers in support of the mission:

In faith and love we children gave
Our gifts to launch thee on the wave.
Our gifts and pray'rs thy way shall wing,
Till every isle crown Jesus King.[104]

Indeed, one of the loci of mission is the family. If domestic values are part of the gospel, the domestic life of the 'heathen' must be evangelized. Ida Glenwood, about whom nothing seems to be known, writes:

84

Go teach the heathen mother
The way of life and truth,
And sow the seeds of wisdom
In tender hearts of youth.[105]

The direction of mission is clear. The underlying culture is that
children and adults in England and America have the gospel. The peo-
ples of the wide world, which was then opening up through commerce
and conquest, were heathen. It behoved the blessed English and American people to give their money and prayers to support their missionaries,
who would carry the gospel, together with all the benefits of civilization
('home, sweet home'), to those who had never known it.

The mission field is described only in terms of need. Sarah Geraldine
Stock's hymn 'A cry as of pain' puts this in its most extreme form. The
first three verses are about the 'cry' or 'call' and each ends,

Oh what—Oh what shall the answer be?

The 'cry' is described in various terms in the long middle lines of the
verses:

A cry from the lands that in darkness are lying,
A cry from the hearts that in sorrow are sighing;
. . .
Come over and help us! in bondage we languish;
Come over and help us! we die in our anguish;
. . .
It comes with a chorus of pitiful wailing,
It comes with a plea which is strong and prevailing.

There is a dreadful irony in the middle verse, where 'bondage' refers to
enslavement to sin, as the previous line makes clear – the call comes to
all:

Whom Jesus hath rescued from sin's deadly thrall.[106]

It has nothing to do with the literal slavery that the missionary nations
had forced on those whom they sought to free from sin.

The Church Missionary Society published its collection around the
same time as the London Missionary Society centenary edition, having produced various smaller hymn and liturgical collections in the

previous fifty years. The book opens with Sarah Geraldine Stock's text quoted above, which is clearly intended to set the tone for the whole collection. Stock was influential in its compilation, as a rather sad note in the Preface makes clear:

> A pathetic interest is attached to the Book from the fact that it is the last literary work in which Miss S. G. Stock was engaged before her summons to a higher service. This gentle and gifted lady, who will ever be remembered as the missionary poetess of our age, took the liveliest interest in the preparation of this Hymnal. Her colleagues gratefully acknowledge how much, under God, they owe to her refined taste, her quick perception of beauty, and her spirit so deeply taught in divine truth.[107]

Greater care in accurate attribution means that the proportion of women's writing can be given with more confidence. Of 242 items, 72 can certainly be attributed to women, with about five of less certain origin, that is, between a quarter and a third of the book, a truly remarkable proportion.

This is a far more 'mainstream' collection, with texts by Cecil Frances Alexander, Frances Ridley Havergal and Fanny Crosby. Interestingly, Guyon's hymn 'All scenes alike engaging prove' appears in the section on 'Consecration'. Its sense of God's presence in every part of the world takes on a whole new dimension in the missionary context:

> My country is in every clime;
> I can be calm and free from care,
> On any shore, since God is there.[108]

Stock has 20 texts, some to her own tunes. Her hymns are full of the urgency and newness of mission. It is the great enterprise of the Church, calling it out of the slumber of apathy and inactivity ready for the eschaton which will come when all the earth has been evangelized.

The passion that wrings the singer's heart in 'A cry as of pain' is more controlled in a text set, in *Church Missionary Hymn Book*, to Sullivan's dramatic tune 'Lux eoi', 'Lord, Thy ransomed Church is waking'. This is essentially a hymn of praise, for the wakening of the Church and the spread of the gospel, which is described in the last quatrain of both verses two and three as 'treasure'. Mission is still one-way:

> Praise to Thee for saved ones yearning
> O'er the lost and wandering throng.

The stirring last verse sets the whole in the context of a double eschatology: the return of the Lord and the homecoming of the faithful
servant:

> Set on fire our heart's devotion
> With the love of Thy dear Name;
> Till o'er every land and ocean
> Lips and lives Thy Cross proclaim:
> Fix our eyes on Thy returning,
> Keeping watch till Thou shalt come,
> Loins well girt, lamps brightly burning;
> Then Lord, take Thy servants home.

The rubric shows the verse starting loud (*f*) with a crescendo starting at line 5 and a rallentando in the last line at *ff*. It must have been
tremendous to sing!

A text by Eva T. Evered Poole tells a very different story. Here, again,
is the one who stays at home and supports the work. Her mawkish
hymn begins, 'I could not do the work the reapers did.' This is followed
by two other verses detailing the singer's perceived failures. Unable to
cast the 'heavy fisher-net',

> I pleaded for the Master's blessing, where
> My brethren toiled upon the world-wide sea.

And again, missing out on the glorious and thrilling battle, because

> The work allotted by the Master's hand
> Kept me at home, while others went to die.

She nevertheless gets to join in the triumph song and share in the spoils.
This is because:

> . . . the tiniest work for Thee
> Finds recompense beyond our highest thought,
> And feeble hands that worked but tremblingly
> The richest colours in Thy fabric wrought.[109]

The text is in the section on 'Service and Conflict', but the biblical text
assigned to it locates it in the experience of women. Mark 14.8, quoted
as 'She hath done what she could', refers to the anointing of Jesus'

head by the woman with the alabaster jar. Far from being a 'tiniest work', the anointing of the head (not the feet as in other similar stories) is very significant. It is the action of anointing a king or priest. Jesus recognizes it as anointing his body for burial (also v. 8), and gives the action a prominent place in the proclamation of the gospel: 'I tell you, wherever the good news is proclaimed in the whole world, what she has done will be told in remembrance of her' (v. 9, NRSV). The phrase 'in remembrance of her', of course, echoes what Jesus says of his own actions at the Last Supper, which is narrated immediately following the anointing (14.22–25), though Mark's Gospel does not use the phrase 'in remembrance of me'. By linking a quotation from this powerful text with such a mawkish hymn, the author entirely reverses the point of the Bible narrative!

However, a fascinating set of three texts by Mary Fawler Maude (1819–1913, best known for the hymn 'Thine for ever, God of love'), specifically headed 'For Women's Meetings', offers a far stronger image of the place of women in mission. The women are 'handmaids of the Lord', a reference to the Magnificat (Luke 1.48).

> O Matchless honour, all unsought,
> High privilege surpassing thought,
> That Thou shouldst call us Lord, to be
> In fellowship of work with Thee!

The language of this first hymn of the three is about 'the lowly mind, the yielded will,/The emptied soul', but the 'feeble hands' of women can achieve much in divine strength:

> Mountains shall vanish, foes shall flee,
> 'All things are possible' with Thee.[110]

The last of the three transcends this rather cautious hold on divine power and authority. The Scripture text is Psalm 68.11 (in the Authorized Version), 'The Lord giveth the word: the women that publish the tidings are a great host.' The first three verses relate to biblical accounts of empowered women:

> The Lord gave the Word,—
> 'Let all my people bless my saving Name!'
> And Israel's women throng,
> With timbrel and with song,
> To spread his fame.

The Christ gave the Word,—
'Go, tell my brethren that I live for aye!'
   And swift the glad feet sped
   Along the path that led
     From Calvary.

The King gave the Word,—
'Go, teach ye every soul in every land!'
   Loud sounds that call, and clear:
   Rabboni! we are here
     At thy command.

The first two verses refer very clearly to women in Scripture: Miriam and the women from Exodus 15.20–21, and Mary Magdalene in John 20.17. The third verse has a more complex relation to Scripture. Matthew 28.16–20 suggests that it was only the eleven that met the risen Jesus in Galilee. But Maude links this with the resurrection appearance to Mary Magdalene, to whom the command in the previous verse was given, to tell the 'brethren' about the resurrection. Her initial response on recognizing Jesus is the 'Rabboni' of the hymn.

These three verses are echoed in verses 4–6, which start, 'The Lord gives the Word', 'The Christ gives the Word', and 'The King gives the Word'. For the most part, the response of the singers is active, though, unfortunately to our eyes, verse 6 ends:

They also serve their King,
Who stand and wait.[111]

The tune 'Ancilla' (handmaid) is written by someone known only by the initials E. J. C., clearly for these words. There is a pause over the fifth note ('Word', in each verse), and a note that the first three verses should use a lower note for the third and fourth note ('gave the', in verses 1–3), and a higher note in subsequent verses, emphasizing the present tense, 'gives the'. Again, it must have been a tremendous hymn to sing.

One anonymous text is in fact by Anne Taylor Gilbert, collaborator with her sister Jane Taylor on the popular children's hymn book *Hymns for Infant Minds*. This text is a classic overseas mission hymn:

Far across the ocean's wave
Brethren, sisters too, we have:
But they have not heard of Thee;
Wilt Thou not their Father be?[112]

But this is by no means Gilbert's usual stance. There is a fascinating collection by the Revd J. Leifchild, which exists in a MS draft[113] in the Congregational Library in London and in published form there and elsewhere. It was not a successful book, despite its claim to be supplying 'a want . . . of a greater variety than was to be found in the collections generally used'.[114] The want is supplied by a set of entirely new texts, many of them by Anne Taylor Gilbert. In three handwritten volumes there are 108 of her hymns, all but seven of which make it into the 370 items that make up the book, about a third of the final published work.

I must say that, reading her texts, I feel that yet another powerful voice was lost to hymnody by the failure of this book. We have her children's hymns, but not what she wrote for adult worship. Four of her hymns appear in Beecher's *Plymouth Collection*,[115] but they are pretty well unknown today. She is clearly influenced by Watts, particularly by his imaginative awe in the presence of God. Her hymn,

> Low at thy feet, Eternal Power,
> Mysterious Infinite, we fall:

clearly depends on Watts. The Eternal Power of this text is the Son of God,

> Great peerless, co-existent Son,

before whom, reason is nothing:

> Oh how shall reason meet the theme,
> Yes, meet it, reason, praise and bow:

> Hang o'er that infinite abyss,
> Thy very soul as nothing laid;
> And shield thy nothingness in this –
> That Son thy Saviour hath been made![116]

Interestingly, the published volume replaces the colon at the end of verse 5 (in the MS version) with a full stop, destroying the relentless drive of the last three verses (which are all one sentence) and making nonsense of the last verse.

Gilbert is rooted firmly in evangelical theology, with a powerful sense of salvation through the cross:

Yes, with my depth of crimson guilt,
My weakness, want and woe,
To that rich blood on Calvary spilt,
I'll look, I'll hope, I'll go.[117]

But this is no faith without works. Many of her texts are calls to a very practical commitment in day-to-day life.

Shall we the loftier truths embrace,
And pass the humble precept by?
Aspire to be a godly race
And fail in worldly honesty?

The answer must be, 'No':

The christian [sic] tradesman,—let him be
A man to put the world to shame!

for

Tis thus that Paul and James agree:
Faith plants the principle within;
Such faith, by holier works we see,
Works, which through love, in faith begin.[118]

The Church, too, must display a practical faith. Her hymns for special occasions are just as trenchant. Her 'Prayer at the dedication of a place of worship' contains the warning verse:

From formal, dull decline,
From schism's destructive root,
From error serpentine,
From foliage void of fruit;
From all that from the truth would swerve,
Head of the church, this church preserve.[119]

Sadly, here again some of the meaning is lost from the MS version, by careless typesetting. The original last line was,

Head of the Church, this church preserve.

As a Congregationalist, she would have appreciated the difference between the 'Church' universal and the local 'church'. Also, the second line of the original verse read, 'From schism's deadly root', which is far easier to sing, and gives 'schism' two syllables.

It is not surprising, then, that Gilbert should have a strong commitment to mission, but should exercise some common sense about the romance of foreign missions. Again and again, she calls for mission at home. She calls for 'Abundant sheaves from British fields',[120] and cries, 'Bone of our bone! the spirit bleeds/For thousands, Britain-born'. This latter text parodies the emotional overseas mission hymn:

> Abroad the glorious tidings spread,
> Fly, missionary, fly!
> But England's fields are heaped with dead,
> And daily still they die.[121]

Leifchild's book includes other texts by women writers, including the American writer Eliza Follen (1787–1860),[122] and a 'Miss East', who has written a lovely, strange text, based on Song of Songs 5.6, 'My Beloved had withdrawn himself, and was gone.' The text is full of desperate searching for the beloved, who has fled. Earthly pleasures are no consolation, as the third verse demonstrates with a powerful image:

> As well the orphan babe may rest
> On some fair statue's marble breast.
> Whence no nutritious virtues flow
> To sooth the hapless child of woe.

She calls upon the happier souls who enjoy his favour:

> O, tell him when he smiles on you,
> I languish for his favour too.

There is no solution to the search, but the hymn ends still on a note of longing:

> Could I ascend, like yonder dove,
> I'd speed my flight to realms above;
> Nor should my hovering spirit rest,
> Till safely sheltered in his breast.[123]

The text is reminiscent of Cowper's 'O for a closer walk with God', to the extent that the sense of loss and longing is almost overwhelming. But Miss East's hymn is expressed in a language and imagery that is tremendously powerful, even erotic, and it is hard to imagine a congregation ever singing it!

There are pencilled attributions to other women. What a shame that it was not more widely taken up!

Teaching children: catechesis

However, the call to mission at home was heeded, especially mission to children, who were seen, in the earliest days of hymn-writing, as natural reprobates in urgent need of salvation and moral guidance.

There were two movements in children's writing. One was catechetical, addressing the children already in the churches, and seeking to teach them the truths of the Christian faith in language that they would understand. The second was the great eighteenth- and nineteenth-century invention of the Sunday school. This started life as a mission movement, parallel to the overseas missions described above.

Isaac Watts falls into the former category. His hymns for children[124] have been criticized and satirized (the latter famously by Lewis Carroll in *Alice in Wonderland*[125]). But they were forward-looking in their intent, which was to help children to learn and apply the catechism taught in dissenting churches, which would have been the Westminster Shorter Catechism.[126]

The Unitarian Anna Laetitia Barbauld (1743–1825) wrote hymns in prose for children, in the 1780s. Her texts raised questions and introduced social as well as moral issues. She did not regard children as naturally depraved from birth, or invoke terrifying imagery of hell for disobedience. Her *Hymns* and *Lessons* were used in work with children in Unitarian churches, and became well known to a generation.[127]

But the majority of hymns written for children were designed to be sung, and, for the most part, supported traditional moral values and expressed soundly evangelical sentiments.

Ann and Jane Taylor's *Hymns for Infant Minds*, published in 1810, was a specific response to Watts' hymns for children, and ran into over fifty editions throughout the century. The hymns were advertised as more suitable for children's minds than those of Isaac Watts, in that they are 'calculated in every instance to win to what is good by love rather than deter from what is evil by terror'.[128] But the terror of hell is, in many cases, replaced by manipulation that is horrifying to twenty-first-century readers.

Susan Tamke cites the hymn 'A child's lamentation for the death of a dear mother', which begins with conventional expressions of grief before a compassionate heavenly Father:

> A poor afflicted child, I kneel
> Before my heavenly Father's seat,
> To tell him all the grief I feel,
> And spread my sorrows at his feet.

It is bad enough that the next verse attributes the death to that same God:

> Since thou art pleased to take away
> So dear, so very dear a friend.

But the hymn goes on to heap guilt upon the child:

> And now I recollect with pain
> The many times I grieved her sore:
> Oh! if she would but come again,
> I think I'd vex her so no more.[129]

With current knowledge of children's readiness to take on guilt for the ills of their families, this appears incredibly cruel and manipulative. Many of the hymns dwell further on the sins that beset children: greed, temper, disobedience and frivolity. This is characteristic of children's hymns of the time. Tamke, again, notes the impossibility of the task placed on children. 'In fact, the image of a perfect Christian child presented by children's hymns is that of a monastic; he is disciplined, he contemplates God continually, he rejects worldly pleasures, and he mortifies himself for any transgressions.'[130] And that's just the boys!

Perhaps the most influential and best known of the catechetical writers for children was Cecil Frances Humphreys, whose married name was Cecil Frances Alexander. Her hymn of the incarnation, 'Once in royal David's city', paints a romantic image of the infancy of Jesus:

> And through all his wondrous childhood,
> He would honour and obey,
> Love and watch the lowly maiden
> In whose gentle arms he lay.

Based on that, which is 'our childhood's Pattern', the young singers are reminded:

Christian children all must be
Mild, obedient, good as He.

The reward for obedience is a place in heaven, where

. . . like stars His children crowned,
All in white shall wait around.[131]

This hymn appears in her *Hymns for Little Children* (1848), whose aim was to help children to grasp and put into practice the catechetical teachings of the Church, in this case the Catechism and Creed of the *Book of Common Prayer*.[132] 'Once in royal David's city' is the fourth of a series on the Creed, headed 'Who was conceived by the Holy Ghost, born of the Virgin Mary'.

Two hymns earlier, 'All things bright and beautiful' illustrates the clause 'Maker of heaven and earth'. Both these hymns are still popular, even in an age that has lost touch with much of its Christian heritage. The rich pictorial language, dreaming up a rural paradise of purple mountains and meadows, flowers with glowing colours and birds with tiny wings, is almost medieval in its jewel-like quality. The point of the hymn lies in the response, in what has become the chorus, and in the last verse – God made them all, and God has given us eyes to see, and lips to praise the Maker.

How odd, then, is the normally omitted verse:

The rich man in his castle,
The poor man at his gate,
GOD made them, high or lowly,
And ordered their estate.[133]

Valerie Wallace, in her rather uncritical biography of Alexander, suggests that, if the reader pays careful attention to the punctuation, he or she will find an alternative to the common understanding of this verse. Instead of seeing it as an affirmation of the social order as divinely ordained, she reads it as a statement that *God made* people of all ranks – a statement of equality, rather than difference.

This may be true of the third line, but the last line reverts to divine ordering. And this is not the only hymn that suggests acquiescence to one's station in life. Another series of hymns illustrates the Ten Commandments. The tenth, 'Thou shalt not covet', gives rise to an extraordinary hymn, 'Saw ye never in the meadows', in which 'children bred in lowly cot' are likened to sweet white daisies growing in the meadow, underfoot, while 'children of the high and great' are compared to lilac or acacia waving high overhead in the sunshine.

The former children are 'modest, meek and quiet/And contented with their lot'; the latter, 'gracious, good and gentle/Serving God in their estate'. For sure, both kinds of flower give glory to God, but the daisy

> [n]ever murmurs, never wishes
> It were hanging up on high.

So the singer is exhorted:

> You must be content and quiet,
> Your appointed station in;
> For to envy, or to covet
> Others' goods is *mortal sin*.

Instead, the singer must wait till 'they shall all meet Him in Heaven'.[134] It is a classic statement of the much-derided 'Pie in the sky when you die'.

However, Alexander's book reached over 100 editions, and rivalled Watts and the Taylor sisters in popularity. The hymns quickly spread into general use in Sunday schools and churches, and throughout the overseas mission field. Those texts that remain popular today demonstrate a clarity of teaching that continues to make dense theological concepts accessible, in a way that other children's writing does not even attempt.

Eric Routley calls her 'the greatest of women hymn-writers in English', and ranks her with the only other woman writer of theological note, to his mind, Caroline Maria Noel (1817–77),[135] as 'a great woman writer of credal hymns – hymns that answer the questions rather than declare experiences'. Her hymns have, he says, 'the simplicity that a Christian person need never grow out of'.[136]

Hymns for Little Children was written when Cecil Frances Humphreys was 25 years old. This was young for such an authoritative collection of texts, but it was not her first. Her *Verses for Holy Seasons* was written two years earlier as a children's companion to Keble's *The Christian Year*.[137] Hook helped her to edit the book and wrote the Preface. Her approach to Keble himself to write a preface for *Hymns for Little Children* elicited what must be the most grudging 'Notice' ever to appear in a publication![138]

Fanny (as she was known) met and married William Alexander when she was 32, and he much younger. She was financially independent and very well connected socially. She was an already published writer, and continued to write and publish after her marriage. She seems to have seen herself very much as a fellow worker in William Alexander's ministry, supporting him in his literary ambitions, and through his elevation to Bishop of Derry (the first Irish-born bishop in that see since the Reformation) and eventually Archbishop of Armagh.

When Gladstone's government disestablished the Church of Ireland, she shared the Church's devastation. She wrote a poem for use on 1 January 1871, the day that disestablishment came into effect, which included the verse

Look down, O Lord of Heaven, on our desolation!
Fallen, fallen, fallen is now our Country's crown,
Dimly dawns the New Year on a churchless nation,
Ammon and Amalek tread our borders down.[139]

While she is best known still for her children's hymns, they are by no means the sum of her poetic output. One of her hymns for adults that has survived to the present day is her version of 'Saint Patrick's Breastplate', 'I bind unto myself this day', written for St Patrick's Day 1889. This is so different from the others of her hymns that are still sung that people are often surprised to find it is by the same author.

Ingrid Hotz Davies comments on this in her fascinating study of English women poets,[140] as the 'creation of a powerful speaking voice' – the 'I' of the hymn. She writes:

For the congregation singing this text, and indeed for the author writing it, the 'I' we are invited to enter in this poem allows access not only to authority ('The word of God to give me speech'), but also to a positively omnipotent, jubilant sense of power. This breastplate is 'strong,' offers 'power,' the 'service' of angels and church fathers, the dynamic force of the material universe, in fact the very power of God himself.[141]

She is right. This is very much the appeal of the hymn, and the experience of singing it. The sense of power is legitimized, as with so much women's writing, by placing its origin outside the singer. This is God's power and authority, assumed by the singer. The unusual and dramatic idea lies in the active, even assertive role of the 'I'. The singer is not cast in the role of passive receiver, overwhelmed by God's actions, but rather actively laying hold on the power of God.

The first words, repeated throughout the text, are incredibly powerful. 'I bind unto myself' – almost a reflexive verb, an action from which any other agent, even God, is excluded. Of course, what is being bound is all of God, but the agency, the activity, is all the singer's.

Saving children: Sunday schools

At the same time as Alexander was writing for Anglican children in Ireland, a new movement was changing the emphasis from children's religious education to mission. The Sunday schools movement was part of the great missionary enterprise of the eighteenth and nineteenth centuries. The impulse to take the gospel to the ends of the earth not only looked outwards to the burgeoning colonies and empire, but took notice of major social changes in Britain, in particular the growth of urban areas based on industrial development.

The populations of new urban centres were uprooted from the structured communities in which they had lived, in the villages from which they had come. Living conditions for the rural poor were by no means idyllic, but urban poverty was truly desperate. Child labour was viewed not with horror, but as a good social provision for all members of a family to contribute to its income.

Sunday schools were quite different from catechism classes. They were an attempt to offer training and minimal education to children for whom the only day on which they were not earning money was Sunday. The initial idea is attributed to Robert Raikes, whose inspiration it was not only to see the need, but also to promote the solution as a contribution to keeping the peace. His advertisement in the *Gloucester Journal* of 1783, and much reprinted after that, claims that Sunday schools are:

> for rendering the Lord's day subservient to the ends of instruction, which has hitherto been prostituted to bad purposes. Farmers, and other inhabitants of the towns and villages, complain that they receive more injury to their property on the Sabbath than all the week beside: this in a great measure, proceeds from the lawless state of the younger class, who are allowed to run wild on this day . . .[142]

He goes on to say that, where these measures are taken, 'the behaviour of children is greatly civilised'. The language of mission is reflected in the implication that children, like people of other lands, are native savages, in need of civilization by the proclamation of the gospel.

This mission field was not without controversy. Teaching the poor and their children to read and write was considered a dangerous innovation by some. The French Revolution raised fears of similar rebellion in Britain, and the production of 200,000 cheap copies of Thomas Paine's *Rights of Man* in 1793 added to the sense of foreboding. The Sunday school movement had to prove that it was a mechanism of stability not an organ of rebellion, even though many Dissenters had in fact supported the French Revolution and American independence.

Stephen Orchard charts the success of the 'spin' given to the movement at this point: 'The declared objective of most Sunday Schools, to combat the idleness of youth and protect private property, complemented the anxieties of the magistracy and their government that Jacobinism should not find a foothold among the labouring classes and the poor.'[143] Philip Cliff cites the French historian Élie Halévy's belief that Methodism saved the British people from the French experience, but goes on to suggest that the Sunday school movement more generally may have averted the possibility by the style of its education.[144]

The other controversy was over what was appropriate to be taught on the Sabbath Day (Sunday being seen as the Sabbath). The Sunday schools may have begun as schools, which took place on Sunday because that was the only day that working children were free. But the accident of the day, together with the missionary emphasis of the movement, began to raise questions about what should be read and what other subjects should be taught.

Clearly, reading material should be religious in nature. In 1799, the Religious Tract Society was formed, and Hannah More, among others, wrote tracts for the children to read. The big argument was whether the children should be taught to write, as writing was seen as work, and therefore should not be undertaken on the Sabbath. Evangelical churches, such as Methodist and some evangelical Anglican churches, would not permit writing to be taught in their Sunday schools. Churches of the Old Dissent, and particularly Unitarian churches, maintained the emphasis on education, and continued lessons in writing as well as reading. This led to wholesale migrations in some cases away from the evangelical Sunday schools to those where writing was still taught.

In this way, the Sunday schools were as culturally imperial in their education of the working classes and urban poor as the missionaries were in the global mission field. While it is true that, 'With the emphasis on cleanliness, neatness, manners, and the proper use of language, the way of life of thousands had altered unbelievably',[145] the slightly more cynical view of Stephen Orchard is also accurate.

The hymns written for the growing movement reflected and reinforced the emphasis on civilization. From their inception, the Sunday schools included a devotional element, simply as part of the mores of the time. They would begin or end with prayers and a hymn, sometimes moving from the rooms in which the teaching took place to the parent church, or a communal worship area.

As the movement grew, local Sunday schools began to publish their own collections of hymns, particularly in the large industrial conurbations where the movement was strongest. The Manchester District Sunday Schools Union was active in this field. Several Sunday schools around Manchester published their own resources. George Leigh Street Sunday School produced a collection of 42 hymns in 1819, and Disley (Cheshire) published a more substantial volume of some 182 items, beginning with versifications of the psalms, in 1839. In neither of these are the items attributed. Some classics by male authors such as Watts and Wesley are recognizable, but the majority are by other hands, many unidentifiable.

Stockport Sunday School seems to have collected its hymns written for special occasions in 1848. They include hymns for the 'Annual Sermon' from 1809 to 1847, mostly didactic in their address to the children and fulsome in praise and prayer for teachers, pastors and sponsors! There are also hymns for anniversaries of the foundation of the school in 1805, and for celebrations in branch schools, such as Heaton Mersey. These were later bound into a larger collection which included the same mixture of classics by male writers, with a mass of hymns by unknown hands.[146]

On the other side of the Pennines, the Committee of the Leeds Sunday School Union published its Sunday School Hymn Book in 1833, and there was even a journal dedicated to Sunday school music, *The Song Service Reporter*, also based in Leeds.[147]

Sunday school hymnbooks gathered the hymns from these smaller, local collections during the nineteenth century, and developed into a positive flood of publications, more in number than any other single category of hymnbooks. Many went through edition after edition.

It is beyond the scope of this book, but it would be interesting to discover how many writers started by writing for local consumption and went on to publication in national and better-known books.

Cecily E. Pike (1878–1960), for example, appears in a pamphlet of eight hymns published for use in the Chapeltown and District Sunday School Union.[148] Her hymn, entitled, 'Your Task', was written specifically for the collection. Her short text, 'Dear little breeze', about world mission, then appears in the 1950 *School Hymn Book of the Methodist Church*[149] with the copyright holder given as the National S. S. Union.

The problem, of course, is that very often their work appeared anonymously, and they remain unrecorded. The *Primitive Methodist Sunday School Union Hymn Book* of 1879 contains 493 hymns of which 107 – nearly a quarter – are 'unsigned'. Of the remainder, 78 are by named women authors. Its Wesleyan counterpart, published in the same year, contains only 23 'unknown' out of 589 hymns, but others are cited as 'American' or by the name of their original publication. Again, there are 78 by named women.

In both collections, well-known writers are represented: Frances Ridley Havergal, Jane Taylor and her sister, and Fanny Crosby from the other side of the Atlantic. But there are hosts of writers represented by single texts.

In a later era, when it was thought proper to acknowledge authorship and people began to be interested in the writers of hymns, the lack of information caused concern. When William Kelynack came to write the *Companion to the School Hymn Book of the Methodist Church* in 1950,[150] he was clearly embarrassed by the lack of information, and even, in some cases, withholding of information, in relation to women writers. He finds a variety of ways to say that more information would be gratefully received.

His list of biographical notes begins with 18 anonymous and 19 untraced hymns. Of 89 women authors listed, he expresses regret at the lack of information in the case of about 40, including the aforementioned Cecily Pike. Sometimes that is because his researches have simply drawn a blank, and later sources often record no more than he was able to discover, as is the case with Pike. Occasionally, information is withheld, either because the author does not think there is anything interesting to say, or because she refuses permission for biographical details to be printed. Kelynack's expressions of regret on these occasions betray an underlying frustration that every researcher must sympathize with!

I was surprised to find that the authors of some of the hymns I grew up with fall into this category. Little is known of Etta Campbell, who wrote 'What means this eager, anxious throng',[151] beyond the fact that she lived in Morristown, New Jersey, and was a teacher. Kelynack records of Doris Gill, who wrote 'Come let us remember the joys of the town',[152] 'A personal request from this hymnist, that no particulars be given either of the hymn writer or her hymns, must be respectfully, but regretfully, complied with.'[153] There is more information extant now, so the ban must have been lifted or otherwise overcome.

The thing is that, even for someone born in the 1950s, when Sunday schools were in deep decline, many of these hymns carry huge emotional weight. I can remember perplexities and mishearings. For instance, I confused Cecil Frances Alexander's concept of children standing around 'all in white' (last verse of 'Once in royal David's city') with a mishearing of Dearmer's hymn 'Praise him, praise him', which I continued as 'woolly little children' (not 'all ye little children'). I thought that we would wear white wool in heaven, like lambs, which we were also mysteriously meant to be.

Anyone who grew up singing hymns has a story like that to tell. My maternal grandmother wondered why the God of Bethel 'Has stole our father's leg' ('Hast all our fathers led'). Slowly, as children matured, the words of hymns became clearer, but the imagery, even half-understood, shaped and formed our imaginations, and provided an emotional structure that is hard to shake off, even should we wish to try.

Stephen Orchard cites Richard Hoggart's record of a survey of elderly working-class women in the 1980s:

> None of those women would know much poetry, if any, except for a few rhymes remembered from school. But their minds were full of a kind of poetry, a comforting and uplifting poetry on which they could without thinking draw, which they could hear in the backs of their heads.[154]

Susan Tamke takes this argument back into the heyday of Sunday schools and hymns, to point out the little-explored centrality of hymn culture:

> It seems indisputable that quantitatively the effect of hymns on the Victorian public was more profound than the literary works which traditionally have been mined so assiduously by cultural historians. In sheer volume, the writing of hymns far outweighed the writing of poetry in the nineteenth century. More important, the people whose lives were affected by hymns far outnumber those who were affected by poetry ... hymns were sung everywhere – on street-corners, at secular meetings, in the nursery, as well as in churches and chapels.[155]

The influence of the Sunday school movement on the shaping of British – particularly English and Welsh – society was incalculable. With such a large proportion of the population attending Sunday schools, and their evident place right at the heart of community life, through Whit walks, anniversaries, concerts and pageants, their influence ran right through the culture of several generations.

During the last quarter of the nineteenth century, three major changes affected the kinds of hymns published for children: the Sunday school movement became more established and conventional; there were advances in educational philosophy and practice; and, particularly, the Nonconformist churches entered a period of liturgical reform, which spread to the use of church music, with attempts to reduce the use of choruses and sentimental language, and to promote higher quality words and music.

The Primitive Methodist book, for example, claims in its Preface:

> If it should be judged that a number of the hymns are beyond the mental grasp of children, let it be remembered that we have all classes of capacity in our Schools, each requiring to be met; that the intelligence of our scholars is advancing and needs to be kept pace with . . .[156]

This shows the changing population and nature of Sunday schools, as well as chiming in with the general movement for liturgical reform.

Many of the later writers came not from the Sunday school movement or from catechesis, but worked in secular education. Their texts appear in the forward-looking books of the twentieth century.

But the nineteenth century retained and retains its power. In 1950, the Methodist Arthur Mills compiled a service of children's hymns, with a narrative commentary, designed to 'introduce children and young people to the rich store of faith and experience in our Christian hymns'.[157] The service was offered for use at Sunday school anniversaries and similar services.

In the optional 'chairman's remarks' at the beginning of the service, he states:

> Many of the early hymns reveal an appalling ignorance of child nature, were full of terrifying images and treated the children of those days as though they were fully-grown adults with a mature Christian Experience. Happily a better understanding of the nature of the child in recent years has produced hymns more suitable to the

child mind and understanding, which express much more naturally the deep religious instincts of the child, and provide him with a fitting means of praising God.[158]

Of the ten hymns chosen for this service, seven are by women. Two are by Cecil Frances Alexander. The hymns are uplifting (Mary Butler's (1841–1916) 'Looking upward every day'), imaginative (Jemima Luke's (1813–1906) 'I think when I read that sweet story of old'), challenging ('Oft in danger, oft in woe', written by Henry Kirke White but completed by Frances Fuller Maitland (1809–77) at the age of fourteen), and oddly (for a children's service) nostalgic ('Tell me the old, old story', by Katherine Hankey (1834–1911)). No writer was living at the time of the service. The story of women's writing for children seems to have ended.

Notes

1 *Hymns Ancient and Modern for use in the Services of the Church*, London: Novellow, 1861.

2 J. R. Watson, *The English Hymn: A Critical and Historical Study*, Oxford: Clarendon Press, 1997, p. 339.

3 Watson, *The English Hymn*, p. 339.

4 Ann Douglas, *The Feminization of American Culture*, New York: Alfred A. Knopf, 1977, p. 12.

5 Sandra A. Sizer, *Gospel Hymns and Social Religion: The Rhetoric of Nineteenth-Century Revivalism*, Philadelphia: Temple University Press, 1978; Philip Bliss and I. D. Sankey (comp.), *Gospel Hymns and Sacred Songs*, Cincinnati: John Church & Co., New York: Biglow & Main, nos. 1–6, 1875–91.

6 Douglas, *The Feminization of American Culture*, p. 13.

7 A. M. Allchin, *Ann Griffiths: The Furnace and the Fountain*, Cardiff: University of Wales Press, 1986, p. 19.

8 Writer of 'Guide me O Thou great Jehovah', he was often known as 'Pantycelyn' after the place where he made his home.

9 Richard Baxter, *The saint's everlasting rest; or, a treatise of the blessed state of the saints, in their enjoyment of God in heaven*, 1650.

10 Ann Griffiths, 'Dyma babell y cyfarfod'. I am using the translations into verse by Alan Gaunt in Alan Gaunt and Alan Luff, *Hymns and Letters: Ann Griffiths*, London: Stainer & Bell, 1997; Gaunt, 'Here we find the tent of meeting', p. 5, v. 1 (l. 6). The 'nesting place' is a reference to Psalm 84.3, where the swallow finds a nest near God's altar.

11 William Morris, *Cofio Ann Griffiths 1805*, Llyfrfa'r Cyfundeb: Caernarfon, 1955, p. 57, v. 4.

12 Gaunt and Luff, *Hymns and Letters*, p. 5, v. 4.

13 Morris, *Cofio Ann Griffiths*, p. 67.

14 Gaunt and Luff, *Hymns and Letters*, p. 24.

15 A. M. Allchin, *Praise Above All: Discovering the Welsh Tradition*, Cardiff: University of Wales Press, 1991, p. 79.

16 For her involvement in the Sunday schools and movement and campaign to abolish the slave trade, see pp. 99 and 115.

17 'To the Reader', Charlotte Elliott, *Hours of Sorrow; or Thoughts in Verse, Chiefly adapted to Seasons of Sickness, Depression and Bereavement*, London: James Nisbett and Co., 1836, pp. 1, 2, ll. 1–2, 23–6.

18 *Memoir of Charlotte Elliott, author of 'Just as I am,' etc*. By her sister E. B. [that is, E. Babington.], London, 1875.

19 James King, *Anglican Hymnology, being an account of the 325 standard hymns of the highest merit according to the verdict of the whole Anglican Church*, London: Hatchards, 1885, pp. 41–4. By comparison, Watts has eight hymns and Wesley ten.

20 King, *Anglican Hymnology*, p. 155.

21 Octavius Winslow, *The King in his Beauty: A Tribute to the Memory of Miss Charlotte Elliott, Authoress of 'Just as I am,' etc.*, London: John F. Shaw, 1871, p. 43.

22 Cited in Julian, *Hymnology*, p. 609.

23 King, *Anglican Hymnology*, p. xi.

24 See below, pp. 86, 94–5.

25 *Havergal's Psalmody and Century of Chants, from 'Old Church Psalmody,' 'Hundred Tunes,' and unpublished manuscripts of W. H. Havergal Edited by Frances Ridley Havergal*, London: Robert Cocks & Co., 1871; Charles Busbridge Snepp, *Songs of Grace and Glory, for Private, Family and Public Worship*, London: W. Hunt & Co., 1872.

26 Cited in Janet Grierson, *Frances Ridley Havergal: Worcestershire Hymnwriter*, Bromsgrove: Havergal Society, 1979, p. 5.

27 Grierson, *Frances Ridley Havergal*, p. 107.

28 Grierson, *Frances Ridley Havergal*, p. 130.

29 Grierson, *Frances Ridley Havergal*, p. 139. Electric light was, of course, then a relatively new phenomenon.

30 Cited in Grierson, *Frances Ridley Havergal*, p 148. The author's emphases.

31 Eric Routley, *Hymns and Human Life*, London: John Murray, 1952, p. 219.

32 Frances Ridley Havergal, 'The Ministry of Song', *The Ministry of Song*, 5th edn, London: J. Nisbet & Co., 1874, p. 4, ll. 53–4 *et passim*.

33 J. Mountain (comp.), *Hymns of Consecration and Faith and Sacred Songs for Missions*, London, 1876. Later editions were compiled by Mrs Evan Hopkins.

34 See above, pp. 34–38.

35 Phoebe Palmer, *Promise of the Father; or, A neglected speciality of the last days. Addressed to the clergy and laity of all Christian communities*, Boston: H. V. Degen, 1859.

36 Catherine Booth Clibborn, 'O Spotless Lamb, I come to thee', *Song Book of the Salvation Army*, 1953, no. 401, v. 1, chorus, v. 3.

37 *Wings of Praise. A Collection of Gospel Songs*. Compiled and edited by The Maréchale [that is, Catherine Booth-Clibborn]. Containing many original

compositions by A. S. Booth-Clibborn and other members of the Booth-Clibborn family, London: Marshall, Morgan and Scott, 1930.

38 Evangeline Cory Booth, *Songs of the Evangel*, new and enlarged edn, London: Salvation Army Publishing and Supplies, 1937.

39 Kidd, *The Great Awakening*, p. xv.

40 Robley Whitson, *The Shakers: Two Centuries of Spiritual Reflection*, London: SPCK, 1983, p. 209.

41 Richard MacNemar, *The Kentucky Revival: or a Short History of the outpouring of the Spirit of God in the Western States of America, with a brief account of Shakerism*, Cincinnati: J. W. Browne, 1807.

42 Richard MacNemar, 'The Testimony of Eternal Truth', Christian Goodwillie with Joel Cohen (ed.), *Shaker Songs: A Celebration of Peace, Harmony & Simplicity*, New York: Black Dog & Leventhal, 2002, p. 27, vv. 2, 8.

43 Goodwillie with Cohen (ed.), *Shaker Songs*, pp. 5–6.

44 Jemima Blanchard, in Roxalana Grosvernor (ed.), *Sayings of Mother Ann and the First Elders* (Sabbathday Lake manuscript, before 1845), pp. 64–5, cited in Whitson, *The Shakers*, p. 273.

45 Goodwillie with Cohen (ed.), *Shaker Songs*, p. 9.

46 *Millennial Praises: containing a collection of gospel hymns in four parts adapted to the day of Christ's second appearing*, Hancock, 1813, http://passtheword.org/SHAKER-MANUSCRIPTS/Millennial-Praises/mpraisesndex.htm.

47 Goodwillie with Cohen (ed.), *Shaker Songs*, p. 57.

48 Goodwillie with Cohen (ed.), *Shaker Songs*, p. 47.

49 Goodwillie with Cohen (ed.), *Shaker Songs*, p. 5

50 George Pullen Jackson, *White and Negro Spirituals: Their Life Span and Kinship*, Locust Valley NY: J. J. Augustin, 1943, p. 86, quoted in Buell E. Cobb Jr., *The Sacred Harp: A Tradition and its Music*, Athens GA: University of Georgia Press, 1989, p. 81

51 George W. Sanville, *Forty Gospel Hymn Stories*, Winona Lake IN: The Rodeheaver Hall-Mack Co., 1943, p. 28.

52 Lelia Morris, 'If you are tired of the load of your sin', http://www.cyberhymnal.org/htm/l/e/letjesus.htm, vv. 1, 4.

53 Mary D. James, 'All for Jesus!', http://www.hymnal.net/hymn.php?t=h&n=444.

54 Kenneth O. Brown, *Holy Ground: The Study of the American Camp Meeting*, New York: Garland, 1992, p. 29.

55 Ira D. Sankey, *Sacred Songs and Solos, New Hymns and Solos and the Christian Choir*, London: Morgan and Scott, 1897, no. 185; *Songbook of the Salvation Army*, 1953, no. 486; *Songbook of the Salvation Army*, 1986, no. 535.

56 Edward S. Ninde, *The Story of the American Hymn*, New York: Abingdon Press, 1921, p. 308.

57 Ninde, *The Story of the American Hymn*, p. 312.

58 June Hadden Hobbs, *'I sing for I cannot be silent'; The Feminization of American Hymnody, 1870–1920*, Pittsburgh PA: University of Pittsburgh Press, 1997, p. 117.

59 Mary Artemesia Lathbury, 'Day is dying in the west', *Redemption Hymnal*, no. 794.

60 Mary Artemesia Lathbury, 'Break Thou the bread of life', *Congregational Praise*, London: Congregational Union of England and Wales, 1951, no. 233.

61 Hobbs, *'I sing for I cannot be silent'*, p. 120.

62 The figure is given in earlier books as 8,000, but a further 1,000 texts were discovered at Hope Publishing Co. in 1972! Wesley Milgate, *Songs of the People of God: A Companion to the Australian Hymn Book/With One Voice*, London: Collins, 1982, p. 213.

63 John Ogasapian, *Church Music in America 1620–2000*, Macon GA: Mercer University Press, 2007, pp. 184–5.

64 Fanny Crosby, 'Blessed Assurance, Jesus is mine', no. 500; 'To God be the glory' 373, *Sacred Songs and Solos, New Hymns and Solos and the Christian Choir*, 1897; nos. 561, 512 in *Church Hymnary*, 4th edn, Norwich: Canterbury Press, 2005.

65 Fanny Crosby, 'All the way my Saviour leads me', no. 131; 'I am thine, O Lord, I have heard Thy voice', no. 165; 'Rescue the perishing', no. 37, *Sacred Songs and Solos*; nos. 421, 309, 359 in *Christian Life Hymnal*, Peabody MA: Hendrickson Publishers Ltd., 2006.

66 Fanny Crosby, 'Blessed Assurance, Jesus is mine', vv. 1 (ll. 3–4), 2 (l. 1).

67 Fanny Crosby, 'Only a little while'.

68 Fanny Crosby, *Memories of Eighty Years*, Boston MA: J. H. Earle & Co., 1906, p. 163.

69 See above, p. 66.

70 Crosby, *Memories of Eighty Years*, p. 141.

71 Hobbs, *'I sing for I cannot be silent'*, p. 81.

72 Crosby, 'Safe in the arms of Jesus', v. 1 (ll. 1–4).

73 Hobbs, *'I sing for I cannot be silent'*, p. 96.

74 Mary de Jong, 'I want to be like Jesus: The self-defining power of evangelical hymnody', *Journal of the American Academy of Religion* 54, Fall 1986, pp. 461–93.

75 Hobbs, *'I sing for I cannot be silent*, p. 24.

76 Hobbs, *'I sing for I cannot be silent'*, p. 24.

77 For example Hosea 2.2–13; alternatively, Jeremiah 2.1–3.

78 Annie Sherwood Hawkes, 'I need Thee every hour, most gracious Lord', http://www.cyberhymnal.org/htm/i/n/ineedteh.htm (accessed 28 August 2009), v. 5.

79 Sarah Addison Pollard, 'Have Thine own way, Lord, have Thine own way!', http://nethymnal.org/htm/h/t/hthineow.htm (accessed 29 August 2009), v. 4.

80 C. Austin Miles (1868–1946), 'I come to the garden alone', chorus and v. 3. 'Silent Worship' describes blackbird and thrush falling silent at the singing of the (female) beloved in the garden: George Friedrich Handel's setting of this anonymous text.

81 Fanny Crosby, 'Blessed assurance, Jesus is mine', ll. 9–10.

82 Hobbs, *'I sing for I cannot be silent'*, p. 136.

83 Judson W. van der Venter, 'All to Jesus I surrender', http://www.cyberhymnal.org/htm/i/s/isurrend.htm, vv. 2 (l. 4), 3 (l. 2), 4 (l. 3).

84 Sizer, *Gospel Hymns and Social Religion*, p. 139.

85 Donald Hustad, *Jubilate! Church Music in the Evangelical Tradition*, Carol Stream IL: Hope, 1981, p. 248.

86 See above, p. 72.

87 Hobbs, 'I sing for I cannot be silent', p. 146.

88 Cited Hobbs, 'I sing for I cannot be silent', p. 146.

89 Hobbs, 'I sing for I cannot be silent', p. 146.

90 Crosby, *Memories of Eighty Years*, p. 140.

91 Crosby, *Memories of Eighty Years*, p. 185.

92 Hustad, *Jubilate!*, p. 248.

93 John Ogasapian, *Church Music in America 1620–2000*, Macon GA: Mercer University Press, 2007, p. 104.

94 The 'Baptist Missionary Society' was founded in 1792 under the name of 'The Particular Baptist Society for the Propagation of the Gospel Amongst the Heathen'; Congregationalists formed the 'London Missionary Society' (until 1818 known as 'The Missionary Society') in 1795 as a non-denominational organization; Wesleyan and Primitive Methodist missionaries were active at the same time, though the churches did not form societies in the same way; the Anglican 'Church Mission Society' was formed in 1799.

95 Isaac Watts, *The Psalms of David Imitated in the Language of the New Testament and applied to the Christian State and Worship*, London: 1776, pp. 204–5, v. 1; See John Hull, 'Isaac Watts and the Origins of British Imperial Theology', *International Congregational Journal*, vol. 4, no. 2, February 2005, pp. 59–79.

96 See below, p. 93.

97 Ann and Jane Taylor, 'I thank the goodness and the grace', *Hymns for Infant Minds*, London, 1810, no. 1, v. 1.

98 Ann and Jane Taylor, 'Are we better than the heathen?', *Hymns for Infant Minds*, London, 1876, no. 49, vv. 1 (l. 3), 4 (ll. 3–4).

99 Cecil Frances Alexander, 'There are strange countries far away', *Hymns for Little Children*, vv. 1–2, ll. 1. Cecil Frances Alexander is treated at greater length at pp. 94–7. Praying to gods of wood and stone is a common theme in hymns of this kind.

100 *Missionary hymns: composed and selected for the services at the annual missionary meetings of the Society in London and for the Monthly Meetings for Prayer in Town and Country*, London, 1801.

101 Mrs Stokes, 'Soon may the last glad song arise', *Missionary hymns: composed and selected for the public services at the annual meetings of the London Missionary Society and for the Prayer Meetings of Auxiliary Societies in Town and Country*, London: London Missionary Society, 1840, no. 32, v. 3.

102 'Give thanks all Christian people', *Centenary Missionary Hymnal*, comp. and ed. Revd Stanley Rogers, London: London Missionary Society, 1895, p. 90 (the hymns are not numbered in the music edition).

103 *Centenary Missionary Hymnal*, Preface, p. iii.

104 Mary J. Wilcox, 'O Mission Ship! Dear Mission Ship!', *Centenary Missionary Hymnal*, p. 129, vv. 1, 2 (ll. 1–2, 6–8), 3 (ll. 5–8).

105 Ida Glenwood, 'God's vineyard is not bounded', *Centenary Missionary Hymnal*, p. 90, v. 2.

106 Sarah Geraldine Stock, 'A cry as of pain', *Centenary Missionary Hymnal*, p. 103, vv. 1–3 (ll. 4–5), 2 (l. 3).

107 H. E. Fox, Hon. Secretary, CMS, Preface, *Church Missionary Hymn Book*, London: Church Missionary Society, 1899, p. iii.

108 Madame Guyon, tr. William Cowper, 'All Scenes alike engaging prove', *Church Missionary Hymn Book*, no. 84, v. 2 (ll. 2–4); see above, p. 34.

109 Eva T. Evered Poole, 'I could not do the work the reapers did', *Church Missionary Hymn Book*, no. 132, vv. 2 (ll. 5–6), 3 (ll. 3–4). 4 (ll. 1–4).

110 M. Maude, 'O matchless honour, all unsought', *Church Missionary Hymn Book*, no. 230, vv. 1 (ll. 1–4), 2 (ll. 7–8).

111 M. Maude, 'The Lord gave the word', *Church Missionary Hymn Book*, no. 232, vv. 1–3, 6 (ll. 4–5).

112 Ann Taylor Gilbert, 'God of love, before Thee now', *Church Missionary Hymn Book*, no. 187, v. 5.

113 John Leifchild, *Original Hymns (many never printed & contributed expressly to these pages)*, MSS, 3 vols.

114 Rev J. Leifchild, *Original Hymns Adapted to General Worship and Special Occasions by Various Authors*, London, 1842, Preface, p. A2.

115 Ann Taylor Gilbert, 'Wearied with earthly toil and care', no. 26, 'I faint, my soul doth faint', no. 831, 'Hark the sounds of joy and gladness', no. 987, 'How happy they who safely housed', no. 1123, in Henry Ward Beecher (ed.), *The Plymouth Collection of Hymns and Tunes for the use of Christian Congregations*, New York: A. S. Barnes & Company, 1856.

116 Ann Taylor Gilbert, 'Low at thy feet, Eternal Power', Leifchild, *Original Hymns* (MS), no. 8, Leifchild, *Original Hymns Adapted*, no. 8, vv. 1 (ll. 1–2), 3 (l. 1), 5 (ll. 3–4), 6.

117 Ann Taylor Gilbert, 'No work of ours, no law fulfilled', Leifchild, *Original Hymns* (MS), no. 91; Leifchild, *Original Hymns Adapted*, no. 62, v. 4.

118 Ann Taylor Gilbert, 'Shall we the loftier truths embrace', Leifchild, *Original Hymns* (MS), no. 263; Leifchild, *Original Hymns Adapted*, no. 143, vv. 1, 2 (ll. 3–4), 5.

119 Ann Taylor Gilbert, 'King of high heaven, whose will', Leifchild, *Original Hymns* (MS), no. 87; Leifchild, *Original Hymns Adapted*, no. 277, v. 6.

120 Ann Taylor Gilbert, 'Can we the gospel feast partake', Leifchild, *Original Hymns* (MS), no. 163; Leifchild, *Original Hymns Adapted*, no. 290, v. 6 (l. 4).

121 Ann Taylor Gilbert, 'Bone of our bone! the spirit bleeds', Leifchild, *Original Hymns* (MS), no. 165; Leifchild, *Original Hymns Adapted*, no. 291, vv. 1 (ll. 1–2), 2 (ll. 1–4).

122 See below, p. 126.

123 Miss East, 'But has my Lord my soul forgot?', Leifchild, *Original Hymns* (MS), no. 314; Leifchild, *Original Hymns Adapted*, no. 203, vv. 3, 4 (ll. 3–4), 5.

124 Isaac Watts, *Divine and Moral Songs Attempted in Easy Language for the Use of Children*, 1715.

125 Lewis Carroll, *Alice's Adventures in Wonderland*, London: MacMillan & Co., 1865.

126 Susan Tamke writes: 'Although Watts' theology in his hymns for adults was often liberal and humane, in his hymns for children he was, at his most characteristic, harshly Calvinistic.' Susan Tamke, *Make a Joyful Noise unto the Lord; Hymns as a Reflection of Victorian Social Attitudes*, Athens, OH: Ohio University Press, 1978, p. 80.

127 *Hymns in Prose for Children*, London: J. Johnson, 1781; *Lessons for Children*, London: J. Johnson, 1778, contains five volumes: I (2–3 years), II (3

years), III (3 years), IV (3–4 years) and a *Little Spelling Book for Young Children*. See below, pp. 113–18.

128 Ann and Jane Taylor, *Hymns for Infant Minds*, Preface to rev. edn, London, 1876, cited in Tamke, *Make a Joyful Noise*, p. 83.

129 Ann and Jane Taylor, 'A poor afflicted child, I kneel', *Hymns for Infant Minds*, London: 1810, no. 30, vv. 1, 2 (ll. 3–4), 3.

130 Tamke, *Make a Joyful Noise*, p. 85.

131 Cecil Frances Alexander, 'Once in royal David's city', *Hymns for Little Children*, London, 1848, no. 11, vv. 3, 4 (l. 1), 7 (ll. 5–6).

132 *Hymns for Little Children* is dedicated 'To my little Godsons . . . 'hoping that the language of verse which children love may help to impress on their minds what they are, what I have promised for them, and what they must seek to be.'

133 Cecil Frances Alexander, 'All things bright and beautiful', *Hymns for Little Children*, no. 9, v. 3.

134 Cecil Frances Alexander, 'Saw ye never in the meadows', *Hymns for Little Children*, no. 30, vv. 2 and 3 (*passim*), 4 (ll. 2–3), 6 (ll. 2–3), 8, my emphasis.

135 Routley calls Noel's 'At the name of Jesus' the only hymn written by a woman 'of a theological, outward looking kind'. Routley, *Hymns and Human Life*, p. 203.

136 Routley, *Hymns and Human Life*, pp. 214–15.

137 *Verses for Holy Seasons with questions for examination by C. F. H.* (this is her maiden name, Cecil Frances Humphreys), ed. Walter Farquhar Hook, London: Francis and John Rivington, 1846.

138 Keble's 'Notice' for *Hymns for Little Children* runs to less than 200 words, noting, 'These few lines . . . are prefixed because the writer of the Hymns wished for some kind of clerical *imprimatur*.'

139 Cited Valerie Wallace, *A Life of the Hymn-writer Mrs Alexander, 1818–1895*, Dublin: Lilliput Press, 1995, p. 153. Ammon and Amalek are archetypal enemies of Israel: see for example, Psalm 83.7.

140 Ingrid Hotz-Davies, *The Creation of Religious Identities by English Women Poets from the Seventeenth to the Early Twentieth Century: Soulscapes*, Studies in Women and Religion, vol. 42, Lampeter: The Edwin Mellen Press Ltd., 2001.

141 Hotz-Davies, *The Creation of Religious Identities*, p. 47.

142 *Gloucester Journal*, 3 November 1783, cited in Philip B. Cliff, *The Rise and Development of the Sunday School Movement in England 1780–1980*, Redhill: National Christian Education Council, 1986, p. 27.

143 Stephen Orchard, 'From Catechism Class to Sunday School', in Stephen Orchard and John H. Y. Briggs (eds), *The Sunday School Movement: Studies in the Growth and Decline of Sunday Schools*, Bletchley: Paternoster, 2007, pp. 1–16, p. 16.

144 Cliff, *The Rise and Development of the Sunday School Movement*, p. 75.

145 Cliff, *The Rise and Development of the Sunday School Movement*, p. 73.

146 *Select Hymns, for the use of the Union Sunday School, George Leigh-Street*, Manchester: The Observer Office, 1819; *Selection of Psalms and Hymns for the use of Disley Church and Sunday School*, Cheshire Manchester: H

Whitmore, 1839; *Hymns for Public and Social Worship, selected chiefly for the use of the Stockport Sunday School*, Manchester: J. Ambery, 1848; notably the 1871 edn was published by The Guardian Steam Printing Works.

147 *Hymns selected and original, principally intended to aid the devotional exercises of children and teachers in the Leeds Sunday School Union*, Leeds: Heaton, 1833; *The Song Service Reporter: A Journal chiefly devoted to Sunday School music, etc.* Leeds: Phlox Publishing Office, 1890 etc.

148 *Hymns for the use of Chapeltown and District Sunday School Union*, British Library E.602.ii(9). This is bound with two copies of hymns for Whitsuntide: *Festival Hymns and Tunes: Union Street Congregational Sunday School Hyde, Hymns for Whitsuntide*, British Library E.602.ii(10); and *Festival Hymns and Tunes: Otley Sunday School Union at the 96th Anniversary Whitsuntide*, British Library E.602.ii(11): both Manchester: Manchester Sunday Schools Union, 1922. The Otley pamphlet shows how important the Whitsun celebration was. The front page advertises a programme over the whole Whit weekend, ending with: 'On Whit-Monday, June 5th, the Annual Out-door Gathering will be held in the Licks at 2.30 p.m., when the Hymns will again be sung to the Accompaniment of the Otley Band. After the singing of the hymns (weather permitting) the Scholars will parade the town, headed by the above band . . .'

149 *School Hymn Book of the Methodist Church*, London: Methodist Youth Department, 1950, no. 16.

150 William Kelynack, *Companion to the School Hymn Book of the Methodist Church*, London: Epworth Press, 1950.

151 Kelynack, *Companion*, no. 123.

152 *School Hymn Book of the Methodist Church*, no. 261.

153 Kelynack, *Companion*, p. 105. Two of her texts appeared in the book: 'In summer fields are grasses green', no. 493, and 'May I rise, may I rise at the break of the day', at no. 332.

154 R. Hoggart, *The Way We Live Now*, London: Chatto and Windus, 1995, p. 271, cited in Doreen Rosman, 'Sunday Schools and Social Change in the Twentieth Century', in Orchard et al. (eds), *The Sunday School Movement*, pp. 149–60, p. 153.

155 Tamke, *Make a Joyful Noise*, p. 2.

156 *Primitive Methodist Sunday School Union Hymn Book*, London: Ralph Fenwick, 1879, p. iii.

157 Foreword to Arthur E. Mills, *Children's Hymns and Hymn Writers*, comp. Arthur E. Mills, London: Epworth Press, 1950.

158 Mills, *Children's Hymns and Hymn Writers*, p. 5.

4

The Nineteenth Century: Political and Social Revolution

While evangelical and revivalist Christian traditions focused on the moral reform of the nations, and on bringing people to salvation in Jesus, or to higher spiritual states, a strong Dissenting tradition also marks the nineteenth century, supporting more radical social change. It is a shame that so little from the women's writing of this range of traditions continues in use. The evangelical hymns are a great treasury, but so much has been lost.

There was an ideological and active resistance on both sides of the Atlantic to the feminization of culture that undergirded evangelical writing. Harriet Martineau (1802–76) objected to the social alliance between women and clergy, and to the identification of women with religion. Harriet Beecher Stowe (1811–96) called it *Pink and White Tyranny* in the title of her 1871 society novel of that name. And, both in Britain and in America, women began to question the misogynistic alliance between religion and society that denied women their full humanity.

At the same time, campaigners such as Josephine Butler (1828–1906) raged against the double standard that laid all the blame and punishment for prostitution on women. Sarah Flower Adams (1805–48), among others, argued for the full equality of women with men. Julia Ward Howe (1819–1910) became a formidable campaigner for women's rights.

English Unitarians

The introduction to *Nineteenth-Century Women Poets* identifies a 'post-Revolutionary radical formation', which 'was extraordinarily powerful at the beginning of the century'[1] and traces 'A questioning dissenting tradition', which 'moves through the century. It can be seen in the work of Sarah Flower Adams, who was associated with the Unitarian and Utilitarian *Monthly Repository*, to which [Anna Laetitia] Barbauld also contributed.'[2]

The *Repository* was read, for example, by Elizabeth Barrett Browning (1806–61), and influenced a group of largely Anglican women writers, including Adelaide Ann Procter (1825–64).[3] The influential *English Woman's Journal*, to which Procter was a principal contributor, was founded by Bessie Raynor Parkes and Barbara Leigh Smith, both from Unitarian backgrounds, and counted among its readership Christina Georgina Rossetti (1830–94).[4]

There were strong links with the United States of America, as many of these women, particularly those from Dissenting traditions, supported the American Revolution, and envied what they saw as a freer and fairer society. Liberal British and American Christians were at the forefront of the campaign for the abolition, at first, of the slave trade, and finally of slavery itself.

Anna Laetitia Barbauld, whose hymns gained great popularity, stands squarely in this tradition. She was the daughter of a Unitarian who took up a post at Warrington Dissenting Academy when she was 15. Although he disapproved of his daughter's scholarly nature (she could read by the time she was two), he reluctantly allowed her to learn Latin and Greek, and she was tutored by Philip Doddridge.

She married the Huguenot, Rochemont Barbauld, and together they set up a boys' school in Stoke Newington in North London. Ironically, as Clara Balfour notes in a sketch of her life, 'She had importunately sought from her father sound and liberal education for herself, and yet she either entertained his prejudices against increasing the range of female education, or her diffidence rendered her objection to [a scheme for educating ladies] insuperable.'[5] She certainly rejected attempts to encourage her to open a school for girls.

On other matters, however, she held extremely radical views. Oddly, these come out more in her hymns for children than in her writing for adult worshippers. The hymns for children are in prose, as she considered that 'it may well be doubted whether poetry *ought* to be lowered to the capacities of children, or whether they should not rather be kept from reading verse until they are able to relish good verse'.[6]

Children are by no means the reprobate savages who are the objects of Isaac Watts and Jane Taylor. Rather, they are encouraged to see the divine in all of life. The theology of the hymns is liberal, almost pantheistic. The children are to offer praise on behalf of nature, which is dumb:

Trees that blossom, and little lambs that skip about, if you could, you would say how good he is; but you are dumb, we will say it for you.

We will not offer you in sacrifice, but we will offer sacrifice for you on every hill, and in every green field, we will offer the sacrifice of thanksgiving, and the incense of praise.[7]

Interestingly, Barbauld twice compares God to the human mother. Her Hymn III asks, systematically, if the shepherd looks after the sheep, who is the Shepherd of the shepherd, and, if the King rules over his subjects, who is the Sovereign of the King? The second stanza is as follows:

The mother loveth her little child; she bringeth it up on her knees; she nourisheth its body with food; she feedeth its mind with knowledge; if it is sick, she nurseth it with tender love; she watcheth over it when asleep; she forgetteth it not for a moment; she teacheth it how to be good; she rejoiceth daily in its growth.

But who is the parent of the mother? who nourisheth her with good things, and watcheth over her with tender love, and remembereth her every moment? Whose arms are about her to guard her from harm? and if she is sick, who shall heal her?

God is the parent of the mother; he is the parent of all, for he created all. All the men and all the women who are alive in the wide world are his children; he loveth all, he is good to all.[8]

Hymn V is all about sleeping, and contains the lovely stanza:

As the mother moveth about the house with her finger on her lips, and stilleth every little noise, that her infant be not disturbed; as she draweth the curtains around its bed, and shutteth out the light from its tender eyes; so God draweth the darkness around us, so he maketh all things to be hushed and still, that his large family may sleep in peace.[9]

However, the theological thought that excites her is to be found in the later hymns in the collection. Hymn VIII is political, and carries out what Barbauld regards as an important piece of education. In her *Civic*

Sermons to the People,[10] she urges working families to discuss politics in the presence of their children, and to teach children that the State is an extension of the small community of the family, each community with its head, its rules and government, its security and responsibilities. This hymn begins in the family of a labourer: the father is seen as the master of the family (her politics may be liberal but they are still patriarchal). The child, who spends his first years in this small (though not nuclear) society, will learn later about the village or town, the kingdom, whose ruler is the sovereign, and the world, whose ruler is God.

The world is varied, and contains much injustice, whose victims, however, must cry to God, in the same way as a child takes its complaints to its father. A major concern of Barbauld is revealed in the stanza:

> Negro woman, who sittest pining in captivity, and weeping over thy sick child; though no-one seeth thee, God seeth thee; though no-one pitieth thee, God pitieth thee: raise thy voice, forlorn and abandoned one; call upon him from amidst thy bonds, for assuredly he will hear thee.[11]

Moira Ferguson calls her 'The first white woman to speak – more or less – in her own voice and engage a slave as interlocutor', and notes that 'Barbauld draws young readers into a crucial moral-political debate. This responsible address to children about slavery stemmed from her Dissenting background. She knew powerlessness and political prejudice at first hand.'[12]

Barbauld and other dissenters came at the anti-slavery debate from a different point of view from the evangelical campaigners of the Clapham Sect, including Hannah More,[13] and other evangelical writers such as Cowper, Newton and, above all, Wilberforce. The evangelical position drew a parallel between redemption from slavery and redemption from sin. The slave is freed into servitude to Christ. The Dissenters, on the other hand, saw slavery as an injustice, to be eradicated on the way to setting society free. Wilberforce, as well as leading the campaign against slavery, was also a vigorous opponent of Dissenters' rights.

In this, Barbauld was allied with fellow dissenter Helen Maria Williams. Williams did not enjoy the popularity that Barbauld did as a poet or hymn-writer. This is attributed to the antipathy she earned by her far more public and lasting support for the French Revolution. She moved to France in 1790, and remained there, with a brief stay in Switzerland in 1795, for fear that her anti-Jacobin writing would put her in danger. She wrote a number of letters and books giving her own eye-witness account of the events of the Revolution.

Before making this public and courageous move, she was already a prominent thinker and writer on a range of radical topics. Ferguson comments:

> For well over a decade Williams commanded a formidable intellectual position within the Dissenting community: like Hannah More she was an eminent figure in London circles, but unlike More her home became a cultural and political gathering place for radical Dissenters and bluestockings alike.[14]

She also says that Horace Walpole told More that he regarded Williams and Barbauld as Deborah and Jael from Scripture![15]

Barbauld was also deeply involved in the political debates of her day, writing under various pseudonyms. She was a pacifist, and argued powerfully for class equality, and for freedom of religion and thought. She was impatient under what she regarded as the outdated restraints of the England of her day, and applauded France and America for their liberalism.

Like Anne Steele,[16] she too responded to national days for fasting and penitence, but not with hymns to be sung in chapel. As well as writing hymns and poetry, she published political pamphlets under the pseudonym 'A Dissenter'.

She wrote two scathing commentaries on National Fasts for penitence appointed in April 1793 and February 1794, during the War with France. The first tract is vehement in its criticism of an unholy alliance: 'an unjust war is in itself so bad a thing, that there is only one way of making it worse, and that is, by mixing religion with it'.[17] In a brilliant piece of satire, she provides the words for an honest prayer before war:

> God of love, father of all the families of the earth, we are going to tear in pieces our brethren of mankind, but our strength is not equal to our fury, we beseech thee to assist us in the work of slaughter . . . Whatever mischief we do, we shall do it in thy name; we hope, therefore, thou wilt protect us in it. Thou, who hast made of one blood all the dwellers upon the earth, we trust thou wilt view us alone with partial favour, and enable us to bring misery upon every other quarter of the globe.[18]

She celebrated the freedoms won and preserved in the American Declaration of Independence, and lamented the tyranny (as she saw it) of the Established Church in England. In her view, public worship is 'the only place, to enter which, nothing is more necessary than to be of the same species; – the only place, where man meets man not only as an equal but a brother; and where, by contemplating his duties, he may become sensible of his rights',[19] and she goes on, 'Every time Social Worship is celebrated, it includes a virtual declaration of the rights of man.'[20]

Unlike the hymns for children, her hymns for public worship rarely strayed from the expressions of conventional piety. They concentrate on conventional moral and pious themes: the life of Jesus, the death of the virtuous, the perils besetting the soul. Only occasionally does her radical theological stand show through. John Beard's book includes a hymn 'for the Lord's Day'. The hymn begins and ends conventionally enough, opening with the question, 'What rites, what honours shall he pay – How spread his Sovereign's name abroad?', and ending with two verses that distance the 'sabbath' from the cares of life.

Verses two and three suddenly round on the pomp commonly associated with worship, and which she satirized so effectively in her prose works:

> From marble domes and gilded spire
> Shall curling clouds of incense rise,
> And gems, and gold, and garlands deck
> The costly pomp of sacrifice?
>
> Vain, sinful man! creation's Lord,
> Thy golden offerings well may spare;
> But give thy heart, and thou shalt find,
> Here dwells a God who heareth prayer.[21]

But the most radical of these hymns is, frustratingly, the least clear in its attribution. Later books give the authors, either with the hymns, or in a separate list. Jeremy Belknap's collection notes the author at the head of each hymn, assigning Barbauld's hymns to 'Barbauld'. Hymn CCCXXII is, however, attributed to 'Aiken'. It is not clear whether this is a mistake, or whether the hymn is by her brother. There is no initial, or other information.

The hymn deals uncompromisingly with the evil of war, and reflects the sentiments of many of her prose writings, but its style is so much more daring than that of most of her hymns that its authorship may well be in doubt. There is no glorification or justification of war, but rather condemnation:

Oh see! with what insatiate rage
Thy sons their impious battles wage;
How spread destruction like a flood,
And brothers shed their brothers' blood!

See guilty passions spring to birth,
And deeds of hell deform the earth;
While righteousness and justice mourn;
And love and pity droop forlorn.[22]

Barbauld's courage and importance in her own time are undeniable. Her prose hymns for children were the staple diet of a generation of Dissenters' children in the newly forming Sunday schools, and in the home, and her hymns for adult worship appeared in Unitarian and other Nonconformist hymnbooks for generations.

One of Barbauld's pupils at Palgrave was the father of another campaigner on equality and human rights, Harriet Martineau (1802–76). Martineau recalls of her childhood, 'in those days, we learned Mrs Barbauld's Prose hymns by heart; and there were parts of them which I dearly loved: but other parts made me shiver with awe'.[23] The direct influence is plain, in Martineau's hymns for families.[24]

She remembers Mrs Barbauld as an occasional visitor to her family home in Norwich: 'It was a remarkable day for us when the comely elderly lady in her black silk cloak and bonnet came and settled herself for a long morning chat', and she retained her deep admiration for the older woman's writings, regarding her as a pattern of female achievement for another generation, writing, 'I still think her one of the first writers in our language, and the best example we have of the benefits of a sound classical education to a woman.'[25] She also met and admired Barbauld's niece, Lucy Aikin, with whom she tried unsuccessfully to set up a periodical devoted to the cause of women.

Martineau was a self-confessed sickly and ungracious child, becoming deaf at an early age, and adoring of her younger brother James, who profoundly influenced her in her adult choice of career, that of professional writing. James Martineau became a supporter of a growing movement to improve the quality of hymns for public worship, and his book *Hymns for the Christian Church and Home* (1840) gained immediate popularity.

It was James who persuaded her to early efforts at writing for the *Monthly Repository*.[26] She wrote an article, 'Female Writers on Practical Divinity', and signed it 'V'. She records her intense embarrassment when her elder brother roundly praised this new writer in her presence, until she was forced to confess her authorship. He sealed her ambition by his proud approval, 'Now, dear, leave it for other women to make shirts and darn stockings; and do you devote yourself to this.' At this, she 'went home in a sort of dream, so that the squares of the pavement seemed to float before my eyes. That evening made me an authoress.'[27]

Four years later, her father's business disintegrated, leaving the family completely impoverished. She writes, 'I, for one, was left destitute; – that is to say, with precisely one shilling in my purse.'[28] But loss of social standing had its compensations:

> In a very short while, my two sisters at home and I began to feel the blessing of a wholly new freedom. I, who had been obliged to write before breakfast, or in some private way, had henceforth liberty to do my own work in my own way; for we had lost our gentility. Many and many a time since then we have said that, but for that loss of money, we might have lived on in the ordinary provincial method of ladies with small means, sewing and economizing, and growing narrower every year: whereas, by being thrown, while it was yet time, on our own resources, we have worked hard and usefully, won friends, reputation and independence, seen the world abundantly, abroad and at home, and, in short, have truly lived instead of vegetated.[29]

She now wrote voraciously about the history and politics of her time. Oppression of any kind incensed her, and she could see no reason for the expediency of gradual reform, once the principle of justice was established. She applied this ruthless logic to the debates on the abolition of slavery and the emancipation of women.

Her series *Illustrations of Political Economy*[30] eventually gave her financial security, and brought her into contact with serving politicians. The series became essential reading for MPs, and Martineau found herself called on for advice. She records that MPs sent their Blue Books to her, and that Elizabeth Fry invited her to a meetings at Newgate, in order to discover from a woman who was in the confidence of the Government, the official position on Poor Law Reform.[31]

She was a fervent supporter of women's full equality, and looked forward with hope:

The best advocates are yet to come, – in the persons of women who are obtaining access to real social business, – the female physicians and other professors in America, the women of business and the female artists in France; and the hospital administrators, the nurses, the educators and substantially successful authors of our own country.

She goes on:

> women, like men, can obtain whatever they show themselves fit for. Let them be educated, – let their powers be cultivated to the extent for which the means are already provided, and all that is wanted or ought to be desired will follow of course. Whatever a woman proves herself able to do, society will be thankful to see her do, – just as if she were a man.[32]

At the close of her *Autobiography*, there is a great sense of excitement at being at the dawn of a new and scientific age, a development away from theological and philosophical to scientific thinking. At the end of her life, Martineau was still capable of being excited and inspired by new ways of thinking.

Some of her excitement comes across in her hymns. Gone is the earlier generation's sense of life's fleeting nature in the face of God's eternal essence. Instead, change is a reason for hope. Her strange and powerful hymn 'Beneath this starry arch' concludes alternate verses with two refrains: 'Moves one, move all:/Hark to the footfall!/On, on, for ever!' and just 'On, on, for ever!' The stars become the symbol of slow but constant change, the passing of the hours. The hymn concludes by setting human life in the context of the longer timespan of the stars:

> They pass the cradle-head,
> And there a promise shed;
> They pass the moist new grave,
> And bid rank verdure wave;
> They bear through every clime
> The harvests of all time,
>   On, on, for ever![33]

Her attitude to worship is different from Barbauld's. Wisdom and reason are not presumptions on the part of the human worshipper, but are to be sought through the din of human life in the still moments of worship or reflection. A lovely hymn on the call of Samuel likens the voice heard by the boy in the Temple to the voice of reason:

E'en such a voice I too may hear,
E'en such a light my soul may cheer;
For wisdom's words by God were given,
And reason is a ray from heaven.

Then will I feed this sacred fire;
For wisdom's precept's still enquire;
Still pray, from pride and folly free,
'Speak! for thy servant heareth thee.'[34]

Where Martineau agrees with Barbauld is in the equalizing power of true worship. Martineau puts into verse the sentiments of Barbauld's article on worship, in her hymn 'All men are equal in their birth'. The third verse of the hymn shows her view of the root of inequality:

'Tis man alone who difference sees,
And speaks of high and low;
And worships those, and tramples these
While the same path they go.

The experience of worship, according to the last verse, ought to recall 'men' to their essential equality. This could not be more different from Cecil Frances Alexander's 'rich man in his castle' verse in 'All things bright and beautiful'![35]

Ye great! renounce your earth-born pride;
Ye low! your shame and fear;
Live, as ye worship, side by side;
Your common claims revere.[36]

Certainly, the words of her most political hymns are designed to recall the singers' attention to the inequalities and evils of the world in which they live. A hymn combining eschatology with pure nineteenth-century optimism calls on the coming of Jesus:

Lord Jesus! come; for hosts
Meet on the battle plain:
The patriot mourns, the tyrant boasts,
And tears are shed like rain.

Lord Jesus! come; for still
Vice shouts her maniac mirth;
And poverty's a crushing ill
While teems the fruitful earth.[37]

The *Monthly Repository* was edited by the Pastor of South Place Unitarian Chapel, Finsbury, in North London, William Johnson Fox, a politician and radical thinker. Two sisters, Sarah and Eliza Flower, close friends of Harriet Martineau, attended the chapel. They were daughters of Benjamin Flower, who was notorious for his advocacy of civil and religious liberty, and an ardent Unitarian lay preacher, keenly opposed to theological dogmatism and spiritual domination. He had been imprisoned for six months for his radical views.

On Flower's death, Fox became the guardian of the two girls, and probably the lover of Eliza. Both sisters showed great creative talent, Sarah in writing poetry and Eliza in composing music.

We know Sarah Flower Adams as a hymn-writer, but she and her sister also wrote popular protest songs in connection with the great political issue of their day. In the nineteenth century as in the folk revival of the 1960s, Christians involved in radical political movements wrote both hymns and songs of protest – indeed, the distinction is blurred by the holistic nature of radical Christian theology. Derek Hyde comments:

> It is no accident that revolutionary movements soon give birth to their protest songs or arousing anthem: the Women's Suffrage Movement in England was no exception. In the protest songs of Eliza Flower connected with the agitation for the 1832 Reform Bill and the repeal of the Corn Laws in 1846 . . . nineteenth-century women used music as a means of protest.[38]

Sarah was also encouraged to write articles and stories for the *Monthly Repository,* for which Martineau was also writing at the time, and her confidence and thinking can be seen developing through her writing. The articles appear in issues during the years 1833–36.

Like Martineau, she cannot see any reason why women should not be equally able to exercise strength and intellect, and, like Martineau, she blames inequality in education for the low expectations and low achievements of women in her day.

Inspired by a visit to Luxembourg, where she viewed works of art by women as well as by men, Sarah wrote:

> And what becomes of woman's intellect and woman's soul, and the courage that prompts her to dare all that may become a woman . . .? We would do away with *mere dependence* which is only gratifying to a man as it ministers to his love of power . . . if men set a value on the dependence which prevents the proper application of power, they must not wonder if the evil recoils upon themselves.[39]

Sarah experienced an intellectual struggle with her faith. In 1827, she wrote to Fox, out of her struggle to retain her beliefs:

> It was in answering Robert Browning that my mind refused to bring forward argument, turned recusant, and sided with the enemy . . . I would give worlds to be a sincere believer; to go to my Bible as to a friend in the hour of trial . . .[40]

This struggle intensified as the years passed, and as her health became more uncertain.

Adams' hymns are nearly all written before her association with the *Monthly Repository*, and are filled with a kind of gentle piety, which barely makes contact with her later radical thinking. She writes a lot about death, but with a kind of sentimental hope familiar from much writing of the time. The dead are not to be mourned; instead they are accompanied on their way by the risen Jesus:

> Then mourn we not beloved dead,
> E'en while we come to weep and pray;
> The happy spirit far hath fled
> To brighter realms of endless day.
> > Immortal hope dispels the gloom!
> > *An angel sits beside the tomb.*[41]

The changing nature of the world is not to be feared, but enjoyed by the individual. She has nothing of the sombre power of Martineau's 'Beneath this starry arch', but rather a song full of sentiment and courage:

> The world may change from old to new,
> > From new to old again;
> Yet hope and heaven, for ever true,
> > Within man's heart remain.
> The dreams that bless the weary soul,
> > The struggles of the strong,
> Are steps towards some happy goal,
> > The story of hope's song.

But the outcome of such courageous hope is not social change in this life, but the promise of a better tomorrow:

Oh no! it is no flattering lure,
　　No fancy weak or fond;
When hope would bid us rest secure
　　In better life beyond.[42]

The hymns have much to say about individual endurance of trouble, but present no challenge to the social and political structures that give rise to suffering. The nearest she comes to tackling social ill is in her two-verse hymn to the Creator. The first verse emphasizes the goodness, wisdom and power of God, a theme repeated in the first two lines of the second verse, which then goes on:

Though by oppression his people sore troubled,
May suffer in bondage, or languish for light;
His mighty right arm, with a power redoubled,
Can tyranny quell, and redeem for the right.[43]

Two of her works postdate these years: The hymn 'Nearer my God to Thee', and a long dramatic poem, *Vivia Perpetua*. The latter is Adams' account of the martyrdom of Perpetua in Carthage in AD 203.[44] The story of spiritual and intellectual struggle mirrors Adams' own.

The only hymn written during the last years of her life is the one for which she is best known. While this hymn deals more maturely with its scriptural reference, being based on the story of Jacob's ladder,[45] the sense is still of one leaving earth for heaven, by a path won through suffering, rather than of God's influence descending to earth.

In the same year (1840), Fox, in collaboration with Eliza and Sarah, published his *Hymns and Anthems*, to which Sarah contributed 13 hymns, and her sister 63 of the 150 tunes. Five years later, Eliza was dead from consumption. Sarah, whose health had never been good, is said to have pined away after her sister's death, and died two years later.

It would have been interesting to see Adams' thought and style develop through the long lifetime of Barbauld or Martineau, both of whom lived for over 70 years, while Sarah stopped writing at 41 and died at 43.

Dissent in America

It was, as Barbauld and Martineau suspected, from America that the writing and hymnody would come that reflected the depth of radical thinking from the nineteenth century.

When Martineau visited America, she stayed with Unitarian friends and attended abolitionist meetings at the invitation of Dr and Mrs Follen and Henry Ware, dedicated campaigners for abolition, remarking, typically, 'some were of the opinion that personal danger was incurred by attending abolition meetings at present. This was, of course, nothing to me in a case where principle, political or moral, was involved, and I said so.'[46] True to her word, she attended meetings at which she was at real personal risk.

Freed, to a certain extent, of the weight of historical convention, American writers could express in songs for public worship some of the frustration and some of the longing for justice in this world that was largely limited to the prose writings or poems for private use among the English.

This was, in fact, a period of remarkable outpouring of hymn-writing and hymn-book publication from Unitarian and liberal writers in America. Between 1830 and 1865, 15 Unitarian hymnbooks were published. Benson recognizes the unusual feel to this, though in fact other eras of radical theology have given rise to similar outpourings:

> The period of Unitarianism covered by these hymnbooks – between the '30s and the Civil War – was precisely the era of religious debate between the historical and the new conceptions of Christianity rather than a time of what is regarded as religious revival. And it is somewhat remarkable that it should have been characterised by a spirit of devotion expressed in a great outpouring of hymns, such as we ordinarily associate with a revival era.[47]

In Henry Ward Beecher's pioneering and influential collection, *The Plymouth Collection of Hymns and Tunes for the use of Christian Congregations*, over 90 of the 1374 texts are by women – and there may be more, since many are unattributed. These include 30 by Anne Steele, who is the only woman writer to merit a special mention in the introduction.

The section on 'Missions and Reform' (hymns 943–1068) contains a number of texts on issues of social concern. Again, this is mentioned specifically in Beecher's introduction:

Much attention has been given to the Great Humanities which the Gospel develops, whenever it is faithfully and purely preached. The hymns of Temperance, of Human Rights and Freedom, of Peace, and of Benevolence, will be found both numerous, energetic, and eminently Christian.[48]

The texts relating to the abolition of slavery include one by Caroline Seward, which relates the release from slavery to Miriam's song following redemption from Egypt:

As Thou of old to Miriam's hand
The thrilling timbrel didst restore,
And to the joyful song her hand
Echoed from desert to the shore; –

O let thy smitten ones again
Take up the chorus of the free . . .[49]

On the following page is a text by Eliza Cabot Follen (1787–1860), a friend of the Beecher family,[50] written from the point of view of the captive; and a couple of pages later is Harriet Martineau's text 'All men are equal in their birth', though unattributed. Martineau's anti-slavery text, 'Lord Jesus come! for hosts/Meet on the battle plain', also appears in this section.[51]

While the anti-slavery movement had begun in the previous century in England, and led to the successful abolition of the Atlantic slave trade in 1807 and slavery in the British colonies by 1838, the issue was still unresolved in America, to the horror of liberals in that country. Vicki Eaklor has collected and commented on the hymns of the American anti-slavery campaigns. These were a major feature of campaign meetings. The texts are passionate and urgent, and, for the most part, written specifically for the campaign.

A number are by women writers. Eliza Follen has five texts, including a longer and altered version of her anti-slavery hymn in *The Plymouth Collection*.[52] Eaklor records the occasions for which the hymns were written, or on which they were used. Follen's text, 'Heart to heart, and hand in hand', was written for the Twelfth Anti-Slavery Fair at Faneuil Hall (Boston), and takes up a common theme, lamenting the presence of slavery in the 'Land of the Free':

To the Pilgrim spirit true
Which nor slave nor master knew,

Onward! faithful fearless few,
Liberty's the prize.

. . .

Will you your New England see
Crouching low to slavery?

. . .

Listen to our solemn call
Sounding from old Faneuil Hall.[53]

Hymns were often written to familiar tunes, many of them secular. Harriet Martineau wrote 'Now's the day and now's the hour' to 'Scots Whae Hae'. It must have been tremendous to sing lines such as:

Gather like the muttering storm!
Wake your thunders for reform!
Bear not, like the trodden worm,
Scorn and mockery![54]

In fact, this tune is the second most popular among the items collected by Eaklor, with 19 uses. There is a suggestion that the resonance with the Scottish battle for liberation is deliberate.

In America, unlike Britain, the anti-slavery campaign was an integral part of the struggle for national identity. Faneuil Hall was nicknamed 'The Cradle of American Liberty', because the patriots met there so frequently during the American Revolution. There was a sense of outrage that America retained slavery, while hidebound Britain had achieved abolition. This means that large social themes run through the hymns, one of which was the contribution and place of women and the rhetoric of the home and family.

The campaign split in 1840 over the issue of the emancipation of women, which some saw as essential to the freedom of the whole nation, while others held it to be a side issue. A rather unwieldy text by Joshua Simpson contrasts the two causes:

Women's rights and annexation
Is the topic by the way,
While poor Afric's sable nation
For mercy, cry both night and day.[55]

Joshua was a free black man, who produced three collections of this own songs, and was a prominent campaigner.

An unknown author, presumably female, as she claims to speak for 'New England's daughters', counters with a text addressed to John Quincy Adams for his visit to Hingham and 'sung with fine effect'.

> May not a woman plead
> That evils be redressed?
> Has God spurned women from his throne?
> Has *He* refused to hear the groan
> Which bursts from woman's breast?[56]

A great many of the hymns, by men as well as women, refer to the special suffering of slave women, and the horror of the disruption of family life as mothers and children are parted. Abby H. Price (1814–73, a prominent supporter of women's rights, and speaker at women's rights conventions in the 1850s) wrote 'The Slave Mother', in which the mother laments her loss of children and family:

> O, who can imagine her heart's deep emotion,
> As she thinks of her children about to be sold!
> You may picture the bounds of the rock-girdled ocean,
> But the grief of that mother can never be told!

The call to end slavery is pictured as the end to her despair:

> Rejoice, O rejoice! for the child thou art rearing,
> May one day lift up its unmanacled form,
> While hope, to thy heart, like the rainbow is cheering,
> Is born, like the rainbow, 'mid tempest and storm.[57]

Henry Beecher's daughters, Harriet and Catharine, responded to their liberal upbringing, and espoused the two great causes of the emancipation of slaves and the emancipation of women. Anne Douglas talks of women like Harriet Beecher Stowe and her sister Catharine as being destroyed by American society of the time. 'Both women', she says, 'were unusually well-versed and interested in Protestant theology; both played a major role in vitiating its intellectual content. Their options were painfully limited.'[58]

Catharine, the elder of the sisters, devoted her life to the cause of women's education. The sisters received only the education considered appropriate to women of their class, while their brothers attended Harvard and Amherst. Catharine Beecher campaigned against the gender exclusivity of the great universities and spent her adult life trying to raise funds to endow a women's college.

For a short time, from 1824, Harriet attended the Hartford Female Seminary, opened by Catharine. Her abilities as a student and writer were quickly evident, and she became involved in decisions over the running of the Seminary. However, in 1832, the whole family, including the two sisters, moved to Ohio, where their former support of the abolition of slavery came up against the realities of slave markets and divided families.

Uncle Tom's Cabin was inspired by two events, one public and one personal. In 1849, Harriet's 18-month-old son Charley died of cholera. She later wrote to Eliza Cabot Follen:

> It was at his dying bed and at his grave that I learned what a poor slave mother may feel when her child is torn away from her . . . I have often felt that much that is in that book had its root in the awful scenes and bitter sorrow of that summer.[59]

The other event was the 1850 Fugitive Slave Act, which enforced the duty to return runaway slaves, and penalized aiding them, causing widespread anger among the abolitionist states, and leading to further suffering for escaping slaves.

The book was an immediate, overwhelming success, and has been credited with the ending of slavery and even blamed for the Civil War!

Relevantly to this study, *Uncle Tom's Cabin* refers to hymn-singing. Hobbs recognizes that hymns are often used subversively in novels, and considers the singing by women and slaves in this light. There is an extraordinary scene towards the end of the book, when the slave Susan and her daughter Emmeline are waiting for the auction, which may well (and, indeed, does) separate them and send Emmeline to a life of abuse at the hands of a cruel master.

Behind bars, through the night, the two women sing 'a wild and melancholy dirge, common as a funeral hymn among slaves'. The hymn is in the style of a camp meeting song, with only the characters in the first two lines changed. Two verses are cited. The first refers to the sorrows of women; the second makes a direct reference to the scene evoked by their situation, the imprisonment of Paul and Silas.

Oh, where is weeping Mary?
Oh, where is weeping Mary?
    'Rived in the goodly land.

She is dead and gone to heaven;
She is dead and gone to heaven;
   'Rived in the goodly land.

Oh, where are Paul and Silas?
. . .
They are dead and gone to heaven.[60]

Like the captive apostles, the mother and daughter sing, but not praises, as in the story from Acts 16.25, but a lament. For them, there is to be no release from their suffering. Stowe depicts the slave market, held the following morning. Following the sale of the mother to a benevolent middle-aged man, Emmeline is the subject of a bidding frenzy which ends: 'the hammer falls, – he has got the girl, body and soul, unless God help her!'[61]

Later, her purchaser, Legree, is shocked and terrified to hear a 'strange and ghostlike' voice, singing. He stops to listen, as 'A wild, pathetic voice, chants a hymn common among the slaves.' This time it is a hymn of judgement, of parting, and he fears that the ghost of his dead mother will appear to judge him.

This may well echo the way hymns 'common among the slaves' were used in a genuinely subversive way to impart meaning. Harriet Tubman (1822–1913) is said to have used hymns and songs to convey clandestine messages to the slaves she was leading to freedom. For example, 'Steal away to Jesus' or 'Go down Moses' were signs that the coast was clear and the escapees could move.[62]

Despite her use of hymns as a subversive device in her book, Beecher Stowe's hymns do not reflect her concern for wider social issues. Instead we see something of her inner life. The loss of her son Charley can be traced in the text 'Far, far beneath, the noise of tempests dieth'.[63] Another, 'Still, still with thee – when purple morning breaketh', recalls the tranquillity of dawn, a time when she liked to walk in her own garden:

As in the dawning, o'er the waveless ocean,
The image of the morning star doth rest,
So in this stillness, Thou beholdest only
Thine image in the waters of my breast.
. . .
When sinks the soul, subdued by toil, to slumber,
Its closing eye looks up to Thee in prayer,
Sweet the repose beneath Thy wings o'ershading,
But sweeter still to wake and find Thee there.[64]

On 23 December 1870, an extract of a letter from Harriet Beecher
Stowe was read at a Peace Meeting held at Union League Hall, New
York, addressed by one Julia Ward Howe (1819–1910). The purpose
of the meeting was to propose a World Woman's Peace Congress, and
Stowe was one of the voices raised in support, as was feminist campaigner and writer Lucretia Mott. Howe's speech to the meeting attacks
the double standard which she sees as responsible for war:

> this bitter custom of war has its source in the doctrine that there
> is one morality for man and another for woman. Women must be
> patient and forgiving; men may be savage and vindictive . . . This
> unequal scale of morals disorganizes the world. If it is wrong for
> women to fight, it is also wrong for men to fight.[65]

Julia Ward Howe was unanimously elected President of the Congress,
with 23 male and female Vice-Presidents, who included Lucretia Mott
and Henry Ward Beecher. Howe was at this point in her early 50s, and a
very powerful voice in a number of causes, including women's suffrage
and women's ministry. She was Founder President of the New England
Woman Suffrage Association, and went on to become President of the
American Association in 1874. She was for 19 years President of the
Association for the Advancement of Women, following (among others)
the astronomer Maria Mitchell and the writer Antoinette Brown. She
was still campaigning publicly for equal rights as late as 1906, and
became the first woman to be elected to the American Academy of Arts
and letters in 1908 when she was in her ninetieth year.

She was a late convert to the cause of women's advancement and suffrage, though the seeds were sown early and germinated throughout the
first half of her life. Her daughter Florence Howe Hall recalls that she
only became interested in her forties, before which, she said, 'I looked
to the masculine ideal of character as the only true one.'[66] She had
found such a masculine ideal in Samuel Gridley Howe, some twenty
years her senior, who was a romantic, Byronic hero. She describes him
in a poem:

A great grieved heart, an iron will,
As fearless blood as ever ran;
A form elate with nervous strength
And fibrous vigor – all a man.
. . .
One helpful gift the Gods forgot
Due to the man of lion mood

A woman's soul, to match with his
In high resolve and hardihood.[67]

He was a powerful, energetic, even driven man, who had been involved in relief work in Paris, was briefly imprisoned in Berlin for 'suspicious activities' and fought in the Greek War of Independence, earning the honour 'Chevalier of the Order of St Saviour', which gave him his nickname 'Chev'.

Julia's father had died following the financial crash of the 1830s, and her brother's wife died in childbirth, losing their baby son, around the same time. Stricken by grief and a feeling of guilt towards her father, she was swept up into the religious fervour of Calvinist revival. But she did not find satisfaction here. She began to read and talk with liberal Protestants and Unitarians. She described the experience: 'I studied my way out of all the mental agonies which Calvinism can engender and became a Unitarian.'[68]

She had, by this means, just come to her own independent understanding of herself in relation to God and the world when she met Chev. When they met in 1842, he was Director of the Perkins Institution and Massachusetts Asylum for the Blind, working with the conviction that blind people should be treated with dignity and offered education. He and Julia entered on a stormy courtship, leading to marriage in April 1843. Samuel was, in fact, a domineering husband, who both admired and crushed Julia's intellectual energy.

Julia's literary ambitions had begun in her childhood, when she handed in a set of poems instead of a prose composition at the age of 11. Three years later, she had several poems published in the New York American.[69] Throughout the turmoil of her life, she expressed herself in her poetry, to the mockery and disapproval of her husband. Her first collection, *Passion Flowers*, was published anonymously about a decade after her marriage, having been worked on in secret.

The book was extremely well received, except, of course, by her husband, once her authorship became known. George Ripley wrote a review for the *New York Tribune*, in which he commented on the poems' 'stern vigor, which betokens an intellect of masculine self-concentration and force'. Were it not for the evidence of a woman's experience, he goes on, 'we should not have suspected these poems to be the production of a woman. They form an entirely unique class in the whole range of female literature.'[70]

The collection is revealing of the author, and full of surprising and dramatic imagery. Although the poems arise from unmistakably female experience, they represent a daring break from nineteenth-century poetic traditions, and, in particular, a shockingly realistic view of domestic life from a woman's point of view. Gary Williams writes, 'From a late twentieth-century feminist perspective, there is nothing to do but cheer at such milestones as the appearance of a work like *Passion-Flowers*', which he compares to the 1848 Seneca Falls convention and the deification of Florence Nightingale.[71]

In relation to her children, she writes of herself not as a steady star, but a comet. As she trudges round the house in the evening, her youngest three children watch her:

> . . . as Astronomers,
> Whose business lies in heaven afar,
> Await, beside the slanting glass,
> The re-appearance of a star.
>
> Not so, not so, my pretty ones,
> Seek stars in yonder cloudless sky;
> But mark no steadfast path for me,
> A comet dire and strange am I.

She develops the theme. Like a comet, she knows time among the shining stars, but also wearying years in the deadness of space. And yet the pull of 'heaven's dear heart' always brings her back. She ends with a prayer:

> And ye, beloved ones, when ye know
> What wild, erratic natures are,
> Pray that the laws of heavenly force
> Would help and guide the Mother star.[72]

Her wandering was literal as well as symbolic, for Chev's restlessness meant that the family was often on the move. They travelled to the South during the Civil War, and Chev was implicated in the activities of John Brown, as one of the 'secret six'. He was forced to flee to Canada after the 1859 raid on Harper's Ferry, returning only after John Brown's hanging.

In 1862, she had ridden out to Bailey's Crossroads, Virginia, to watch a review of the troops, when a battle broke out between Confederate and Union troops and the carriages drove back to Washington to the sounds of war. As she rode, she heard the song 'John Brown's Body' and one of her companions, James Freeman Clarke, urged her to write some new words for the tune.

The experience of writing 'The Battle Hymn of the Republic' was intense and exciting for Julia. The words sprang from her long study of Scripture, particularly the writings of the prophets, and drew on a sense of a realized eschatological vision that was circulating among writers and thinkers such as John Greenleaf Whittier. The original poem piles up image on image:

> I have seen him in the watchfires of a hundred circling camps,
> They have builded him an altar in the evening dews and damps,
> I can read his righteous sentence by the dim and flaring lamps
> His day is marching on.
>
> I have read a burning Gospel writ in fiery rows of steel
> As ye deal with my contemners, so with you my grace shall deal
> Let the hero, born of woman, crush the serpent with his heel
> Our God is marching on.

The line that we now generally sing, 'As he died to make men holy, let us live to make men free', was originally 'let us die to make men free', and refers to the issue at the heart of the War, the abolition of slavery. And the verse,

> He has sounded out the trumpet that shall never call retreat,
> He has waked the earth's dull bosom with a high ecstatic beat
> Oh! be swift my soul to answer him, be jubilant my feet
> Our God is marching on.[73]

in which the second line was revised in the published version to read, 'He is sifting out the hearts of men before his judgment seat', moves powerfully through the experience of the biblical judges (for example Judg. 3.27), where the trumpet call is answered by the armies of ancient Israel.

For Julia, the writing of the Battle Hymn made sense of the War. She could not accept the bloody loss of life as a glorious part of the abolitionist cause. But casting war in this religious mould gave a purpose to the dying. As Jesus died for 'men', so the deaths of those who fought in this cause could have a literally redemptive effect, in the battle against slavery.

Gary Williams sees in it a response to 'conditions that underline the particular challenges faced by *women* writers'.[74] Julia was involved in the War only as a supporter and admirer of the men in her life: 'I seemed to live in and along with the war . . . with these two brave men, Dr. Howe and Governor Andrew.'[75] She was a wife and mother, and felt the restriction of her position:

> I could not leave my nursery to follow the march of the armies, neither had I the practical deftness which the preparing and packing of sanitary stores demanded. Something seemed to say to me, 'You would be glad to serve, but you cannot help any one; you have nothing to give, and there is nothing for you to do.'[76]

Not only was she not a man, able to govern or fight, but she was not a heroic woman like Florence Nightingale, whom she much admired, or Dorothea Dix, who was Superintendent of Women Nurses for the Union Army. Her Battle Hymn recognizes what her own talent can do, at the same time as expressing her strong desire to answer the call. It is that fervour that calls from the hymn to the hearts of singers to this day.

The text was published in the *Atlantic Monthly* in February 1862, and was an instant success. Julia found herself called on to retell the dramatic story of its composition on many occasions. Gary Williams concludes: 'By the end of the war, it held a place in the popular imagination equivalent to that afforded *Uncle Tom's Cabin* a decade earlier.'[77]

Mary Grant's book *Private Woman, Public Person* ends in 1868 with what she calls Julia's 'conversion' to woman suffrage (as she calls it) as a fundamental element in the reform and reconstruction of society after the War. The energy of reform gave her the intellectual and emotional drive that took her onto the public platform and into print for the rest of her life.

The English women's movement

The women's movement in England was complex. Excluded from the male sphere of intellectual debate in coffee houses and from politics, women began to form literary societies in which they could debate the new ideas of the day.

At 19 Langham Place, London, was the office of the feminist publication *The English Women's Journal*, which ran from 1858 to 1864, with a small circulation but wider readership and influence, and the location of a women's reading room. The women who contributed to the journal and met at the reading room were known as the Langham Place Circle. The Portfolio Society was a group of women (and some men) artists and writers, who met informally to discuss their work, and to explore social and political themes. Adelaide Anne Procter and Christina Georgina Rossetti were associated with both. Rossetti was also part of a 'trio' of women poets, including Jean Ingelow and Dorothy (Dora) Greenwell.

Adelaide Anne Procter (1825–64) was one of the best-selling poets (male or female) of her age. She came from a well-connected literary family. Her mother, Anne Procter (née Skepper), attracted Charles Dickens among others to the salon that she hosted, and her father Bryan Waller Procter was an established poet.[78]

She herself began publishing her poems under a pseudonym, Mary Berwick, around which she had constructed the character of a shy, elderly governess. It was Dickens who discovered the true identity of the author, in 1854, and from then on her work was published under her own name.

In her mid-twenties, she converted to Roman Catholicism, and her religious poetry demonstrates the influence of the Tractarian Movement. John Henry Newman had converted only five or six years earlier. Many of the poems in her A Chaplet of Verses[79] focus on Mary. 'The names of Our Lady' is a purely devotional poem, ending with the hope that 'Mary' will be 'the last we sigh of earth, – /The first we breathe in heaven'.[80]

She would also have come under the influence of Christian Socialism as a student at Queen's College in Harley Street in 1850, where F. D. Maurice and the evangelical, anti-Tractarian Charles Kingsley, both Christian Socialists, taught.

Through the Church, she became involved in work with homeless people, particularly women and children. The proceeds of A Chaplet of Verses were devoted to the Providence Row Catholic Night Shelter for Women and Children, the first such shelter open to homeless Roman Catholics as well as Protestants.[81] Her confessor, Monsignor Gilbert, founded a bed at the shelter in her honour, and the poem 'Homeless', which ends the book, was written at his request.

This text poignantly contrasts society's concerns for its pet animals, for criminals and for possessions, with its indifference to the needs of homeless people. The pairs of verses ask whether the various noises and shadows on the street are those of animals or thieves, or even a pack left lying against a wall. The answer is, in each case, that we would not ignore any of those. Instead, we ignore women and children:

(Those are only the homeless children
Who are wandering to and fro.)

. . .

That is only a sister-woman
Who has got neither food nor bed –
And the Night cries 'Sin to be living'
and the River cries 'Sin to be dead'.[82]

She expressed the same sentiments in the Preface to the book, comparing the offer of shelter, 'a boon we could hardly deny to a starving dog',
with the human homeless,

> without food to eat, with their poor rags soaked in rain . . . women
> and children utterly forlorn and helpless, either wandering about all
> night, or crouching under a miserable archway, or, worst of all, seek-
> ing in death or sin the refuge denied them elsewhere.[83]

Procter's concern for the lives of women, as we have seen, extended
beyond those who were destitute and homeless. Through her contact
with feminist writers and activists, she became involved in campaigns
for the working rights of women. She was a prominent member of the
committee of the Society for Promoting the Employment of Women,
and in 1861 she edited *The Victoria Regia*,[84] a collection of writing,
including pieces by Tennyson, Thackeray and Trollope, and a number
of women writers, including Harriet Martineau.

The work was produced by the Victoria Press, which had been established by Emily Faithfull in 1860 and was entirely staffed by women,
including compositors, printers and binders, jobs that were fiercely
defended by men and considered entirely unsuited to the capacities or
strength of women.

Procter died young, from consumption, which had troubled her for
some years. But during a short life, she met and responded to the challenges of her era. In the Introduction to her biography, Gill Gregory
describes the chronological story told by her poetry as that 'of a Victorian woman who slowly moved from the position of dutiful daughter
and retiring, ladylike poetess to that of a woman who challenged mid-
Victorian mores and conventions and championed the cause of single
and homeless women'.[85]

Her best-known hymn text, 'My God I thank Thee, who hast made/
The earth so bright',[86] is typically vigorous and honest. The poem is
entitled 'Thankfulness', and the original opening is 'I thank Thee, oh

my God, who made/The Earth so bright'. Its view of a life that was 'full of splendour and of joy', but also sharp with 'yearning for a deeper peace,/Not known before',[87] proved too much for hymn-book compilers. For example, the *Companion to Congregational Praise* notes:

Two verses are omitted, including the unfortunate lines:

I have enough, yet not too much
To long for more.[88]

They have also altered the beginning of verse three from 'I thank Thee *more* that all our joy/Is touched with pain;', substituting, 'too' for 'more'. *Hymns & Psalms* changes to 'I thank Thee, too, that often joy/Is touched with pain.'[89]

But the forthright nature of the hymn confronts joy and pain head on. It rejoices

that in the darkest spot of earth
Some joy is found'

but also

that shadows fall on brightest hours;
That thorns remain;
So that earth's bliss may be our guide
And not our chain.[90]

She is not glorifying suffering, but facing the imperfection of the present world in lively hope of the fulfilment of the longing it inspires. There is a challenging pathway through the original text, which maintains its integrity.

Part of the same cultural milieu, and sharing the same radical concerns, was a poet and social activist, Dorothy (Dora) Greenwell (1821–82). There is a fascinating mismatch in assessments of Greenwell's life. On one hand, it is supposed to have been 'entirely uneventful'.[91] On the other hand, it is clear that she became wholeheartedly involved in work among, and concern for, some of the most marginalized elements of society.

She was a friend of Josephine Butler, who campaigned for women's rights and particularly for the rights of prostitutes, in the face of injustices like the Contagious Diseases Act.[92] A rather verbose and complex biography by Constance Maynard, first Principal of Westfield College, celebrates her work among 'the really *poor*' and goes on, 'We don't see them because we don't want to see them . . . But there *they are*, and this woman of unblinking sincerity and world-embracing heart could not rest until the best of human resources had been expended upon them.'[93]

Her poems, as opposed to her prose works, define an inner landscape. When her collection *Carmina Crucis* was published, she wrote to Christina Rossetti that the poems were 'of an inwardly historical character, connected, though the thread may not be always apparent'.[94] This is no 'ministry of song' such as Frances Ridley Havergal's, meant to comfort, convert and cheer. The poems are sometimes very bleak. 'Oh amiable, lovely death', for example, contrasts human life, which 'stands up in strength and anguish; a blind giant wrapt in an envenomed mantle', with the traces of love in the natural world. The poem ends:

> But the life that was formed for love and joy is blighted, and the heart of man wanders and hath not found its home.[95]

The only answer lies in God who suffers with us. In 'Summa Theologiae', she finds in God

> . . . a need divine
> That meeteth need of mine;
> . . .
> I see my God who turns
> And o'er his creatures yearns, –
> Upon the cross God gives, and claims the tear.[96]

The collection ends with the long poem from which the lovely hymn 'And art thou come with us to dwell' is taken. The poem is prefaced with a quotation from Bunyan's *Holy War*, describing the town of Mansoul's preparation to receive Emmanuel, with garlands and music. The first verses are full of judgement, laid out in gory, Old Testament terms, the treading down and defeat of all that 'wrought thy people shame'.

The thirteenth verse turns to healing, with a 'Then' – following all that has gone before. Now the warhorse feeds on young shoots; this 'Saviour of the world and heart' will not 'hurt the oil and wine'. The 'Earth's wild story . . . Its broken tale of wrong and tears', comes to an end, and we turn towards a new beginning.

The verse that begins the familiar hymn is verse 23, and it brings the eschatological language of the earlier verses into the present time: 'And art thou come with us to dwell?' All the language turns now to the opening and flowering of what has been blighted and repressed.

> Each heart's deep instinct unconfess'd;
> Each lowly wish, each daring claim;
> All, all that life hath long repress'd.
> Unfolds, undreading blight or blame.[97]

Maybe it is her own sense of limitation that she is expressing here. In her essay 'Our Single Women', she expresses the freedom that can come out in writing, in comparison to the strictures on women's lives:

> It is surely that woman, bound, as she is, no less by the laws of society than by the immutable instincts of her nature, to a certain suppression in all that relates to personal feeling, should attain, in print, to the fearless, uncompromising sincerity she misses in real life.[98]

No wonder Routley comments on the hymn based on these verses: 'If you try to disentangle time from eternity in it, you will be in trouble.' But this is not accidental. He says that the poem 'shows excellently the new approach to this doctrine which advancing Christian social thinking was producing in the middle of the nineteenth century'.[99]

Maynard regards Greenwell as, 'the one woman theologian of the last hundred years and perhaps for long before that',[100] and also as a prophet, whose tolerance of thought could rejoice in the preaching of the American evangelists when they visited, and even write hymns for their campaigns, but also engage with the biblical criticism of her day as 'that clearing away which is the first sign of improvement'.[101] She is certainly a million miles from the dreamy poetess living the uneventful life that contemporary sources described!

Her friend and correspondent Christina Rossetti suffered even more at the hands of biographers and commentators. Her brother wrote a memoir after her death, which the editors of *Nineteenth-Century Women Poets: An Oxford Anthology* describe as 'unintentionally demeaning',[102] and which set the scene for later writing about her. The memoir describes her as unassuming and pious, casting her in the mould of religious women writers, whose internalized view of the place of women causes them to silence their own voices.

However, Rossetti's corpus of poetry and prose is too large, too diverse and too brilliant to be silenced and, once it had been released from the accretion of patriarchal interpretation, her work was recognized as a major and powerful critique from within the religious culture to which she was committed. She was a considerable poet, publishing in Italian as well as in English. Ingrid Hotz-Davies' assessment is that she, 'would undoubtedly become the central figure in an as yet unwritten canon of religious women authors'.[103]

Like other women writers in this book, she did not marry. In fact she broke off her relationship with the painter James Collinson and, later, the poet Charles Bagot Cayley, in each case because their beliefs conflicted with her own deeply held faith. This has been seen as a determining factor in her life and poetry. On limited evidence, others have suggested that her poetry derives from other failed love affairs or childhood abuse.[104]

On the other hand, in the Victorian era, no less than in earlier times, marriage largely obliterated women's identity and freedom of choice. Hotz-Davies suggests that

> there was enough in Victorian society to convince a thinking woman that romantic entanglements, even the 'world,' could turn out to be a trap . . . Her first-hand experience with Dante Gabriel's women or with the fates she would have encountered in her work for a Magdalen House might also have been less than reassuring.[105]

In fact, Rossetti's work reveals a radical and intelligent dialogue with the strongly gendered theology of her own church. Like Greenwell and Procter, her literary development was shaped by practical experience of need and injustice. She was involved with the establishment of the St Mary Magdalene Penitentiary for prostitutes on Highgate Hill in north London in 1854, and remained so till 1870 when failing health prevented her.

Lynda Palazzo has written a powerful analysis of the feminist theology to be found in Rossetti's writing. She reads the poem 'Goblin Market' within the framework of feminist theology and Christology.[106]

The poem describes the 'fall' of one of two sisters, Laura, through eating the fruit offered by the goblin men. The remaining sister, Lizzie, seeks to redeem her by going out into the goblin market herself. Though the goblins press the fruit to her lips, Lizzie does not eat, but goes back covered with the pulverized fruit, which will satisfy and save her sister. On her return, she urges Laura:

Come and kiss me.
Never mind my bruises,
Hug me, kiss me, suck my juices
Squeezed from goblin fruits for you,
Goblin pulp and goblin dew.
Eat me, drink me, love me.

Laura obeys:

Shaking with anguish fear and pain
She kissed and kissed her with a hungry mouth.

Lizzie is shown as a redeemer, putting herself into the clutches of the powers of evil for the sake of her sister, but remaining sinless herself.

The poem has been criticized for its denouement, which sees Laura and Lizzie enter not the kingdom of heaven, but domestic bliss, in which they instruct their children to remain close: 'For there is no friend like a sister.'[107] However, Palazzo draws parallels with the powerful female figure of Wisdom in the book of Proverbs, where the domestic setting becomes a symbol of divine abundance and blessing.

What is outstanding is the female redeemer. Palazzo writes: 'Rossetti's capacity to envisage a "female saviour" from within Christian theology . . . allows her to continue living and writing within the tradition of the Church without sacrificing her integrity as an active worker against woman's oppression.'[108] This figure is not unique to this poem in Rossetti's writing, but can be found again and again, as the poet intricately constructs female space for female spirituality.

Palazzo comes to 'In the bleak midwinter' in this context, a poem that, 'more than any other of hers, claims once and for all the acceptability of womanhood to Christ'.[109] Within the various landscapes – wintry earth, cosmic splendour – the mother and child remain in intimate relationship.

Enough for Him whom cherubim
Worship night and day,
A breastful of milk
And a mangerful of hay.

And again

Angels and archangels
May have gathered there;

Cherubim and seraphim
Thronged the air.
But only his mother
In her maiden bliss
Worshipped the Beloved
With a kiss.[110]

This powerful and intense poem has become a much loved Christmas carol. A survey of church music directors and choir leaders in the UK and USA in the winter of 2008 put this carol, in Harold Darke's 1911 arrangement, at the top of the list of favourites. Jeremy Pound, deputy editor of *BBC Music Magazine*, asked, 'Does any other song get to the very heart of Christmas as understatedly but effectively as "In the Bleak Midwinter"?', adding that it was 'nigh-on perfect as a carol text'.[111]

On the other hand, a contemporary source apparently described it as 'a little poem . . . wise in a sort of child-wisdom, sweet and clear and musical'.[112] Its vivid female language is dismissed by Eric Routley as he mentions in passing Harold Darke's setting, in which 'one slightly embarrassing line in the original' is altered to read, 'A heart full of mirth/And a manger-full of hay', which Routley says 'For general use . . . is commendable'.[113]

These are as shocking a distortion of the text's value as is William's memorial of her life. It is tragic that so many generations have passed before Rossetti's place in the 'canon' of women's writing has begun to be recognized.

Rediscovering the German hymns

Among the nineteenth-century sources seen by Richard Watson as major contributors to *Hymns Ancient and Modern* was the rediscovery and translation of German Protestant hymnody. This had regained its popularity among English-speaking worshippers in the nineteenth century, in translations by mostly women writers. These include Catherine Hannah Dunn (1815–63), Jane Montgomery Campbell (1817–78), Emma Frances Bevan (1827–1909) and Elizabeth Rundle Charles (1828–96).

In 1841, Frances Elizabeth Cox published *Sacred Hymns from the German*. This was followed in 1855 by Catherine Winkworth's first series of *Lyra Germanica* and her second in 1858. Almost contemporary with these was *Hymns from the Land of Luther*, published anonymously under the pseudonym 'HLL', the work of the Scottish sisters Jane Borthwick (1813–97) and Sarah Findlater (1823–1907).[114]

Despite the prevalence of women's writing and the importance of women's contribution to the hymnody of the German Protestant Reformation, none of the nineteenth-century women translated very many of their texts. Nor did they make any conscious link through their gender, or mention the gender of the writers.

Of course, the best known and most frequently translated writers of the German Protestant traditions were the men: Count Nicholas von Zinzendorf, Gerhard Tersteegen, Paul Gerhardt and, of course, Luther himself. The women writers suffered, as women have through the ages, through anonymity and doubtful attribution. The only text of the prolific Emilia Juliana, Countess of Schwazburg-Rudolstadt (1637–1706), who is said to have written 587 hymns, to have been translated by Winkworth, was claimed at the time by G. M. Pfefferkorn (1646–1706), a pastor.[115] However, the only manuscript evidence is a copy of the text initialled by her, as are her other hymns. Even Creutziger's text, *Herr Christ, der einge Gottes Sohn*, was mistakenly attributed to Andrew Knophe in a translation in A. T. Russell's, *Psalms and Hymns*.[116]

Catherine Winkworth did translate the Creutziger hymn.[117] She also translated single texts by Maria of Hungary, Elizabeth von Senitz (1629–79) and Henrietta Louisa von Hayn (1724–44), and two by Louisa Henrietta, Electress of Brandenburg (1627–67).[118] Frances Cox translates another by the Electress, '*Ich will von meiner Missethat*', as 'With sorrow now for past misdeeds', the only text attributed to a woman in her later collection *Hymns from the German*.[119] This is a passionate hymn of repentance, with nine verses lamenting the singer's sinful ways. These sins are brought to Jesus, at the turning point of the hymn:

Lord Jesus Christ, to Thee I flee,
In Thy deep Wounds to hide;
O let my soul's safe refuge be
Thy pierced and gaping side;
Since in my stead, Thou Lamb of God,
Thou hast endured the chastening rod,
And on the Cross hast died.

The theology is fully substitutionary: Christ has died in the sinner's place, and taken on the punishment that should have been hers. This is her only, but her sure, hope:

Thy holy Father's Throne before,
This Ransom, Lord, present;
Remembering then my sins no more,
His justice will relent,
And in the depths of ocean vast
Thy self-inflicted load will cast,
If truly I repent.[120]

A gentler and more comforting text, Katherina Amalia Dorothea von Schlegel's text 'Stille, mein Wille! dein Jesu hilft siegen', appears in translation in *Hymns from the Land of Luther* translated as the popular hymn 'Be still my soul!', marked 'unbekanntes' – 'anonymous' or 'author unknown'. The book contains no translations of texts attributed to women writers, but ten further texts marked 'unbekanntes' and three without named attribution.

However, later editions of the volume include the texts published as *Alpine Lyrics*, the translator's versions of the texts of Meta Heusser (1797–1876), whom, she says, she has 'the happiness to call a personal friend'.[121] She notes that some of the texts will be recognized, since they have already appeared in *Hymns from the Land of Luther* and *Thoughtful Hours*, and indeed five of Heusser's texts do appear in translation in *Hymns from the Land of Luther*, though marked 'unbekanntes' there.

It is perhaps not surprising that they appear with anonymous attributions. Borthwick says that she came across them as 'perfect gems in the "Liederschatz"'. Like many women writers, Heusser was reluctant to release her writing into the public domain, and her texts were published by Albert Knapp, first over the name 'einer Verborgenen' ('a hidden one'), in his Almanac, and later, with her hard-won permission, in a volume entitled, *Lieder einer Verborgenen* (*Songs of a hidden one*).[122] Borthwick cites Heusser's daughter in saying, '"What she had sung in her quiet chamber, to relieve her own full heart, has now become a common treasure."'[123]

Many of the texts reflect day-to-day life: the child's first step, yearning for lost childhood, the beauty of the mountains. This reflects Borthwick's interests: Kübler notes that she deals 'mostly with hymns of a more modern and less congregational cast',[124] in contrast to Winkworth's concentration on the earlier classics.

A more objective text was 'written for the Zurich Hymn-book', and uses the conventional language of the Reformation:

Though all of hope and promise
On earth may pass away,
One source of joy unfailing
Shall ever with me stay; –
Christ lives, my portion sure!
Let what is mortal perish, –
My treasures are secure![125]

The best known and most enduring of the translators in this group was Catherine Winkworth. Her texts are true to the sense of the originals, and carry their evangelical intensity through into what have become accepted as English hymns. This is partly due to the complexity of her own journey of faith and thought.

Catherine was born into a family deeply involved in the evangelical movement in the Anglican Church. Her paternal grandfather was incumbent of St Saviour's, Southwark, a passionate evangelical, friend of John Newton, among others. Two uncles on her mother's side were lifelong deacons in the Countess of Huntingdon's Connexion.

Hymn-singing would have surrounded her throughout her childhood. She is likely to have been familiar with *Olney Hymns* and also the hymnbook of the Connexion, which Leaver calls 'a basic anthology of Evangelical hymnody'.[126] However, she was taught by the Unitarians William Gaskell and James Martineau, both also connected to hymn-writing.

Following her mother's death in 1841 and her father's remarriage four years later, Catherine and her sister Susanna were sent to stay with relatives in Dresden. She returned from Germany having become acquainted with the language and literature, but spiritually very confused. It was Martineau who, though she never espoused his Unitarian views, helped her to sort out her faith and thoughts. At this point, she was nearest in her understanding to liberal Anglican theologians. Her sister Susanna wrote: 'when by degrees her notions of theology grew clearer and firmer they rather crystallized into forms of thought, more or less resembling those held by such men as Maurice, Hare, Kingsley or Baldwin Brown'.[127]

Susanna was already working on translations from German into English, and mentioned this fact to the novelist Mrs Gaskell, the wife of the sisters' tutor. Through her, they were introduced to the German Ambassador, Chevalier Bunsen, a pioneer in German hymnbook reform, who was to have a great influence on them.

Susanna published *Theologia Germanica* in 1854, and suggested that her sister should publish a companion volume, which she did, as *Lyra Germanica*, in 1855, to instant acclaim. The translations are based on Bunsen's 1833 collection, but the order of the hymns demonstrates that they are intended to be used in public worship. They follow the seasons and lections of the church year. Leaver mentions others who were beginning to make similarly ordered compilations, but notes:

> Catherine Winkworth surpasses them all in her choice of appropriate and suitably devotional hymns for the Sundays and seasons. Indeed, in doing so she was many years ahead of her time ... Catherine Winkworth was not only a careful translator of German hymns: she was also a thoughtful hymn book compiler.[128]

The second series of *Lyra Germanica*, and later compilation *The Chorale Book*,[129] show Catherine widening her knowledge of German hymns beyond Bunsen's collections. This led to her publication in *Christian Singers of Germany*,[130] the first book to view the texts hymnologically rather than offering them for devotional use. This book gives an overview of the history of German hymnody with brief biographies of the authors.

The only woman writer to feature is Louisa Henrietta, Electress of Brandenburg, whom she lists as one of the admirers of Paul Gerhardt. Recognizing that the Electress was 'a hymn-writer of no mean ability', Winkworth says that she 'shines out upon us from the confused and tragic scenes of that seventeenth century, as almost the ideal of a noble Christian lady'.[131] She cites two of the Electress's hymns: 'Jesu meine Zuversicht' ('Jesus my Redeemer lives'), of which she gives the first line only, but notes that it 'ranks among the most popular of German hymns';[132] and 'Ich will von meiner Missethat' ('I will return unto the Lord'), which, being less well known, she gives in full, in 11 verses.[133]

'Jesus my Redeemer' can be found in *Lyra Germanica*, first series, and is full of confidence, even defiance. Drawing its inspiration from the text in Job 19.25, the verses look forward to a triumphant bodily resurrection at the end of time, and the hymn is set for the Tuesday in Easter Week:

> Shall I fear then? Can the Head
> Rise and leave the members dead?

The bodily nature of the resurrection is proclaimed in a strange address to the mortal flesh:

Body, be thou of good cheer,
In thy Saviour's care rejoice,
Give not place to gloom and fear,
Dead, thou yet shalt know His voice.

This leads to a triumphalist last verse:

Laugh to scorn then death and hell,
Laugh to scorn the gloomy grave;
Caught into the air to dwell
With the Lord who comes to save,
We shall trample on our foes,
Mortal weakness, fear and woes.[134]

The hymns best known to us have become embedded in English hymnody, and not many people, singing them, would think of them as
translations. They have been sung at national and royal events, from
Queen Victoria's Diamond Jubilee (when 'Now thank we all our God'
was used) to the present day.

As well as the hymns, Catherine Winkworth translated a life of Amalie
Sieveking (1794–1869), a pioneer of women's emancipation through
social involvement, in Germany, and Pastor Fliedner, the founder of
the Lutheran order of deaconesses.[135] Her admiration for Sieveking is
evident, though she acknowledges her faults. She sees her as the practical demonstration of a resource that is being wasted by the Protestant
churches:

what an amount and variety of female energy is at the command of
the Christian congregation, whenever the Church shall display the
courage, or rather the faith, no longer to resist her Lord, but to suffer
the congregation to attain an organic life and become in truth the
body of Christ.[136]

She admires not only the example, but also the convictions of the 'Ham-
burg Tabitha', noting in her conclusion to the *Life*:

[Miss Sieveking] certainly did not err in believing that most women
underrate their own power, and that besides attending to the duties
most immediately under their hand, they would do well to develop
a different kind of activity, in schools, charitable societies, etc., and
thus might obtain generally a wider mental horizon.[137]

Both sisters had been appalled at the social conditions in Clifton, Bristol, where the family had moved following the collapse of her father's business. Susanna threw herself into work for the improvement of housing, and set up a company, of which she was managing director, which built and managed two housing projects.

Catherine's interests lay in education for women. In 1868, she was instrumental in forming the Committee to Promote Higher Education of Women, which eventually succeeded, among other things, in establishing a University College in Bristol that extended the same educational rights to women as to men, the first in England to do so. The Committee went on to set up a scholarship fund for women at the College.

In 1874, the sisters attended a congress of women workers in Darmstadt, organized by Princess Alice, Grand Duchess of Hesse, where Catherine was one of three British delegates. Despite all this, Catherine was no feminist. She was not in favour of women's suffrage, and knew that some found her support of women's rights less than wholehearted.

Catherine and Susanna were thoughtful and critically engaged. They moved within the theological and literary world of their time, and were accepted as translators and writers. Catherine pursued her own journey to an honest and open evangelicalism, which comes out both in the hymns she chose to translate and in the translations themselves, which echo her own faith as well as that of the original texts.

She describes the German hymns and their writers:

> The Christian sacrifice of entire self-surrender to God, the union of the Church in Christ, reliance on God in trouble, these thoughts, which the circumstances of their own career must have brought very close to their hearts, meet us again and again in their hymns.[138]

This is well illustrated in the passion and commitment of the original hymns and her translations.

Towards the twentieth century

Around the middle of the century, the huge diversity of hymn collections began to coalesce into more or less official books, which consciously attempted to encompass a broad range of material. The archetype of these collections was *Hymns Ancient and Modern,* published in 1861.

As we have seen, Richard Watson sees the proliferation of women's writing as a major element of its publication. He also sees it as a 'pivotal moment in the history of nineteenth-century hymnody', and quotes Nicholas Temperley's comment that it was 'indisputably the representative book of Victorian hymnody'.[139] At its height, the book was used by over half the parish churches in England.

Although it was known by some as a 'Tractarian Manifesto', it represented a conscious attempt to draw on a wide range of resources. Its immediate success can be seen from its subsequent development. The 1868 appendix included a section, 'For the Young', so bringing the best of the burgeoning area of writing for Sunday schools and catechists within its range, including Cecil Frances Alexander's 'Once in royal David's City'. A revised and enlarged edition appeared in 1875, which itself was supplemented in 1889. Watson comments: 'These editions established *Hymns Ancient and Modern* as a standard book, unchallenged in its universal adoption until the early twentieth century.'[140]

The major Free Church denominations were also busy publishing collections for use in their churches. This marks the last part of the century as a period of consolidation, a series of 'official' attempts to garner and control the chaotic development of the century.

The *Congregational Church Hymnal* was compiled by a committee of the Congregational Union of England and Wales, itself an organization bringing together independent churches, which had been formed in 1831. The Committee worked from 1883 till the book's publication in 1887. The *Hymnal* professed three aims: the first was breadth and quality – a mixture of 'the best of the older hymns that had been found to minister to the faith and devotion of the past generations', plus recent hymns, 'especially . . . those in which the Evangelical faith and spiritual life of the present day have found expression'; the second was an attempt to establish a denominational yardstick, 'consistent with the retention of the classics of Evangelical and Congregational worship'; the third was to include hymns, chants and anthems in one book.[141]

In 1898, a collection authorized for the use of the Church of Scotland, The Free Church of Scotland, the United Presbyterian Church and the United Presbyterian Church in Ireland, brought together a committee from each of those churches, and started a tradition of (at least limited) ecumenical publication. *Church Hymnary* has now passed through four editions, and eventually blazed a trail of increasing inclusivity in hymnbook publication. Its preface claims: 'It is catholic, as including hymns by authors belonging to almost every branch of the Church from the second century to the present day, and comprehensive, as intended for the use of various Churches and congregations.'[142]

As the Victorian era drew to a close, the mood of the nation was changing. The great mission fields at home and abroad were now well organized, and there was not the same evangelical fervour for the conversion of the world. With the rise of a moneyed middle class came a desire for respectability, an appreciation of quality in worship as elsewhere.

The aesthetic movements of the last quarter of the nineteenth century influenced the worship of the Nonconformist churches. The churches were turning away from subjective, sentimental hymnody, which was associated with women's writing, and seeking something more objective, more 'manly', more energetic and of higher quality. The drive for higher quality coincided with a backlash against the perceived feminization of hymnody, which belonged to an earlier age.

This was reinforced by the rise of both Christian Socialism and fundamentalism. Fundamentalism reclaimed evangelical Christianity for masculine control and leadership, restating the patriarchal order of creation; Christian Socialism focused on the public worlds of politics and work, which had been characterized as masculine in contrast to the feminine world of the home.

June Haddon Hobbs chronicles this period. She comments on the irony of women's disappearance at this stage. Both evangelical and liberal women had been deeply involved in public works. There had been real advances in the understanding of injustice and victimization as social mechanisms. Women had worked alongside the poorest and most marginalized, had challenged the double standards for men's and women's lives, and called for equality of education and opportunity. But the backlash simply ignored these advances. Women were redefined as emotional and home-bound at precisely the time that Christianity was seeking objectivity and a public face.

Hobbs cites Walther Rauschenbusch's *Christianity and the Social Crisis*,[143] in which he characterizes evangelicalism as female and Christian Socialism as male and blames the Church's neglect of social needs on the 'feminization' of Christianity and churches. She comments: 'Rauschenbusch's association of community and material concerns with public, masculine religion, then, ignores what women had actually been doing and, worse, appropriates the model of spirituality that fuelled what Baptist women then called "personal service".'[144]

She looks at the 1914 hymnbook *Social Hymns of Brotherhood and Aspiration* (1914), edited by Mabel Hay Barrows Mussey. Despite the fact that the compiler is a woman, Hobbs notes ruefully that most of the 111 hymns are by men:

The social gospel hymns themselves are dominated by references to ... the 'outward world' of masculine Christianity: descriptions of cities and the problems of 'the mill and the mart' rather than homes and domestic concerns. Nearly every hymn refers to war in some way ... The evangelical vision of God as a lover, mother, or bosom companion is also missing; instead the hymns describe a creator God 'from [whom] all skill and science flow' ... Many hymns focus entirely on humanity or 'men', and the phrases 'the Fatherhood of God' and 'the brotherhood of man' are social gospel clichés. In fact, women are almost non-existent in these hymns.[145]

Both the newly masculine evangelicalism and Christian Socialism were to define Christianity and its worship for the next half-century. They were inimical to each other, and locked in an intellectual and political war of great intensity. What everybody seems to have missed at the time was that the real losses were to women, whose voices were effectively and brutally silenced.

Notes

1 Isobel Armstrong, Joseph Bristow and Cath Sharrock (eds), *Nineteenth-Century Women Poets: An Oxford Anthology*, Oxford: Clarendon Press, 1996, p. xxxi.

2 Armstrong, Bristow and Sharrock (eds), *Nineteenth-Century Women Poets*, p. xxxiii.

3 See below, pp. 136–38.

4 See below, pp. 140–43.

5 Clara Balfour, *A Sketch of Mrs Barbauld*, London: W. & F. G. Cash, 1854, p. 11. Clara Balfour wrote many works about women and women's issues, including works on temperance, maternal solicitude, and working women.

6 *Hymns in Prose for Children*, p. iv, her emphasis. See above, p. 93.

7 *Hymns in Prose for Children*, Hymn II, last two stanzas.

8 *Hymns in Prose for Children*, Hymn III, stanza 2.

9 *Hymns in Prose for Children*, Hymn V, stanza 11.

10 A. L. Barbauld, *Civic Sermons to the People*, London, 1792.

11 *Hymns in Prose for Children*, Hymn VIII, stanza 7.

12 Moira Ferguson, *Subject to Others: British Women Writers and Colonial Slavery, 1670–1834*, London: Routledge, 1992, p. 133.

13 See above, pp. 62 and 99.

14 Ferguson, *Subject to Others*, p. 157.

15 Ferguson, *Subject to Others*, p. 164. For a fuller treatment, see Janet Wootton, 'Hymns and Slavery', *Hymn Society Bulletin* 254, vol. 18, no. 9, January 2008, pp. 306–18, continued in *Hymn Society Bulletin* 255, vol. 18, no. 10, pp. 305–15. For Deborah and Jael, see Judges 4—5.

16 See pp. 48–51.

17 A. L. Barbauld, *Sins of Government, Sins of the Nation Etc., A Discourse for the Fast Appointed on April 19th 1793*, by A Volunteer, p. 33.

18 Barbauld, *Sins of Government*, p. 31.

19 A. L. Barbauld, 'Thoughts on Public Worship: Thoughts on the devotional taste, on sects, and on establishments', in Jared Sparks, *A Collection of Essays and Tracts in Theology from Various Authors*, Boston, 1823–26, vol. IV, 1823, pp. 310–11.

20 Barbauld, 'Thoughts on Public Worship', p. 313.

21 Anna Laetitia Barbauld, 'What rites, what honours shall he pay', in John R. Beard, *A Collection of Hymns for Public and Private Worship*, London: John Green, 1837, no. 86, vv. 2–3.

22 Aiken, 'While sounds of war are heard around', in J. Belknap, *Sacred Poetry, consisting of Psalms and Hymns, adapted to Christian Devotion, in public and private, selected from the best authors*, Boston: Thomas & Andrews, 1797, no. CCCXXII, vv. 3–4.

23 Harriet Martineau, *Autobiography with memorials by M. W. Chapman*, Windermere, 1877, vol. 1, p. 34.

24 Harriet Martineau, *Addresses with Prayers and Original Hymns For the Use of Families and Schools*, London, 1826.

25 Martineau, *Autobiography*, vol. 1, p. 302.

26 See above, p. 113.

27 Martineau, *Autobiography*, vol. 1, p. 120.

28 Martineau, *Autobiography*, vol. 1, p. 141.

29 Martineau, *Autobiography*, vol. 1, p. 142.

30 Harriet Martineau, *Illustrations of Political Economy*, vols 1–9, London, 1832–33.

31 Martineau, *Autobiography*, vol. 1, pp. 179, 229–30.

32 Martineau, *Autobiography*, vol. 1, pp. 402.

33 Harriet Martineau, 'Beneath this starry arch', in William J. Fox, *Hymns & Anthems*, London: 1841, no. LIX, v. 4.

34 Harriet Martineau, 'When Samuel heard, in still midnight', in Beard, *A Collection of Hymns*, no. 437, vv. 2–3.

35 See above, p. 95.

36 Harriet Martineau, 'All men are equal in their birth', in Beard, *A Collection of Hymns*, no. 288, entitled 'Human Equality', vv. 3, 5.

37 Harriet Martineau, 'Lord Jesus! come, for hosts', in Beard, *A Collection of Hymns*, no. 205, vv. 2–3.

38 Derek Hyde, *New-Found Voices: Women in Nineteenth-Century English Music*, Aldershot: Ashgate, 3rd edn, 1998, p. 9.

39 *Monthly Repository*, 1834, p. 61 (her emphasis).

40 Cited in Harold W. Stephenson, *The Author of Nearer my God to Thee – Sarah Flower Adams*, London: Lindsey Press, 1922, pp. 23–4. Browning was a great friend of both sisters, and his 'Pauline' is said to have been inspired by Eliza.

41 Sarah Flower Adams, 'The mourners came at break of day', in Fox, *Hymns & Anthems*, no. 52, v. 3.

42 Sarah Flower Adams, 'The world may change from old to new', in Fox,

Hymns & Anthems, no. 127, vv. 1, 3 (ll. 1–4).

43 Sarah Flower Adams, 'Sing to the Lord, for his mercies are sure', in Fox, *Hymns & Anthems*, no. 40, v. 2 (ll. 3–6).

44 See above, p. 3.

45 Genesis 28.10–22.

46 Martineau, *Autobiography*, vol. 2, p. 25.

47 Louis F. Benson, *The English Hymn: Its Development and Use in Worship*, London: Hodder & Stoughton, 1915, p. 468.

48 Henry Ward Beecher, 'Introduction', in Henry Ward Beecher (ed.), *The Plymouth Collection of Hymns and Tunes for the use of Christian Congregations*, New York: A. S. Barnes & Company, 1856, pp. iii–vii, p. iv.

49 Caroline Seward, 'Lo, in these latter days, our land', Beecher (ed.), *The Plymouth Collection*, no. 1034, vv. 3, 4 (ll. 1–2).

50 Mrs Follen, 'May the captive's pleading fill', Beecher (ed.), *The Plymouth Collection*, no. 1037.

51 Harriet Martineau, 'All men are equal in their birth', no. 1059; 'Lord Jesus, come! for hosts', no. 1014, in Beecher (ed.), *The Plymouth Collection*.

52 E. L. Follen, 'Lord Deliver! Thou canst save', in Vicki L. Eaklor, *American Antislavery Songs: A Collection and Analysis*, New York: Greenwood, 1988, no. 30. The first verse in *The Plymouth Collection*, 'May the captive's pleading fill', appears here as the second verse.

53 No. 79, ll. 8–11, 15–16, 22–3.

54 Harriet Martineau, 'Now's the day and now's the hour', in Eaklor, *American Antislavery Songs*, no. 248, v. 2 (ll. 1–4).

55 Joshua Simpson, 'O'er this wide extended country', in Eaklor, *American Antislavery Songs*, no. 93, v. 3, ll. 5–8.

56 Anon. 'Thrice welcome, hoary sage', in Eaklor, *American Antislavery Songs*, no. 237, v. 2.

57 Abby H. Price, 'The Slave-Mother', in Eaklor, *American Antislavery Songs*, no. 315, vv. 2, 8.

58 Douglas, *The Feminization of American Culture*, p. 142.

59 Harriet Beecher Stowe, 'Letter to the Abolitionist Eliza Cabot Follen', in Harriet Beecher Stowe, *Uncle Tom's Cabin*, Norton Critical Edition, ed. E. Ammons, New York: W.W. Norton, 1994, p. 413.

60 Harriet Beecher Stowe, *Uncle Tom's Cabin, or Negro Life in America*, Leipzig: Bernhard Tauchnitz, 1852, vol. II, p. 140.

61 Beecher Stowe, *Uncle Tom's Cabin*, p. 146.

62 http://www.harriettubman.com/itsharriet.html.

63 Beecher (ed.), *The Plymouth Collection*, no. 675.

64 Harriet Beecher Stowe, 'Still, still with thee, when purple morning breaketh', in Beecher (ed.), *The Plymouth Collection*, no. 676, vv. 3, 5.

65 Proceedings of a Peace Meeting held at Union League Hall, New York, December 23d, 1870, For the purpose of Free Consultation on the subject of a Woman's Peace Congress for the World as Proposed by Mrs Julia Ward Howe of Boston', Philadelphia: John Gillam & Co., Printers, 1871, pp. 7–8.

66 Florence Howe Hall, *Julia Ward Howe and the Woman Suffrage Movement*, Boston: Dana Estes & Company, 1913, p. 11.

67 Mary Grant, *Private Woman, Public Person: An Account of the Life of*

Julia Ward Howe from 1819–1868, Brooklyn NY: Carson, 1994, p. 55, citing Julia Ward Howe *Reminiscences 1818–1899*, Boston: Houghton Mifflin & Co., 1900, p. 82, vv. 1, 6.

68 Untitled reminiscence, cited in Grant, *Private Woman, Public Person*, p. 50.

69 Deborah Pickman Clifford, *Mine Eyes Have Seen the Glory: A Biography of Julia Ward Howe*, Boston: Little, Brown, 1979, p. 23.

70 George Ripley Review, *New York Tribune*, 10 January 1854, cited in Gary Williams, *Hungry Heart: The Literary Emergence of Julia Ward Howe*, Amherst: University of Massachusetts Press, 1999, p. 137.

71 Williams, *Hungry Heart*, p. 171.

72 Julia Ward Howe, 'The heart's astronomy', in *Passion Flowers*, Boston: Ticknor, Reed, and Fields, 1854, pp. 100–2, ll. 9–16, 65–8.

73 *Reminiscences*, between pp. 276 and 277, cited in Williams, *Hungry Heart*, p. 138, vv. 2–4, 5 (l. 3).

74 Williams, *Hungry Heart*, p. 209.

75 *Reminiscences*, p. 265, cited in Williams, *Hungry Heart*, p. 210.

76 *Reminiscences*, p. 274, cited in Williams, *Hungry Heart*, p. 210.

77 Williams, *Hungry Heart*, p. 209.

78 See Gill Gregory, *The Life and Work of Adelaide Procter*, Aldershot: Ashgate, 1998, pp. 38–55.

79 Adelaide Anne Procter, *A Chaplet of Verses*, London: 1862.

80 Adelaide Anne Procter, 'The Names of Our Lady', *A Chaplet of Verses*, pp. 14–17, ll 67–8.

81 Adelaide Anne Procter, Preface, *A Chaplet of Verses*, pp. vii–xiv, p. viii.

82 Adelaide Anne Procter, 'Homeless', *A Chaplet of Verses*, pp. 125–6, ll. 11–12, 21–4.

83 Preface, *A Chaplet of Verses*, p. vii.

84 Adelaide Anne Procter (ed.), *The Victoria Regia: A Volume of Original Contributions in Poetry and Prose*, London, 1861.

85 Gregory, *The Life and Work of Adelaide Procter*, p. xi.

86 Adelaide Anne Procter, 'I thank Thee, oh my God, who made', *Legends and Lyrics: A Book of Verses*, London, 1858, pp. 207–8.

87 Adelaide Anne Procter, 'I thank Thee, oh my God, who made', ll. 3, 29–30.

88 Kenneth Lloyd Parry (ed.), *Companion to Congregational Praise*, London: Independent Press, 1953, p. 39, referring to Adelaide Anne Procter, 'I thank Thee, oh my God, who made'; *CP* first line, 'My God, I thank thee, who hast made', v. 5 (ll. 3–4), which actually read, 'We have enough . . .'

89 *Hymns & Psalms*, no. 564, *HP* first line, 'My God, I thank thee, who hast made'; the altered lines are Adelaide Anne Procter, 'I thank Thee, oh my God, who made', v. 3 (l. 1), emphasis hers.

90 'I thank Thee, oh my God, who made', vv. 2 (ll. 5–6), 3 (ll. 3–4).

91 Note printed in the *Academy*, 1885, cited in Armstrong, Bristow and Sharrock, *Nineteenth-Century Women Poets*, p. 439.

92 For Josephine Butler, see above, p. 112.

93 Constance L. Maynard, *Dora Greenwell: A Prophet for our Own Times on the Battleground of our Faith*, London: H. R. Allenson Ltd., 1926, p. 81.

94 Cited in William Dorling, Introduction to *Poems by Dora Greenwell (Selected) with a Biographical Introduction by William Dorling*, London: Walter Scott, 1889, p. xviii.

95 Dora Greenwell, 'Oh amiable and lovely death!', in Dora Greenwell, *Carmina Crucis*, London: Bell and Daldy, 1869, pp. 29–41, ll. 87, 94.

96 Dora Greenwell, 'Summa Theologiae', *Carmina Crucis*, pp. 66–70, ll. 73–8.

97 Dora Greenwell, 'Veni, veni, Emmanuel!', *Carmina Crucis*, pp. 129–36, ll. 48, 51, 57–8, 105–8.

98 Dora Greenwell, 'Our Single Women', in Dora Greenwell, *Essays*, London and New York, 1866, pp. 1–68, cited in Armstrong, Bristow and Sharrock, *Nineteenth-Century Women Poets*, p. 438.

99 Routley, *Hymns and Human Life*, p. 214.

100 Maynard, *Dora Greenwell*, p. 11.

101 Dora Greenwell, *Two Friends*, edited with an Introduction and Summary by Constance L. Maynard, London: R. Allenson, Ltd., 1926 p. 89, cited in Maynard, *Dora Greenwell*, p. 18.

102 Armstrong, Bristow and Sharrock, *Nineteenth-Century Women Poets*, p. 519, referring to Christina Georgina Rossetti, *Poetical Works of Christina Georgina Rossetti, with a Brief Memoir and Notes &c. by W. M. Rossetti*, London: MacMillan & Co., 1904.

103 Hotz-Davies, *The Creation of Religious Identities*, p. 2.

104 See, for example, Lona Mosk Packer, *Christina Rossetti*, Cambridge: Cambridge University Press, 1963; Jan Marsh, *Christina Rossetti: A Literary Biography*, London: Jonathan Cape, 1994.

105 Hotz-Davies, *The Creation of Religious Identities*, p. 210, n. 16.

106 Lynda Palazzo, *Christina Rossetti's Feminist Theology*, Hampshire: Palgrave, 2002.

107 Christina Georgina Rossetti, 'Goblin Market', in Christina Rossetti, *Goblin Market and other Poems*, London and Cambridge: MacMillan & Co., 1865, ll. 466–71, 491–2, 562.

108 Palazzo, *Christina Rossetti's Feminist Theology*, p. 27.

109 Palazzo, *Christina Rossetti's Feminist Theology*, p. 45.

110 Christina Rossetti, 'In the bleak midwinter' *The Poetical Works of Christina Georgina Rossetti, with Memoir and Notes by William Michael Rossetti*, London: MacMillan and Co. Ltd., 1904, pp. 246–7, vv. 3 (ll. 1–4), 4.

111 http://news.bbc.co.uk/1/hi/entertainment/arts_and_culture/7752029.stm (accessed 9 September 2009).

112 The American journal, *Scribner's Monthly*, cited in Palazzo, *Christina Rossetti's Feminist Theology*, p. 45.

113 Eric Routley, *The English Carol*, London: Herbert Jenkins, 1958, p. 187.

114 Frances Elizabeth Cox, *Sacred Hymns from the German*, London: William Pickering, 1841; Catherine Winkworth, *Lyra Germanica: Hymns for the Sundays and Chief Festivals of the Christian Year*, London: Longman, Brown, Green and Longmans and Roberts, 1855, *Lyra Germanica: Second Series, The Christian Life*, London: Longman, Brown, Green, Longmans and Roberts, 1858; Jane Borthwick and Sarah Findlater, *Hymns from the Land of Luther*, Edinburgh, 1854.

115 'Wer weiss wie nahe mir mein Ende', tr. Winkworth as 'Who knows how near my end may be', *Lyra Germanica*, second series, pp. 204–6, Catherine Winkworth, *The Chorale Book for England*, London: Longman, Green, Longman, Roberts and Green, 1863, p. 187. For the claim by Pfefferkorn, see Kübler, *Historical Notes to the Lyra Germanica*, p. 274.

116 'The only Son from heaven', a translation of the first three verses of the hymn, Arthur T. Russell, *Psalms and Hymns partly original, partly selected, for the use of the Church of England*, Cambridge: John Deighton, 1851, no. 41, attributed to 'A. Knophe, around 1520', in the numerical index to the hymns; see Kübler, *Historical Notes to the Lyra Germanica*, p. 290.

117 See above, pp. 39–41.

118 Maria, Queen of Hungary, 'Mag ich Unglück nicht widerstehn', tr. 'Can I my fate no more withstand', *Lyra Germanica*, second series, pp. 178–9; Henrietta Louisa von Hayn, see p. 45; Louisa Henrietta, Electress of Brandenburg, see below, p. 147.

119 Frances E. Cox, *Hymns from the German, Translated by F. E. Cox*, London: SPCK, 1890, no. 48.

120 Cox, *Hymns from the German*, no. 48, vv. 10–11.

121 Jane Borthwick, Preface, *Alpine Lyrics: A Selection from the Poems of Meta Heusser-Schweizer, Translated by H. L. L.*, London: T. Nelson and Sons, 1875, p. ii.

122 Albert Knapp, *Lieder einer Verborgenen*, Leipzig, 1858.

123 Fraülein Schweitzer, sketch written for the Preface, cited in Preface, *Alpine Lyrics*, p. v.

124 Kübler, *Historical Notes to the Lyra Germanica*, p. xii.

125 Jane Borthwick, 'O Christ, my Life, my Saviour', *Alpine Lyrics*, pp. 69–71, v. 4.

126 Robin A. Leaver, *Catherine Winkworth: The Influence of her Translations on English Hymnody*, St Louis MO: Concordia Publishing House, 1978, p. 24. John Newton and William Cowper, *Olney Hymns*, in three volumes, London, 1779; *The collection of hymns, sung in the Countess of Huntingdon's Chapel*, comp. Selina Hastings, Countess of Huntingdon, Bath: T. Mills, 1770.

127 Susanna Winkworth and M. J. Shaen, *Letters and Memorials of Catherine Winkworth*, Clifton: privately printed, 1883–86, p. 21, cited in Leaver, *Catherine Winkworth*, p. 13.

128 Leaver, *Catherine Winkworth*, p. 31.

129 Winkworth, *The Chorale Book for England*.

130 Catherine Winkworth, *Christian Singers of Germany*, London: MacMillan & Co., 1869.

131 Winkworth, *Christian Singers*, p. 219.

132 Winkworth, *Christian Singers*, p. 221 (this is translated in *Lyra Germanica*, first series, p. 93, with this first line, and in *The Chorale Book*, no. 59, with the first verse 'Jesus Christ, my sure Defence').

133 'Jesus, my Redeemer lives' is cited on p. 221; 'I will return unto the Lord' is quoted in full on pp. 221–4, under the heading 'Penitence'.

134 *Lyra Germanica*, first series, pp. 93–5, vv. 2 (ll. 5–6), 6 (ll. 1–4), 7.

135 Amalie Wilhemine Sieveking, *Life of A. W. Sieveking*, tr. Catherine Winkworth, London, 1863; Theodor Fliedner, *Life of Pastor Fliedner*, tr. by

Catherine Winkworth, London, 1867.

136 Catherine Winkworth, 'Preface to the German Work', in Winkworth (tr.), *Life of A. W. Sieveking*, pp. xi–xxi, pp. xx–xxi.

137 Catherine Winkworth, 'Conclusion', in Winkworth (tr.), *Life of A. W. Sieveking*, pp. 513–20, p. 517, cited in Peter Skrine, *Susanna and Catherine Winkworth: Clifton, Manchester and the German Connection*, Croydon: The Hymn Society of Great Britain and Ireland, Occasional Paper Second Series, no. 2, 1992, p. 12.

138 Winkworth, *Christian Singers*, p. 136, cited in Johansen, *Moravian Hymnody*, p. 7.

139 Watson, *The English Hymn*, p. 340, citing Nicholas Temperley, *The Music of the English Parish Church*, Cambridge: Cambridge University Press, 1979, I, p. 301.

140 Watson, *The English Hymn*, p. 391.

141 Arthur Hannay, Preface, *Congregational Church Hymnal*, London: Hodder & Stoughton, 1887, pp. iii–vi, p. iii.

142 Preface, *Church Hymnary*, Glasgow, Belfast: Henry Frowde, 1898, pp. v–xii, p. v.

143 Walther Rauschenbusch, *Christianity and the Social Crisis*, New York: Macmillan & Co., 1907.

144 June Hadden Hobbs, *'I sing for I cannot be silent': The Feminization of American Hymnody, 1870–1920*, Pittsburgh PA: University of Pittsburgh Press, 1997, p. 150.

145 Hobbs, *'I sing for I cannot be silent'*, pp. 154–5.

5

Explosions and Outpourings

Hymns Ancient and Modern, which was such a landmark publication of the mid-nineteenth century, tried to respond to the changing mood at the century's turn with a new edition in 1904.[1] This, however, disappointed those who continued to love the *Ancient and Modern* tradition, without satisfying those who desired something different. Percy Dearmer, who initially proposed a supplement to the 1904 edition, when he saw the unpopularity of the new book, suggested publishing an entirely new and different resource. This was *The English Hymnal*.[2]

Dearmer was an interesting character, who would have a profound influence on the next generation of hymn-writers and hymnbook compilers. He had been at Oxford during the late 1880s amid a ferment of new ideas. His first wife was an artist, and brought him into contact with the Arts and Crafts Movement and William Morris.

Donald Gray captures the cultural milieu of the couple: 'With many friendships in both the artistic and literary scene and their commitment to political causes, not least feminism, the Dearmers were at the cutting edge of cultural life and far from being imprisoned in any ecclesiastical ghetto.'[3]

The preface to *The English Hymnal* shows how this intellectual rigour and social conscience govern the style of the new book:

> the best hymns of Christendom are as free as the Bible from the self-centred sentimentalism, the weakness and unreality which mark inferior productions. The great hymns, indeed, of all ages abound in the conviction that duty lies at the heart of all Christian life – a double duty to God and to our neighbour.[4]

So, while *The English Hymnal* seeks 'manly' texts, such as the sadly altered John Bunyan text, 'He who would valiant be',[5] it also introduces Cecil Frances Alexander's 'I bind unto myself to-day', an energetic and powerful text by a woman writer, whom people would more normally associate with children's writing, and Christina Rossetti's poem 'In the bleak midwinter', with the 'breastful of milk' line unchanged. Both hymns were very successful.[6]

Dearmer went on to publish *Songs of Praise* in 1925, which sought to take the advances made by *The English Hymnal* to a wider audience. *Songs of Praise* was a consciously forward-looking book. The Preface praises the 'magnificent prose' that Coverdale and Cranmer contributed to English-speaking worship, but laments the fact that this 'has never adequately been matched by the hymns in common use . . . Our English hymns . . . most of which were the product of the Victorian era, have not been altogether worthy of the English Bible and the English Prayer Book.'[7]

The book acknowledges its debt to *English Hymnal*,[8] but expresses the hope that this collection 'will be found especially suitable for young people, and may prove not unacceptable to those who bear the responsibility of our national education'.[9] The paragraph describing its use by young people is carefully worded. There is a children's section, but this comprises only hymns for very young children, 'nor do they form a large section, when mawkish and misleading pieces are excluded'.[10] Hymns suitable for young people are marked in the index, but the whole book is intended for use across the generations, on the principle that 'Even young children should be brought up on the standard hymns, and it is supremely important that they should know and love the best hymns and tunes that are sung by adults.'[11]

The book was successful in these aims, and was quickly taken up in the context of education. Dearmer's own abridged edition for schools appeared in 1927, and was immediately popular, some schools producing their own selections.

The enlarged edition of 1931[12] included a text by Maria Matilda Penstone (1859–1910), whose background was not the Sunday schools but secular education. Following a period as head of St Jude's National School in Southwark, she went on to work in teacher training. She was influential in improvements in education, and, Dearmer notes in *Songs of Praise Discussed*, 'It was the work of such women that freed children's hymnals from matter like . . .', and he quotes a dire verse which warns against the profligacy of youth by reminding them of mortality.[13]

Instead, the Penstone text is rooted in the daily life of fishing communities, where the boats go out to sea 'when night comes down'. The children are enjoined to pray for the fishermen, when they (the children) go to rest. There is no great theological theme; the sea is not the symbol of evil or danger; neither the fishermen of the Bible nor Jesus' comparison between fishing and mission are mentioned. Simply, at the end of the hymn:

> God hath watched o'er the fishermen
> Far on the deep dark sea,
> And brought them safely home again,
> Where they are glad to be.[14]

Penstone's down-to-earth hymn sits opposite a children's classic, 'When a knight won his spurs', by a new writer, a discovery of Percy Dearmer. She was one of two women who stand out as almost the only new writers of their era of either gender.

Several writers and compilers of new books comment on the dearth of new writers during this period. John Wilson, writing about recent editions of the *Public School Hymn Book*,[15] remarks: 'We are not privileged to live in a great age of hymn-writing, and our selection must draw chiefly on the fine things of the past.'[16] And Robin Leaver cites a similar reminiscence by Erik Routley, referring to the compilation of *Congregational Praise*: 'Well do I remember how difficult it was to find any new texts that were fit to use: we reckoned we were clever to find about a dozen . . .'[17]

Voices in the desert: Jan Struther and Eleanor Farjeon

Richard Watson attributes the longevity of the hymnbooks published at the turn of the twentieth century to this phenomenon. He mentions only four new writers, published in *Songs of Praise*: Eleanor Farjeon, Jan Struther, Geoffrey Dearmer and Percy Dearmer. Percy Dearmer was the compiler of the resource and father of Geoffrey, and Farjeon and Struther were both aquaintances. But the two women were far more interesting characters than the singers of their hymns ever imagine!

Singers of 'Morning has broken' (by Eleanor Farjeon) or 'Lord of all hopefulness' (by Jan Struther) would be astonished by the unconventional lifestyle of the two women. In fact, Jan Struther's granddaughter, Ysenda Maxtone Graham, writes: 'Lovers of these hymns who discover that their author was not herself a churchgoer feel a sense of betrayal. The favourite hymn sung at their own wedding or their grandfather's funeral turns out to be, so to speak, a fake.'[18] Jan Struther was a *nom de plume* adopted by Joyce Anstruther (J. Anstruther) for her considerable body of writing. She was a regular contributor to a number of journals, including the *Evening Standard, Daily Express, Eve: The Lady's Pictorial* and, later, *Punch* and the *New Statesman*.

Jan's parents were what should have been a powerful combination of old money and political power. Her mother Eva was the daughter of a wealthy Baron, and her father, at the time of their marriage, a Liberal MP with bright prospects. However, just before the birth of their first child, Eva's father was ruined, and her husband, Jan's father, resigned as an MP to take up the directorate of the North British Railway Company. Her parents barely spoke.

Her much-loved nanny, nicknamed 'Lala', encouraged her to learn at her own pace, rather than following an educational programme. Cut out of her parents' lives, Jan spent a great deal of time below stairs, or playing solitary games.

As a child, she would have preferred to have been a boy. She learnt a love of carpentry from her father, who, she surmised, would have been happier earning his living as a jobbing carpenter.[19] It is not surprising, then, that the 'labours' at 'the noon of the day', in her best-known hymn, are typified by the work of Jesus, the carpenter, 'whose strong hands were skilled at the plane and the lathe'.[20]

Jan was an independent, modern young woman in the 1920s. She worked part-time as a secretary at Scotland Yard, and lived a life of dances and parties. Her first love committed suicide, supposedly because of gambling debts, and she married his friend, Anthony Maxtone Graham, who was heir to an ancient Scottish title. The marriage was initially happy, but eventually both parties had affairs and they were divorced in 1947.

The divorce was made doubly painful by the popularity of Jan Struther's creation, Mrs Miniver. She had started out as a character in a column for the Court pages of *The Times*. The stories were brought together into a popular book and film. The film starred Greer Garson, and was a picture of homely English life in danger of destruction by Nazi Germany, which played a great part in convincing the American audience that it was worth America entering the War. Mrs Miniver, the central character, was more or less the perfect wife. The exposure of her creator's unhappy marriage, ironically in the same year that Greer Garson also ended her marriage, only added to the painfulness of the situation.

Jan then married Adolf Placzek, a Jewish refugee from Vienna, whom she met at the beginning of the war in London. They married in 1948, in a civil ceremony. 'Dolf', as he was known, was 13 years Jan's junior, and outlived her by half a century. She died in 1953 of a brain tumour.

He remarried five years later, and enjoyed over forty years in his second marriage, till his death in 2000.

Jan Struther's hymns formed a very small interlude in her complex life. They were written at the request of Percy Dearmer for the 1931 enlarged edition of *Songs of Praise* which contains 12 of her texts. Her granddaughter suggests that her lack of involvement in Christianity gave her the freshness of expression that people value in the hymns: 'It was perhaps because Joyce was so unholy that she wrote such good hymns. She could stand back from Christianity and express its essence with childlike simplicity and refreshing vocabulary, from a distance.'[21]

She took an active role in proofreading and editing material for the new book, but as Maxtone Graham records, dishearteningly for lovers of the hymns: '"My dear Percy", she said one morning when he was fretting about the theology of Heaven and Hell in one of Isaac Watts' hymns, "surely you don't believe all this stuff?"'[22]

And yet the hymns speak straight to the experience of faithful Christians. At a recent training weekend for Christian ministries, one of my students came across her words, 'Round the earth a message runs', unexpectedly, as he was looking through *Congregational Praise*. He thought the words (while archaic in expression) just the thing we needed to hear. The young musician, who was asked to play for the service, had never met the hymn, but he noticed that it was by the author of 'When a knight won his spurs', and I was amazed that he had sung this at school and felt a sentimental attachment to it.

The hymns use almost no explicit Christian language. 'When a knight won his spurs' uses the imagery of medieval pageantry to refer to moral precepts.

When a knight won his spurs in the stories of old,
He was gentle and brave, he was gallant and bold;
With a shield on his arm and a lance in his hand,
For God and for valour he rode through the land.

No charger have I, and no sword by my side,
Yet still to adventure and battle I ride,
Though back into storyland giants have fled,
And the knights are no more and the dragons are dead.

Let faith be my shield and let joy be my steed,
'Gainst the dragons of anger, the ogres of greed;
And let me set free with the sword of my youth,
From the castle of darkness, the power of the truth.[23]

Jan Struther is writing the kind of hymn she would have liked to sing as a romantic, tomboy child. The imagery throughout is that of knightly chivalry. 'God' only appears as part of the romantic background, the counterpart to the valour that was the knight's quest. The second verse is clear, that the stories are nothing more than that. The hymn might have gone on to set the story of Jesus over against the mythology of storyland, as still living and true. However, it continues with the romantic imagery. After the poignant recognition that the dragons are dead, comes the rallying cry to kill moral dragons and ogres.

The last verse is terrific to sing. It places all the power in the hands of the singer. Borne along by faith and joy, the singer has the power to storm the castle and free the power of the truth – truth is bound and captive, but powerful.

This is in direct contrast to the way these words and images are used in the New Testament. Paul draws on military imagery in Ephesians 6.10–18. Here the enemy is 'the evil one' with his fiery darts, and the embattled Christian bears a shield of faith and the sword of the Spirit. Truth is part of the equipage, holding all in place as the belt buckled around the waist.

John's Gospel refers to the truth as itself a liberator: 'And you shall know the truth and the truth shall set you free' (John 8.32). In both these passages, the believer needs truth, faith and the word as external aids. The hymn turns this round, and gives the singer the daring challenge to use his or her own youthful vigour to set the truth free.

The best known of her hymns, 'Lord of all hopefulness', links the narratives of the earthly Jesus with the narratives of daily life. This is not the heavenly Christ, nor even the miracle worker and teacher, but the carpenter of Nazareth, who was swift to welcome and embrace the people around him.

Part of its freshness at the time was its almost unprecedented use of 'you' as an address to God. This sounds so natural in the hymn that it is hard to remember how the debates about 'thee' and 'you' raged through liturgical discussion in the mid-twentieth century. Gordon Wakefield, writing about the previous fifty years in a *Hymn Society Bulletin* article of 1968, calls her 'romantic, chivalrous and, indeed, girlish, with her blushing use of the second person plural in address to God and her anapaestic lilt'.[24]

In fact, this was the herald of a new era of hymn-writing, and Jan Struther's unselfconscious use of the second person plural opened the way for the writers of the 1960s and beyond to use this form of address. Her hymns helped to give voice to the liberal Christianity of the 1940s and 1950s in worship. The liberal-minded *Congregational Praise*[25] contained three of her hymns, and they appeared in School hymn books that were based on *Songs of Praise*. So several generations of children grew up singing and loving them and imbibing their theology (or lack of it).

The other author mentioned by Richard Watson as writing at this time was Eleanor Farjeon, the writer of 'Morning has broken'. Her life was no less colourful than Jan Struther's. Eleanor's parents were middle class, but she, like Joyce Anstruther, was educated at home.

She was one of four children, and closest to her eldest brother Harry. The other two brothers, Bertie and Joe, formed another close relationship. Harry invented a game called 'TAR', which seems to have enthralled Eleanor right into her adult years. It was a fantasy game, incorporating fictional characters. Eleanor grew up surrounded by a world of books. She wrote:

Our nurseries upstairs were full of books. Downstairs my father's study was full of them. They lined the dining room walls and overflowed into my mother's sitting room and up into the bedrooms. It would have been more natural to live without clothes than without books, as unnatural not to read as not to eat.[26]

The title of the memoir from which this quotation is taken, *Magic Casements*, shows how her reading fed into her fantasy world. The 'Magic Casements' were the books, which provided windows through which she escaped into other worlds.

Harry withdrew from the TAR game rather abruptly, when he took on a teaching post at the Royal Academy of Music. Joe had also married, so Eleanor and Bertie formed a close relationship which included literary collaborations throughout their life. Bertie introduced her to a group of writers, including Rupert Brooke and D. H. Lawrence. Through them, she met the poet Edward Thomas, and fell in love with him.

Later, she was adamant that they had not had an affair. Though she was aware of her own feelings, she also knew that what Thomas wanted from her was friendship. She wrote part of her autobiography in the form of a memoir of their time together. In the Preface, she writes: 'He counted on me for friendship, and I loved him with all my heart.' She knew that she had to keep her feelings controlled and hidden, and that she could never declare herself: 'If I had, our friendship must come to an end.'[27]

Farjeon admired Thomas's writing. She took on the task of typing up his poetry, and encouraged him to submit it for publication. Her niece considers that Eleanor's contribution to Thomas's recognition as a poet has been underplayed in favour of that of the American poet Robert Frost.

> Frost has been given credit for the discovery of Thomas as a poet while Eleanor's earlier discernment, her help and encouragement, have been lightly dismissed. But Thomas was one of the first in a long list of men and women to benefit from the perspicacity of the now confident Eleanor.[28]

Tragically, Thomas was killed in 1917 in France. Eleanor moved to a small cottage in Sussex where she lived alone for a time. This was a period of self-discovery, and the Sussex countryside formed a background for her writing. She wrote books and poems for children, and also novels and poems for adults, some in collaboration with Bertie. She wrote comic verse for the *Daily Herald* (as 'Tomfool') and for *Punch*.

In 1920, she met a teacher and lover of literature, called George Earle, nicknamed 'Pod'. Eleanor knew that her emotional maturity had been stunted by her years in the fantasy world or TAR and reading as escapism. She knew nothing of sex, and had no experience of a mature adult loving relationship.

Earle was married with children and they decided to elope together. They arranged to meet each other on Paddington Station. Eleanor waited for several hours before finally giving up, only to turn and find that Earle had been waiting for her elsewhere on the station. Having found each other, they did elope, and, as Farjeon writes, 'sealed as true a marriage as could be without benefit of clergy'.[29]

She and Earle lived together, with only a couple of breaks, till his death in 1949. The first break followed a miscarriage. Eleanor wanted children, but Earle had children by his first marriage, and did not. The miscarriage devastated her – her sonnet 'Farewell, you children that I might have borne'[30] expresses the depth of her pain, but he was unsympathetic.

Eleanor sought some time away, and went to Tuscany for an extended trip. When she returned, they resumed their relationship. Her failed pregnancy drew Eleanor further into the field of writing for children.

Eleanor's family, for the most part, deeply disapproved of her life-style, though Bertie maintained his closeness to her, and collaboration with her. As with Jan Struther, one may speculate how the singers of her hymns, particularly those written in the 1920s while she was still with George Earle, would respond to knowing the facts about her life at the time.

She converted to Roman Catholicism in her later years, and was received into the church at the age of 70. She was wryly aware of how her family would react, given the way she had lived.

Farjeon is best known as a prolific and creative writer for children. The year after her death in 1965, the Children's Book Circle established a prize for children's writing in her honour. The prize has been awarded annually ever since.[31]

Again, as with Jan Struther, Farjeon's hymns form a small part of her biography. Her niece mentions the early hymns only in passing, noting that 'In the early 1920s Eleanor was asked to write some hymns and readily produced three for which the fee was nine guineas.' She comments on the rise of 'Morning has broken' to Top of the Pops, sung by Cat Stevens, 'with a blast of notoriety and royalties that would have amused and delighted its author'.[32] Even though the biography is named after the hymn, there is no other reference to this or Farjeon's other hymns.

It was Dearmer who asked her to write the text to the tune 'Bunessan' for the 1931 edition of *Songs of Praise*. He comments: 'There being no known hymn in this short dactylic metre, and something being also wanted on the theme of Thanksgiving for each day as it comes, Miss Farjeon was asked to make a poem to fit the lovely Gaelic tune.'[33]

She wrote three other texts at Dearmer's request, for *Songs of Praise*. One has a tune by her brother Harry. When Dearmer turned his attention to the tradition of carol singing, in collaboration with R. Vaughan Williams and Martin Shaw, he turned to her again. She translated carols from French and German, and, again, wrote an original text to a tune of her brother's.

Only one of her other texts has found wider use, though by no means as wide as 'Morning has broken'. 'People, look East', which appeared in *The Oxford Book of Carols*, was written for an old Besançon carol tune, to which 'Shepherds, shake off your drowsy sleep' had also been set. Her text draws on the contrast between the dark infertility of winter and the new life beginning in the Christ-child.

The first verse calls on people to look East to welcome 'Love the Guest'. Then nature is called to shake off winter:

Furrows, be glad. Though earth is bare,
One more seed is planted there:
. . .

Birds, though ye long have ceased to build,
Guard the nest that must be filled.
. . .

Stars, keep the watch. When night is dim
One more light the bowl shall brim.
. . .

Each verse ends with two lines that echo the theme of the verse:

People, look East, and sing today:
Love the Rose (or Bird, or Star) is on the way.

The last verse brings in the angel chorus, announcing to 'man and beast/
Him who cometh from the East' (see Isa. 41.2) and ends:

People, look East, and sing today:
Love the Lord is on the way.[34]

Several others of her carols appear in *The Oxford Book of Carols*,
some of them paraphrases of French or German texts.

Richard Watson says of Jan Struther's text, 'High o'er the lonely
hills',[35] 'This is hymnody of the English water-colour.'[36] The same
could be said of Farjeon's texts. Their appeal lies in a romantic view
of the English countryside: dewy gardens in which blackbirds speak
at dawn, and even rainfall is sweet; barren furrows and frosty starlit
nights. There is more of theological and biblical reference in these texts
than in Jan Struther's, but the setting is here and now. We are rooted in
the present time, with no eschatological reach.

An exclusive explosion

The move away from gospel hymns and choruses to a hymnody that
was more poetically and theologically intelligent was also a move
towards a more liberal hymnody. Biblical studies, preaching and theological teaching at this time were all taking on a more liberal stance.
Writing about the first half of the twentieth century, Kenneth Long was
able to speak of

a gravitational pull [in the Anglican Church] towards the high
church position, 'moderates' tending towards 'high' and Evangeli-

cals becoming slowly more liberal until, at the present time, the true Evangelicals are only a small, if sometimes vociferous, minority.[37]

The 'present time' was 1971: he was writing on the eve of the charismatic revival! But he was true to the era that was then ending when he wrote, 'Subjectivity is giving way to objectivity; concepts of the Church Universal and the Christian brotherhood of man are now thought more important than "I, me and mine".'[38]

The book he quotes as the most excellent example of this type of theology and hymnody is *Congregational Praise*.[39] H. Davies also holds this book in high esteem. He says that the work of Eric Thiman and Erik Routley 'helped to make this the finest of the Free Church hymn books for literary and musical quality'.[40]

Certainly, this book, whose gestation was interrupted by the Second World War, and so came out later than intended, has all the characteristics of its time. We have seen that Erik Routley mourned the lack of new texts and texts by living writers.[41] The book owes as much to *The English Hymnal* and *Songs of Praise* as to its denominational predecessors or those of the evangelical revivals.

This was the tradition I grew up with. I sang from various school versions of *Songs of Praise* each weekday morning and from *Congregational Praise* on Sundays at church. These books, with the intelligent, liberal preaching of the time, formed my own early theology and relation with God. Though *Congregational Praise* expressed the desire in its Preface to be a book, like the 1916 *Congregational Hymnary*, for its own generation,[42] there was a sense of permanence about it. New writing had practically ceased. The corpus of hymnody seemed to be complete, set in stone – nothing so modern as concrete! There was no hint that new hymns could be written, no suggestion of the riot of creativity that was about to begin, or the opportunities that were about to be lost.

The next few years were tremendously exciting for a young, and then teenage, Christian, as new hymns and songs were written in both traditional and folk-revival form, with challenging and radical words and ideas. These two were very much in the social gospel mould, as we shall see, and therefore masculinizing. But there were two other sources of new music for worship that were far more inclusive. The charismatic revival of the 1970s brought in a great wave of songs that drew on the emotional feel of the gospel era, but in the musical style of the folk revival. And the Second Vatican Council released a completely new set of voices, though not in the official responses of the Roman Catholic Church.

The beginning of new writing came in the so-called 'hymn explosion', from the 1960s onwards. At its beginning, the explosion was deliberately orchestrated and encouraged, and, in part at least, it is characterized by the aims and liturgical interests of its instigators. Among these was Eric Routley. As early as 1946, he opened a discussion at the Hymn Society Conference in Bristol, on the way in which the art of new hymn-writing was suffocated by the rise of the 'official hymnbook'. A series of articles in the *Hymn Society Bulletin* pursued this theme.

Although he had been involved in the making of a new 'official' book, he expressed his frustration at the innate conservatism of the exercise in his own generation. The *Hymn Society Bulletin* of 1962 carried reviews of *The English Hymnal Service Book* and *Baptist Hymn Book*,[43] both published earlier that year. Cyril Taylor, reviewing *The English Hymnal Service Book*, laments that the book, 'which blazed so magnificently daring a train [*sic*] in 1906 has in 1962 repudiated the ancestry, and dared nothing at all'.[44]

Routley comments on both books:

Need we be so cautious? Need we be so terrified of our congregations? Need we exclude what will rarely be sung? Need we be quite so polite? Need we be so unsure, where V-W and Dearmer were in their generation so sure? Must we be so much more afraid than they were that posterity will write us down fools for our judgement?[45]

Both Routley and Caryl Micklem, reviewing *Baptist Hymn Book*, express interestingly prophetic hopes for the next generation of writers. Micklem comments:

In the century since *Hymns Ancient and Modern* first appeared, the centrally-published corpus of hymns-with-tunes has reached and passed its apogee, and is now, one hopes, reaching the end of the line . . . Up with local enterprise, loose-leaf books, and *ad hoc* hymnodists![46]

And Routley asks the question: 'Could a book edited by a couple of young enthusiasts with a handful of chosen friends round them get published now?'[47]

The answer, of course, was 'Yes'! It was exactly that kind of enterprise and that kind of publication that was to hold centre stage for the next quarter of a century. The influences were manifold and complex. New translations of the Bible had brought the freshness of a variety of contemporary language forms into worship, and not only offered alternatives to the Authorised Version, but challenged the very concept of a single authoritative translation. The Second Vatican Council made an even more extraordinary leap from Latin to contemporary vernacular language, and brought about major liturgical changes, which empowered laypeople and women. The Church of England was, at first timorously, moving away from the *Book of Common Prayer* and experimenting with new versions of the liturgy.

The 1960s were, in any case, a strange decade, with new freedoms and a wholesale rejection of old manners and social orders. Globally, the era saw the demise of British imperialism and the rise of new mass communications. By the end of the decade, the world had seen itself from the depths of space, and the fragility of the planet was becoming evident.

A new generation of Christians sought forms of worship, including hymns and songs, that responded to this new world. A mass of publications of different kinds, loose-leaf booklets, hymnbook supplements, single author collections and short thematic collections poured off the presses. And what nobody seems to have noticed, amid this welter of creativity, is that, with a few exceptions, the voices of women were almost completely excluded.

Eric Routley commented, prophetically, as it turned out, back in 1952, that in comparison with the positive effect of women's emancipation on the quality and number of women's writing in other spheres,

> the coming of that age corresponds exactly with a virtual drying-up of the gift of hymn-writing in women. The only qualification of that generalization that we can admit is to say that women are still writing good things for children; but nothing at all is coming from the women of the present generations in the way of universal hymnody.[48]

During the writing of this book, I searched through the hymn resources of the 1960s up to the turn of the millennium, for living women hymn-writers, that is, women who were alive at the time each book was published. I experienced a sense of deepening shock as I discovered the minuscule contribution of living women writers in book after book, hovering between 2 and 3 per cent in most cases, and going below 1 per cent in more than one supplement. This had an effect on the denominational books published later in the century. *Hymns & Psalms* has fewer than 2 per cent of texts by living women writers, *Rejoice and Sing*, 3.5 per cent, and *Baptist Praise and Worship* 4.75 per cent. A century before, the picture had been very different.

The thing is that no one, as far as I could see, had noticed or commented on this, with the exception of Routley's throwaway line in the 1950s. It seemed worth bringing it to people's attention, so I wrote an article giving the statistics, in the *Hymn Society Bulletin*. I ended the article very bitterly:

> This is not a matter for mild regret and a shrug of the shoulders. I, for one, feel it sharply and bitterly, and I know others who would have blossomed and perhaps offered what would become some of the great hymns of the twenty-first century. The church's loss is their stifled talent – the first irredeemable and the second unforgivable.[49]

I received some interesting responses from writers who had been involved at the time. Brian Wren wrote a thoughtful letter, comparing institutional sexism with institutional racism. His book *Hymns for Today*,[50] to be published as this book goes to press, will explore the writing and writers of what he calls the 'English language hymn renaissance', and may well throw further light on its gender imbalance. In his letter, he expresses the hope that, 'your work will irrevocably put on the agenda (a) how to encourage good new hymn and song writing (b) by women, but also by other voices not heretofore heard'.[51]

I am aware that, in working on this era, I am writing now from my experience of having lived and sung my way through many of these initiatives, fired with the excitement of each new genre; as a member of various editorial committees, and therefore responsible for some of the selection that excluded women; and as a writer, whose experience mirrors that of women during this era.

What Routley describes as the drying-up of the gift is more likely to be the result of disempowering circumstances. It is unlikely that women suddenly lost the gift of writing itself, when they had so patently had it 50 years earlier! And I would love to know what happened.

Some reasons are evident. Much of the impetus to the writing of new hymns originated in the ministerial training colleges or among church leaders. I was a student at Mansfield College, Oxford,[52] in the late 1970s. The College was well known for producing hymn-writers – among them, David Goodall, Caryl Micklem, Brian Wren, Peter Cutts and George Caird, largely under Routley's influence. In December 1965, the *Hymn Society Bulletin* printed a call, 'Wanted! New Hymn-writers', by Hugh Cunliffe-Jones, Principal of Northern Congregational College, Manchester.[53]

In the period in question, not many women were students at these institutions, and the call and encouragement would have been heard –

as the list of writers produced by Mansfield College demonstrates – by men. Many of these went on to produce hymns as a resource for their own congregations. Fred Kaan, among others, talks of writing hymns to supply a need for a particular service, where the pace of change in worship had outstripped the resources available. Again, though there were ordained women and women church leaders at this time, they were few indeed.

Another element is the nature of the revolution that took place in the theology of the hymns. There was a desire for theology and language that would meet the needs of a fast-changing world. Michael Hewlett captured the prevailing mood when he wrote:

> This is a world-affirming age; its hymns must reflect it. It is also an age when we know much more about our fellow-men all over the world; its hymns must not be too parochial – God must not be thanked too glibly for a good harvest in England if there is persisting famine in India. Congregations need hymns about the lack of time, about being an untriumphant and tiny percentage of the world, about a post-Darwinian, post-Einstein, post-Teilhard doctrine of creation, about war as an evil thing . . .[54]

The world that was affirmed in the first instance was the world of work and of science. Margaret Leask quotes from the report on the working party on hymn-writing that assembled at Dunblane, that 'hymns which arose from the life of men today had to take account of the industrial context in which people lived'.[55] There was a conscious move away from the glorification of a rural idyll in which few people lived, towards the reality of town and city life, the world of concrete and steel.[56]

Leask's research mentions only male writers from the hymn explosion, without comment on the inequity. She contacted 15 contemporary hymn-writers as part of her research. The only female writer was Ruth Micklem, mentioned alongside her husband Caryl. This is overwhelmingly the case with all commentators on this period in hymn-writing in Britain. Without comment on the gender pattern, they list only, or almost entirely, male writers, partly because the women were not writing, or not being published, and partly, I guess, because men's writing was seen as normative or exemplary.

Normative human experience, from which the new hymnody was drawn, was now seen as masculine experience. The new incarnational language and theology of hymnody exacerbated the masculine gender bias of hymns and worship language in general. The words 'man', 'men' and 'brothers' now populated these hymns of human life. No one noticed the shift from 'man' as generic term for human, to the dominance of male experience. Female experience was (with very few exceptions) nowhere to be seen. It would be a long time before women's lives were recognized and celebrated in worship with the novelty and creativity that marked these hymns.

A toe-curling interchange recorded at the 1968 Hymn Society conference captures the atmosphere of this time. The closing session of the conference consisted of a panel discussion between six hymn-writers, three male and three female. The women were Mrs Dickie (of the Dunblane group), Joan Rogers and Rosamond Herklots. At one point, the discussion turned to the subject of rhyme, with one member asking what would rhyme with 'strife'. The record goes on: 'came a quick response, "wife". Much laughter. But what the hymn-writer was looking for came out as "gun and knife".'[57] I wonder how that exchange felt to the three women writers, who were speaking within a largely male institution, alongside three far better known, ordained, male writers, the Revds A. F. Bayly, M. Hewlett and F. Pratt Green!

Incidentally, this would be tragic if the experience had remained in the 1960s. Horrifyingly, I encountered the same kind of misogynist ribaldry during the writing of this book. As chair of a church music organization, I commented on the absence of material by women writers in the 2009 programme. Two male committee members turned to each other and sniggered – 'We wouldn't have noticed, would we?' Later in the meeting (which took place in the summer of 2008), one of those gentlemen summed up the discussion with the comment, 'I take it we accede to our chairman's [sic] wish to have a *lady writer* in the programme.' Clearly, this was seen as the 'lady chairman's' eccentricity, to be snidely indulged, rather than a matter of concern for any other reason. Forty years between the two incidents, and what hope is there?

Once the new hymns began to be collected into supplements and hymnbooks, and organized by denominational and other institutions, the editorial committees, whether groups of enthusiasts, denominational appointees or representatives of ecclesiastical interests, were almost entirely male. There was no incentive or motivation to encourage women writers. Other under-represented groups are tentatively encouraged, or at least acknowledged. Compilers nod towards world music, for example, or young people. But the scandal of women's absence is not even remarked upon.

In 1963, a number of initiatives set the tone for future developments in hymnody. Ian Fraser called together a working party in Dunblane, with the aim of producing new hymns and tunes. Sydney Carter joined the group in 1964, bringing his very individual style of songwriting and theology. *Dunblane Praises 1* was published in 1965.[58]

One specific area of interest for the 1965 Dunblane working party was that of children's hymns. Existing children's hymns were seen as 'adult control devices – suggesting that God's great desire was to keep children in line and get them to be meek and mild like Jesus; tidy, colourless conformists'.[59] Gracie King (1919–) was put in charge of the production of a volume of hymns for children, which came out in 1970.[60] King had visited schools, collecting material and trialling the hymns. Only hymns that the children remembered and asked for were considered for inclusion.

But the group consisted almost entirely of men, and many of the great names of the hymn explosion are there. Their influence on the development of mainstream hymnody runs straight through the denominational hymnbook supplements and into the major hymnbooks published in the last decades of the twentieth century.

Two denominational supplements came out at this early stage in the hymn explosion: *Hymns & Songs* was a supplement to the *Methodist Hymn Book*; *100 Hymns for Today*, a supplement to *Hymns Ancient and Modern*. Both were published in 1969.[61] Only *100 Hymns for Today* lists its committee, which comprises five men.

The book *100 Hymns for Today* included hymns by only two living women writers: Emily Chisholm (1910–91) and Rosamond Herklots (1905–87), with one text each (2 per cent of the book). By contrast, there were 59 texts out of the 100 by 29 living male writers (more than half the book). *Hymns & Songs* did slightly better, with two hymn texts and a choral poem by Emily Chisholm, a song by the Evangelical Sisters of Darmstadt ('I come ever singing') and the text of Herklots (just under 4 per cent). In comparison, out of 99 hymns and songs, there are 42 texts by 22 living male writers.

Rosamond Herklots and Emily Chisholm are long-lived, so that their presence slightly distorts the proportion of women's writing in later supplements. Also, the same two texts of theirs appear in most collections – 'Forgive our sins as we forgive' by Herklots and 'Peter feared the cross' or sometimes an advent hymn by Chisholm. This hides the fact that there are no texts by women writers who belong to the same up and coming generation as the new male writers, and no stream of new writing as there was coming from the men.

A significant input into the hymn explosion had come from writers in the Congregational tradition, Brian Wren, Alan Gaunt and Fred

Kaan among them. A majority of Congregational churches in England and Wales joined with the Presbyterian Church of England to form the United Reformed Church in 1971. The new Church had a radical and liberal theology, derived from its academic roots in its training colleges, specifically, in this regard, Mansfield College, Oxford, which had a tradition of liturgical innovation and hymn-writing. Both the aforementioned writers were at Mansfield.

Work began almost immediately on a supplement to *Congregational Praise*, which would tap into the creativity of the URC writers. *New Church Praise*, quite literally the praise of the new Church, was published in 1975. This drew on a wider range of material, and thus included more by women.

Of 109 texts, 14 are by living women writers (11 per cent). These include Marian Collihole (1933–)[62] and Valerie Dunn (1932–) from the folk tradition; Gracie King, the only woman to have been involved in the early years of the Dunblane process; two collaborations from *Cantate Domino*, a translation by Ruth and Caryl Micklem, and a Doreen Potter tune to Brian Wren's text 'Christ is alive!' There are 76 texts by 27 living male writers.

This is a higher proportion of women's writing than any other of the supplements of this era. There were two women on the initial search committee: Ruth, the wife of Caryl Micklem, and Carolyn Brock, the wife of the Chaplain at Mansfield College, Oxford. Carolyn Brock taught hymnody at Mansfield, and the Micklem family had a long association with the College. Among the new writers they found was Ann Phillips, who went on to serve on the Committee to *Hymns & Psalms* which had the intention to be Methodist and ecumenical, and was the only woman on the words committee of *Rejoice and Sing*.[63]

Her text 'Into a world of dark' is a powerful exploration of God's dramatic eruption into the darkness before creation, the darkness of doubt and death. The short 6666 four-line verses, with a strong downbeat at the beginning of each verse, contain and control the theological depth of the hymn. Typically of hymn explosion texts, particularly those in the liberal reformed tradition, the hymn tackles doubt and grief, but (unlike some) ends with a strong sense of hope. After the verse on doubt, she writes:

From empty wastes of death
on love's disordered grief
light in the darkness blazed
and kindled new belief.

The reference is to the resurrection appearances (for example Luke 24.4) but the hymn touches the rawness of grief in the singers as well. The last verse brings the hymn very precisely into its own time:

> Still, with creative power
> God's Spirit gives to men
> a pattern of new life –
> and worlds begin again.

We are precisely at the time when hymns began to open up the reality of human life in worship, and to challenge old prejudices and stereotypes, but while 'men' were still considered the overarching norm of humankind. *Rejoice and Sing* has altered the verse to:

> Still, with creative power,
> God's Spirit comes to give
> a pattern of new life –
> our world begins to live.[64]

Another supplement was published a year later by the Church of England. *English Praise* was a supplement to *The English Hymnal* and drew in some of the great names from Anglican hymn-writing of the explosion era. There are 11 texts by George Timms, who was also on the all-male compiling committee, three by Timothy Dudley Smith, five by Michael Hewlett, and so on – 34 texts by living male writers.

Of the 120 texts, astonishingly only four are by women, living or dead! This is an abysmally low proportion even by 1970's hymn-supplement standards. Of these, only one is by a living writer: Rosamond Herklots' 'Forgive our sins as we forgive'.

Meanwhile, the Church of Scotland was contemplating a third edition of *Church Hymnary*.[65] The Church made a deliberate, but abortive attempt to work ecumenically and internationally. In fact, only Presbyterian churches participated, though these included English-speaking churches from other parts of the world. Like many well-meaning attempts to be inclusive of world music, this also foundered, because the music had to be 'singable', by which I imagine the committee meant that it had to be familiar to people used to singing hymns in a European style. However, the presence on the committee of representatives from the Presbyterian churches of the Pacific would bear fruit when the hymn explosion took off in that part of the world.

The committee was very large, being representative of a number of Presbyterian bodies. Of 40 people, the only woman was the Revd

Elizabeth B. Barr, one of the two representatives of the United Free Church of Scotland. I wonder what that was like!

The book contains 10 texts by 9 living women writers, out of 695 items. There are 46 texts by living male writers, so about a fifth of recent texts are by women. Most of them are for children, with one or two in a traditional style by women of an older generation, for example, Violet Nita Buchanan's (1891–1975) 'O day of joy and wonder'.

There is one text that is new in style, and by a relatively young writer. Carol Rose Ikeler (1920–) was the first woman to be received into the Presbytery in Philadelphia, when she joined the staff in 1958, having been ordained in 1955. She served on the Board of Christian Education of the United Presbyterian Church of the USA, and wrote hymns for children. However, her text, first written for primary children, 'The church is wherever God's people are praising', has become popular, and found its place at the cutting edge of new language in hymnody.

It is set to a folk tune ('The Bard of Armagh'), and describes the Church very much in terms of the people, rather than in institutional or theological terms. Each verse starts,

The Church is wherever God's people are . . .

She sees it as an enterprise, where God's people are striving with imperfection, finding forgiveness,

where all are accepted, whatever their background,
whatever their past and whatever their pain.

There is room for joy and challenge too, in seeking to convey the gospel:

. . . its joy and its comfort,
to challenge, refresh and excite and inspire.[66]

There is a high proportion of texts by women (living or non-living) because of the book's policy on children's hymns. The committee took the then radical decision not to have a separate section of hymns for children. I can still remember the outcry when the *Hymns & Psalms* committee took the same decision a decade later.

The view was that children should not be asked to sing 'hymns which adults thought children ought to sing, rather than children's hymns', nor be 'confined . . . to their "own small corner" of the hymnary'.[67] Rather, in this, as in other fields, it is better that a child's reach should exceed his grasp than that he should be encouraged to sing what is banal or below his best capacity. Many of the great hymns of the Church are admirably suited for children's enjoyment and use, so that their omission from children's worship is a serious lack.[68]

Miss Carrie M. Barnett, Sunday School Organizer in the Presbyterian Church in Ireland was therefore asked to find about four hymns suitable for younger children, to be included at the end of each section of the book. Thus, not only did children sing hymns from the main body of the book, and perhaps become familiar with the other hymns in those sections, but the writing of a number of women, who had previously been confined to children's resources or the children's sections of hymnbooks, was now included alongside established hymn-writers, and perhaps people became familiar with their names.

These included a number of writers from within the children's work of the Presbyterian churches in Britain and abroad. Elizabeth McEwan Shields (1879–1962) served as Director of the Department of Religious Education for the Committee of Publication of the Southern Presbyterian Church USA. Her simple three-verse text, 'I like to think of Jesus',[69] sits among a group of children's hymns at the end of the section on Jesus' ministry, which includes D. Helen Stone's 'I can picture Jesus toiling', and Margaret Cropper's 'Jesus' hands were kind hands',[70] but also surrounded by the texts of the incarnation and passion of Jesus: 'O love how deep, how broad, how high' at no. 223, and 'Praise to the Holiest in the height' at 238.

The odd thing about a book that aimed, albeit imperfectly, at inclusivity, was that Church Hymnary (third edition) made a policy decision not to include hymns in contemporary idioms. They drew texts from publications since Church Hymnary Revised,[71] but published only seven new texts submitted to them in manuscript, none by women. This was because contemporary writing was felt to be ephemeral, and there was a danger that the book would be out of date as soon as it was published.

So the Church of Scotland's committees on Public Worship and Youth were asked to convene a working party under the Revd John D. Ross, which published Songs for the Seventies in 1972,[72] a year before Church Hymnary (third edition) came out. This was co-published with Galliard, which had produced the Faith, Folk and Clarity series, books of Sydney Carter's hymns, and other similar collections. Carter was well represented, as were Fred Kaan and other hymn-explosion writers.

In common with other hymn-explosion publications, the book contained very little writing by women – only two texts (4 per cent), in fact: 'Think of a world' by Doreen Newport and Valerie Dunn's 'Bursting into Life'. Of the 52 items, 43 were by living male writers, 12 by Sydney Carter (nearly a quarter), demonstrating the book's affinity with the music of the folk revival.

Folk revival

The folk revival was a secular movement which influenced a generation of young Christian worshippers. Peter Smith brought together three collections of traditional and new folk-style songs during the 1960s. In the Preface to *Faith, Folk and Clarity*,[73] the first of these, he comments on the contribution of folk:

> With its roots in the people, [folk song's] disregard for the party line, its refusal to court low commercial standards, its simplicity and tradition and its association with many of the great religious and humanitarian movements, it is proving an excellent medium for expressing Christian faith and concerns.[74]

The tone of the book is earthy and full of protest about poverty, racism and the marginalization of communities. Although the language is overwhelmingly male ('The family of man'[75]), there are some interesting texts by contemporary women writers. Marian Collihole's (1933–) story appears on pp. 235–43 of this book. Her text 'Woman racked and torn with pain' begins with this startlingly realistic description of childbirth and goes on to describe the stages of human life. The woman's experience rivets the singer's attention in the first two lines,

> Woman racked and torn with pain,
> soon to bring new life,

but the action thereafter moves to her husband:

> husband pacing anxiously,
> suffering with his wife.
> 'Where is God?', says the man,
> 'Where is God in this?'
> 'Here I am,' God replies,
> through a new-born infant's cries.

The child is a son, whose journey through crime and drugs, through witness to tragedy and experience of hardship, to gradual realization and discovery of God and home, shares the mindset of Victorian piety:

> Man comes trudging home at night,
> knows fog and flood and snow;
> begins to see beyond the mist
> the waiting firelight glow.
> 'Where is God?' says the man,
> 'Where is God in this?'
> 'Nearer, son,' God replies,
> 'Love is opening your eyes.'[76]

The firelight of home represents safety and salvation, in comparison with the wild weather outside the home, which is where the man encountered the evils and temptations of the world. But, whereas a Victorian hymn might have had the female voice of the author calling the wayward son home to safety and to God, there is no further female influence in this text. It is God who calls the son home.

Judith Piepe's (fl. 1966) text 'Come down Lord from your heaven', subtitled 'A Soho de Profundis', calls Jesus to return to the hell of the clip joint and strip club, 'Where only love is blind'. Making powerful links between modern human dereliction and the gospel narratives, the hymn deals with the 1960s' world of drug addiction and crime. Here, women's experience of degradation is taken seriously. The prostitutes are real and vocal. Also, unlike hymns of an earlier – and also a later – age, there is no 'happy ending'. The hymn does not find its climax in assurance, but ends:

> So come down, Lord, from your heaven, you whom we can't confess,
> And be the resurrection from this our living death.[77]

A poignant text about female adolescence is written by Susan Tuck, herself a young woman at the time: 'Just on the threshold they tell you you're waiting', with its second verse bringing the message home:

> Just on the threshold I know I am waiting . . .
> Now, while the dreams of a child can still find me,
> I take reality too in my gaze.[78]

I had sung and admired this text in my teenage years, and was therefore thrilled to meet Sue Gilmurray (1950–), as she now is, a few years ago, through *Worship Live*. I am equally thrilled that she agreed to write her story for this book. She sees herself very much as within the folk tradition. If she had found fame and fortune, she would rather it had been as a folk singer than as a hymn-writer.

Her current writing is spurred by her involvement with the peace movement, and *Worship Live* has included a number of her texts on this theme. Indeed, the editorial committee was inspired to produce an issue on the theme of peace and war, partly by the power of Gilmurray's writing.[79] In 2007, the bicentenary of the abolition of the Atlantic slave trade, we published a song that compared slavery to warfare. The first verse starts:

> It used to be normal to buy and sell people
> To use them as cattle to exploit or to kill.

It goes on to describe the common reaction to the early anti-slavery campaigners:

> 'You're a fool, that's just the way the world's made.'

But we know that change did come:

> And then the tide turned,
> A new light dawned . . .

The second verse suggests that we are in the early stages of the same kind of change of attitude with regard to war:

> Today it is normal to justify warfare
> In spite of its evils that are clear to be seen.

This time the chorus is a challenge:

> Because the tide turns,
> A new light dawns . . .[80]

In common with nineteenth-century hymn-writers in radical traditions, Gilmurray's music draws from and supports her social campaigning.

Faith, Folk and Clarity also contains work by a couple of hymn-writing partnerships: Alan and Barbara Vanderstock (fl. 1966) contribute the anti-racism text, 'They settled down in Manchester', and

Brenda Stringfellow writes the tunes for Jim Stringfellow's texts, 'Let's share the food my brother'[81] – a deeply ironic song, in which the vast inequity of the share is laid bare – and 'I've got a million sisters'.[82] These make a fascinating pair. The experience of the 'brother' in 'Let's share the food' is poverty, apartheid, war – the masculine is clearly intended to encapsulate the general ills of the human race. In 'I've got a million sisters', her lot is the loss of home and man in war, the death of her child through famine, and being mixed up beneath her make-up. Her experience is specifically female, while that of the 'brother' is normative.

Faith Folk and Nativity followed in 1968, and *Faith Folk and Festivity* in 1969. There are more contributions by Marian Collihole, including 'Was I really once a child',[83] in which she looks at Christmas through the eyes of a lonely old man living in poverty. As in her text 'Where is God', the narrative is that of a male, whose experience, while challenging norms of cosy family life at Christmas time, is still taken as normative for men and women.

Muriel Smith's (fl. 1967) 'Carry on sister, high up the hill' brings the nativity into the present day. The sister, the brother and the children are invited to the manger. The first verse, rather oddly, seems to equate the sister with the shepherds:

Carry on, sister, high up the hill.
'Twon't be long afore you're filled
With heavenly light, O so bright!
God is giving a gift tonight![84]

The brother, more conventionally, symbolizes the wise men, in the modern guise of 'Bankers, lawyers all kneeling to praise'.

However, very few writers from the folk tradition came into the mainstream. Sydney Carter is the best known, and his 'Lord of the Dance', among other texts, has become a staple of turn-of-the-millennium worship. Some of the sensitive and creative women writers are among those whose light flared with the folk revival, and died with it. However, the folk style continued and continues its influence, as we shall see, through Roman Catholic charismatic music and through the Presbyterian world church.

Post-Vatican II

The Catholic Church was being rocked by a different kind of hymn explosion in the 1970s, with the advent of Vatican II. This had a profound effect on the shape of the liturgy, with a huge increase in lay participation, through the introduction of the vernacular, which produced a sudden requirement for suitable hymns. *New Catholic Hymnal*,[85] published in 1971, was an official and conscious response to the demand. Recognizing that there was not the same tradition of hymn-singing as in the Churches of the Reformation, the book drew enthusiastically on a variety of sources, and commissioned a number of new musical settings and texts or translations by living writers.

Elizabeth Poston, who had been the music editor of the *Cambridge Hymnal* of 1967,[86] contributed three tunes, and there were two more by women composers. However, of the 305 items, only 20 texts are by women writers, and these include six translations by Catherine Winkworth. There are only three living women writers, less than 1 per cent of the book.

In the same year, a revised and enlarged edition of *Praise the Lord*[87] was published. The first edition, of 1966, had contained very little new material, apart from Gelineau Psalms. That had been a response to a rise in congregational singing at Mass in Catholic parishes and schools, but it predated both Vatican II and the impact of the hymn explosion on Catholic worship.

The revised edition was published only five years later, but the Introduction acknowledges that 'in that time the whole liturgical life of the Church has undergone a drastic reform'.[88] Cardinal Heenan's foreword describes it as 'a sign that the hitherto Silent Church is on its way to becoming a Singing Church'.[89]

The cover of the book is amazing. It is a photograph of a crowd, from above, showing a mass of faces, intent on something that is happening in front of them – possibly a football crowd. This mass of humanity is evidently intended to locate the book in the 1960s' incarnational tradition of hymn-writing, which it does very successfully, since, with one or two *possible* exceptions if you look really hard, there is not a single female face. The picture conveys unequivocally that the mass of humanity is overwhelmingly and normatively male.

The hymn-explosion writers are reasonably well represented: Fred Kaan, for example, with two hymns and Sydney Carter with three. Valerie Dunn (1932–) is the only female writer from this tradition, with her text 'Man more than man'.[90] There are a number of new Catholic writers. Stephen Dean, a third of the all-male editorial group, has 16 tunes in the book. His texts appear in the 1999 book, *Laudate*.[91]

The living women writers are a very interesting group. While the editorial committee consisted of three men, there was a consulting group of seven, including one woman, Sister Winifred Wilson RSCJ. It was largely religious sisters who were to provide the female voice in the Roman Catholic hymn explosion. Many of these are very traditional, such as the text by Sister Agnes, 'Hail glorious St Patrick, dear saint of our isle', which also appeared in the *New Catholic Hymnal*.[92]

There are one or two texts by religious sisters that point to the more radical theology of the hymn explosion, though rather tentatively. Sister Margarita has three texts, including 'Jesus Christ our Lord and God', with its chorus:

'*I have been among you as one who serves.*'

The text is based on John 13.1–17, Jesus washing the disciples' feet. The last verse brings the Bible story into the realities of the 1960s:

Let us serve each other then,
Seeing Jesus in all men,
Banish from our Christian life
Colour, class or racial strife.[93]

Almost nothing is known about the sisters who contributed to this and other books. Their dates of birth and death are not given. Sometimes they appear anonymously within a group, for example the Anglican 'Benedictine nuns of West Malling'.[94]

The voice that was about to burst onto the scene would take this more radical theology further. As the folk revival and Charismatic Renewal swept through newly liberated Catholic worship, Estelle White (1925–) began to publish not in these official or semi-official books, but on the margins of the Church.

Faith, Folk and Festivity included her texts 'There is a world' and 'Harvey's in his forties' (title, 'And he listens with his hands').[95] This is a purely secular text, and sharply divided opinion even among the singers of the new hymns. Harvey, a miner, is not explicitly Christian, but he is a 'listening man', to whom people turn in all the seasons of life.

'There is a world' is typical of the challenge in much of her work. The 'world' of the first line of each verse is filled with the injustice, hardness and violence of life, expressed in very dense and powerful terms, carried by the relentless march of the tune. The people of this world

. . . never care to know
That every step they take is placed on roads
Made out of men who had to carry loads too hard to bear.

The chorus is in dialogue with the text:

'That world's not ours,' that's what we always say,
'We'll build a new one, but some other day.'
When will we wake from comfort and from ease,
And strive together to create a world of love and peace?[96]

I was privileged to interview Estelle White for *Feminist Theology* journal in 1999.[97] She had developed her musical gifts alongside a variety of other employments – as a saxophonist in an Army Band, through training at Corpus Christi under the care of a Carmelite order, and teaching music and religious education in secondary schools.

She wrote this text, her first, while at Corpus Christi, which, she says, was 'in the 1960s when protest was in the air'. She continues: 'I was asked if I would go and sing at the youth club, and I wrote a protest song for the occasion: "There is a world where people come and go".' As it happened, Kevin Mayhew was at the youth club when she performed the song, and asked her to write another 11 songs. The conversation took place just before Christmas, and he asked her for the 12 songs by the first week in January.

She managed to get them to him by the second week in January! She comments on the experience: 'It was absolutely amazing. They were nearly all written in the middle of the night. I just sat up and wrote them down, including the melodic line. The arrangement came later.'[98]

'Harvey', she says, comes from her background, having gone to school in Seal Harbour, which was surrounded by pits. This text, too, 'came in one fell swoop in the night', but took a further month to refine.

Her texts began to appear in collections such as *Folk Praise*, published in 1977,[99] but it was with *Celebration Hymnal*,[100] an instantly popular book both inside and outside Roman Catholicism, that her writing became widely known and sung. *Celebration Hymnal* was a phenomenon born from the charismatic movement in the Roman Catholic Church. It was an outpouring of informal song, much like the Spirit-filled music of the Fisherfolk.[101]

The original book, published in 1976, includes 20 of her texts, and was known colloquially as the 'Estelle' book. Her writing is fresh and original. Many of the texts are written with children or young people in mind, for example 'Moses I know you're the man', with its chorus:

So every day, we're on our way,
For we're a travelling wandering race,
(or, in v. 4, wandering, vagabond race)
We're the people of God.[102]

But there are hymns for adults as well, both simple and challenging. A more recent hymn to the Holy Spirit consists of four-line verses, with a single line repeated twice and a petition in the last line:

Breath of God, O Holy Spirit,
breath of God, O Holy Spirit,
breath of God, O Holy Spirit,
breathe on us now.

. . .

Light divine, and flame eternal,
burn in us now.[103]

A much earlier text begins from the healing of the blind man in John 9, or Mark 8.22–26, and is told from the point of view of the man who was healed. The name of Jesus is not mentioned, nor is there any direct reference to the story. Instead, the text compares the man's newfound sight, and the things he sees, with the moment he opened his eyes and looked at Jesus. When he looks at human faces, and sees his own reflection, he recognizes

the line of envy round the lips
and the greed and the hate in the eyes.

In the first two verses, he turns away,

for I had seen the perfect face of a real and proper man,
the man who'd brought me from the dark
into light, where life began.

In the last verse, what he sees in the 'faces of men' was not envy and hate but

the lines of sorrow round their lips
and the child looking out from their eyes.[104]

And now the memory of seeing Jesus leads him to turn to them, not turn away.

The text assumes a reasonably thorough knowledge of the biblical story, and also the sophistication to be able to follow a line of reasoning through a fairly complex song, in which the repeated pattern in the verses carries the progression of thought.

Estelle White is a thoughtful and careful writer, who addresses serious issues in her hymns. When I interviewed her, I asked about her attitude to feminism. She said that she had really been a feminist all her life, and her mother had been too. Her mother had been a great admirer of the suffragettes and Estelle remembers being thrilled when her mother went to vote.

But she had not been aware of the feminist movement, or of issues such as inclusive language. She had revisited some of her texts in the light of this, though some – such as the text just quoted – could not be changed.

There was a supplement to *Celebration Hymnal*, then a second volume published in 1984, and a third collection, *New Songs of Celebration*, in 1989. It is interesting to see the changes in women's contributions through the various publications.[105]

The 1976 book included a number of texts by religious sisters, some of which had first appeared in *Praise the Lord*. There were also older texts by women writers, such as Julia Ward Howe's 'Mine eyes have seen the glory' and Dorothy Gurney's 'O perfect love'.[106] By the time of the second volume, the influence of the charismatic movement and the Fisherfolk can be seen in texts like Mimi Farra's 'Alleluia, sons of God arise' and 'We cry hosanna, Lord', and Karen Lafferty's 'Seek ye first the kingdom of God'.[107]

World music is also beginning to enter the collection, with Fred Kaan and Doreen Potter's 'Break not the circle'. Some of the sisters from volume 1 are still writing, but their work is less central to the collection. There are five items by Estelle, in comparison with the 20 items in the first collection.

New Songs of Celebration has far fewer texts by women writers. Estelle has disappeared. Instead, the writers of the hymn explosion have moved in: Christopher Idle, Fred Pratt Green, Fred Kaan, Brian Wren and Timothy Dudley Smith have a dozen texts between them. Now the voice of the worship song tradition is Graham Kendrick with three texts, and there are some emerging Catholic writers: Martin Haugen with 10 texts, Chris O'Hara and Anthony Sharpe. Taizé is represented by seven items.

But a new and powerful female voice is also emerging at this point. Three of Bernadette Farrell's texts and tunes appear in this collection.

Bernadette is a musician and social activist. Her material has been published by OCP[108] in the United States since the 1980s, and she is a member of the Thomas More Group of composers.[109]

Her text 'Come to set us free' was published in *Let's Praise* (1987) and *Carol Praise* (1988),[110] and appears in *New Songs of Celebration* at no. 733. Both this text and 'Praise to you, O Christ our Saviour' are Christocentric, focusing on the incarnate God:

> You are the Word who calls us to be servants;
> you are the Word whose only law is love;
> you are the Word-made-flesh who lives among us:
> glory to you, Lord Jesus Christ.[111]

Many of her hymns are settings of psalms or passages of Scripture. A lovely setting of Psalm 139, 'O God, you search me and you know me', appears in a wide range of books published since the millennium, including the Kevin Mayhew publication *The Source*, and *Church Hymnary* (fourth edition), both published in 2005.[112] The hymn is true to the psalm, and captures the sense of complete absorption in God's presence, complete knowing by God. The last line of the last verse breaks out of the psalm into the new creation:

> For you created me and shaped me,
> gave me life within my mother's womb.
> For the wonder of who I am I praise you:
> safe in your hands, all creation is made new.[113]

Other hymns have a sharper social message. 'Longing for light, we wait in darkness' contrasts the many kinds of darkness in the world with the light of Christ. The verses deal with war, hunger and homelessness. In each case, the answer lies in a response drawn from the imagery of the people of God, mirroring or serving Christ:

> make us your bread, broken for others,
> shared until all are fed.
> . . .
> make us your building, sheltering others,
> walls made of living stones.[114]

Bernadette runs seminars and workshops, and is still making a tremendous contribution to the hymnody of today as one of the most creative and challenging voices of our time.

Charismatic revival and worship songs

The other tradition that broke the male domination of the hymn explosion was the charismatic revival in evangelical churches, which burst into the British churches when Betty and Graham Pulkingham brought the Fisherfolk from the USA, and we were introduced to the songs that were soon to be published in *Sound of Living Waters* and *Fresh Sounds*.[115] The foreword to *Sound of Living Waters* makes the provenance clear:

> *Sound of Living Waters* is a book with many fresh sounds reflecting the cascade of joyous praise, of awesome wonder, of sincerity and hope, which accompany the Holy Spirit's renewal in the Church today.[116]

I can remember a visit by the Fisherfolk to Oxford, where I was studying in the 1970s. I was struggling with the contrast between my liberal Christian upbringing, under which I had received a firm call to the ministry, and the rather old-fashioned evangelical teaching of the Oxford Christian Union, which had only male officers, ran debates on issues such as girls wearing short skirts, and took a very dim view of my sense of calling.

The Fisherfolk erupted into that rather sterile environment like a volcano. The songs were evangelical in theology, lacking the radical edge of the folk revival, but they expressed their spirituality in a completely contemporary idiom. Many of them were simple worship songs; others were lively and dramatic, exciting to sing. We had simply never heard anything like them.

There was a great deal to appeal to adolescent and young adult singers: Alliene G. Vale's 'The joy of the Lord is my strength'[117] had the nonsense chorus 'Aha ha ha ha ha ha', designed to show that joy could be expressed in laughing. Laughter in worship was a controversial issue, with Christian clowning growing as a movement and the musical *Godspell*[118] gaining notoriety for showing Jesus telling the parables with humour.

As well as contemplative songs, like the round 'Father we adore you' by Terrye Coelho,[119] there was music with a very contemporary idiom, driving rhythms and dramatic chord sequences, such as Priscilla Wright (later Porter)'s 'Fear not, rejoice and be glad'.[120] This is interesting, as the words use archaic language: 'the vine beareth fruit', 'Ye shall eat in plenty', and refers to the Authorised Version of the Bible (Joel 2 and 3), but is set to lively, modern music. Its musical pattern, with a big dramatic chorus and verses that could be sung by a soloist or group, was practical for learning new music, and became very popular.

Betty Pulkingham's concern for breadth and practicality, which she mentions in the interview,[121] is evident in the Foreword to the collection. She writes that 'On the whole, the songs included here were chosen because of their proven usefulness in worship', and 'Vaughan Williams and Bortniansky do have their say. So do a secretary named Sylvia, a young college student, and the four-year-old son of one of the editors!'[122]

However, the balance is definitely weighted in favour of living writers, of both genders, and captures the outpouring of creativity from this group of people.

The two books were compiled not by earnest committees of male clerics, but by two women, Betty Pulkingham and Jeanne Harper. As Betty Pulkingham says in the interview in this book, she did a great deal of arranging music, as new material was produced. A lot of the new songs were by women. Of 133 items in *Sound of Living Waters*, 31 are by women, 26 by living women writers, about a fifth of the book.

Sister Miriam Therese Winter (1938–) is there, from the *Celebration Hymnal* tradition. Others were members of the Fisherfolk, travelling with the group and writing new songs, for example Mimi Farra (1938–) who has four songs in the collection. Her text 'Alleluia, sons of God arise'[123] also appeared in *Celebration Hymnal* volume 2. There is a certain amount of cross-fertilization between the charismatic movement in these two traditions.

Fresh Sounds was published two years later and, as is common with the development of a tradition of this kind, increased numbers of texts by individual writers demonstrates careers beginning to develop. Mimi Farra has four more texts, including the dramatic performance song 'I will arise'.[124] Jodi Page, a new writer here, has six texts.

In a book of 108 items, 39 are by women, all living at the time of the book's publication. When I interviewed Betty Pulkingham, I asked why the charismatic tradition was so successful in encouraging women writers, given the abysmal failure of the hymn explosion in this respect. Her reply is on page 311, but I remember the laugh in her voice when she said, 'Well, the Spirit brings freedom!'

Certainly, there is a wealth of writing by women, and it is full of delight and fun. However, these texts, like those of the folk revival or hymns explosion, retain an overall masculine cast to the language. It is the 'sons of God' who are invited to arise. The Body of Christ will set 'mankind' free.[125]

The Foreword to *Fresh Sounds* ends with an invitation,

> to explore some of the infinite variety and musical resourcefulness of God's creative Spirit and to expect him to use you as a vehicle for his power and praise as you sing, that others may hear and follow on to know for themselves his creativity and blessing.[126]

The Spirit of God here is uncompromisingly masculine, as is common in the evangelical traditions.

Indeed, the next wave of evangelical hymnody to sweep in from the United States was less playful and far more patriarchal. In 1984, Billy Graham set out on 'Mission England', a series of evangelistic rallies at football stadia and other mass venues. The hymnbook to accompany the mission was *Mission England Praise*. This lost its 'England' reference and was joined by *Mission Praise 2* in 1987. The initial collection of 282 pieces was designed to resource the campaign, but it was widely taken up in churches of all denominations.

Under the same banner were *Junior Praise* (1986), *Carol Praise* (1987) and *World Praise* (1993). *Junior Praise* has gone through a number of editions and now has its own complete edition (2008), and a new edition of *Carol Praise* was published in 2006. A combined edition of *Mission Praise* was published in 1993, with two 'complete' editions, one in 1999 and the second in 2005, with 1,144 items.[127]

The original book contained a number of traditional hymns, with some nineteenth-century gospel songs and choruses. Of the 282 items, 124 were by living writers – nearly half. Of those, 94 were by male writers and 30 by women. So just over 10 per cent of the book was by living women writers, but they were outnumbered three to one by the men. Christopher Idle, Fred Pratt Green and Michael Saward are present, from the hymn explosion, but not the more radical writers: no Sydney Carter or Fred Kaan at this stage. Timothy Dudley Smith, on the other hand, has four hymns. And there is a young Graham Kendrick, with six texts.

The women writers come from the Fisherfolk (Priscilla Wright and Terrye Coelho (1952–), for example), and from American evangelical and Pentecostal traditions. As the later *Mission Praise* books were published, new names arose. Marilyn Baker (fl. 1980) was published first in the Supplement of 1990, and her texts have come into the combined and complete editions.

Noel and Tricia Richards (1960–) met when Noel visited Tricia's school on a Youth for Christ team. Over the years they have coauthored a number of songs, which have featured in the Christian arts festival *Spring Harvest*[128] and appeared in later editions of *Mission Praise*. Their texts are eschatological and full of confidence. For instance, 'Called to a battle, heavenly war' (surely an extraordinary first line! The hymn is subtitled 'Thunder in the skies') has the chorus '*By the blood of the Lamb we shall overcome, see the accuser thrown down . . .*'. The text appears in *New Mission Praise* (1996) and then in the two *Complete Mission Praise* books. It is also taken up into *The Source* (1998) and *The Source Combined Words* (2005) and *Songs of Fellowship* 2 (1998). [129]

Many of the copyrights for new music in *Mission Praise* have been held by Thankyou Music, Maranatha Music and Kingsway Music, a linked group of publishers. In 1991, Thankyou Music Publishing brought out the first of a new series of *Songs of Fellowship*,[130] with an editorial committee of 18, including Dave Bilbrough, Chris Bowater, Rob Frost and David Peacock, well known in the publication of evangelical music. There was only one woman, Jackie Williams, of JAW Music in Sheffield.

Three more books came out as *Songs of Fellowship* 2 (1998), *Songs of Fellowship* 3 (2003) and *Songs of Fellowship* 4 (2007).[131] The numbering runs consecutively through all four books, ending with 2,200 items. These have been immensely popular, and used by churches of all denominations.

The four books chart a move from congregational singing to songs by recording artists. Vicky Beeching (fl. 2002) was born in Canterbury and studied theology at Oxford. While there, she attended the Oxford Vineyard church, affiliated to the charismatic evangelical Vineyard movement. She worked and recorded with Soul Survivor, before moving to Nashville, Tennessee. Her songs appear in *Songs of Fellowship* 4 and in the Kevin Mayhew *Source*, which itself now runs into a number of books.

These are songs of worship, awe and wonder. God is 'Awesome God, holy God', who humbles us by 'your majesty and the mystery of your great love for me'.[132] There is little in the way of prophetic or social concern. One text refers to human needs:

You lift the needy from the ashes
and seat them high up with the princes.
You give the barren woman healing;
she'll dance for joy like the mother of children.[133]

This is a lovely reference to Isaiah (61.3; 54.1), but there is no sense that the needy have a right to justice at our hands, or the woman might dance for joy in her own identity. This whole set of resources pretty well ignores issues of inclusivity. Very little attention is paid to inclusive language for humans, and God is overwhelmingly King, Father, Lord almighty, before whom the singer is kneeling and trembling, or amazed and overcome.

A quest for inclusivity

Alongside this development, and following on from the male-dominated hymn explosion, a new and different kind of language, imagery and theology was emerging. If the hymn explosion formed the background to my growing up, the quest for a true inclusivity in hymns, as in other language, has accompanied my adult years. It took a further generation, and the emergence of second-wave feminism before the human experience of women was accepted as valid material for worship and hymnody.

I was ordained in 1979, and was almost immediately delegated by the Congregational Federation as its representative on the committee for what eventually became *Hymns & Psalms*. This was the first British denominational hymnbook to be published for some time and saw itself as a consolidation of material published in small collections and supplements with a core of traditional hymns.

Leask sees this as the first of a new generation of hymnbooks: 'Beginning with *Hymns & Psalms* (1983), the next generation of hymn books consolidated the developments in congregational hymnody. The Methodist book became a benchmark hymnal.'[134]

Among the contemporary issues with which it grappled was inclusive language, not, at this early stage, for God, but for human beings. I can remember a consultation with a group of women at an editorial meeting, following which we made a very few, tentative changes. Some authors had already changed their texts, and other changes were making their way into contemporary sources.

Elizabeth Cosnett, whose story appears in this book,[135] reflected on the complexities of adjusting to inclusive language. Her article is written in response to a request from an American hymn committee to consider altering the first line of 'Can man by searching find out God?' She is honest enough to start from her own 'initially puzzled and hurt reaction', but she goes on:

I came increasingly to see the force of the basic feminist argument that there is a mutually causal relationship between accepted linguistic conventions and accepted social norms. Once this is admitted we are certainly treading in a minefield but retreat is not an option. New ways of looking at language put us in a position like that of our first forebears facing the question, 'Who told thee that thou wast naked?' New awareness may be regrettable, problematic, even horrifying, but there is no way back to a time before we had it. [136]

This lays a burden of responsibility on the hymn-writer.

Reluctantly I must now avoid, or use as sparingly as possible, certain resources of the English language on which I could once draw freely. And if I thus contribute in a tiny way to the loss of such resources in the future, so be it. The price is high but necessary.[137]

In the case of the particular text, the alteration of 'man' was not simple. The first line, 'Can man by searching find out God?' establishes a dynamic between 'man' and 'God' as two objective entities. The replacement, 'we', says something quite different, and involves the singers as subjects in the hymn, not as participants in the human race, about which a question is being asked.

'Man' is also a very strong syllable, and 'Can man by searching', a strong beginning to the hymn. 'We' is a far weaker sound, coming as it does on the first stressed syllable of the hymn. 'Can we by searching' is far less satisfying a start. This is part of the high price to which Cosnett refers. Those of us who support the use of inclusive language, and even campaign for it, have to recognize the weight of what is lost to gain what we believe to be justice.

Interestingly, Cosnett's argument is misrepresented quite seriously by Donald Webster, in a lecture given to the Church Music Society in 1992. He deprecates the hymn explosion for its roots in the social gospel, as 'little more than political propaganda, in which God is brought in as an after thought, if at all'. He goes on:

In earlier times 'Son of God, eternal Saviour' and 'O God of earth and altar' satisfied most people's needs on this subject, and there is obvious sympathy for the New English Hymnal's point of view that the social duty of Christians can often be better expressed in sermon and prayers – as well as in action – than by merely singing about it.[138]

But he saves his most outspoken condemnation for the inclusive language: 'Even more disturbing is the objection to the use of Man or Men or Mankind when referring to the entire human race.'[139] He quotes Elizabeth Cosnett's honest report on her shock at being asked to change the word 'man', but not her equally honest recognition of the necessity of it.

One of our other storytellers, Marian Collihole, takes a view nearer to Webster's. She expresses her irritation with 'feminists' who do not accept the inclusivity of the word 'man' and she tells of being encouraged by June Boyce-Tillman to consider using female language for God. Her response is to reject the notion entirely.[140] On the other hand, Shirley Erena Murray (1931–) speaks of nailing her colours to the mast of inclusivity, and happily uses male and female language in referring to humans and to God.[141]

In the same year as the publication of *Hymns & Psalms*, Brian Wren, Fred Kaan and Fred Pratt Green (the last then 80 years old) held a conversation about 'New Hymnody: Some Problems and Prospects'. The conversation was published in Robin Leaver and James Litton's memorial volume to Eric Routley, *Duty and Delight*.[142]

The conversation between these three men (their gender is a fact not lost on Brian Wren) turned to language, and inclusive language. Wren saw it as simply a matter of fact that masculine language could no longer be taken as inclusive of women. He was the only one of the three to see this as part of a larger issue of human identity: 'Who am I? What do I know, experience, and believe? Who am I in society? What is my social position? Am I one of those who benefit or suffer from injustice? another basic question is: Who am I as male or female?'[143]

He also wants to explore a diversity of terms for God, not jettisoning 'Father', for example, but adding 'Mother', so that both genders of God-language will appear in the context of a hymnbook or resource. This is extremely far-reaching for its time, and Wren would go on to explore it further in his ground-breaking study *What Language Shall I Borrow?*, published in 1989.[144]

The feminist theology of the 1970s and 1980s predates the development of feminist hymnody. Rosemary Radford Ruether's groundbreaking book *Sexism and God-talk*[145] laid the foundations. She later drew out the implications of this theology for church and worship in *Women-Church: Theology and Practice of Feminist Liturgical Communities*.[146] The first half of the book deals with the history of the Church and possibilities for Women-Church engaging with and transforming the existing institutions.

In Part II, she turns to liturgical life. In this, she draws from Jewish and Christian traditions, which are based on an historic timeline that looks towards an eschatological future:

> The core of the Christian calendar is eschatological or messianic. It builds upon the future dimension of Hebrew hope. But it also sees itself as already empowered by the advent of this final deliverance of the world from sin and death even while looking forward to its future completion. This element of foretaste of things to come is the key dynamic of Christian ritual.[147]

But she also recognizes the value of liturgies that mark the seasons of life. There is a danger in cutting ourselves off from nature and its cycles, because 'the actual existence and survival of humanity is still based on the cycles of nature'.[148] For women, the cycles of nature include menstruation and, for many, birth-giving and nurturing, as well as the seasons of the year, and the natural stages of growing and ageing.

However, she points out a danger in turning away from the historical focus of liturgy towards 'a romanticism that suggests that a world without sin can be easily recreated simply by reverencing and celebrating nature cycles',[149] since this will lack the prophetic and ethical dimension that arises from the tension between historical reality and the eschatological vision of traditional Christianity.

The hymnody of the folk revival and hymn explosion was already grappling with the ethical and social demands of historical religion, as we have seen. But this had led to the exclusion of women's stories and women's lives. The 'family of man' had to recognize its systematic sexism and break through another barrier.

There were three major elements of exclusivity to overcome. The lived human experience of women had to be recognized and seen as equally part of human life. Some hymns of the folk revival had mentioned prostitution, for instance, or birth-giving, or female adolescence, but they were few, and the overwhelming message of the movement was that humanity was expressed in masculine terminology and experience.

This extended into secular folk song's tradition of celebrating individuals. Not many Christian songs in the tradition did this, but Sydney Carter's 'There's a light that is shining in the heart of a man',[150] for example, honours George Fox, founder of the Religious Society of Friends (Quakers). It was for writers in the feminist tradition to bring women's experience and female heroes to our attention.

The second element was the recovery of a female tradition, from the

Bible onwards. This was hampered by the patriarchal nature of Scripture, the anonymity of many women (for example, in encounters with Jesus) and their absence from the record. The births of very few daughters are recorded in the narratives of Genesis, or the books of Samuel and Kings. There are almost no female leaders or prophets in Israel. Deborah is a noble exception, but Athaliah gets a very bad press, and Huldah barely a mention.[151]

In the New Testament, Jesus' unusually open attitude to women is largely ignored in scholarship or worship. This is partly due to the marginalization of the actual life of Jesus (apart from his birth and passion) in the early creeds, which has an effect on Christian teaching and worship for two millennia.[152] The few hymns about Jesus' life and ministry have tended to focus on dramatic events such as stilling the storm and feeding the five thousand, and his welcoming of the 'little children'. Jemima Luke's 'I think when I read that sweet story of old' is typical of this section in most of the old traditional books.

This is exacerbated by ignoring almost wholly the women whom Jesus met: for example, Martha and Mary, the Syro-Phoenician woman, the woman at the well, among many others.[153] Mary the mother of Jesus is well represented, though not as a human figure, but rather as the semi-divine mother of God, who assented readily to divine impregnation and gave birth 'how silently' in a sanitized stable; whose obedience and virgin motherhood, indeed, set the tone for the impossible and crippling demands on femininity for generations.

The other major female figure in the Gospels, Mary Magdalene, is depicted as a penitent, fallen woman, by conflating her with other Marys and other female characters in Scripture. This has the feel of a deliberate campaign to remove any power or authority from one in whom Jesus seems, even in the four canonical Gospels, to have placed a great deal of trust.

On the other hand, songs like the anonymous 'Fisherman Peter', which appeared in a number of children's hymnbooks in the 1970s and 1980s, celebrates the call of Jesus to Peter, the rich young ruler, Zacchaeus, Nicodemus and Doubting Thomas, but no female figures.

The third and most controversial element in the development of feminist hymnody is female language for God. This begins from the rare scriptural female descriptions of God as mother eagle, mother bear, the female figure of Wisdom, the fact that the Hebrew word for 'Spirit' is feminine in gender, and moves on to explore other female images. Brian Wren explores this in *What Language Shall I Borrow?*, in a section on 'Meeting God as She'.[154]

He begins from the word 'Mother', the obvious place to begin in suggesting an alternative to 'Father', but he calls us to go beyond this, 'lest our relationship with God continue in permanent babyhood'.[155] He does go beyond, naming God as Sister, Midwife and simply She (using the feminine pronoun).

None of these elements of feminist hymnody is uncontroversial. I have experienced hostility on a couple of occasions, once when a church music festival included my text 'With Miriam we will dance', and on an earlier occasion when I included in my service of induction to the Presidency of the National Free Church Women's Council Judith Driver's (1965–) 'Dance, dance, dance, let the Spirit move you', with its last verse:

> Celebrate all the Spirit does!
> Celebrate all she does with us!
> Dance and sing, join us on the way,
> dance and sing with us today![156]

On the latter occasion, the objector wrote not to me, but to the (male) General Secretary of the Free Church Federal Council, Geoffrey Roper, who was supposed to be in authority over the women's organization and its feckless leader. Geoffrey asked me to respond, as a biblical scholar, with the news that 'Spirit' in Hebrew is feminine.

The beginnings of feminist hymnody were tentative. A book from the Netherlands, *Eva's Lied* (*Eve's Song*),[157] appeared in 1984, a deliberate attempt to use feminist ideas in hymn-writing. In the UK, the impetus towards inclusive worship focused on liturgy and prayer, rather than hymnody at first.

This is because the early initiatives were driven by women and men's reaction to Church of England legislation about the ordination of women. The St Hilda Community was formed in 1986, following the Church of England Synod's rejection of legislation that would permit women ordained in other Anglican Communions to preside at the Eucharist in England. The community was not schismatic, but began to explore the use of 'non-sexist liturgy', 'that gave full space and authority to women, without apology, secrecy or shame'.[158]

A small collection of worship resources was published by the Movement for the Ordination of Women (MOW) and Women in Theology in September 1986, edited by Janet Morley and Hannah Ward. *Celebrating Women* starts with 'A Story of Creation' by Kathy Galloway (fl. 1988),[159] a retelling of the seven days of Genesis 1 as the narrative of a birth, from the breaking of the waters to the rest after labour.

There are poems, meditations and prayers by a number of women, including two hymns by Anna Briggs (b. 1947). 'In love revealed', in the section 'Reclaiming the Word', celebrates Jesus' encounters with women. Each verse ends 'she was (or all were, or we are) healed,/Behold God's grace in love revealed'.[160] Her other text, 'We lay our broken world' is not specifically feminist, but a prayer for all the brokenness of the world. It was included in *Reflecting Praise*, but also in *Songs of God's People*, from where it has been taken into *Common Ground* and then *Church Hymnary* (fourth edition).[161]

Janet Morley was at the forefront of thinking and practice in feminist liturgical development. Her collection *All Desires Known* was first published in 1988.[162] In the preface, she lays out her position as a feminist seeking ways of worshipping:

> I have . . . tried, in my writing, to integrate my faith and my feminism. For me, as for many others in recent years, the women's movement has been the place where my Christian faith has been most strongly challenged, and yet has also been the most important resource for its renewed growth and energy.[163]

She acknowledges that altering existing texts can produce awkward language. She is writing about prayers, not hymns, and so the weight of existing well-loved texts is slightly less than in hymnody. But she prefers the option of writing 'new texts in vigorous language, which also respected and inhabits ancient worship forms, evocative biblical imagery, and familiar cadences and rhythms'.[164]

The Preface gives careful thought and expresses pastoral insight concerning the use of feminine language and imagery for God. There is a sense of liberation in addressing God as female. As Morley says, it can open the way to a whole wealth of biblical language, and at the same time, 'the very range of possible imagery forbids us to *identify* God with any limited form of words'.[165]

On the other hand, the more common masculine language undoubtedly has a distancing effect for women:

> Feminine imagery not only affirms a comfortable closeness for women to the God in whose image we are made: it also prevents us from distancing ourselves – as we can do with 'male' language – from the uncomfortable, even frightening closeness of the difficult God who is not made in our image.[166]

So she urges caution in the communal use of the psalms and poems in the book, because of that sense of exposure, as well as its unfamiliarity. The rest of the book is designed for use in public worship. I can remember its impact. It is clear sighted and uncompromising as well as creative and vigorous. There are collects that bring biblical women, such as the Syrophoenician woman of Mark 7.24–30 out of the shadows into the centre of worship. God is praised as Eternal Wisdom. And the book contains a Litany of penitence for the denial of women's authority, which recognizes both male and female complicity in the sin.[167]

The St Hilda Community told its own story and produced a collection of worship material as *Women Included* in 1991. Again, most of the material is for liturgy in spoken words or actions. The short section on 'Music' is prefaced by the comment:

> We use traditional hymns and carols, Taizé chants, and sometimes other chants e.g. Peruvian taught us by members. We are beginning to think about making up dances to music we particularly enjoy, but have not got very far in writing our own hymns.[168]

There follows a short collection of texts, including some from the sources mentioned, and two original hymns: F. Gerald Downing's translation of a Latin text (which is also given but not attributed), 'Rage, Wisdom, and our lives inflame', had appeared in the MOW journal *Chrysalis* in June 1987; and a version of 'For all the saints', which is also unattributed. Hymn-writing had a considerable amount of ground to make up.

In 1988, the World Council of Churches had declared a Decade for the Churches in Solidarity with Women. A group of women's organizations in the UK decided to explore the possibility of a London launch. Alan Luff, the then Precentor of Westminster Abbey, and a hymn-writer, was known to June Tillman (b. 1943 – later, June Boyce-Tillman), and invited us to use the evening service on Low Sunday of that year.

A small committee formed to prepare worship, including Nicola Slee, Suzanne Fageol, June Boyce-Tillman and me. June's story is on pp. 321–36 of this book. Several of the other stories refer to her encouragement in their own writing. She had collaborated with Peter Smith to produce *New Orbit*[169] some 15 years earlier, and was developing an interest in feminist hymn-writing.

The committee produced a small collection of hymns and liturgical material, called *Who are you looking for?*[170] While the collection was aimed at the launch service, there was more material than was used there, and it was offered for wider use.

There are four groups of hymns: opening hymns, sermon hymns, closing hymns and eucharistic hymns. There are some imaginative choices, for instance, Graham Kendrick's 'Led like a lamb to the slaughter', which focuses on the encounter between Jesus and Mary Magdalene in the garden (John 20.10–18).[171] My own translation from the Greek *Pentecostarion*, 'At break of day three women came', is among the opening hymns.[172]

Here, also, are intentionally inclusive texts by hymn-explosion authors: Fred Pratt Green's 'What tale is this our women bring?', Colin Hodgetts' 'The Guardian', and Brian Wren's 'Woman in the night' and 'Who is She'.[173] There was clearly a vein of emerging feminist hymnody to be tapped and developed.

During the first half of the decade, June Boyce-Tillman and I worked together on a hymn resource that would focus on writing by and about women. *Reflecting Praise* was somewhat eclectic, but included a reasonable range of resources.

Lois Ainger (1928–), a member of Women in Theology, contributed some strong texts. Her 'We know the songs of Zion from our youth' is a big dramatic piece, comparing the experience of refugees with Psalm 137. The mockery of the captors and the Israelites' resistance through silence lies at the heart of the song. But silence eventually entails the loss of the songs and their language as the years of exile pass:

> If we forget our roots and destiny,
> we lose our faith in our identity,
> so our language is our secret
> in a strange land:
> *by the rivers of Babylon, we listen and remember,*
> *we hang our harps on the willow tree*
> *and the music of our grief is in the silence.*[174]

Lois herself was not exiled, but was evacuated from Guernsey just before its occupation in the Second World War, and must have grown up knowing refugees from that conflict, as I did.

Cecily Taylor's (1930–) story appears in this book. Her lively Easter Sunday hymn, 'Alleluia, Christ, is risen', with its driving tune, contains the verse:

> All our doubts come crashing downwards,
> darkness melting into light,
> death's horizon just becomes the
> limit of our sight.[175]

This contrasts with her haunting

> Some days the fog comes creeping
> through mountains of my doubting
> and question marks climb peering
> through windows of my soul:
> asking, stealing,
> fighting in my mind.[176]

The breadth of her spiritual experience echoes my own, and surely that of many others. Glorious moments when doubts crash down are highlights, inner struggle is a reality, in the wholeness of a life of faith. So Charlotte Elliott's classic, 'Just as I am', moves from

> With many a conflict, many a doubt,
> Fightings and fears within, without (originally 'Fightings within and fears without')

to the denouement in

> Just as I am, of that free love
> The length, depth, breadth and height to prove,
> Here for a season, then above,
> O Lamb of God, I come.[177]

Taylor's Pentecost hymn, 'The bright wind is blowing, the bright wind of heaven' appears in *Church Hymnary* (fourth edition).

Lois Ainger's and Cecily Taylor's texts are honest and incarnational, but they are not feminist. *Reflecting Praise* did include hymns that were feminist in fulfilling each of the elements mentioned earlier.

June Boyce-Tillman's 'It was dark in the dawn of time' explores darkness as a place of creating, from the 'darkness' of Genesis 1.2 onwards. The fifth verse enters the darkness of the 'sheltering womb':

> Where the baby for nine months lies,
> curved like a moon near a warm woman's heart
> till the waters roll aside.[178]

The chorus to this hymn is

> *then the rest in the dark was transfigured with light*
> *as the Spirit worked out her plan.*

There is, of course, a danger that the feminine gender of the Spirit in Hebrew may serve to locate any femaleness in God in the third person of the Trinity, away from the very masculine Father and Son. Other hymns address this, but there is also a freedom in singing about this aspect of the godhead, which is linked in Scripture with mystery and playfulness. The Spirit whisks Ezekiel away without warning,[179] and Jesus talks of the Spirit like the playful wind (which of course is the same word in Greek).[180]

Judith Driver's 'Dance, dance, dance', already mentioned, picks up on this sense of playfulness. The feminine pronoun appears only briefly in the last verse of the hymn, but by the time the singer reaches the 'she', it is already clear that this is not the same image of the Holy Spirit as can be found in traditional hymn texts. Here, the Spirit overcomes anger and hate, frees prisoners[181] and gives courage. The response is the powerful chorus, 'Dance, dance, dance, let the Spirit move you'.[182]

This is not an explicit reference to women's experience, as the Boyce-Tillman text is, but it relates the Spirit of God to a lively, ecstatic experience, which has been part of the experience of women throughout the tradition of women's writing. It is another delicate thematic pairing. There is a danger of relegating women's experience to the emotional rather than the rational part of human nature. This was the tendency in earlier hymn-writing and was not altogether positive. On the other hand, women have rarely had the chance to express their spirituality in vigorous and bodily form.

The text that finishes the book is June Boyce-Tillman's 'We shall go out with hope of resurrection'.[183] The hymn is a passionate call for the kind of joy that fully includes others. In two verses, Boyce-Tillman stirs up a range of emotions, from anger to commitment, in the context of the celebration of resurrection and new hope. The second verse promises

> We'll give a voice to those who have not spoken,
> we'll find the words for those whose lips are sealed,
> we'll make the tunes for those who sing no longer,
> vibrating love alive in every heart.
> We'll share our joy with those who are still weeping,
> chant hymns of strength for hearts that break in grief,
> we'll leap and dance the resurrection story
> including all within the circles of our love.

The silent, grieving ones who are to be included are doubtless the millions of abused and poverty-stricken people in the world. But women have taken this text to their hearts, recognizing the heart-breaking reality of the silencing of women throughout human history and into the present day. The dance language of the penultimate line not only introduces a metaphor of inclusivity and joy, but offers the chance for people rendered immobile by all that silences them and makes them weep, to celebrate in an unrestrained and physical way. Tradition has often enjoined quietness and modesty on women, so that even if they do gain freedom of expression, it is still restrained by cultural expectations.

Boyce-Tillman herself does this by translating a medieval woman writer, who was up to this point very little known. Hildegard has been given back her voice and her place in the history of the Church and its song in recent years. Peter Dronke's study of medieval women's writing helped to break the ground. June Boyce-Tillman has brought her poetry to life in translation and in live performances of her songs. *Reflecting Praise* includes Boyce-Tillman's celebration of Hildegard, which uses images and ideas drawn from her writing: she is 'Feather on the breath of God', for example.[184]

Another translator of medieval women's texts is New Zealander Betty Wendelborn, whose version of words by Julian of Norwich was sung in Westminster Abbey when I conducted a 'Come and Sing' in May 1993, based on texts by or about women, many from *Reflecting Praise*, published that year. Wendelborn rejoices in the dramatic image of Jesus as a lactating mother, offering nourishment to the worshipper. The jazzy tune adds to the celebratory feel of the hymn:

> O mother Jesus, lead me to your breast,
> to drink your nature, on your wisdom to feast.
> 'See how much I love you, on me you can feed.
> Enter through my open side, to take whatever you need.'
> My mother Jesus leads me to her breast,
> to drink her nature, on her wisdom to feast.[185]

Elizabeth Cosnett gives a voice to a particular woman, a hero in the annals of women's lives, in her text, 'For God's sake let us dare to pray like Josephine'. The text is quoted in full on page 249. In four four-line short-metre verses, she conveys the spiritual and social range of Josephine Butler's life.

It was her prayer life as a committed Christian that led her to move beyond compassion, and the sense of the personal sin of 'fallen women', to engage with the social injustices behind prostitution. She headed the campaign against the Contagious Diseases Acts of the 1860s, which permitted genital examination of any women accused of prostitution. Famously, she referred to the examination as 'surgical rape'.

What she understood was that the 'sin' involved in prostitution lay deeper in society than was currently believed. By criminalizing the prostitutes, society allowed the men, who resorted to them, moral and social licence. This was part of the nineteenth-century dichotomy between male and female, which made women responsible for the moral health of home and nation. It meant that men and women were judged by the law according to what came in the 1950s to be known as a 'double standard'. Butler's outspoken campaigning forced her contemporaries to recognize the injustice in this, and the Acts were repealed in 1886.

Reflecting Praise also collected a number of hymns that celebrate biblical women. Ruth Thomas sang of Miriam dancing in 'The bangles were jangling';[186] there are a number of texts about Mary, the mother of Jesus. These are incarnational, focusing on her experience as a human mother, rather than her status as mother of God. However, the contribution of Orthodox worship is recognized by two of my own translations: 'At break of day' and 'In all truth it is a worthy act'.

The former of these is a translation of sections from the third-century *Pentecostarion*, the Easter liturgy of the Greek Orthodox Church.[187] I was impressed with the interweaving of biblical female persons and imagery. The first verse follows the journey of the three women to the tomb, their joy at finding the tomb empty, and their action:

They run to take the good news back
And share their holy joy.

In the second verse, Mary the mother of Jesus is likened to the city of Jerusalem, which, in Isaiah 60, receives back its sons and daughters:

Lift up your eyes, look round and see
With radiant faces, strong and free,
Your children come to find their home
For all eternity.[188]

A lot has happened in this area of writing since the publication of *Reflecting Praise*. I don't think we would now accept uncritically a text like Elizabeth Cosnett's 'For God's sake let us dare', which uses Mary Magdalene as an example of prostitution. More recent scholarship has exposed this for the smear campaign that it was, using a conflation of New Testament characters to focus on the supposed penitent sinner, and away from one of the few facts about her in the canonical Gospels, the fact that Jesus commissioned her to announce the good news first.[189] My translation shows the women rushing from the tomb to tell the others the good news of the resurrection, but does not interpret this as an evangelistic or apostolic act, as later theology and later texts have done.

The only character from the Hebrew Scriptures to be celebrated in song in *Reflecting Praise* is Miriam. Again, a good deal has been written since 1993. I have written texts in celebration of Leah (Gen. 29—30), Shiprah and Puah the Hebrew midwives (Ex. 1.15–21), Deborah (Judg. 4—5) and Esther (book of Esther), and mourned with the wives and concubines of David (1 Sam. 18 right through to 1 Kings 1), and with Jephthah's daughter (Judges 11.30–40).[190]

In the song 'Jacob, he has a voice', I have tried to explore the double discrimination against Leah, but also the cultural pressure on Rachel:

Rachel, pretty, petite,
Jacob thinks you're so sweet –
you gotta live up to his dreams,
gotta be part of his masculine schemes.

But the story tells us that God honours Leah. She is one of the few people in the Bible to name her daughter (Gen. 30.21). So in the end, she is

Leah, sacred and strong,
we will carry your song –
sing to the ends of the earth
a woman who knows what her worth and ours is.[191]

The Iona Community has also explored the women of the Bible. John Bell's 'There is a line of women' moves through the Hebrew Scriptures into the New Testament, to 'Sing a song of women'.[192]

One area in which *Reflecting Praise* does very well is in the exploration of female language and imagery for God. Brian Wren recognizes the seriousness of the challenge:

By speaking of God as She . . . we are going against the grain of the society that has formed us. Since that society downgrades and disvalues what it labels 'feminine', naming God as She means facing that down-grading head-on and hoping to break through it.[193]

This makes some sense of the extreme reactions to feminist hymnody. They come from a gut reaction which feels that their God is being devalued, debased, even dirtied, by the use of female language. Wren recognizes the need to counter this: 'If we use female images, we must make sure that they are being *revalued into equality*. Otherwise all that will happened will be the incorporation of a devalued femaleness into the godhead.'[194] He does this, for example, in 'Bring many names' in which consecutive verses praise

> Strong mother God, working night and day,
> Planning all the wonders of creation,
> Setting each equation,
> Genius at play:
> Hail and Hosanna,
> Strong mother God

> Warm father God, hugging every child . . .[195]

The language of the mother God verse refers to Proverbs 8.22–31, where Wisdom is planner, architect and playmate (depending on the translation) in creation.

The final image Wren looks at is 'Bag Lady God'.[196] Here the revaluing is a challenge to our attitude to humans as well as ways of meeting God:

> To think of God as a Bag Lady means taking both God and bag ladies seriously. She is our Mother, our Sister, the Christ in our neighbor. She has the waywardness of the Holy Spirit. The whole Trinity meets us . . . in the last and the least . . . Using the metaphor means loving the real bag lady as one in whom God meets us.[197]

Reflecting Praise begins with my hymn, based on Deuteronomy 32.11 and Isaiah 40.31, 'Dear mother God', and includes texts such as Judith Driver's 'My God is woman', Brian Wren's 'Who is She, neither male nor female', and Colin Hodgetts' lovely revisioning of Psalm 121, 'If I raise my eyes to the hills', in which the guardian is female, not male.[198]

More understated, but equally radical, is Jan Berry's hymn 'Praise to God, the world's creator', which is a hymn of praise to the Trinity. The first verse is explicit: the creator is described as

> Cradling in her arms her children,
> Holding them from birth to death.

The second person of the Trinity is praised as 'our saving Wisdom'. This is a perfectly traditional identification between Jesus and Wisdom, but in context we are reminded that this is a female figure in the Hebrew Scriptures. While the feminine gender is not used again (indeed, pronouns are avoided), the text keeps a radical edge:

In our hurting, in our risking,
In the thoughts we dare not name,
God is present, growing with us,
Healing us from pride and shame.[199]

Here is a hymn text fulfilling Ruether's vision of worship that maintains a prophetic and ethical witness. The theology of God is also radical, in that it shows God not as immutable, but growing and changing with us.

Meanwhile, two other traditions, on opposite sides of the world, but inspired by the experience of *Church Hymnary* (third edition), were also beginning to explore the issues raised by feminist hymn-writing. On the island of Iona, John Bell and Graham Maule began to gather hymns and worship material. Through Wild Goose Publications, they put together the sketches *'Eh Jesus'* . . . *'Yes Peter'* in 1987, and the *Wee Worship Book* in its various incarnations.

They compiled *Love and Anger: Songs of Lively Faith and Social Justice*, published in 1997, a mixture of world music and their own texts, with a strong social and prophetic message, and a series of *Wild Goose Songs*.[200] Many of the texts were set to Scottish folk melodies, and they became hugely popular. The mixture of Scottish folk and world music was exciting, and John Bell has become a world renowned speaker and worship leader.

Common Ground, published in 1998, was the first move towards a book for more general church use, published by the Church of Scotland's Saint Andrew Press rather than Wild Goose. There is the same mixture of new writing, folk style and world music, with a bias, stated in the Foreword, towards new material and material not readily accessible elsewhere.

John Bell has eight texts, and a further 16 written in collaboration with Graham Maule. This is equal in number to the sum of texts by living women writers. Nevertheless, this is a creditable 16 per cent of the total number. Living women writers include the American, Ruth Duck, whose story appears in this book at pages 263–75, Scottish writer Kathy Galloway, whose story is on pages 276–86, English-born

Bernadette Farrell, whose story I never quite got, and New Zealander Shirley Erena Murray, who appears at pages 295–307 – all prominent, or to become prominent, in the field of hymnody.

Ruth Duck tells the story of her text 'We cannot own the sunlit sky' on page 266. Like other writers in these traditions, she is inspired by a sense of justice and social need. She says that she started writing out of her shock at the way the Church treated women, and in response to hymns such as 'Rise up O men of God'.[201]

Kathy Galloway, too, speaks of the need 'for women to name and be named'. Her text 'She comes with a mother's kindness' does not make explicit who 'she' is, but an editor's note at the bottom of the page explains: 'It may seem unusual in one collection to have two hymns which allude the Holy Spirit in the feminine. This is not to say that the Spirit is a woman, but to encourage deeper thinking about the nature and work of the Spirit.'[202]

In fact, the hymn's reference is wider than the third person of the Trinity, and the first two verses speak of sacrificial giving, closer to the offering of Jesus:

> She comes with a mother's kindnesses
> and bends to touch and heal.
> She gives her heart away in love
> for those who cannot feel.
>
> She comes with a lover's tenderness
> to answer love's appeal.
> She gives her body with her heart
> to make her passion real.[203]

The text is strongly incarnational. The 'She' who is the subject comes as worker, artist, child and sister, inhabiting the flesh of those who labour, create, trust and support. The hymn invites us to look for sisterhood in God, and, by unspoken inference, to look for God in workers and sisters and children.

Here, as in the other two texts in *Common Ground*, Galloway celebrates creation and speaks for justice. Shirley Erena Murray talks of New Zealand hymns expressing their landscape, and Kathy Galloway's hymns seem to draw on her Scottish setting:

> the changing of seasons in mountain and valley,
> the stars and the bright restless sea.[204]

But this is a world that requires justice:

> Sing of God's justice
> disturbing each easy illusion,
> tearing down tyrants
> and putting our pride to confusion.[205]

'Mothering God'[206] by the American Jean Janzen, with a tune by Janet Peachey, very explicitly describes the three persons of the Trinity in female language. The three verses start: 'Mothering God', 'Mothering Christ' and 'Mothering Spirit'. As with many similar texts, Janzen is reaching back into the writings of medieval women mystics and writers. Here, she consciously echoes the language of Julian of Norwich.

The text in *Common Ground* that does focus on the Spirit as female is John Bell's 'She sits like a bird, brooding[207] on the waters'. This is significant, because it marks feminist, or feminist-inspired, hymn-writing moving closer to the mainstream. Here are male authors recognizing and celebrating the feminine gender in relation to the godhead. Female language and images run through the whole text:

> she nests in the womb, welcoming each wonder,
> nourishing potential hidden to our eyes.

> She dances in fire, startling her spectators,
> waking tongues of ecstasy where dumbness reigned;
> she weans and inspires all whose hearts are open,
> nor can she be captured, silenced, or restrained.[208]

I came across this text when I was preparing to lead the 'Come and Sing' in Westminster Abbey in 1993. I was thrilled to see such a thoroughly feminist text written by someone whose voice was heard and respected around the world. I wondered how they got away with it. I think it was because Iona was still, in a way, on the margins, and their voice was a voice calling from the edges of the Church, rejoicing in their marginal status.

But it is only when the voices from the margins begin to be heard that they can make a difference. The voice of Iona was heard because of the popularity of their resources and the integrity of their vision. They produced worship material that enjoyed its liminality (*Eh Jesus* was written in a Scottish idiom), and they made contact with other margins by enthusiastically embracing world music. Because of this, people listened with fascination and learned to let go of their certainties; and also the Iona writers picked up on the marginalized but exploratory field of feminist writing, and invested it with its own sense of legitimate adventure.

In addition, the worship coming out of Iona had a very incarnational and prophetic message. While nearly all hymnody up to this point had followed the bias of the historic creeds and barely mentioned the life and teachings of Jesus, John Bell and Graham Maule's texts frequently focused on the Jesus of the Gospels. One of their earliest texts, 'Inspired by love and anger', begins from human need and suffering and the singer's frustration (love and anger) in the face of this. The fourth verse begins

> To God who, through the prophets,
> proclaimed a different age,
> we offer earth's indifference,
> its agony and rage.

The verse ends with a very human view of Jesus, and one which makes a direct link between his teaching and that of the prophets:

> Amused in someone's kitchen,
> asleep in someone's boat,
> attuned to what the ancients
> exposed, proclaimed and wrote,
> a saviour without safety,
> a tradesman without tools
> has come to tilt the balance
> with fishermen and fools.[209]

Putting Jesus in someone's kitchen (a reference to the story of Martha and Mary in Luke 10.38–42), paints a picture of him comfortable in a female setting. In a sense, the logical outcome of the strongly incarnational and prophetic tone of the folk revival and its successors should be a recognition of the humanity of women.

As second-wave feminism began to gain an influence, any call for justice must begin to recognize the injustices meted out to women on the grounds of gender. Any close engagement with the Jesus of the Gospels must at least notice his extraordinary dealings with the women he encountered.

John Bell went on to chair the committee for the 2005 production of *Church Hymnary* (fourth edition). The Preface makes specific mention of changes in the place of women since the publication of the third edition in 1973 – though some are oddly anachronistic. He refers to equal pay legislation: 'Women were still to be paid the same as men for doing the same job' – though the first two Equal Pay Acts preceded the publication of the earlier book. And the changes in the Church, 'New translations of scriptures, the ordination of women . . .'[210] both predate the third edition of *Church Hymnary*. I am surprised that a Scottish publication should appear to support the prejudicial view that no women were ordained until they were ordained in the Church of England.

The Foreword sets out the policy on archaic or inclusive language:

> Broadly speaking, where a text could be sensitively amended by the contemporizing of archaic language or by having an exclusive term replaced by an inclusive one, that was done. But where that was not possible, either the whole text was reworked or it was left intact.[211]

The fourth edition of *Church Hymnary* combines the new material and sources from *Common Ground* with the historic tradition represented in the third edition. Of the 825 items, 142 are by women (17 per cent), 93 (just over half, and 11 per cent of the total) by living women writers. By comparison, John Bell has 61 hymns, two-thirds of the total sum by living women.

Bernadette Farrell has seven texts, concentrating on liturgical texts and settings of psalms and Scripture passages. Ruth Duck is well represented with eight texts. Her writing explores the wealth of scriptural language and imagery for God. This is another rediscovery of recent hymn-writing. The Bible has many ways to speak of God, not only male and female, but animal, vegetable, mineral and abstract! So Duck enables us to sing of God as 'womb', 'brooding Spirit', 'Artist', 'wisdom', 'lamp', 'truth', 'vine', 'wellspring', and so on.[212] She follows through the female imagery where it occurs, for example, in 'Womb of life and source of being', she calls on the 'Brooding Spirit' to

> Labour with us, aid the birthing
> of a new world yet to be,
> free from status and division,
> free for love and unity.[213]

She also provides a lovely alternative to the doxology, with its heavily masculine language. Sung to the same tune as the traditional text:

Praise God, the Source of life and birth;
praise God, the Word, who came to earth;
praise God, the Spirit, holy flame:
all glory, honour, to God's name.[214]

By replacing the pronouns with 'God', the text avoids the repetition of 'him' quite naturally, and the recasting of the Trinity as Source, Word and Spirit, remains scriptural, but again replaces the heavily masculine 'Father, Son'. The text is set alongside the traditional form of the doxology, so is intended to supplement rather than oust Thomas Ken's text.

There is an American voice new to British publications, Mary Louise Bringle, with four texts. These include a hymn of human solidarity, 'When the hungry who have nothing share with strangers',[215] and a lovely text that deals with ageing. This begins with perhaps the most feared aspect of growing old, mental frailty:

When memory fades and recognition falters,
when eyes we love grow dim and minds confused.

It ends by setting the finitude of passing lives in the context of eternity:

All joys remain, with heavenly light pervading;
no valued deed will ever be undone.
Your mind enfolds all finite acts and offerings,
held in your heart, our deathless life is won![216]

But the strongest presence among the living women writers – and one of the strongest in the book – is the New Zealand writer, Shirley Erena Murray, whose story appears in this book. The third edition of *Church Hymnary* had attempted to be global and ecumenical. In the end, neither aim quite succeeded, but the vision of a hymnody that was inclusive in purpose did not go away.

In Australia, an ecumenical committee had been formed as early as 1968, representing Anglican, Congregational, Methodist and Presbyterian Churches, with the Roman Catholics joining in 1974. The three 'Free Church' denominations joined together in June 1977, and the *Australian Hymn Book* was published that autumn. It was republished in 1979 as *With One Voice* with a Catholic supplement.[217]

This was an inspirational collection. It provided a springboard for later work in New Zealand, as we shall see. And when the committee for *Hymns & Psalms*[218] started to meet, with its aim of producing an ecumenical book for British churches, it was to *Church Hymnary* (third edition) and *With One Voice* that we looked for inspiration.

It was one of the first books to achieve some success in the ambitions of *Church Hymnary* (third edition), to be both ecumenical and global. There are a number of translations of texts from the non-English-speaking world, drawn from *Cantate Domino*[219] and World Council of Churches' publications. Some of these are translated by women, either missionaries or people from the communities from which the songs come.

Helen Taylor (1915–93, so still living when *With One Voice* was published), a Presbyterian missionary teacher in what was then Nyasaland (now Malawi), had already translated a number of texts by Malawian writers, and published them in her 1959 collection, *Tunes from Nyasaland*,[220] some set to traditional tunes. The publisher, the Overton Institute of the Livingstonia Mission, had a commitment to the publication of material from the non-English-speaking churches. Her translation of Tembo E. Maweleva's 'O praise the King of heaven' was first published in *Cantate Domino* IV[221] and then in *With One Voice* at no. 101.

Other texts were translated by people from the language community that the hymn came from. Kim Yung Oon (fl. 1950), Korean born, but educated in Canada, translated Tai Jun Park's text 'The Saviour's precious blood'.

The development and inclusion of world Christian music is a subject for another book! But it is part of the success story of the musical tradition that developed through the World Council of Churches and *Canatate Domino* IV, edited by Fred Kaan and Doreen Potter. The vision of *Church Hymnary* (third edition) brought people from the English-speaking Presbyterian churches onto its committee, and, through their publications, the dream of opening the treasure chest of global song has begun to be realized.[222]

With One Voice was too early to address issues of gender inclusivity. The Preface expresses a desire to be ecumenical and global, and talks about alterations to texts to eradicate archaisms, but makes no mention of gender. The main committee was all male, as was the music committee. There were two women on what they called the literary committee: Lady Hope Hewitt and Honor Mary Thwaites.

Of the 624 items, 67 are by women, just over 10 per cent. These include a large number of translations, by Borthwick, Cox and Winkworth, as well as translations of world hymns. There are 18 texts by living women writers. These appear rather eclectic. Valerie Dunn's 'Man more than man' comes in from the folk tradition, and Pat Uhl's 'O what a gift' from the Fisherfolk. There are a couple of new writers. Catherine Arnott's (1927–) text, 'God who stretched the spangled heavens', addresses contemporary issues that were at the forefront of people's minds in the 1970s:

> We have ventured worlds undreamed of
> since the childhood of our race;
> known the ecstasy of winging
> through untravelled depths of space;
> probed the secrets of the atom,
> yielding unimagined power,
> facing us with life's destruction
> or our most triumphant hour.[223]

Five of the texts (about a third of the texts by living women writers) are new translations of German hymns by committee member Honor Mary Thwaites.

The best known is her translation of Karl Johann Philipp Spitta's 'O selig' Haus', as 'Happy the home'. This gained currency as a wedding hymn, and appears in Jubilate Hymns' *Wedding Book*.[224] The image of the home has an old-fashioned feel to it. It consists of 'man and wife', and children, and culminates when domestic bliss enters the heavenly home:

> until each one, their work on earth completed
> comes to your Father's house to meet him there.[225]

Her translation of Luther's 'Ein' feste Burg', 'A mighty stronghold is our God', is heavily masculine in language: 'but for us fights the rightful Man', for example. The last verse is different from Thomas Carlyle's translation except for the notorious lines:

> And though they take our life
> goods, honour, children, wife.

Fascinatingly, the Carlyle translation is retained unchanged in the fourth edition of *Church Hymnary*. I can remember long discussions about alterations to this verse in the *Hymns & Psalms* committee, where the first person we asked to change it failed to understand the point. In the end, Rupert Davies proposed an acceptable text, which did not suggest that the singers were all married men!

Thwaites did write one original text, which seems to have broken free of her rather backward-looking style. This was a collaboration with her husband Michael Rayner Thwaites, and was published only in the HarperCollins short collection, *Sing Alleluia*.[226] It is an interesting text, as it focuses on the spirituality of Australia, and in the middle of the three verses makes an attempt to honour the indigenous inhabitants and recognize some of the implications of European settlement:

People of the ancient Dreamtime,
they who found this country first,
ask with those, the later comers,
will our dream be blest or curst?[227]

Along with the slow rediscovery of world Christian music, this text demonstrates a desire, in Australia and New Zealand, to recognize the uniqueness of this part of the world. From the days when Edmund Hillary's conquest of Everest was acclaimed as a British triumph (to say nothing of people's attitude to Sherpa Temsing!), to the bicentenary of Australia in 1988 and 150th anniversary of the New Zealand Treaty in 1990, attitudes have undeniably and justifiably changed.

Shirley Erena Murray describes this as part of her own awakening as a hymn-writer. The hymns she grew up with were located in the ethos and natural environment of the Northern hemisphere, in which, at the very least, the strong connection between Christmas and winter was totally unnatural in the South. She also wanted to speak from the bicultural politics of New Zealand, but there was nothing in hymnody either to express the vision or to make it possible for other voices to be heard.

Murray also took inspiration from the Australian *With One Voice*, but went on to work with the New Zealand Hymnbook Trust to produce *Alleluia Aotearoa*.[228] Shirley's husband John Murray wrote the Preface to the first edition in 1993, in which he acknowledged the book's debt to the New Zealand Supplement to *With One Voice* of 1982.

The aim of *Alleluia Aotearoa* is 'to include all traditions, languages and styles, both of word and music, found in our Churches'.[229] The book focuses on new texts and tunes, and many of the committee members contributed items. The committee was ecumenical and three of the eight members were women. The vision of cultural inclusivity was not quite achieved, though there are certainly a substantial number of texts by Maori and Island writers or groups of writers. There were advisers representing the Pacific Island and Maori community, but I have had some email correspondence with Shirley Erena Murray regretting the fact that they were not more systematically involved.

John Murray addresses his wife's concern for hymns that arise from their New Zealand setting:

> What makes a New Zealand hymn? . . . not just the use of natural imagery . . not just the use of Maori words . . . but perhaps more importantly, our belief as a people, in a society that is fair and equal, doing justice and loving peace, in a country that is green and godly . . .[230]

The book draws on a relatively small number of authors and composers. It is interesting that Shirley Erena Murray comments on the lack of text-writers in comparison with composers. My own experience in editing resources is the opposite, but here there is a sense of a few people, full of creativity and ideas, but not part of a wider pool of writers. Of 162 items, Shirley Murray has written words or tunes or both for 62, a massive proportion of the material. Cecily Sheehy has 15 texts, so between them they make up nearly half the book.

Betty Wendelborn is also represented, with translations from Julian of Norwich, Mechthild of Magdeburg, and Hildegard.[231] She draws on Hildegard's concept of greening, *viriditas*, as the healing of the earth, a topic just then coming into prominence, particularly in the Southern hemisphere.

> In the shaking of God's mantle,
> by the drops of precious dew:
> so the gentle rain on earth life will renew.
>
> May the Spirit of creation
> by whose breath we are as one,
> heal our body with the gift of compassion.[232]

The hymns are lively and fresh. They certainly have a different feel from the hymnody of the Northern hemisphere. Christmas is confidently claimed by the South:

> Here where the sheep are grazing,
> where summer sun is blazing,
> harvests for others ripen –
> food for the world can grow:

Christ of a cold December,
quicken us to remember
poverty in a stable,
need, like the sting of snow.[233]

The cold, dark Northern Christmas is a reminder to the summer of
poverty and need. There is a passion for justice and concern for the
health of the natural world.

Let there be greening,
birth from the burning,
water that blesses and air that is sweet,
health in God's garden,
hope in God's children,
regeneration that peace will complete.[234]

One of the joys of the book is the unselfconscious juxtaposition of children's and adult texts, thrown together by the alphabetical ordering of
the hymns. We have enjoyed singing Cecily Sheehy's 'Colour me free'
and 'One, two, three, alleluia', but also her thoughtful text of the Holy
Spirit, 'O the Spirit she moves on the water', with its strong feminine
language about the third person of the Trinity.

O the Spirit she's dark and she's brooding,
unpredictable, wild without fear,
she can roar with the power of a hurricane wind.
Do you see, do you hear?
And her silence becomes so profound we forget
she is there.[235]

The other tradition to make a concerted effort to use inclusive language
and imagery comes from North America, in the liberal churches of
Canada and the USA. Leask comments particularly on *Voices United*,[236]
published by the United Church of Canada, which

drew substantially from the work of a growing number of women
hymn writers, including Sylvia Dunstan and two other Canadian
writers whose work is known outside Canada – Judith Fetter and
Margaret Clarkson. Hymns by women writers from Great Britain,
the United States and New Zealand, most of whom have published
separate collections of their work, are included.[237]

This was one of the few books to look specifically at hymn collections published by women, including *Reflecting Praise*. Of 974 items, 179 are by women, about 20 per cent, and there are 105 texts by 58 living women writers. It is very exciting to see so many new living writers. A number of those no longer living have died during or not long before the publication of the book. Most have one or two texts, but there are 10 by Ruth Duck and 13 by Sylvia Dunstan (who died during the gestation of the book). Shirley Erena Murray has 12 texts.

The Preface and Introduction lay a strong emphasis on inclusivity, both in the use of world music and in gender language. They have not shrunk from female language for God, having included my own text 'Dear Mother God'.[238]

This text is typical of feminist hymns that explore female imagery of God. It is a scriptural exploration of the image of God as a mother bird in Deuteronomy 32.11, and the way in which humans, in the image of God, may also find their wings, as promised in Isaiah 40.31. The hymn ends with hope of freedom for all people.

> Dear Mother God, your wings are warm around us.
> We are enfolded in your love and care.
> Safe in the dark, your heartbeat's pulse surrounds us,
> you call to us, for you are always there.
>
> You call to us, for we are in your image.
> We wait on you, the nest is cold and bare –
> high overhead your wingbeats call us onward,
> filled with your power, we ride the empty air.
>
> Let not our freedom scorn the needs of others.
> We climb the clouds until our strong heart sings.
> May we enfold our sisters and our brothers
> till all are strong, till all have eagles' wings.

Where next?

Richard Watson ended his book *The English Hymn* with the gloomy prediction: 'I have written this book in the hope of earning some respect for the hymn while it is still a part of a popular culture, before it becomes a subject of study for Church historians and antiquarians.'[239] But hymn books are still being published in huge numbers. The early years of the new millennium have seen a kind of consolidation in some of the most active areas of writing, in very large books (over 1,000 texts in many) called, 'Combined' or 'Complete' editions, for example *Complete Mission Praise, Complete Celebration Hymnal* and *Complete Anglican Hymns Old and New*.[240]

This is a little like what seems to have happened towards the end of the nineteenth century, and represents a desire to grasp and organize the creativity of a very prolific period. But in this case it does not mark the end of hymn-writing in the extraordinary way that the beginning of the twentieth century did. As editor of *Worship Live* I receive a constant stream of new writing. We are never short of material – and good, creative material – for our thrice-yearly issues.

There is also a lot of activity in specialist fields, including that of women's or feminist hymnody. In 2003, the Episcopal Church in the USA brought out *Voices Found: Women in the Church's Song*, not just as an academic resource but in a pew version for public worship.[241] Women's voices are very much heard now. Many writers are bringing out their own collections of texts. Mary Louise (Mel) Bringle published *Joy and Wonder, Love and Longing* in 2002; June Boyce-Tillman's *Rainbow to Heaven* came out in 2006; and my own hymns and other worship material were collected in *Eagles' Wings and Lesser Things* in 2007.[242]

But there are also changes in the way that music is used and resourced in worship. Many of my students now are simply not used to singing hymns as part of worship. If they sing, it is worship songs, but congregational singing is itself in decline. Emerging church, or fresh expressions of church often include very different worship styles. Quite apart from oddities such as 'Skate-boarding church', many worshipping communities are turning to performance music, or contemplative worship styles, in which it would seem eccentric to invite everyone to stand up and sing a hymn together. Where this does still happen, often the words are digitally projected, and drawn from large electronically held collections such as *Songselect* or *Hymnquest*[243] which contain thousands of texts and are constantly updated.

The internet provides an enormous resource. Every publisher and supplier of words and music for worship has a presence on the net. Out-of-copyright texts are available from sites such as The Cyberhymnal,[244] and authors are as likely to publish their texts on specialist sites as in books or collections.

Music for worship is still a vivid and vital world. I am delighted that women are finding their voices again, though I mourn the lost years.

And I am proud to count many wonderful women writers among my friends. I honour them.

Notes

1 *Hymns Ancient and Modern for use in the Services of the Church*, London: William Clowes and Sons, 1904.

2 *The English Hymnal*, London: Henry Frowde, 1906.

3 Donald Gray, 'The Birth and Background of the English Hymnal', in Alan Luff (ed.), *Strengthen for Service: 100 years of the English Hymnal 1906–2006*, Norwich: Canterbury Press, 2005, pp. 1–30, p. 3.

4 Preface, *The English Hymnal*, pp. iii–ix, p. v.

5 *The English Hymnal*, no. 402. The original Bunyan text starts 'Who would true valour see', which Dearmer thought too bold a statement for a congregation to sing.

6 'I bind unto myself to-day', no. 212; 'In the bleak midwinter', no. 25, *The English Hymnal*. See also pp. 97–8, 142–3.

7 *Songs of Praise*, Oxford: Oxford University Press, 1925, p. iii.

8 Preface, *Songs of Praise*, pp. iii–ix, p. iv

9 Preface, *Songs of Praise*, p. v.

10 Preface, *Songs of Praise*, p. v.

11 Preface, *Songs of Praise*, p. v.

12 *Songs of Praise: Enlarged Edition*, London: Oxford University Press, 1931.

13 Percy Dearmer (comp.), *Songs of Praise Discussed: A handbook to the best-known hymns and to others recently introduced*, London: Oxford University Press, 1933, p. 479.

14 Maria Penstone, 'When lamps are lighted in the town', *Songs of Praise: Enlarged Edition*, no. 378, vv. 1 (l. 3), 2 (l. 1), 4.

15 *The Public School Hymn Book*, edited by a committee of the Headmasters' Conference, London: Novello & Co., 1949, 1959.

16 John Wilson, 'The Public School Hymn Book 1949 and 1959', *Bulletin of the Hymn Society* 89, Summer 1960, pp. 1–10, p. 9.

17 Eric Routley, 'Hymns. Stop the Plane, I want to get off', in Lionel Dakers (ed.), *English Church Music*, Croydon: RSCM, 1974, p. 11, cited in Robin Leaver, *A Hymn Book Survey 1962–80*, Bramcote, Nottinghamshire: Grove Worship Series, no. 71, January 1980, p. 3. Leaver cites Routley in an article in the *Hymn Society Bulletin*, vol. 5, no. 14, January 1965, p. 245, saying, 'At present the words are just not there to be had', Leaver, 'A Hymn Book Survey', p. 3, n. 1.

18 Ysenda Maxtone Graham, *The Real Mrs Miniver: Jan Struther's Story*, London: John Murray, 2001, p. 57.

19 Maxtone Graham, *The Real Mrs Miniver*, p. 12.

20 Jan Struther, 'Lord of all hopefulness', *Songs of Praise*, 1931, no. 65.

21 Maxtone Graham, *The Real Mrs Miniver*, p. 56. It is interesting that Fred Kaan says something similar about his own writing – not that he stands at a distance from Christianity, but that his writing gains in freshness from the fact

that he has not grown up with the weight of the English hymn tradition on his pen.

22 Maxtone Graham, *The Real Mrs Miniver*, p. 59.

23 Jan Struther, 'When a knight won his spurs', *Songs of Praise*, 1931 no. 377.

24 Gordon S. Wakefield, 'The Hymnody of the Past Fifty Years', *Hymn Society Bulletin*, no. 114, Winter 1968, pp. 239–51, p. 242.

25 Jan Struther, 'Lord of all hopefulness, no. 534, 'When a knight won his spurs', no, 535, 'Round the earth a message runs', no. 728, *Congregational Praise*.

26 Eleanor Farjeon, *Magic Casements*, London: Allen & Unwin, 1941, p. 10, cited in Anne Harvey, *A Life Kept Always Young: An Introduction to Eleanor Farjeon*, Cheltenham: Dymock Poets Archive & Study Centre, Occasional Papers Series, no. 7, 1999, p. 2.

27 Eleanor Farjeon, *Edward Thomas, the Last Four Years: Book One of the Memoirs of Eleanor Farjeon*, London: Oxford University Press, 1958, p. x.

28 Annabel Farjeon, *Morning has Broken: A Biography of Eleanor Farjeon*, London: Julian MacRae, 1986, p. 183.

29 Eleanor Farjeon, unpublished memoir, cited in Farjeon, *Morning has Broken*, p. 140.

30 Farjeon, *Morning has Broken*, p. 142.

31 http://www.childrensbookcircle.org.uk/farjeon.asp (accessed 29 June 2009).

32 Farjeon, *Morning has Broken*, p. 154.

33 Dearmer, *Songs of Praise Discussed*, no. 30, p. 16.

34 Eleanor Farjeon, 'People look East, the time is near', in Percy Dearmer, *The Oxford Book of Carols*, Oxford: Oxford University Press, 1928, no. 133, vv. 2 (ll. 1–2), 4 (ll. 1–2), 6 (ll. 1–2, 5–6).

35 *Songs of Praise: Enlarged Edition*, no. 63

36 J. R. Watson, *The English Hymn: A Critical and Historical Study*, Oxford: Clarendon Press, 1997, p. 528.

37 Kenneth Long, *The Music of the English Church*, London: Hodder & Stoughton, 1971, p. 384.

38 Long, *The Music of the English Church*, p. 402.

39 Long, *The Music of the English Church*, p. 402.

40 H. Davies, *Worship and Theology in England 1900–1965*, Princeton: Princeton University Press, 1962, vol. V, p. 116.

41 See above, p. 161.

42 Preface to *Congregational Praise*, London: Independent Press, 1951, pp. iii–iv, p. iiii.

43 *The English Hymnal Service Book*, London: Oxford University Press, 1962; *The Baptist Hymn Book*, London: Psalms and Hymns Trust, 1962.

44 Cyril Taylor, Review, *The English Hymnal Service Book*, in *Hymn Society of Great Britain and Northern Ireland Bulletin* 96, Summer 1962, pp. 111–18, p. 118.

45 Eric Routley, 'Comment', *The English Hymnal Service Book*, in *Hymn Society of Great Britain and Northern Ireland Bulletin* 96, Summer 1962, pp. 120–4, p. 123. V–W is Ralph Vaughan Williams, the music editor of *The English Hymnal* of 1906; Percy Dearmer was the instigator and overall editor.

46 Caryl Micklem, Review of *Baptist Hymn Book*, in *The English Hymnal Service Book*, in *Hymn Society of Great Britain and Northern Ireland Bulletin* 96, Summer 1962, pp. 118–20, p. 120.

47 Routley, 'Comment', p. 124.

48 Routley, *Hymns and Human Life*, p. 203.

49 Janet Wootton, 'Hymn-writing: The Lost Generation', *Hymn Society Bulletin* 257, vol. 19, no. 1, January 2009, pp. 9–16, p. 16.

50 Brian Wren, *Hymns for Today*, Louisville KY: Westminster John Knox Press, 2009.

51 Letter from Brian Wren to Janet Wootton, by email, 10 February 2009, quoted by permission.

52 At that time a Permanent Private Hall of the University, of Congregational Foundation, offering ordination training to United Reformed Church and Congregational ordinands.

53 Hugh Cunliffe Jones, 'Wanted! New Hymn-Writers', in *The English Hymnal Service Book*, in *Hymn Society of Great Britain and Northern Ireland Bulletin* 105, December 1965, pp. 56–8.

54 Michael Hewlett, 'Thoughts about words', *Hymn Society of Great Britain and Northern Ireland Bulletin* 115, Spring 1969, pp. 11–14, p. 12.

55 Margaret Anne Leask, 'The development of English-language hymnody and its use in worship 1960–1995', University of Durham, 2000, thesis, DX214549, p. 99, citing 'Music in the Church: Consultation at Scottish Churches House, Dunblane'.

56 As in for example Richard Granville Jones' text 'God of concrete, God of steel', which appeared first in the *Boys' Brigade Hymnbook*, Hemel Hempstead: Boys' Brigade, 1958, no. 3, and was included in many of the supplements and short collections of the 1970s and 1980s.

57 Arthur S. Holbrook, 'Annual Conference 1968', *Hymn Society of Great Britain and Northern Ireland Bulletin* 114, Winter 1968, pp. 235–9, p. 238.

58 See Eric Routley, *A Panorama of Christian Hymnody*, Collegeville MN: Liturgical Press, 1979; also 2nd edn, ed. and expanded by Paul Richardson, Chicago IL: GIA Publications, 2005.

59 Ian Fraser, 'Beginnings at Dunblane', in Robin Leaver and James H. Litton (eds), *Duty and Delight: A Memorial Tribute to Eric Routley (1917–1982), Ministry, Church Music, Hymnody*, Norwich: Canterbury Press, 1985, pp. 171–90, p. 180.

60 *Dunblane Praises for Schools: I Juniors*, Dunblane, 1970.

61 *Hymns & Songs: A Supplement to the Methodist Hymn Book*, London: Methodist Publishing House, 1969; *100 Hymns for Today: A Supplement to Hymns Ancient and Modern*, London: William Clowes & Sons, 1969.

62 Marion Collihole tells her story at pp. 235–43.

63 *Rejoice and Sing*, London: Oxford University Press, 1991.

64 Ann Phillips, 'Into a world of dark', *New Church Praise*, no. 43, vv. 5–6, *Rejoice and Sing*, no. 325, v. 6.

65 *Church Hymnary*, 3rd edn, Oxford: Oxford University Press, 1973.

66 Carol Rose Ikeler, 'The Church is wherever God's people are praising', *Church Hymnary*, 3rd edn, no. 427, vv. (1 (l. 1), 2 (ll. 3–4), 3 (ll. 3–4).

67 John M. Barkley, 'The Revision, 1963–1973', in James Moffatt (ed.),

Handbook to the Church Hymnary, Third Edition, London: Oxford University Press, 1927, pp. 55–67, p. 58.

68 Introduction to *Church Hymnary* 3rd edn, p. xi.

69 *Church Hymnary*, 3rd edn, no. 229.

70 *Church Hymnary*, 3rd edn, nos. 227 and 228.

71 *Church Hymnary*, revised edition, London: Oxford University Press, 1927.

72 *Songs for the Seventies: A Collection of Contemporary Hymns*, Great Yarmouth: Galliard, Edinburgh: Saint Andrew Press, 1972.

73 Peter D. Smith (ed.), *Faith, Folk and Clarity*, London: Galliard, 1967.

74 Peter D. Smith, Preface, *Faith, Folk and Clarity*, p. iii.

75 Karl Frederick Dallas, 'The Family of Man', in *Faith, Folk and Clarity*, p. 20.

76 Marion Collihole, 'Woman racked and torn with pain', *Faith, Folk and Clarity*, p. 16 (ii), vv. 1, 4.

77 Judith Piepe, 'They say you've gone to heaven, but I have heard them tell', *Faith, Folk and Clarity*, p. 40, vv. 2 (l. 4), 5 (ll. 3–4).

78 Susan Tuck, 'Just on the threshold they tell you you're waiting', *Faith, Folk and Clarity*, p. 37, v. 2 (l. 1, 6–7).

79 *Worship Live* 44, June 2009.

80 Sue Gilmurray, 'It used to be normal to buy and sell people', *Worship Live* 38, October 2007, p. 3, vv. 1 (ll. 1–2, 9–10), 2 (ll. 1–2, 9–10).

81 *Faith, Folk and Clarity*, p. 31.

82 *Faith, Folk and Clarity*, p. 34.

83 Marian Collihole, 'Lament of an old age pensioner', in Peter D. Smith (ed.), *Faith, Folk and Nativity: A New Collection of Songs*, London: Galliard, 1968, p. 27.

84 'A Christmas Spiritual', *Faith, Folk and Nativity*, p. 4, v. 1 (ll. 1–4).

85 *New Catholic Hymnal*, London: Faber Music Ltd., 1971.

86 D. Holbrook and E. Poston (eds), *Cambridge Hymnal*, Cambridge: Cambridge University Press, 1967.

87 Wilfrid Trotman (ed.), *Praise the Lord: Hymns, Psalms and Canticles for Community Use*, London: G. Chapman, 1966; John Ainslie, Stephen Dean and Paul Inwood (eds), *Praise the Lord, revised and enlarged*, London: Geoffrey Chapman, 1972.

88 Introduction, *Praise the Lord, revised and enlarged*, pp. vi–vii, p. vi.

89 Cardinal Heenan, Foreword, *Praise the Lord, revised and enlarged*, p. v.

90 Valerie Dunn is a Canadian Presbyterian; three of her texts appear in Peter D. Smith (ed.), *Faith, Folk and Festivity*, London: Galliard, 1967. 'Man more than man' appeared in *Faith, Folk and Festivity* on p. 17 (ii), and is no. 202 in *Praise the Lord, revised and enlarged*.

91 *Laudate*, Brandon: Decani Music, 1999.

92 *Praise the Lord, revised and enlarged*, no. 253, *New Catholic Hymnal*, no. 301.

93 Sr Margarita, 'Jesus Christ our Lord and God', *Praise the Lord, revised and enlarged*, no. 87, chorus and v. 4.

94 *Praise the Lord, revised and enlarged*, nos. 310, 311 and 315, hymns for times of day, are attributed to them.

95 Smith (ed.), *Faith, Folk and Festivity*, 'There is a world', p. 28, 'Harvey', p. 30.

96 Estelle White, 'There is a world where people come and go', v. 1 (ll. 2–4) and chorus.

97 Janet Wootton, 'Interview with Estelle White', *Feminist Theology*, vol. 8, January 2000, pp. 85–9.

98 Wootton, 'Interview with Estelle White', p 87.

99 *Folk Praise*, Leigh on Sea: Kevin Mayhew, 1977.

100 *Celebration Hymnal*, Great Wakering: Mayhew-McCrimmon, 1976.

101 See below, pp. 190–2. Several writers refer to the influence of the Fisherfolk in their own accounts in this book.

102 Estelle White, 'Moses I know you're the man', *Celebration Hymnal*, no. 197, chorus.

103 Estelle White, 'Breath of God, O Holy Spirit', *Hymns Old and New*, Roman Catholic edn, Stowmarket: Kevin Mayhew Ltd., 1989, no. 71, vv. 1, 4.

104 Estelle White, 'I saw the grass, I saw the trees' *Celebration Hymnal*, no. 140, vv. 2 (ll. 7–8, 10–12), 3 (ll. 7–8).

105 Stephen Dean (ed.), *Celebration Hymnal*, vol. 2, Great Wakering: Mayhew McCrimmon Ltd., 1984; Stephen Dean (ed.), *New Songs of Celebration*, Great Wakering: Mayhew McCrimmon Ltd., 1989.

106 *Celebration Hymnal*, nos. 195 and 243.

107 *Celebration Hymnal*, vol. 2, nos 394 and 593.

108 http://www.ocp.org/ (accessed 19 September 2009).

109 http://www.ocp.org/artists/840 (accessed 30 September 2009).

110 *Let's Praise*, London: Jubilate Hymns, 1988, no. 23; *Carol Praise*, London: Jubilate Hymns, 1987, no. 74.

111 Bernadette Farrell, 'Praise to you, O Christ our Saviour', *New Songs of Celebration*, no. 788, v. 3.

112 *The Source 3*, Stowmarket: Kevin Mayhew, 2005, no. 1454, *Church Hymnary*, 4th edn, Norwich: Canterbury Press, 2005 no. 97.

113 Bernadette Farrell, 'O God, you search me and you know me', *The Source 3*, no. 1454, v. 5.

114 Bernadette Farrell, 'Longing for light, we wait in darkness', *The Source 3*, no. 1409, vv. 3 (ll. 3–4), 4 (ll. 3–4).

115 Betty Pulkingham and Jeanne Harper (comps), *Sound of Living Waters Songs of Renewal*, London: Hodder & Stoughton, 1974.

116 Betty Pulkingham and Jeanne Harper, 'Foreword' (the book actually says, 'Foreward' which could be a mistake or a deliberate pun), *Sound of Living Waters*, pp. 7–8, p. 7.

117 *Sound of Living Waters*, no. 83.

118 *Godspell*, musical by Stephen Schwartz and John-Michael Tebelak, 1971; the Foreword to *Sound of Living Waters* mentions the musical.

119 *Sound of Living Waters*, no. 26.

120 *Sound of Living Waters*, no. 59.

121 See below, pp. 308–12.

122 Pulkingham and Harper, Foreword, p. 7.

123 *Sound of Living Waters*, no. 86.

124 Betty Pulkingham and Jeanne Harper, *Fresh Sounds*, London: Hodder & Stoughton, 1976, no. 33.

125 Mimi Farra, 'Alleluia, sons of God arise', *Sound of Living Waters*, no. 86; Priscilla Porter, 'Fear not, rejoice and be glad', *Sound of Living Waters*, no. 59, last line.

126 Betty Pulkingham and Jeanne Harper, Foreword, *Fresh Sounds*, p. 5.

127 Roland Fudge, Peter Horrobin and Greg Leavers (eds), *Mission England Praise*, Basingstoke: Marshall, Morgan & Scott, 1983; Peter Horrobin and Greg Leavers (eds), *Junior Praise*, Basingstoke: Marshall Pickering, 1986; M. Perry and D. Peacock (eds), *Carol Praise*, London: Jubilate Hymns/Marshall Pickering/ HarperCollins Religious, 1987; David Peacock and Geoff Weaver (eds), *World Praise*, London: Jubilate Hymns/Marshall Pickering, 1993; Peter Horrobin and Greg Leavers (eds), *Complete Junior Praise: The Best-selling Songbook for Children and Young People*, London: Collins, 2008; M. Perry and D. Peacock (eds), *Carol Praise 2006*, London: Harper Collins, 2006; Peter Horrobin and Greg Leavers (eds), *Complete Mission Praise*, London: Marshall Pickering (HarperCollins), 1999; Peter Horrobin and Greg Leavers (eds), *Complete Mission Praise*, London: Collins, 2005.

128 http://www.springharvest.org/ (accessed 28 September 2009).

129 Noel and Tricia Richards, 'Called to a battle, heavenly war', in Peter Horrobin and Greg Leavers (eds), *New Mission Praise*, London: Marshall Pickering, 1996, no. 13, *Complete Mission Praise* (1999), no. 811; *Songs of Fellowship 2*, Eastbourne: Kingsway Music, 1998, no. 681, ll. 5–6. Graham Kendrick (ed.), *The Source*, Stowmarket: Kevin Mayhew, 1998, no. 61; Graham Kendrick (ed.), *The Source, Combined Words Edition*, Stowmarket: Kevin Mayhew, 2005, no. 61.

130 *Songs of Fellowship*, Eastbourne: Kingsway Music, 1991.

131 *Songs of Fellowship 3*, Eastbourne: Kingsway Music, 2003; *Songs of Fellowship 4*, Eastbourne: Kingsway Music, 2007. Kingsway had been publishing *Songs of Fellowship* since 1982.

132 Vicky Beeching, 'Your voice is the voice that', *Songs of Fellowship 3*, no. 1680, chorus (ll. 1, 5–6).

133 Vicky Beeching and Steve Mitchinson, 'There's no-one like our God', in *Songs of Fellowship 3*, no. 1554, v. 2.

134 Leask, 'The development of English-language hymnody', p. 361.

135 See below, pp. 244–53.

136 Elizabeth Cosnett, 'Language in Hymns: One Woman's Experience', *Bulletin of the Hymn Society* 182, January 1990, pp. 158–63, p. 159.

137 Cosnett, 'Language in Hymns', p. 159.

138 Donald Webster, *The Hymn Explosion and its Aftermath*, Croydon: Royal School of Church Music, 1992, p. 4.

139 Webster, *The Hymn Explosion and its Aftermath*, p. 6.

140 See p. 239.

141 See p. 295.

142 Brian Wren, Fred Kaan and Fred Pratt Green, 'New Hymnody: Some Problems and Prospects', in Leaver and Litton (eds), *Duty and Delight*, pp. 217–88.

143 Wren, Kaan and Pratt Green, 'New Hymnody', p. 224.

144 Brian Wren, *What Language Shall I Borrow? God-talk in Worship: A Male Response to Feminist Theology*, London: SCM Press, 1989.

145 Rosemary Radford Ruether, *Sexism and God-talk: Towards a Feminist Theology*, London: SCM Press, 1983.

146 Rosemary Radford Ruether, *Women-Church: Theology and Practice of Feminist Liturgical Communities*, London: Harper and Row, 1985.

147 Ruether, *Women-Church*, p. 103

148 Ruether, *Women-Church*, p. 105

149 Ruether, *Women-Church*, p. 106

150 Sydney Carter, *Songs of Sydney Carter in the Present Tense*, Book 1, London: Galliard/Stainer & Bell, 1968, no. 12.

151 For Deborah, the judge of Israel, see Judges 4—5; for Athaliah, the only Queen, see 2 Kings 11; for Huldah, the prophet, see 2 Kings 22.14–20.

152 See Janet Wootton, 'Jesus Creed' and notes, in Janet Wootton, *Eagles' Wings and Lesser Things*, London: Stainer & Bell, 2007.

153 For Martha and Mary, see Luke 10.38–41, John 11.1–44; for the Syro-Phoenician woman, see Mark 7.24–30; for the woman at the well, see John 4.1–42.

154 Wren, *What Language*, pp. 160–70.

155 Wren, *What Language*, p. 161.

156 Judith Driver, 'Dance, dance, dance, let the Spirit move you', in Janet Wootton and June Boyce-Tillman (eds), *Reflecting Praise*, London: Stainer & Bell and Women in Theology, 1993, no. 34, v. 6.

157 Wil van Hilten, Marijke de Bruijne and Eileen Silcocks (eds), *Eva's Lied: 42 nieuwe liederen, onstaan binnen de feministische theologie*, Kampen: J. H. Kok, 1984.

158 Monica Furlong, 'Introduction: A 'Non-Sexist Community', in the St Hilda Community, *Women Included: A Book of Services and Prayers*, London: SPCK, 1991, pp. 5–15, p. 6.

159 Janet Morley and Hannah Ward (eds), *Celebrating Women*, London: Women in Theology and Movement for the Ordination of Women, 1986.

160 Morley and Ward (eds), *Celebrating Women*, p. 15

161 *Songs of God's People*, Oxford: Church of Scotland/Oxford University Press, 1988, no. 113, *Reflecting Praise*, no. 52, *Common Ground: A Song Book for All the Churches*, Edinburgh: Saint Andrews Press, 1998, no. 143, *Church Hymnary*, 4th edn, no. 721.

162 Janet Morley, *All Desires Known*, London: Movement for the Ordination of Women and Women in Theology, 1988.

163 Preface, Morley, *All Desires Known*, pp. 5–6, p. 5.

164 Preface, Morley, *All Desires Known*, p. 5.

165 Preface, Morley, *All Desires Known*, p. 5.

166 Preface, Morley, *All Desires Known*, p. 5.

167 Morley, *All Desires Known*, The Syrophoenician woman is the subject of the collect 'O God whose word is life' on p. 13; 'Eternal Wisdom' is the opening prayers, pp. 36–7, 38–9, 40–1, 42–3 and 44–5; Litany of penitence for the denial of women's authority is on pp. 34–5.

168 'Music', in *Women Included*, pp. 83–5, p. 83.

169 Peter Smith (ed.), *New Orbit: Songs and Hymns for Under Elevens*, Great

Yarmouth: Galliard, 1972. June Boyce-Tillman was the music editor. Her story appears at pp. 321–36.

170 *Who Are You Looking For? Easter Liturgies for the WCC Ecumenical Decade, Churches in Solidarity with Women, 1988–1998*, London: British Region of the Ecumenical Forum of European Christian Women and the Women's Interchurch Consultative Committee, 1988.

171 *Who Are You Looking For?*, p. 42.

172 *Who Are You Looking For?*, p. 6.

173 Fred Pratt Green, 'What tale is this our women bring?', p. 7, Colin Hodgetts, 'The Guardian', p. 17, Brian Wren, 'Woman in the night', p. 28 and 'Who is She', p. 30, *Who Are You Looking For?*

174 Lois Ainger, 'We know the songs of Zion from our youth', in Wootton and Boyce-Tillman (eds), *Reflecting Praise*, no. 53, v. 3 and chorus.

175 Cecily Taylor, 'Alleluia, Christ is risen', in Wootton and Boyce-Tillman (eds), *Reflecting Praise*, no. 30, v. 2.

176 Cecily Taylor, 'Some days the fog comes creeping', in Wootton and Boyce-Tillman (eds), *Reflecting Praise*, no. 46, v. 1.

177 Charlotte Elliott, 'Just as I am without one plea', vv. 3 (ll. 2–3), 7.

178 June Boyce-Tillman, 'It was dark in the dawn of time', in Wootton and Boyce-Tillman (eds), *Reflecting Praise*, no. 32, v. 5 (ll. 2–4).

179 See for example. Ezekiel 11.1.

180 John 3.8. *Ruach* in Hebrew and *pneuma* in Greek both mean 'breath' or 'wind' as well as 'spirit'.

181 As in Isaiah 61.1–2 and Luke 4.18–19.

182 Wootton and Boyce-Tillman (eds), *Reflecting Praise*, no. 34.

183 June Boyce-Tillman, 'We shall go out with hope of resurrection', in Wootton and Boyce-Tillman (eds), *Reflecting Praise*, no. 82, also now in *God is Good, God is Truth, God is Beauty, Praise Him*, Stowmarket: Kevin Mayhew, 2005, no. 547. See below, p. 331.

184 June Boyce-Tillman, 'Hildegard of faith unbending', in Wootton and Boyce-Tillman (eds), *Reflecting Praise*, no. 43.

185 Wootton and Boyce-Tillman (eds), *Reflecting Praise*, no. 26.

186 *God is Good, God is Truth*, no. 75.

187 *Pentecostarion*, The Easter Liturgy of the Greek Orthodox Church.

188 Janet Wootton, 'At break of day three women came', in Wootton and Boyce-Tillman (eds), *Reflecting Praise*, no. 31, vv. 1 (ll. 7–8), 2 (ll. 5–8).

189 John 20.17. This wins for her the title 'Apostola Apostolorum' (Apostle (female) of the apostles), given to her by Hippolytus, Bishop of Rome (c. 170–235).

190 Janet Wootton, 'Jacob, he has a voice', p. 50, 'Welcome Sophia', pp. 48–9, 'Esther in the palace, dreaming', p. 56, 'I am Abishag', pp. 52–4, 'The God of Jephthah and his daughter', p. 52, in Wootton, *Eagles' Wings*.

191 Wootton, 'Jacob, he has a voice', vv. 2, 4.

192 John Bell, 'There is a line of women', *One is the Body*, Glasgow: Wild Goose Publications, 2002, no. 60.

193 Wren, *What Language*, p. 162.

194 Wren, *What Language*, p. 163, his emphasis.

195 Brian Wren, 'Bring many names', vv. 2, 3 (l. 1).

196 Wren, *What Language*, pp. 169–70.

197 Wren, *What Language*, p. 169.

198 Janet Wootton, 'Dear Mother God', no. 1, Judith Driver, 'My God is woman', no. 4, Brian Wren, 'Who is She', no. 9, Colin Hodgetts, 'If I raise my eyes to the hills', no. 3, in Wootton and Boyce-Tillman (eds), *Reflecting Praise*.

199 Jan Berry, 'Praise to God the world's Creator', in Wootton and Boyce-Tillman (eds), *Reflecting Praise*, no. 2, vv. 1 (ll. 2–3), 2 (ll. 5–8).

200 John Bell and Graham Maule, '*Eh Jesus ... Yes Peter ...*', Glasgow: Wild Goose Publications, 1987; *A Wee Worship Book*, Glasgow: Wild Goose Publications, 1999; John Bell and Graham Maule, *Love and Anger: Songs of Lively Faith and Social Justice*, Glasgow: Wild Goose Publications, 1997; John Bell and Graham Maule, *Wild Goose Songs*, vols 1–3, Glasgow: Wild Goose Publications, 1987, 1988, 1989.

201 William Pierson Merrill, 'Rise up O men of God'.

202 *Common Ground*, no. 109.

203 Kathy Galloway, 'She comes', *Common Ground*, no. 109, vv. 1–2.

204 Kathy Galloway, 'Oh the life of the world', *Common Ground*, no. 97, v. 1 (ll. 3–4).

205 Kathy Galloway, 'Sing for God's glory', *Common Ground* no. 111, v. 3 (ll. 1–4).

206 Jean Janzen, 'Mothering God', *Common Ground*, no. 88.

207 This is a reference to one possible translation of the action of the Spirit of God in Genesis 1.2, as the action of a bird, brooding over her eggs or chicks.

208 John Bell, 'She sits like a bird, brooding on the waters', *Common Ground*, no. 32, vv. 2 (ll. 3–4), 3.

209 John Bell and Graham Maule, 'Inspired by love and anger', *Heaven Shall Not Wait*, Glasgow: Wild Goose Publications/The Iona Community, 1987, no. 124, vv. 4 (ll. 1–4), 6.

210 John Bell, 'Introduction', *Church Hymnary*, 4th edn, pp. vii–x, p. vii.

211 Bell, 'Introduction', p. ix.

212 *Church Hymnary*, 4th edn, no. 118, 247, 707.

213 Ruth Duck, 'Womb of life and source of being', *Church Hymnary*, 4th edn, no. 118, v. 3 (ll. 5–8).

214 Ruth Duck, 'Praise God, the source of life and birth', *Church Hymnary*, 4th edn, no. 809.

215 Mary Louise Bringle, 'When the hungry who have nothing share with strangers', *Church Hymnary*, 4th edn, no. 258.

216 Mary Louise Bringle, 'When memory fades and recognition falters', *Church Hymnary*, 4th edn, no. 701, vv. 1 (ll. 1–2), 3 (ll. 5–8).

217 *With One Voice: A Hymn Book for All the Churches*, London: Collins, 1979.

218 See above, p. 194.

219 *Cantate Domino*, 4th edn, Oxford: Oxford University Press, 1980.

220 Helen M. Taylor, *Tunes from Nyasaland*, London: Overton Institute of the Livingstonia Mission, 1959.

221 *Cantate Domino*, 4th edn, no. 18.

222 See Janet Wootton, 'Singing the land strange with the Lord's song', given to the joint meetings of the Hymn Societies in Opole, Poland, July 2009, to be

published in the *Bulletin of Internationale Arbeitsgemeinschaft für Hymnologie*, Spring 2010.

223 Catherine Arnott, 'God who stretched the spangled heavens', *With One Voice*, no. 112, v. 3.

224 *The Wedding Book*, London: Jubilate/Harper Collins, 1989, no 59; *With One Voice*, no. 495.

225 Honor Mary Thwaites, 'Happy the home that welcomes you, Lord Jesus', *With One Voice*, no. 495, v. 5 (ll. 3–4).

226 *Sing Alleluia*, London: HarperCollins, 1987.

227 Michael Rayner Thwaites and Honor Mary Thwaites, 'Lord of earth and all creation', *Sing Alleluia*, no. 62, v. 2.

228 *Alleluia Aotearoa*, Palmerston North: New Zealand Hymnbook Trust Inc., 1993.

229 Introduction, *Alleluia Aotearoa*, pp. vii–ix, p. vii.

230 Introduction, *Alleluia Aotearoa*, p. viii.

231 Betty Wendelborn, 'All will be well', no. 2, 'Great is the love that is divine', no. 56, 'In the shaking of God's mantle', no. 71, and 'We are a wheel, the circle of life', no. 145, in *Alleluia Aotearoa*.

232 Betty Wendelborn, 'In the shaking of God's mantle', *Alleluia Aotearoa*, no. 71.

233 Shirley Erena Murray, 'Come to this Christmas singing', *Alleluia Aotearoa*, no. 28, v. 3.

234 Shirley Erena Murray 'Touch the earth lightly', *Alleluia Aotearoa*, no. 143, v. 3.

235 Cecily Sheehy, 'Colour me free', no. 21, 'One, two, three alleluia', no. 111, 'O the Spirit she moves on the water', no. 109, v. 2, *Alleluia Aotearoa*.

236 *Voices United: The Hymn and Worship Book of the United Church of Canada*, Ontario: The United Church Publishing House, 1996.

237 Leask, 'The Development of English-Language Hymnody', p. 367.

238 Janet Wootton, 'Dear Mother God, your wings are warm around us', *Voices United*, no. 270.

239 Watson, *The English Hymn*, p. 532.

240 *Complete Anglican Hymns Old and New*, Buxhill: Kevin Mayhew, 2000 and 2002.

241 *Voices Found: Women in the Church's Song*, New York: Church Publishing Incorporated, 2003.

242 Mary Louise Bringle, *Joy and Wonder, Love and Longing*, Chicago: GIA Publications, 2002; June Boyce-Tillman, *A Rainbow to Heaven*, London: Stainer & Bell, 2006; Wootton, *Eagles' Wings*.

243 http://www.ccli.co.uk/songselect/, http://www.stainer.co.uk/hymnquest/.

244 http://www.hymntime.com/tch/.

Part Two

6

Ten Portraits of Contemporary Hymn-Writers

Marian Collihole

How it all began

'Please Miss, the bull's gone!' was my first published short story, well more of a snippet really, sent into a true story competition in the *Sunday Companion* magazine. The story began with an assumption on my part that the people of Smethwick spoke the same Queen's English that I had been brought up to speak in South Wales! I had mistakenly believed that a bull was a beast with four legs to be found in a field and of which one should be extremely wary.

Since I was only two weeks into my first teaching post, I was also blissfully unaware of all the rules, specifically the one that allowed the children to dispense with orderly lining up, should it be raining. Apparently, once the local factory hooter had sounded, the children could come in en masse. In my defence for what transpired, I must also point out the proximity of a slaughter house opposite the school, albeit out of sight.

So, when the children raced into my annex classroom, breathlessly explaining 'Please miss, the bull's gone', my imagination had gone into overdrive. Visions of a frightened, snorting animal charging into the playground came to mind. I hastily counted the children, locked them safely into the classroom and, armed with a metre-long ruler, crossed over to the main building and raced up the stairs to the Headmaster's room.

'Sir, a bull has escaped from the slaughter house', I announced, feeling rather brave and noble. In my excitement, I barely registered his bemused expression when I explained how I knew. Neither did the twinkle in his eye fully register. With one hand on the telephone to ring the police, he solemnly advised me to return to my children. Should I hear nothing further, it would be a false alarm and the children could be let out at playtime.

Because of the rain, it was in the afternoon before I was able to re-enter the main building. It was then that the reason for the twinkle became all too obvious. The 'bull' of course was the aforementioned hooter and every spare inch of space around the walls of the school hall was covered with paintings of rampaging bulls and myself and my board ruler being tossed up in the air or stuck on the sharpest-looking horns! However, I was paid a small fee for this story and so I think the last laugh was mine.

This story is relevant because it spurred me on to look out for other writing competitions. So it came about that I eventually saw a hymn-writing competition on the television. It was the time of the Aberfan landslide disaster, so I wrote my first hymn, 'Where is God?' It only reached the last 24, but Peter D. Smith was one of the judges, and he wrote asking if he could put my words to one of his tunes. I was delighted and even more so when it was published in the first of his *Faith, Folk* books. I think it fair to point out here that, in retrospect, I have not always liked what I have written. At the time, I was pleased with the words:

Understanding has been slow, but surely it has come,
Oh what grace to face the dark, yet only see the sun.[1]

Now, however, I worry that people might find those words rather glib. Words come easy. Life does not. I doubt whether the parents of the buried children would have felt empathy with those words of mine. We can only live and learn.

Peter, then, was my main source of encouragement in the early stages. He subsequently invited me to contribute my words to his three following books in the *Faith Folk* series and later to the *New Life*, *New Orbit* and *New Horizon* books, all published by Galliard, later taken into Stainer & Bell.

Other encouraging factors around this time were switching on the radio one morning and hearing my words being sung on the BBC *Services for Children* programme and also being told that one of my hymns was being sung in Australia at a Scout's jamboree. Also, Stainer & Bell were holding workshops in Bristol. On being invited to lead a folk-hymn-composing group there, I was delighted to find a minister and his wife were often singing my words at various concerts. They showed me the dates when mine had been sung. This gracious couple then told me two favourites were 'Away, away' and 'Love to a stable low'. I include here a line or so from each.

> To Joseph in a warning dream,
> The angel came at night,
> 'Take Mary and her little child
> From Herod's cruel blight'
> *Away, away, where can we go . . .*

> There was no guiding spirit
> To warn the Vietnamese,
> Just bullets from the sniper's gun,
> Smoke rising through the trees.
> *Chorus*[2]

The rest of the text interweaves the flight of Mary and Joseph with that of a Vietnamese family fleeing the guns and bombs of war.

And the other favourite:

> Heavenly Love came down
> Blazing along a star-lit beam,
> Warming its way through the town,
> Wrapping the earth in the fold of a dream.
> *Love to a stable low,*
> *Love through the world will grow.*

> Earthly love new-stirred,
> Waking to a different morn,
> Thrilling to the spreading word,
> Word of an infant, lowly born.
> *Chorus*

> Had that message come
> Through the television screen,
> Or with supersonic hum
> Would its impact so have been?
> *Chorus*

> Would that burning light,
> Coming to an age of science,
> Fizzle out the self-same night,
> Switched off in sophisticated defiance?
> *Chorus*

Yet that light still burns,
Though it came in ancient days,
Sometimes faint, then strong it turns,
In human hist'ry mapping its ways.
Chorus

Thus will it go on;
In our hearts ever refired.
Steadying to grow more strong,
Faith and hope and love inspired.
Chorus[3]

It was about this time that John Bailey, who was to prove as encouraging as Peter, approached me to contribute to his *Blueprint* series under prescribed headings. One of my favourites here was also under the theme of refugees and again the tune was written by Peter:

I saw the country's greedy fist,
Reaching out towards our land,
For all I saw, this much I missed,
'Twas our destruction being planned.

This was inspired by a political cartoon showing countries under threat as one of the major power's grasping hand hovered over them. As usual the words are simple, but the second and third verses hint at the despair of the outcasts and the complacency that can override our well-meaning attempts to help:

I guess some place will offer us
A Displaced Persons' Camp
A tent set out on barren fields
Or huts grown cold and damp.

Or they may even say to us,
'Come in and live, feel free'
But will they let us once forget
Such generosity?[4]

Throughout this time, Bernard Braley, who was then the Managing Director of Stainer & Bell, treated me with the utmost courtesy and friendliness, as did Peter and John, so it was a happy time for me. My last contact with Peter was when we were both invited to be on the panel responsible for choosing hymns for a new book called *One World Songs*.[5] I really enjoyed reading through all the entries, although we did have one amusing experience, when Peter pointed out that the words of 'Where is God', slightly updated, had been sent in under someone else's name. I did give my permission for it to be included, but at the same time I thought it would have been more courteous to have been asked to update it myself!

A friend lost my one and only copy, but I remember one of those that I had wished I had written:

Jesus was a baby,
Yours and mine and everyone's.[6]

Simple words that say such a lot.

I heard no more from Peter but now my new contact, John Bailey, was a great encouragement. He was about to edit a book for school assemblies called *Theme work*,[7] and gave me a list of headings for which he was seeking a mixture of poems, hymns/songs, stories and biographic entries. Since I was on a fortnight's holiday in my home town of Pontypridd at the time, I was able to produce an assortment and was greatly warmed when he included them all.

I was back into full-time teaching as my daughter was growing up. I had always loved teaching and now found myself with very little free time. I had a couple of tunes and words printed in June Tillman's *Oxford Assembly Book*,[8] published by Oxford University Press, which had published a singing game of mine a year of two before. But when June asked me to write about God as a woman, I declined. I understood the reasoning behind it of course, and sympathised, but two factors were behind my decision. First, I was teaching more and more children who rarely saw their fathers. I hoped that the words 'Our Father' might be a measure of comfort for them. Second, I think of God as asexual, more parent, than of one sex or another, and like to think that across the world people are saying the same words of prayer.

I might comment here that, as a woman writer, I can't honestly say that I have noticed any prejudice against me. If anything, I had more trouble trying to get feminists to understand that when I wrote the word 'Man', as in 'Man is and was and is to be', or 'Primitive Man, squatting in the earth',[9] I was meaning mankind or, even better, humankind. There was no intention of excluding the feminine race. Rhythmically the word sits better within the verses.

Influences and content

The content of my published hymns was of course, in part, directed by the headings I was given. But overall, it was governed by three influences in my life. First, being Welsh, I had a love of words, spoken, written or sung, but I also had the nostalgia or *hwyl* common to the Welsh, for my home town. Examples of this are evident in verses such as:

I walked up and up to where the mountain met the sky
I sat on a rock and I watched the world go by,
I wondered if the people in the valley down below,
Would stop to look up, as they hurried to and fro.

If they look only in front of them, they see the old pit wheel,
To some it may be ugly, but to most it means a meal,
To some it means a story told and many yet to tell.
They work beneath that signpost and they've come to know it well.

And if they look behind them, they see the huddling streets
The houses grey and grimy, set close in narrow pleats,
And here there is a river, a sudgey waste-filled stream,
Sullied by the dustlings from that daily cracking seam.

And yet I know they look up and see beyond the grime,
I know it from their laughter, their singing and their rhyme,
From the tiny stubborn flower thrusting from the backyard wall,
Defiant daub of colour in the greyness of it all.

© Marian Collihole

Again the words used are simple, but there is thought behind them. It speaks of our ability to rise above what is ugly in our lives and how we reach out for something to feed the spirit, whether it be poetry or music or the beauty of a humble flower. I remember visiting Sheffield in my student days and looking down at rows of long black factories. It looked so grim from the hilltop, but the guide told us an amazing fact, that Sheffield had more musical societies, choirs, bands and drama groups than any other town in the North. The parallel between the factory workers and the miners was easy to see and is immensely heartening.

Another song stems from the nostalgia for childhood and the dreams we had. So, in 'Walk with me', I wrote:

My childhood's in the flowers and the glade,
My teens are in the sunshine – and the shade.

And later:

Here a prince was wed or danced a budding star
Tho' the stage of life yet beckoned from afar.

© Marian Collihole

The second major influence on my content was an awareness of so
much injustice all around the world. My favourite on this theme is
the following, which picked up on the sympathy I felt as a child when
watching westerns at the 'Tuppenny Rush' cinemas, sympathy not for
the pioneers but for those who were hounded out of their homes.

Solitary, in its stillness,
Sits the bird upon the tree,
Looking down where once was laughter,
Once proud home of Cherokee.

Sings he out across the prairie,
Sings he out across the plain,
'Has the Redskin gone for ever,
Can't you feel his bitter pain?
Has the Redskin gone for ever,
Can't you feel his bitter pain?'

The second and third verses depict the emptiness of the lodge and the
disappearing buffalos from the prairie:

Once the prairie in its stillness,
Was but deceiving to the eye,
Many herding beasts it sheltered,
Many dreams so soon to die.

The fourth and fifth verses home in on demoralization of the proud and
the noble, and ends:

Desolate now, in its stillness,
For many a spirit's whispered on,
Left their sons to face indifference,
Just a bird to sing their song.

© Marian Collihole

The last line is the reason that I included the chorus when quoting from this one.

This was written in 1970, and it is hard to realize that the struggle for power, or greed or whatever it is that impels one country or race to bully another, still goes on.

Lastly, the influence underlying most of my writing is of course my love for God, my need for him and the comfort and uplift I can get only from him or those inspired by him.

> A Star singing, sings in the silence,
> Tuning its song from the hum of its light,
> The clouds muffle the sound of the singing,
> But the Star sings on, as pure as its light.
>
> © Marian Collihole

I used the star to personify the light of Jesus many times, as in this verse about Mother Teresa:

> Finding its way from Israel to Yugoslavia,
> A splinter of starlight entered the child,
> Who grasped it and held it until she could raise,
> The cross in its centre for lost ones to praise.
>
> They grasped it and held it until she could share.
> The Love of the Father with those without care.
>
> © Marian Collihole

I would like to finish with someone else's words. I mentioned before coming across words I wish I had written and this simple hymn by someone called Carey Landrey is definitely on my wish list. I find it incredibly beautiful. I play it at weddings, funerals, during communion and before services. I have only a copy of the page and have no idea of its source:

> The love I have for you, my Lord,
> Is only a shadow of your love for me,
> Only a shadow of your love for me
> Your deep, abiding love.[10]

I wish, I wish, I wish!

Notes

1 Marian Collihole, 'Woman racked and torn with pain', in Peter D. Smith (ed.), *Faith, Folk and Clarity*, London: Galliard, 1967, p. 16.

2 Peter D. Smith (ed.), *Faith, Folk and Nativity: A New Collection of Songs*, London: Galliard, 1968, p. 25.

3 Smith (ed.), *Faith, Folk and Nativity*, p. 31.

4 John Bailey (ed.), *Blueprint*, a series of reference books for use in secondary school assemblies, religious education and liberal studies classes, project work, church worship and Sunday school, adult education, four vols, London: Galliard, 1976, vol. 4.

5 *One World Songs*, London: Methodist Church Division of Social Responsibility/Methodist Publishing House, 1978.

6 Olive Grimsey, *One World Songs*, no. 59.

7 John Bailey (ed.), *Theme Work: Assembly Material for Junior, Middle and Lower Secondary Schools*, London: Stainer & Bell, 1981.

8 June Tillman (ed.), *The Oxford Assembly Book: Songs, Readings and Discussion for Primary and Middle School Assemblies*, Oxford: Oxford University Press, 1989.

9 Bailey (ed.), *Blueprint*, vol. 4.

10 Carey P. Landry, 'The love I have for you, O Lord', *Laudate*, no. 1999, v. 1.

Elizabeth Cosnett

During my childhood and adolescence, from the late 1930s to the 1950s, the idea of feminism was, of course, known but it was usually associated with the suffragettes and many assumed that women had automatically achieved equality along with the vote. The contribution of women to the war effort was appreciated but the profound effect it had had on their aspirations was not really understood. Equal pay for equal (not in those days 'equivalent') work was strongly opposed, partly by employers but also by many altruistic people of both sexes, who genuinely believed that a woman's health and fulfilment lay exclusively in the calling to serve her husband and children at home. When I started teaching in 1959, it was being phased in over a seven-year period.

One or two of our neighbours had expressed mild surprise that my parents had bothered with sending a girl to university. Fortunately for me, my family thought differently. I had enjoyed an excellent education at the type of girls' grammar school that would nowadays be considered very old-fashioned. All the senior posts were held by women, and the headmistress was particularly keen on debating and the ability to address an audience. Years later I was talking to a much younger and staunchly feminist colleague, who had attended a large, mixed, comprehensive school. By this time, nearly all senior posts in such schools were held by men.

My colleague was surprised that I had spoken in challenging terms to a male-dominated meeting. She assumed that a woman of my generation would have had no female role models in youth and would have been actively discouraged from public speaking, as she felt she had been. She was quite shocked when I described my education. Nevertheless, I grew up knowing that in order to get a university place, I should probably have to be better than a male candidate. I simply accepted this without resentment as a fact of life. It was not until much later, with the change to mixed-sex schools and colleges, that I became sensitized to the idea of systematic or cultural prejudice as distinct from individual injustice, and later still that the whole question of prejudice embedded in language became an issue.

Looked at in one way, the writing of hymns has played only a very small part in my life. I did not start until I was middle-aged, and it took me about twenty-five years to produce the collection of thirty-two hymns and four brief graces which was published by Stainer & Bell in 2001 and entitled *Hymns for Everyday Saints*.[1] I still write from time to time, usually in response to specific requests, but do not expect to produce enough in my lifetime to fill another volume. This does not bother me in the slightest. I see myself as a person who occasionally writes a hymn, rather than as a hymn-writer. This somewhat odd habit is, however, important to me in that it brings together my lifelong love of English literature, especially lyric verse, my interest in language and my commitment to the Church.

For many years, I taught English, and therefore see hymn-writing as a craft and take a professional pride in writing clearly and in getting the technical details of versification correct. I am also very aware of the community for which I write and of the vital distinction between expressing my own thoughts or feelings and fulfilling the needs of my fellow Christians whom I invite to make my words their own in worship. God demands integrity of a hymn-writer while the Church demands a certain self-effacement. The latter definitely excludes any hint of using other people's worship to propagate one's own political ideas, however worthy, but it does not exclude bringing one's passions and convictions before God in prayer. There is a fine balance to be struck and, as always, room for argument.

Luck or Providence, in the form of happening to meet the right people at the right time, played a large part in getting my work published. In the 1970s, my colleague and friend Ian Sharp, who was composing hymn tunes for various radio and television competitions, suggested that, as I had written an MA thesis entitled 'The Poet as Hymn Writer',[2] I might produce some texts for him. He also introduced me to the Hymn Society of Great Britain and Ireland and its annual conferences,[3] at which I met people concerned with writing, composing, editing and publishing. I was keen to learn and these people helped me enormously. I remember listening to Fred Pratt Green chatting in a completely informal way about his work, and the sessions on hymn tunes led by John Wilson. I am not a very musical person, and he helped me to understand the structure of traditional hymn tunes and the importance of where the climax comes.

One of my first texts for Dr Sharp was an early version of what later became 'Can man by searching find out God?'

Can man by searching find out God
or formulate his ways?
Can numbers measure what he is
or words contain his praise?

Although his being is too bright
for human eyes to scan,
his meaning lights our shadowed world
through Christ, the Son of Man.

Our boastfulness is turned to shame,
our profit counts as loss,
when earthly values stand beside
the manger and the cross.

We there may recognise his light,
may kindle in its rays,
find there the source of penitence,
the starting-point for praise.

There God breaks in upon our search,
makes birth and death his own:
he speaks to us in human terms
to make his glory known.[4]

This represented a personal effort on my part to get to grips with the idea of the Trinity and I do find something exciting and inspiring in theological ideas, usually fairly conventional ones.

At about the same time, I wrote a hymn for the patronal festival of my own church, Our Lady and Saint Nicholas, Liverpool, and persuaded the then Rector, Canon Donald Gray, to try it out on the congregation. Some weeks later, he asked me to show him any other hymns I had written. Months after I had forgotten all about this, I learned to my great surprise that he had shown my little folder of work to Canon Vincent Taylor, who was interested in including 'Can man by searching' in *More Hymns for Today* (1980),[5] the second of two supplements to *Hymns Ancient and Modern* (*A&M*) There followed quite a lengthy correspondence between myself and the *A&M* editors, who wanted some alterations, but were very ready to take into account my concerns and suggestions.

This searching critique by experts was sometimes painful but hugely benefited the final text. After publication by *A&M* it was taken up by other editors and noticed by Erik Routley, who introduced it into the USA. Then one of my joint efforts with Dr Sharp, 'However loud the shout' (tune 'Voice of love'),[6] was featured on television in the finals of the BBC *Songs of Praise* festival in 1985, and another, 'Praise the Lord with sound waves' (tune 'Sound waves'),[7] in 1988. This encouraged us and led to further requests and inclusion in more books. These occasions also involved a trip to London and the chance to chat with and learn from the other finalists. Several of my later texts were written at the request of our next Rector, Canon Nicholas Frayling. One of these, 'Round orange, round orange you serve as a sign', is designed for a Christingle service, and was greatly improved by some expert criticism from Brian Wren. I did not take all of his advice but I thought hard, even about the parts I did not actually implement.

Nicholas Williams regularly represented Stainer & Bell at annual conferences of the Hymn Society. He had copies of my hymns on file and had several times expressed an interest in publishing a collection. In the year 2000, I felt I might have enough material and sent him my proposed preface, together with samples of the sort of notes I felt appropriate to accompany the texts. He replied in positive terms and the collection was then quite quickly completed and published. Nowadays computers play their part in dissemination, and some of my work has appeared on the internet and in the software programme *HymnQuest*.[8]

The strong feminist reaction to 'Can man by searching' surprised me greatly at first. The initial objection was to the word 'man' in the first line. The whole line was a quotation from the Authorized Version and I assumed, as I always had done, that the generalized 'man' included women. I personally had no feeling of exclusion. It was not until some time later that the even thornier question arose of 'he' and 'his' in reference to God.

At about this time major changes were affecting my professional life. University departments of English were coming to terms with modern literary theory, which demanded some understanding of semiotics and of Marxist, feminist and psychoanalytical approaches to literary criticism. I had to absorb these new ideas myself and mediate them to students, a significant minority of whom were mature women of various social and ethnic backgrounds who were coming freshly to higher education and felt hugely excited and liberated by left-wing and feminist thinking. Seminars usually included also other students who felt threatened by the intrusion of politics into the 'safe' area of literature. I could see the force of the new arguments and the passion behind them, as well as some of their disturbingly atheistic implications, and I also felt deeply for those students who were bewildered and angered by what seemed to them an utterly unjustified and very hurtful attack on their personal morality.

This combination provoked some challenging and emotional arguments and a great deal of thought on my part, which still continues today.[9] Neither my personal faith nor my hymn-writing could remain unaffected. I have increasingly used language that is inclusive as regards people and not gendered as regards God, but the latter does involve some potentially damaging limitations. I do use 'Lord' occasionally, and have no objection on principle to calling God 'Father', as indeed Jesus did. I should, however, feel much happier with this metaphor if our culture accepted more readily the use of 'Mother' in a similar way. The problem is complicated both by the difficulty many people have in understanding that metaphor conveys truth, not fact (although no single metaphor can ever convey the whole truth), and by the fact that the same metaphor can have radically different associations for different individuals or groups.

As regards the text that first raised these issues, I agreed fairly soon to allow, albeit reluctantly, the alteration of 'man' to 'we' in the first line. There are some disadvantages. 'We' is a much weaker-sounding word than 'man' and is ambiguous in that its meaning can be wider or narrower according to the speaker. 'Man' certainly used to refer to the whole human race whereas 'we' may refer to any group to which the speaker belongs, and in a Christian context there is always a danger of narrowing it down to Christians only or to a particular denomination, congregation or faction, without being aware of what one is doing. However, our changing perception of the word 'man' inevitably began to change its meaning and effect so that it could no longer be used as innocently as it had once been. I therefore accepted 'we', although the loss of the generalized 'man' causes technical problems that hymn-writers have not yet fully solved.

Later I had several requests from America to change 'he' and 'his' to 'God' and 'God's' throughout. These I refused because I had used the offending words very frequently and mainly in metrically unstressed positions. 'Man' takes more readily than 'we' to a heavy stress. The total effect of the proposed changes to this particular text sounded to me, and still does, like bad English and less than perfect metre. I am happy for any congregation that likes my hymn to continue singing it, but I should write a different one today. One of the problems for any writer is that although language is constantly changing it does so in unpredictable ways. For complex reasons it may yield immediately to one change yet stubbornly resist another.

My hymn-writing has been 'occasional' in both senses of the word. Often I have noticed or had pointed out to me a specific need, such as a hymn for a Candlemas procession, for a 'family service' type baptism of children, or for the nine-hundredth anniversary of Chichester cathedral. Others are more obviously personal to me in that they represent my own effort to see what Christian teaching actually means to me and how it could be expressed in a contemporary way. Verses such as

> I can be myself here,
> no-one here pretends,
> for we are accepted;
> you have called us friends[10]

or

> Teach me, my God, to love myself
> as truly and as tenderly
> as you have done in your dear Son
> who lived and died and rose for me[11]

were actually quite deeply felt, but I would not offer them for publication unless I thought they might also have meaning for others, nor if I knew of existing texts that seemed to me to say the same thing better. It is very easy to go on writing without thinking why and to produce careless and self-indulgent work that benefits nobody.

Seeing myself as a person first and foremost, I do not deliberately introduce gender into my hymns, but of course I am also a woman, so it sometimes seems to arise quite naturally, especially when I am writing about other women. For instance I have written a text about the nineteenth-century social reformer Josephine Butler,[12] who is now included in the Anglican calendar of remembrances.

> For God's sake let us dare
> to pray like Josephine,
> who felt with Christ the world's despair
> and asked what love could mean.
>
> He was her truth, her way,
> through her he spoke again
> for each exploited Maggie May,
> each modern Magdalen.

She forced her age to face
what most it feared to see,
the double standards at the base
of its prosperity.

Grant us, like her, no rest
in systems which degrade
at once oppressors and oppressed,
by grace for glory made.[13]

She would probably disagree deeply in many ways with the twentieth-century women's liberation movement but some feminists more radical than myself have expressed their appreciation of my text and such appreciation gives me pleasure. Having read a couple of biographies and spoken with someone who saw herself as one of her followers, I tried simply to give a true picture of her importance. Despite vicious campaigns against her, she worked to help prostitutes and also declared clearly, publicly and repeatedly that male pimps and clients were equally morally responsible with the women.

Josephine Butler incurred great obloquy, whereas her twentieth-century successor, Marguerite (Sally) White, at whose request I wrote the hymn, was honoured in her old age with an MBE. Miss White, who saw herself as one of Mrs Butler's followers, was a social worker and for many years secretary of the Liverpool Diocesan Board of Moral Welfare. Most of her work was with what were then called 'unmarried mothers' and 'illegitimate children'. In her younger days, before I knew her, she had campaigned unsuccessfully to have the words 'prostitute' and 'prostitution' applied legally to the male clients of prostitutes and their activities, as well as to the women involved. All I did was to draw out some of the implications of Josephine Butler's work as I saw them.

Our Lord's mother interests me very much and I was delighted when asked to write a hymn about her which would be suitable for both Anglicans and Methodists to sing. The text reads:

For nine months Mary held
her Saviour in her womb,
while in her thought strange prophecies
were also given room:
but after all the fuss,
the angels and the star,
the child was simply one of us,
a boy as all boys are.

At twelve he made a break,
for home was growing small;
he longed to hear the rabbis teach
but not his parents call:
and as the years went on
they brought a deeper smart;
how could she ever understand
a love that broke her heart?

Dear God of Mary, grant
that we, like her, may know
both how to treasure your good gifts
and how to let them go:
So shall the things of earth
be touched with Heaven's grace
and charity begin at home
its journey into space.[14]

I did have a broadly political aim in that I wished to subvert the traditional image (in my view a stereotype) of Mary, which sometimes
implies that her womb is the only part of her which matters. To do this
I drew upon an aspect of her that had appealed to me imaginatively
long before I started to think about feminism. The Bible stresses that
she also had a brain and was prepared to use it. On first seeing Gabriel,
'she was much perplexed at his words and pondered what sort of greet-
ing this might be' (Luke 1.29, NRSV Anglicized). She was interested
in how God's purpose would be achieved, enquiring, 'How shall this
be, seeing I am a virgin?' (Luke 1.34), and after the visit of the shepherds she 'treasured all these words and pondered them in her heart'
(Luke 2.19). All this suggests that she was thoughtful, perhaps not a
quick thinker but one who took her time to mull things over, and that
she could fuse thought and feeling without losing sight of the distinction between them. In the succeeding verses I tried to imagine how she
might have used a similar approach as she later faced the hard task of
letting go this sacred gift of her Son.

Not at the time of writing but looking back later, I realized that I had
seen something of myself in the Bible story. I believe that Fred Kaan
may have done the same thing when, in *Magnificat Now*, he drew a
picture of a revolutionary Mary.[15] Both pictures are true to aspects of
the Bible narrative, both serve a purpose in the modern world and each
reflects something of its author. I do not believe, however, that the

pondering Mary necessarily indicates a woman writer and the revolutionary one a man. Janet Wootton's 'When Mary heard her cousin say'[16] is considerably closer to Fred Kaan's picture of her than to mine. It is probably impossible to tell from a text alone the sex of the writer.

I have been fortunate in that I have never felt myself on the receiving end of any particular act of injustice against me because of gender, either in my professional life or as a writer of hymns. I have already shown that most of the people who have encouraged and helped me, especially in the early stages, have been men, to whom I am most grateful. This may be partly because it was men who were in the sort of positions that enabled them to do so. If so, this may involve structural and largely unconscious discrimination, which is a different matter and hard to eradicate, although happily one of which we are becoming increasingly aware and therefore more able to tackle.

People sometimes ask me why there have been so few women hymn-writers, especially during what is often called the hymn 'explosion' or 'renaissance' of the late twentieth century, and the honest answer is 'I do not know'. Although I have a strong feeling that the usual feminist arguments about men in influential positions do apply here, they do not give a complete answer. Religion and spirituality are areas in which there is a tradition of women's writing. I believe that, at least until very recently if not still today, it would have been much easier for a woman writer to have had hymns taken seriously than, for instance, an academic work on applied mathematics. In the past, a noticeably high proportion of hymn-writers have been clergy and many of the nineteenth-century women writers were married or closely related to clergy. Among living writers Janet Wootton and June Boyce-Tillman are ordained, while Shirley Erena Murray is a clergy wife.

It may be just that this gives them more access to encouragement and publication, but I wonder if there may also be another factor involved. It is equally noticeable that many hymns are written for particular occasions or to satisfy perceived new needs. This is absolutely clear in the 'hymn renaissance' works of Albert Bayly, Fred Pratt Green, Brian Wren, Fred Kaan, Michael Saward and Christopher Idle, all of them ordained. Could part of the explanation be that clergy are strongly motivated by pastoral feeling, some of which may rub off on their families, who live very close to these concerns? I personally have no clerical connections whatsoever, but I have been for the past few years a eucharistic minister in my own congregation and know from experience a special feeling for those to whom one gives the communion.

It is possible that as more women are given pastoral responsibilities, whether lay or ordained, we shall see an increase in their contribution to hymnody. I also welcome developments such as the increasing practice of conducting hymn searches so that the judges do not know the writers' names. It would be good to see still more women involved in editing major collections and in the choice at local level of hymns for particular services. It may be helpful that female organists and music directors, while still a minority, are commoner than once they were. Even though some questions are not fully answered, I believe the signs are hopeful.

Notes

1 Elizabeth Cosnett, *Hymns for Everyday Saints: 36 Hymns with Commentaries*, London: Stainer & Bell, 2001.

2 Elizabeth Cosnett, 'The Poet as Hymn Writer: A Study of the Hymns of George Wither, William Cowper and Robert Bridges', unpublished thesis, 1975.

3 http://www.hymnsocietygbi.org.uk.

4 Cosnett, *Hymns for Everyday Saints*, p. 2.

5 *More Hymns for Today: A Second Supplement to Hymns Ancient and Modern*, Canterbury: Hymns Ancient and Modern Ltd., The Canterbury Press, 1980.

6 Cosnett, *Hymns for Everyday Saints*, p. 33.

7 Cosnett, *Hymns for Everyday Saints*, p. 34.

8 *HymnQuest*, published for the Pratt Green Trust by Stainer & Bell Ltd. http://www.methodist.org.uk/index.cfm?fuseaction=opentogod.content&cmid=1699.

9 See Elizabeth Cosnett, 'Language in Hymns: One Woman's Experience', *The Hymn Society of Great Britain and Ireland Bulletin* 182, vol. 12, no. 9, January 1990, pp. 158–63; and 'A (female) Bookworm Reads Some Hymns', *HSGBI Bulletin* 205, vol. 14, no. 8, October 1995, pp. 172–84.

10 Cosnett, *Hymns for Everyday Saints*, p. 78.

11 Cosnett, *Hymns for Everyday Saints*, p. 26.

12 See above, p. 205.

13 Cosnett, *Hymns for Everyday Saints*, p. 12. Josephine Butler's date in the Anglican calendar is 30 May.

14 Cosnett, *Hymns for Everyday Saints*, p. 8.

15 Fred Kaan, 'Sing we a song of high revolt', *The Hymn Texts of Fred Kaan*, London: Hope Publishing Company/Stainer & Bell, 1982, no. 93.

16 Janet Wootton, 'When Mary heard her cousin say', in Janet Wootton, *Eagles' Wings and Lesser Things*, London: Stainer & Bell, 2007, p. 20.

Marjorie Dobson

I was four years old. I was standing on the platform at the local Friends' Meeting House, hardly able to see over the front rail, and waiting for the Sunday School Anniversary to begin. For several weeks, I'd been rehearsing the poem I was to recite, and had tried to learn the songs from the special Anniversary hymn sheet, but I was too young to read all of the words and only had a vague idea of how to join in with the singing.

There was a great deal of shuffling and chattering going on in the congregation, but as the conductor of the choir stood up and raised his arms there was silence. And that's when it happened. Suddenly, all around me there was this glorious sound. 'All hail the power of Jesu's name', sung to the tune 'Diadem',[1] with all its repeated

> Crown him, crown him, crown him
> Crown him, Lord of all.

I had never heard such an amazing sound before and I believe I spent the whole hymn gazing open-mouthed at these very ordinary people creating such magnificent music.

It was my first introduction to the power of hymns and hymn-singing.

None of my family were churchgoers. My father was a nominal Anglican, attending rarely, and my mother's family had only one tentative link with the Friends' Meeting House, because one of my uncles had married a Quaker. He died before I was born, but my Aunt Hilda encouraged my mother to send me to the Sunday school, and I was taken along by the older girls who lived in our street. From my earliest childhood, I had loved rhyming verse and had the ability to memorize it easily. That was how I came to be reciting poetry at the age of four. After that first experience I soon began to learn hymns for myself and loved to join in each new one that came my way. We sang hymns at school too, although I must admit that the experience gave me a life-long dislike of 'Immortal, invisible, God, only wise',[2] probably because our juvenile voices murdered it at the time.

Sunday school and anniversaries – big events, with four separate services over two Sundays – figured in my life until about the age of ten, when I announced that I was too old to go there any more and promptly left. But in my early teens I started to attend the little Methodist 'tin chapel' that was at the bottom of our street and there made a personal commitment to Christ as a result of a stirring sermon and an appeal from a Methodist local preacher, who was a teacher at the local boys' grammar school and knew how to encourage young people. There were several obstacles along the way, not the least being the attitude of my family who thought I had caught a bout of religious mania and would soon grow out of it. They were to be proved wrong.

At the age of 17, I felt a strong calling to become a local preacher and qualified and was recognized as such just a few days after my twentieth birthday. I was married just a few months later. As a young woman preacher, I did encounter some strange reactions when I appeared at the door of a church for the first time and met someone who didn't know me. The most frequent question I heard was, 'Are you the preacher?' In fact that statement became so familiar to me that I wrote an article that was printed in the *Youth* magazine being published by the Methodist Church's Youth Department at the time.[3] By now, I was beginning to realize that I could write things that people would want to read, although it was to be many years before that talent was used to any great effect.

My husband and I were leading a youth fellowship at this time and it had some very talented youngsters among its members. One was a natural musician, and he and a friend wrote a musical play entitled *Pilate*, which they performed with some of their friends. It was a great local success. David also asked me to write some Christian words to popular songs of the day and we sang them in our group. It was becoming increasingly evident that there was a demand for new words to sing. The *New English Bible*[4] had just been published, and it was the first time that young people recognized that the Christian faith did not always need to be expressed in archaic language, but was relevant to their everyday world. The seeds of my own dissatisfaction had been sown. I still have in my files a hymn text I wrote in those early days, but thankfully it is buried so deep that it may never be found again.

Time passed. We moved around the country a couple of times, and then a new minister came to the church we attended on the outskirts of Bradford. His name was Peter Smith and we soon learned that his interest was in folk music, especially when it could be applied to songs of faith. He had already compiled two of his collections, *Faith, Folk and Clarity* and *Faith, Folk and Nativity*, and was in the process of working on his third collection, *Faith, Folk and Festivity*,[5] which was published shortly after his arrival with us. Recognizing my interest in making hymns and worship relevant to the young people – and older ones – in the church, he encouraged me to examine this new material and to begin to write my own. Only now do I recognize how privileged I was then to see some of the early work of Fred Kaan just as it was becoming known to a wider audience.

Through Peter I became involved in the religious input to local radio, so my early writing was mainly 60-seconds' worth of 'Morning Messages' and input into the Sunday morning worship slot. No hymns had yet been written, although I had produced some of my morning messages in rhyming verse and had thus been christened 'the Idle bard' by one of the presenters – Idle being the name of the village I lived in at the time. Then the local Methodist Church Music Society promoted a hymn-writing competition and I decided to try out my skills. Thankfully, my entry to that competition has sunk, but not entirely without trace. I have been known to use it in hymn-writing workshops as an example of how not to do it! But my interest had begun; helped along by a kind critique from one of the judges of the competition, who was obviously a very understanding woman and determined to encourage anyone who showed any kind of ability at all.

I continued to write, but hardly any hymns at all at this stage. My main output was prayers, poetry and the occasional sketch to be used in worship. It was some years later that another minister encouraged the church to take part in a creative arts weekend based on the theme of 'Light'. For some forgotten reason, I travelled alone, by train, to this weekend and found myself needing to write a hymn on the subject to the tune 'Little Cornard', always a favourite tune of mine. The hymn began:

> Light from the darkness came,
> when first the world began.
> Sun sent its glorious flame,
> part of God's master plan.
> Then order out of chaos grew
> and life was clean and pure and new.[6]

As I look at that text now, it is full of inversions and rhyme-led line endings, but I still have a great affection for it. When I joined the others at the weekend retreat I was very wary of showing the text to anyone, but was finally persuaded to allow a singing friend to use it in the Saturday evening concert. It was surprisingly well received and I began to wonder if I could do it again, but better.

So I began to write more hymns. I had always been troubled by the lack of hymns expressing the Christian faith in twentieth-century language and began to recognize that if I couldn't find them, then I should try to write something myself. This, I know, is the most common motivation among hymn-writers. I wrote one or two hymns for special occasions, though whether they actually made the occasion special is perhaps a topic for debate. But I was asked to write a hymn for a student group by its chaplain. He requested that the 'fairy-tale' elements of the Christmas story should be left out. So there would be no stars, shepherds or angels; simply the story of the incarnation and its implications for the world. After much thought, this was the text I wrote:

Birth brings a promise of new life awaking,
dawning of hope through a child's open eyes.
Uncharted future is there for the making,
challenge and change in a baby's first cries.

Every new life changes those who are round it
making demands of commitment and care,
calling for love to enfold and surround it,
reshaping patterns by claiming a share.

Jesus the new-born crossed time's moving stages
changing their course by the act of his birth,
translating God from the mystery of ages,
rooting our faith by his presence on earth.

Wonder and worship were waiting to greet him,
love and devotion were his to command,
life was transformed for the ones sent to meet him,
touching their God in a child's outstretched hand.

Birth gives a promise of new life awaking.
Jesus the new-born calls us to new birth.
All that he promised is ours for the taking
when our commitment brings God down to earth.[7]

I still have great affection for this text and personally consider it one of my best.

Not long after this, the minister of our church was moved to another church to fill a vacancy for a circuit superintendent's job. It was an unexpected move and caused disruption and distress to the family, who were happily settled in our community. I had already been asked to write a hymn that would reflect something of the nature of the City of Bradford and had just begun a text with the theme of 'God the Weaver'. Into that text I then wove the theme of the complexities of life and the dark threads of the unexpected that can cause tension and sadness. The hymn was dedicated to Peter and Rosemary and sung at their fare-well service. The words that were particularly poignant and relevant to them were contained in the third verse:

When we see the pattern changing
and a new direction starts,
let us know your love unbroken
winds through life in all its parts
by the threads of love and friendship
closely woven in our hearts.[8]

I did not know it at the time, but this text was to open up a whole new world to me.

One of the other local preachers in our circuit was a man named David McCarthy, a wonderful musician and composer of hymn tunes. He had been asked to go to a neighbouring circuit to do a music work-shop at their creative weekend. I had also been asked to go to work with a drama/dance group. We arranged to travel to the planning meet-ing together. Taking my courage in both hands I decided to let him see my 'God the Weaver' hymn text, but only had enough courage to thrust the envelope into his hands as he drew his car up at our front door. I didn't see him again until the next planning meeting, when he returned the envelope to me without a word, as I got into the car. I hardly dared to open it, but when I did I found that he'd written a tune to my hymn and was anxious to find a piano at the church so he could play the tune for me. On the way back he encouraged me to contact Stainer & Bell, to ask about publication of my texts. Although there was no outlet for them immediately, I was soon linked into the *Worship Live* network, also run by Stainer & Bell, and my work began to be published in 1996. The first two hymn texts being 'Birth brings a promise' and 'God the Weaver'.

Since then I have written many texts. Some have gone into competi-tions, some have been written to fit a particular Bible story or lectionary lesson. Sometimes the texts have been written to fit a special tune. I am not a musician and can neither read nor write music, so most of my hymns have been written to known tunes. Occasionally the texts have then been set to commissioned tunes – notably when Stainer & Bell published the first collection of my work, *Multi-coloured Maze*, in 2004.[9] The title was taken from 'God the Weaver'.

Publication was a problem initially. When you come from an ordinary working-class background, only have a grammar school education, and leave school at 16 because your parents can't see the point in further education, unless you want to become a teacher, then it doesn't exactly inspire confidence in your own ability, especially if you're shy by nature and not driven by ambition. Lack of confidence has always been my problem. My family background led me to believe that 'making something of yourself' was for other people, not for 'the likes of us'. This attitude has hampered me all my life. I had an outsize inferiority complex about the world of academia – and there are still remnants of it hanging round me now. Too many people judge others by what academic qualifications they can display and usually have no idea how that affects those of us who did not, or could not, take that route to achievement. And I am not a cleric either. So what would I know about the deeper things of the Christian life and the structure of worship and what it takes to make a good hymn? Believe me, I have had to battle such prejudices, as well as coping with the fact that I was born a woman – and what would women know about writing hymns, unless they were sweet little ditties for the children to sing?

But I was greatly encouraged by the *Worship Live* editorial team, who knew nothing at all about me, except for the quality of my work. Yet they published almost all of the early material I submitted to them and gave me enough confidence to continue writing. They have since become personal friends, and I joined their ranks many years ago. It was through meeting such people and being encouraged by other creative workshop leaders that I now have work published and used and – through the doorway of the internet – in many countries of the world. It has also led to co-operative work with a fellow writer, Andrew Pratt, and we have produced two books of material together, with – we hope – more on the way.[10] We are fierce critics of each other's work, but it is good to find someone you can trust to be honest about the quality of the work you produce. It is an essential step on the road to confidence and ability.

I have often been asked whether I write differently because I am a woman. That's not easy to answer. There are some images in my work that I may not have used otherwise, although most of them could be equally used by men. But I wrote a hymn in response to a request for Christmas texts for Australia and perhaps some of the personal experiences of giving birth to a child are strongly reflected there. I have been told that it is not the kind of text that most men would write on the subject.

> Sun beats down on travelling strangers,
> weary from the dusty track.
> Pregnant woman, close to labour,
> clings hard to a donkey's back.
> Anxious husband seeks for shelter,
> knowing that the birth is near.
> Looks for safety before sundown;
> fights to quell his rising fear.
>
> Drained by heat, exhausted Mary
> tries to hold her pain at bay.
> Joseph, worried by her anguish,
> cannot find a place to stay.
> Then, at last, someone takes pity,
> as the night is falling fast;
> chill creeps through the darkened stable
> where they find their rest at last.
>
> Through the blood and toil of childbirth,
> Mary gives a cry of joy;
> drenched in sweat and pale with effort,
> welcomes her expected boy.
> As the sun, in all its glory,
> blazes through the cattle stall,
> Jesus cries, to greet the morning;
> brings a new hope for us all.[11]

I have also written a hymn for situations of bereavement, which, with its constant repetitions of 'God, hold us, enfold us', is much more of a cradling, motherly image than the usual fatherly portrayal of God.

> God, hold us, enfold us, through desolate loss.
> The sign of your love is your own empty cross.
> The shock and the anger, the hopeless despair
> are echoes of Calvary. God, meet us there!

God, hold us, enfold us, through long empty days,
when living is pointless, a meaningless maze.
We need you to listen to raging and tears,
to anguish and doubt, to remorse and to fears.

God, hold us, enfold us, by friends who can share
our sorrow and pain with compassionate care.
By their words, you speak out your loving concerns.
They hold us for you, while the tide of grief turns.

God, hold us, enfold us, till weeping has passed;
when flickering hope parts the shadows at last.
One step at a time you will help us to move
to face new horizons, held safe in your love.[12]

But my motivation for writing hymns is principally to provide words
that are relevant to the everyday life and problems and joys of being a
Christian in the twenty-first century. I am also a passionate advocate of
the priesthood of all believers. Everyone has a place in God's mission
and work. Whether you are an academic, or someone who doesn't feel
that you have much to offer; whether you are ordained or not; whether
you have recognizable talents and skills, or are always somewhere in
the background; female or male; young or old – it doesn't matter. God
welcomes you, and our singing ought to reflect that. Let me sum up
how I feel in one final hymn:

Lord, you call us to your service,
each in our own way.
Some to caring, loving, healing;
some to preach, or pray;
some to work with quiet learning,
truth discerning,
day by day.

Life for us is always changing
as your work we share.
Christian love adds new dimensions
to the way we care.
For we know that you could lead us,
as you need us,
anywhere.

Seeing life from your perspective
makes your challenge plain,
as your heart is grieving over
those who live in pain.
Teach us how, by our compassion,
we may fashion
hope again.

Lord, we set our human limits
on the work we do.
Send us your directing Spirit,
pour your power through,
that we may be free in living
and in giving
all for you.[13]

Notes

1 Text, Edward Peronet (1726–92); tune, James Ellor (1819–99).

2 W. Chalmers Smith (1824–1908).

3 *Youth* magazine, published for a few years in the 1960s by the Methodist Youth Department, London.

4 *The New English Bible*, Oxford: Oxford University Press/Cambridge: Cambridge University Press, 1961.

5 Peter Smith (ed.), *Faith, Folk and Clarity*, London: Galliard, 1967; *Faith, Folk and Nativity: A New Collection of Songs*, London: Galliard, 1968; *Faith, Folk and Festivity*, London: Galliard, 1967.

6 Marjorie Dobson, *Multi-coloured Maze*, London: Stainer & Bell, 2004, p. 88.

7 Dobson, *Multi-coloured Maze*, p. 2.

8 Dobson, *Multi-coloured Maze*, p. 180.

9 Dobson, *Multi-coloured Maze*.

10 Andrew Pratt and Marjorie Dobson, *Poppies and Snowdrops*, Peterborough: Inspire, 2006; *Nothing Too Religious*, Peterborough: Inspire, 2008.

11 *Worship Live* 36, October 2006, p. 18.

12 Pratt and Dobson, *Poppies and Snowdrops*, p. 52.

13 Dobson, *Multi-coloured Maze*, p. 96.

Ruth Duck

My love for the Church's song began at home. I was born 21 November 1947, in Washington DC, to Jesse Thomas Duck and Louise Farmer Duck, both of whom had grown up in West Tennessee, though they met in Washington. We moved to Annapolis MD when I was four, and then to Memphis when I was sixteen. My parents were committed evangelical Christians. My mother was raised in a Southern Baptist church, while my father grew up in the Methodist Church. Both were baptized by immersion and confession of faith, and so was I, since they were careful to communicate their faith to me and to make sure I took part in the life of a church all my years at home. So I am grateful for their Christian witness, and also their love for words. Scrabble was our favourite game. My father, who could recite great poems at length, used to play guitar and sing on the radio when he was a young man growing up in rural Tennessee. He complained that I was a gifted writer but needed to take more care in refining my work. My parents loved music and hymns; with their encouragement I studied piano and guitar. My mother loved to play hymns such as 'Whispering Hope'[1] on the piano, and in her eighties, when her memory was severely impaired, staff at the retirement home were startled when she began singing and playing hymns she had loved since childhood. Though my relationship with my parents (who died in the 1990s) was difficult in some ways, it is unimaginable that I would have become a hymn text writer without their influence.

The other experience of my youth which most shaped my hymn-writing was living in Memphis from 1964 to 1969. Here my evangelical faith was tempered by fine teachers in the religion department at South-western-at-Memphis College (now Rhodes College). New Testament teacher Dr Richard Batey might have inwardly groaned to see my hand rise with yet another conservative challenge, yet through his patience and fine scholarship he broadened my thinking beyond the rigid beliefs with which I arrived at college. And, even more important, through the profound ministry of Dr Martin Luther King in Memphis, and the impact of his life and death, I learned that justice is at the heart of faith and Christian practice. Ron Klusmeier (a Canadian composer with whom I have collaborated) once said that all my hymns have some message of social justice and peace.

As it turned out, advocacy for justice for women in the Church was the impetus for my first hymn-writing. In the spring of 1972, as I moved toward completing my coursework at Chicago Theological Seminary, I began preparing for ordination and a call to a congregation. I discovered, not without tears and anger, that the Church had a long way to go to be just toward women and other humans, and I wanted to make a difference. I began to make connections between the Church's many masculine images for God and its historic exclusion of women from ministries.[2] Therefore I volunteered for the committee for *Because We Are One People*, the first collection of hymns adapted or chosen for their 'non-sexist language' (as we called it), sponsored by the Ecumenical Women's Center of Chicago.[3] My work on adapting hymns led to my first original texts, 'Lead On, O Cloud of Presence'[4] and 'Arise, Your Light Has Come' (inspired by 'Lead on, O King Eternal' and 'Rise up, O men of God').[5] These were first published in 1974 (in *Because We Are One People*). I found I enjoyed writing hymn texts, which, over time, I came to believe is a central part of God's call to me.

Here are these first two texts. 'Arise, your light is come' is inspired by portions of Isaiah 60 and 61. 'Lead on, O cloud of presence' used images of the Exodus journey (especially Num. 9.15–23) as well as reflecting the impression the civil rights movement had on me.

Arise, your light is come!
The Spirit's call obey;
show forth the glory of your God
which shines on you today.

Arise, your light is come!
Fling wide the prison door;
proclaim the captive's liberty,
good tidings to the poor.

Arise, your light is come!
All you in sorrow born,
bind up the broken-hearted ones
and comfort those who mourn.

Arise, your light is come!
The mountains burst in song!

Rise up like eagles on the wing;
God's pow'r will make us strong.

Ruth Duck, 1974, © 1992 GIA Publications Inc.
Used by permission.
Suggested tune: 'Festal Song'

Lead on, O cloud of Presence;
the exodus is come;
in wilderness and desert
our tribe shall make its home.
Our bondage left behind us,
new hopes within us grow.
We seek the land of promise
where milk and honey flow.

Lead on, O fiery pillar;
we follow yet with fears,
but we shall come rejoicing,
though joy be born of tears.
We are not lost, though wand'ring,
for by your light we come,
and we are still God's people.
The journey is our home.

Lead on, O God of freedom,
and guide us on the way,
and help us trust the promise
through struggle and delay.
We pray our sons and daughters
may journey to that land
where justice dwells with mercy
and love is law's demand.

Words by Ruth Duck, 1974, 1989, © 1992 GIA Publications Inc.
Used by permission.
Suggested tune: 'Lancashire'

By 1974 I was ordained in the United Church of Christ (UCC), first
serving at Pilgrim Congregational Church UCC in Oak Park, Illinois,
then in two churches in Wisconsin: St John's UCC in Hartford (1975–
79) and Bethel-Bethany UCC in Milwaukee (1979–84). For the next

few years I continued writing hymn texts, some as an expression of my Christian spirituality ('In solitude' and 'With my own breath I formed your life'), two for hymn competitions ('As a fire was meant for burning' and 'The earth and all who breathe'), and a few (including 'We cannot own the sunlit sky' and 'God of endless life unfolding') for the United Church of Christ's fundraising for the One Great Hour of Sharing.

In 'We cannot own the sunlit sky' I sought to speak of supporting world relief and development (through One Great Hour of Sharing) in a way that did not separate givers and receivers but lifted up our shared partnership with God in caring for one another, 'that all may have abundant life' (John 10.10):

We cannot own the sunlit sky,
the moon, the wildflow'rs growing,
for we are part of all that is
within life's river flowing.
With open hands receive and share
the gifts of God's creation,
that all may have abundant life
in ev'ry earthly nation.

When bodies shiver in the night
and, weary, wait for morning,
when children have no bread but tears,
and war-horns sound their warning,
God calls humanity to wake,
to join in common labor,
that all may have abundant life
in oneness with their neighbor.

God calls humanity to join
as partners in creating
a future free from want and fear,
life's goodness celebrating.
That new world beckons from afar,
invites our shared endeavor,
that all may have abundant life
and peace endure forever.

Suggested tune: 'How can I keep from singing?'

As I was beginning my ministry in local churches, I discovered the paucity of good worship resources for churches like mine that printed prayers in a bulletin. Some official worship books featured beautifully written words for worship that did not, however, reflect sensitivity to inclusive language or to the more contemporary language used in churches since the publication of the Revised Standard Version of the Bible.[6] Other worship resources used contemporary and sometimes even inclusive language, but it seemed to me that many of these prayers lacked beauty and theological depth. So I began writing my own. Later I asked a group of clergywomen if they were interested in gathering a collection of worship resources. With their encouragement and advice I began working on a manuscript, which I presented one hot New York day in June 1980 to Marion Meyer, senior editor at United Church Press. The previous General Synod of the UCC had mandated that the press publish a book of inclusive hymns and worship resources by 1981, and the project had been delayed. For this reason, after looking over the manuscript, she accepted my proposal immediately, as well as my suggestion to publish the worship materials and hymns separately. Michael Bausch, a UCC pastor in my area who was hoping to publish an inclusive-language hymn supplement for his congregation, agreed to work on the hymn collection with me. The books appeared in 1981 as *Bread for the Journey: Resources for Worship* and *Everflowing Streams: Songs for Worship*.[7] When people ask me how to find a publisher, I often say I don't know because I didn't have to search; I happened to present my manuscript to a publisher who urgently needed just what I had to offer. Marion Meyer was an excellent editor, and I am grateful not only that she accepted the books for publication, but that she taught me much about writing.

By 1980, I also realized that I wanted to undertake academic study of worship. First, that led me to the summer MA programme in liturgy at the University of Notre Dame. I was able to study liturgy and theology with such outstanding scholars as John Baldovin, Nathan Mitchell and Catherine LaCugna. Moreover, John Ferguson opened up the world of hymnody to me from a historical perspective, while also teaching me excellence in crafting hymn texts. With Don Saliers, the world of the psalms came alive to me; for his class I created my first psalm paraphrase ('Rejoice in God, all earthly lands', Ps. 100). One comment he made about writing based on Scripture has remained with me always; he compared lifting up the images of Scripture to the way a frame can bring out the beauty of a painting. While an inspiring high-school teacher had interested me in imagery in poetry long before, Don (who since has become a dear friend) taught me the importance of scriptural imagery in worship and hymn texts. At Notre Dame I also first met Sister Delores Dufner, a gifted hymn text writer, who has become a writing partner.

My studies at Notre Dame, as well as the many requests to write and speak growing out of my two 1981 publications, whetted my appetite for more study. In 1984, I began a ThD degree in theology and worship at Boston University School of Theology. My studies there were fascinating, and my work with Linda Clark particularly influenced my growth in writing hymns. I took a course with her and Elizabeth Bettenhausen in theology and the arts – which gave me the opportunity to reflect on the meaning of both words and music – and then took a course in hymnody with Linda Clark. I delved deeper into the history of hymnody, researching the history of congregational song at First Church, Cambridge (UCC), since its beginning in 1636.[8] The class was required to write hymns, including one that we would like to have included in our denomination's next hymnal. Given my study of trinitarian theology with LaCugna, Bettenhausen and Marjorie Scott, and my passion for inclusive language, I wrote what is probably my most famous (or infamous) text, 'Womb of life and Source of Being', expressing a fully trinitarian theology using male, female and non-gendered imagery in balance. Although some make objection to the way the first line and title names the first person of the Trinity, several denominations, including my own, have decided to include it in their hymnals.

I graduated from Boston University School of Theology in 1989, the same year I began as a faculty member in the field of worship at Garrett-Evangelical Theological Seminary.

Around this time I began thinking of publishing a single-author collection of my hymn texts, partly inspired by the groundbreaking new hymns of Brian Wren, whose first collection appeared in 1983.[9] (Jeffery Rowthorn, a professor at the Yale Institute of Sacred Music, put it in my hands soon after its publication). I could see the difference Wren was making by providing alternative language for God and Christian faith. I wanted to follow his example – and learn from his excellence – to bring new ways of singing to more people. I also had the opportunity to meet Wren in 1988 and to learn from him at several workshops in the following years. So I began to prepare my growing sheaf of hymns for publication. Naturally I turned to Hope Publishing (Wren's publisher), but my texts (and tune choices) still needed more work and Hope did not choose to publish them. During this time I asked Brian Wren to look over my texts and, amazingly, he took the time to critique all 58 of them! He made many suggestions for improvement, while also encouraging me greatly. He challenged me toward excellence in every way. I was still uncertain where to publish my songs, so I sent copies of the manuscript to a number of friends to receive their advice. I sent a copy to Sue Seid-Martin, musician, scholar and colleague in the feminist liturgy seminar of the North American Academy of Liturgy. She liked what she saw, and asked for permission to send it to Bob Batastini at GIA Publications Inc., Chicago. To my delight, Batastini accepted my hymns for publication. He and Randall (Randy) Sensmeier edited the collection for me, and it was published in 1992 as *Dancing in the Universe: Hymns and Songs*.[10]

My next hymn collection, *Circles of Care*,[11] was published by The Pilgrim Press (Cleveland, Ohio) in 1998. I decided to publish this collection with my denomination's press, since Arthur Clyde, gifted editor of the *New Century Hymnal*[12] of the United Church of Christ, would be music editor. I had been intentional about making time for writing hymns in the six years since *Dancing in the Universe*, making it a regular spiritual practice to work on my hymns each Sunday afternoon. These texts tend to dig deeper into my heart and spirit than the ones that preceded and followed them. While I can't judge whether they are better in quality or usefulness for the Church, they are particularly honest and adventuresome among my texts. Inspired by words from feminist liturgical scholar Marjorie Procter-Smith, I spent a year intentionally praying with feminine images for God, and that practice is reflected in some of the texts. I also had the privilege of serving as UCC representative on the committee that formed the *Chalice Hymnal*[13] of the Disciples of Christ (Christian Church), and I am sure that my years of service (1992–95) sharpened my skills and inspired my creativity as well.

As my life as a seminary professor and leader in my academic field has become more demanding, it seems that I write hymns for a commission or special occasion, and less out of my daily life. Still, in early 2005, when I was sorting through my files, I realized how many hymn texts I had written since 1998, and by summer, with the editorial support and expertise of Randy Sensmeier, these were published by GIA Publications as *Welcome God's Tomorrow*.[14] I have continued to write hymns in the last few years. In all (since 1974) I have written around 150 hymn texts. As I look forward, I am inspired by the great English hymn text writer Fred Pratt Green, who wrote most or all of his hymns after retirement; I hope that I will be able to devote more time to writing in coming years.

In the early 1980s, I was stuffing envelopes to help my friend Dorothy Dean, who was running for the Milwaukee County Board. She asked, 'Ruth, is there anything you aspire to achieve in your life?' I thought about her question and responded, 'I would like to have a hymn in a denominational hymnal someday.' It was not too long before Erik Routley, church musician par excellence, wrote and asked to include one of my first two hymns, 'Arise, your light is come', in *Rejoice in the Lord*, the hymnal of the Reformed Church in America published in 1985.[15] To my amazement, around thirty different texts of mine (and one of my tunes) have found their way into denominational hymnals and supplements in the USA, Canada, Scotland, New Zealand and Australia.

It is a mystery to me which texts will be chosen and sung in many contexts. One big surprise was 'God, we thank you for our people', written for a family reunion of my friend Hal McSwain Jr., based partly on an interview with his father (Hal McSwain Sr.). Like my meditative text, 'In solitude', written soon after the death of my mother, it seemed to be so related to a particular situation that it might not speak to very many people. Yet, 'God, we thank you' was published in the hymnals of the United Church of Christ (USA) and the United Church of Canada. 'In solitude' was published in the UCC Hymnal. 'Creative God, you spread the earth', which I thought was important in raising issues of ecology, has rarely been sung, while 'We cannot own the sunlit sky', not written for the purpose, has sometimes been listed as one of a few 'green' hymns. More recently, seven of my texts appeared in the United Methodist supplement *The Faith We Sing*,[16] including the more recent 'Sacred the body', written at the request of a colleague to apply Paul's concept of the body as the temple of God (1 Cor. 3.16; 13.4–7) to issues of difference and abuse:

Sacred the body God has created,
temple of Spirit that dwells deep inside.
Cherish each person; nurture creation.
Treat flesh as holy, that love may abide.

Bodies are varied, made in all sizes,
pale, full of color, both fragile and strong.
Holy the difference, gift of the Maker,
so let us honor each story and song.

Love respects persons, bodies, and boundaries.
Love does not batter, neglect, or abuse.

Love touches gently, never coercing.
Love leaves the other with power to choose.

Holy of holies, God ever loving,
make us your temples; indwell all we do.
May we be careful, tender, and caring,
so may our bodies give honor to you.

Words by Ruth Duck, © 1997 The Pilgrim Press.
Used by Permission.[17]
Suggested tune: 'Tenderness'

I do have some hunches about why my texts have spoken to so many people. First, my early religious training focused on the Bible. Baptists and Catholics, Lutherans and Presbyterians, Moravians and Methodists (and others) sing my songs because (as Don Saliers taught me) they bring forth the images of Scripture and evoke the memory of key passages beloved by many. I use Scripture in a number of ways. Some texts paraphrase a psalm or canticle, while others tell a story from Scripture. Still others, like many hymns by Charles Wesley, allude to several Scripture passages; for example, 'Womb of Life' refers to at least eight passages. The Scripture resonance of my hymns[18] makes my words recognizable to people who might not want to sit at the same table.

Another reason may be my search for honesty of expression. As I've noted above, some of my texts seem to come from deeper places within myself, and I love these texts. My experiences of exalted praise and painful chronic disease, betrayal and abuse, joy and love are material for my hymns. So are the stories of people I have walked beside in joy and sorrow, such as a friend whose young son died in a hiking accident. My response was 'When earth is changed':

When earth is changed and waters roar,
and mountains tremble, strong no more,
when tumult floods our lives, our homes,
God, be our help when trouble comes.

When death takes those we love the best,
when illness robs our ease and rest,
O Holy Lover, hold us fast
as long as grief and trouble last.

When answers die on silent lips
and truth slips through our fingertips,

God, stay beside us in our hell,
that we may live the questions well.

God, keep us safe till peace returns,
and raised from ashes, new hope burns.
Through change and tumult be our guide.
God, shelter us till storms subside.

Words by Ruth Duck, 1998, © 2005 GIA Publications Inc.
Used by permission.
Suggested tune: 'Deo gracias'.[19]

These challenging experiences may not be on the surface of a hymn, but in Don Saliers' words about prayer and worship, I do bring the 'full stretch of the humanity'[20] I share with other people into my hymn-writing. And all my hymns come from the struggle to express what I believe, or feel, or want to say into the most precise and engaging words possible. (Here I acknowledge the influence of Brian Wren, who in his teaching always insists that each word convey its meaning precisely and thoughtfully – but also of Gracia Grindal, who critiques 'hymnisch', the language in which people string together fragments of all the hymns they've ever heard without figuring out what they want to say themselves!) I have learned that the authenticity and depth of a particular experience – even when it seems private or idiosyncratic – may touch the authentic depths of others.

My third hunch about the widespread use of my words relates to the convoluted and laborious way in which I compose texts. I almost never write a hymn text without a tune in mind. My process is something like this: I identify the basic subject and direction of the text, then brainstorm about ways to develop it, then come up with some key phrases. This may suggest a basic rhythm or bring a tune to mind, whether my own or a tune sung by Christians for centuries. (For 'Are you a shepherd', the theme music to the BBC comedy *The Vicar of Dibley* came to mind). Then the text develops in close relationship to the tune. If I'm creating the tune as well as the text, they develop mutually – an idea about the text changes the tune, and vice versa. If I am using an existing tune, I find the printed music and then conform my rhythms to the rise and fall of the tune's rhythms and even the pitch and length of the notes. Then, once the rhythm becomes clear I concentrate on the text for several more hours, crafting it carefully, rarely out of touch with the tune. While this process takes a long time, and my tunes are rarely publishable, it does make for texts that sing, flowing with the music.

A final important characteristic of my hymns is the breadth of imagery I use for God. Dee Brauninger, a UCC clergywoman and author, discovered more than seventy ways of naming God in my hymns.[21] For centuries the Church has worshiped and sung using only a few, mostly masculine, names and images for God, but in the last thirty years, many churches are expanding their repertoire of language from Scripture, tradition and contemporary experience. I have been a part of that expansion, so much so that when many people hear my name they think of me – with joy or disgust – as that woman who has helped to make the language of the Church more inclusive. Sometimes the criticism has stung. One Conference of the UCC even refused to publish announcements that I would be speaking at a local college and church because (I suppose) they saw me as heretical. When I wrote to the Conference minister and sent him the reasonably orthodox text of my speech, he would not even answer my letter. Still, I have received much affirmation and appreciation from those who welcome the words I bring. Even more important, I am blessed to know that my work has encouraged many, nurtured their faith, and (I hope) made their understanding of God deeper and broader.

As I tell this story, I am grateful once more for all the people who have encouraged me, taught me, made spaces for me, and gently challenged me to grow. And I am grateful to God, who has placed this gift of words within me and made it possible for me to share it with others. Writing hymns has been one of the greatest joys of my life. I am proud in this book to be a part of such an illustrious company of women who have shared this labour and this joy.

I close with a stanza from a hymn I wrote in celebration of the twentieth anniversary of the first ordinations of Episcopal women in the United States:

We praise you, God, for women
who ventured paths unknown
with faith that you had called them there
and claimed them as your own.
When we lose heart, then bring to mind
the courage you bestow.
The saints surround, a witness cloud
to cheer us as we go.[22]

Words by Ruth Duck, © The Pilgrim Press, 1996.
Used by permission.
Suggested tune: 'Hildegard of Bingen' by Joy Patterson.

Notes

1 Alice Hawthorne (author and composer), 'Whispering hope', in B. B. McKinney (ed.), *The Broadman Hymnal*, Nashville TN: The Broadman Press, 1940, no. 466.

2 Three sentences adapted from Dee Brauninger's interview of me, 'Birth of a Hymn,' published as a web article in 2007 at http://www.ucc.org/assets/pdfs/duck.pdf, pp. 5–6.

3 *Because We Are One People*, Chicago: Ecumenical Women's Center, 1974.

4 The first line and title were originally 'Lead on, O cloud of Yahweh', but I changed them after learning that it might be more respectful of Jewish people not to use 'Yahweh' to name God aloud in worship. These texts first appeared in *Because We Are One People*, nos. 32 and 53, and were published in Ruth Duck, *Dancing in the Universe*, Chicago: GIA Publications Inc, 1992, nos. 39 and 50, and also in a number of hymnals. They are printed here by permission of GIA Publications Inc.

5 'Lead on, O King Eternal', Ernest Warburton Shurtleff (1862–1917); 'Rise up, O men of God', William Pierson Merrill (1867–1954).

6 See *The Book of Worship for Church and Home*, Nashville TN: The Methodist Publishing House, 1965, and Luther Weigle et al. (eds), *Revised Standard Version of the Bible*, New York: Thomas Nelson, 1952.

7 Ruth C. Duck, *Bread for the Journey*, New York: The Pilgrim Press, 1981, and Ruth C. Duck and Michael G. Bausch, *Everflowing Streams: Songs for Worship*, New York: The Pilgrim Press, 1981.

8 See Ruth Duck, 'First Church Sings', *The Hymn*, vol. 43, no. 3, July 1992, pp. 20–7.

9 Brian Wren, *Faith Looking Forward*, Oxford: Oxford University Press, 1983.

10 Ruth C. Duck, *Dancing in the Universe*, Chicago IL: GIA Publications Inc, 1992.

11 Ruth C. Duck, *Circles of Care*, Cleveland OH: The Pilgrim Press, 1998.

12 United Church of Christ, *New Century Hymnal*, Cleveland OH: The Pilgrim Press, 1995.

13 Daniel B. Merrick (ed.), *Chalice Hymnal*, St Louis, MO: Chalice Press, 1995.

14 Ruth Duck, *Welcome God's Tomorrow*, Chicago: GIA Publications Inc, 2005.

15 Erik Routley, *Rejoice in the Lord: A Hymn Companion to the Scriptures*, Grand Rapids MI: Eerdmans, 1985, no. 418. This text is sometimes published as 'Arise your light has come'.

16 Hoyt L. Hickman (ed.), *The Faith We Sing*, Nashville TN: Abingdon Press, 2000.

17 First published in Duck, *Circles of Care*, no. 39, later in *The Faith We Sing*, no. 2228.

18 Routley, 'Scriptural Resonances in Hymnody', *Reformed Liturgy and Music*, vol. 16, no. 3, summer 1982, pp. 120–5.

19 Ruth Duck, in *Welcome God's Tomorrow*, pp. 56–7.

20 Don E. Saliers, *Worship as Theology*, Nashville TN: Abingdon Press, 1994, p. 198.

21 Brauninger, interview.

22 From 'We praise you, God, for women', in *Circles of Care*, no. 27.

Kathy Galloway

My mother was always singing . . .

Heredity

When I was a child,
my mother sang songs.
Old songs, about goodwives and fishwives and stockings of silk:
I know where I'm going, and I know who's going with me . . .
songs from the radio,
take my hand, I'm a stranger in Paradise . . .
and
que sera sera, whatever will be will be . . .
songs from the shows,
tonight, tonight, won't be just any night,
tonight there will be no morning star . . .
sacred songs,
I know that my Redeemer liveth . . .
My mother was always singing.

When I was a child,
my grandmother told stories,
about long-ago weddings
we drove round the loch in a pony and trap, and the driver had
white satin ribbons on his whip
and brothers who went off to long-ago wars
that was your great-uncle Jack, he died in
the Boer War . . .
and never-met cousins in far-away places
there's Patsy in Melbourne and Harry in Canada . . .
and people she'd talked to in stations and tearooms
I met this awful nice young man while I was waiting for the bus, he
gave me his address
and asked me if I'd write to him . . .
My grandmother was always telling stories.

When I was a child,
my father was always going to meetings,
I'll be late tonight, Janet
getting people to do things,
believing that they could,
riding off on an old bike round the place.
Everybody knew him,
hi, Mr Orr . . .
implacable with MPs
that communist minister . . .
about the Bomb and South Africa.
When he had time, he followed the Hearts,
but my father was always going to meetings.

I see now that football
has been my main dissent from heredity![1]

I am the Leader of the Iona Community,[2] an ecumenical community with a justice and peace commitment and spirituality. I am a theologian, editor, liturgist, singer-songwriter and poet. I am also a minister of the Church of Scotland. I am neither an academic theologian (though I do some occasional lecturing in universities and theological colleges), nor a dogmatic theologian (though from time to time I serve on church committees engaged in theological reflection). I am a practical theologian working in the community.

That is to say, I engage in theological reflection and writing from a perspective of engagement in the life and work of local neighbourhoods and community groups, and especially of the Iona Community. As someone with a justice orientation and a commitment to the inclusiveness of the gospel, I have had significant engagement with women's groups and movements, with people living in poverty in Scotland, with campaigns and networks working for justice in global economics such as Christian Aid, with people who have had mental health problems and people who are marginalized because of their sexual orientation or marital status. In these groups and movements, I am engaged with Christians of many traditions, with people of other faiths and with people of goodwill who would not identify themselves as belonging to any religious community.

As a theologian, I am a poet, and a lover of poetry. In both my writing and editing (books, articles, and the magazine of the Iona Community, *Coracle*[3]), poetry, both my own and other's, features significantly. As a liturgist undertaking a considerable amount of liturgical work and writing both within and beyond Scotland, I am a poet. As a preacher I am a poet. As a singer, I write both hymns and song lyrics. As a community activist, I am a poet. As a mother of three, I am a poet. Poetry is inseparable from who I am, it is part of my identity, my mother tongue, if you like.

Song, poetry, story are in my DNA, as the poem above tries to communicate. But they are also in my geography, my culture, my gender and my faith background. I have been shaped as a poet since early childhood by the language of the Bible, of psalms and of hymns, by stories and songs, especially those of Scotland, by popular culture (I am a child of the 1960s, a child of the Beatles and of Bob Dylan). I was a singer before I was a songwriter, especially the songs of Robert Burns and the traditional songs of my country; I was a reader before I was a writer . . .

Child's heaven

I remember, I remember
the first time I visited Helensburgh Public Library
(staying with my gran);
the wood panelling,
the musty smell,
the sun falling along the floor
in long shafts of shimmering dust,
and all those books!

My insides dissolved
and flooded with ecstasy.
I thought I had arrived in heaven.[4]

. . . I was a writer of prose before I was a writer of poetry, of stories, articles, essays, lectures, speeches and above all of sermons, because I am a preacher. I did not begin to write formal poetry until I was nearly 40. I served a long apprenticeship. But long before my first poems and song lyrics were published, poetry and songs were forming in me:

- as a minister of the Church of Scotland, involved in creating liturgical and informal rites of passage – for weddings in gardens, on beaches, on islands, in the People's Palace; for hundreds of funerals and memorials; for the dedication of children, interfaith ceremonies, blessings for same-sex couples, blessings of houses, new jobs, new ventures; in healing rituals for survivors of sexual and domestic abuse and broken relationships,

- as a radical theologian, especially involved in reinterpreting the Christian and religious traditions from the margins, in rediscovering and re-imagining the history not part of history, in the memory of suffering, marginalization, reclaiming lost histories,
- as a community activist, as someone sympathetic to people's search for meaning, justice and value – at nuclear bases, outside embassies, in vigils, poverty hearings, acts of resistance and witness, in liturgies for racial, gender, economic justice.

As a theologian working in the community, I am committed to working corporately because it is consistent with my theological understanding that wholeness, holiness, is found not in the recesses of the individual soul but in the belonging of the body personal within the body politic and the Body of Christ. It is in the sharing of our gifts and our wounds that we find healing, experience the challenges of our divided world and receive encouragement to resist evil, to work for justice and to be peacemakers.

So, if as a theologian I am also a poet, as a poet I am also a theologian. Creative writing is a major part of the work I am engaged in with others, and I observe it to be for others, as I have discovered it to be for myself, a source of healing, encouragement, empowerment and solidarity. Creative writing, whether poetry, prose or song, is often thought of as a solitary art form, and certainly most writers will at some point be working alone. But in reality, it is more accurate to describe it as an activity that involves the interplay of solitude and community, of being alone and being with others. All of the contexts I have mentioned were corporate ones. After I started writing poetry, I joined a local writers' group; I found this encouraging, challenging (it was mostly composed of elderly male, West of Scotland trade unionists) and a helpful discipline. I was initially encouraged to write poetry by a comment made by the feminist theologian Rosemary Radford Ruether, who, hearing me preach a sermon in Iona Abbey, said that I was a poet, an identification I had not previously made but was then inspired to explore.

Art is one of the ways in which people seek both to select the features of real significance, to discern and express what is meaningful for them, and to order the signs and symbols, to shape and participate in the world they live in. The attempt to make sense of our lives, to articulate our truth, our story to live by, is a crucial one, for when people lose meaning, when their lives drift into meaninglessness, they lose other things as well. They lose a sense of belonging, a place or people or context where they are at home; and they lose a sense of identity, of knowing who they are. Of course, these things are not static, they are dynamic, always in the process of coming into being, only becoming self-conscious as we attempt to name them.

> Who are we, trapped in our ways
> 　Of dying towards the fact
> of only once having been, together
> or separate in our own being
> 　But never wholly separate, only a part
> of the time we live in, and with others occupy.[5]

Art is a naming. The songs and stories and myths, the paintings and sculptures and architecture and design, the plays and poems and dances, the gardens and public spaces, the ceremonies and rituals and sacraments of a society all communicate something of the meaning of its life, its values, its relationship to place and geography, its identity and historical self-understanding. They are its representation of the past, its presence to itself and others, its hopes and dreams for the future. People express all of these things through their art. The great artists express them in ways that communicate powerfully across time and even culture, the rest of us participate in them in solidarity with our community, with delight at the refreshment they offer us, in the expectation of being challenged to go beyond ourselves and our own narrow horizons, in resistance to the diminishment of life, in gratitude that being a human being contains the possibility to sing, to dance, to write, to paint, to play. We write, sing, paint, dance, dream ourselves back to life and meaning. To participate in art is to hope once again.

At a time of great change for women, for example, both in the world and in the Church, it has been important for women to name and be named. The rediscovery and revaluing of the stories and creativity of women in the past (the 'history not part of history'), the envisioning of new ways of being and of 'being-in-relationship' in music, visual arts, creative writing, dance, working with natural elements, film, theatre and so much else, has helped women to make transitions and find new names for their future. At the same time, the very act of doing this has thrown into sharp relief, has raised to a new visibility the huge injustice, violence and economic marginalization that affects so many women worldwide, and that has so often in the past been unnoticed, invisible where the history of women was simply incorporated into that of men.

Real

I'm not a symbol.
I'm not a statistic.
I'm not the inches in somebody's column.

I'm not admirable, but
I'm not pitiable either.
I'm simply human.

If you turned me inside out,
you'd find fury, fear, regret and sorrow
struggling with the love and longing,
hope and wonder,
and all my neediness.

Please take these things seriously.
Don't pietize or glamorize or trivialize or sermonize.
They are the marks of my life,
gift and loss,
wound and offence.
Please respect them.

I am at odds with all that requires me to be a symbol.
I insist on being real.[6]

In my creative writing, by which I mean my poetry, my songs and hymns, some (though not all) of my public speaking and prose writing and some of my editing (I do not differentiate among them, but see them all as simply using slightly different modes of expression characterized by rhythm) I am motivated by several imperatives.

Proclaiming and reclaiming the word

There are many ways in which poetry is already a part of faith. One of the most vividly evident is in liturgy and worship. I have sometimes, especially in the past, written songs out of desperation, having failed to find appropriate and contemporary words for such subjects as intercession, the environment, justice and everyday life. I have written poetry, story, drama and songs on biblical texts, the Christian year, the seasons of the earth's year and as homily or sermon. I regularly sing in my

preaching. I have written psalms, collects, blessings, curses, lamenta-
tions, wise words, benedictions, journey prayers, closing responses,
words to carry as icons.

Writing to save our lives

Another important dimension of creative writing is its therapeutic
potential. Often in my life and work I am with people who are deeply
wounded; and I carry my own wounds. Sometimes the wounds are
those which are part of the tragic nature of human life, they are deeply
personal yet also universal. We love, and the loved one dies or is absent
or lets us down; we are anxious about our children; we let go of long-
cherished but unrealized hopes and dreams; we age and must let go of
strength and vigour. The very ordinariness of these wounds does not
make them any the less painful.

And sometimes the wounds are the result of preventable human folly
or cruelty. They attack physical, mental, emotional and spiritual health
and wellbeing. The wounds may go back to early childhood or may
have been sustained last week. The task of healing is central to the
gospel. Where love and mercy are (where healing is), there is God.

Rejoicing in heaven

She sings like a raucous angel.
The Blessed Patsy Cline of Pollokshields;
and heaven applauds.
Earth, on the other hand,
whose taste is in its arse,
has not been so appreciative,
and has rewarded her with
abusive men,
crummy houses,
rotten jobs
and a tendency to badmouth her
when she drinks too much.
However, I have it on good authority
that when Celia sings
saints start swaying their hips
and archangels go all dreamy.
They like a bit of attitude in heaven.[7]

Poetry and song almost always comes from an urgency, from a deep need to express and communicate something about the human condition, or at least, about *our* human condition, something we are passionate about. When people are writing expressively, they are using an artistic medium. There is always a learning value to this. There is a value in terms of human communication and exchange, and often in empowerment, encouragement and self-worth. There is a value in the human right to express one's truth in the written word and take pleasure and pride in that. Accomplishment, however, requires further work, learning the disciplines of writing in a particular form, crafting and redrafting and reshaping my initial expression. But just because I am not a proficient and skilled poet does not mean that it is not a good and life-enhancing thing for me to do. I am healed by it.

Writing to make a new world possible

The power of writing has always been recognized in political change and struggles for justice. The singer, poet, the playwright, the journalist have all been on the front line of liberation movements, for example, and are often the first to be imprisoned or otherwise silenced. They are dangerous because they question received wisdom, they present an alternative truth, they are nonconformists and dissenters. In the Church too there have always been those who sang, spoke and wrote and those who silenced them.

When people experience marginalization and silencing, finding their own voices again is not just an act of resistance, it is an act of *insistence*. It is a way of stating, 'You cannot continue to ignore and overlook me. I will be heard.' And remarkably often, people find their voices through writing. This can be a long and painful process, may even require the discovery of a new language. Marlene Nourbese Philip, an African-Caribbean woman, uses her writing to struggle with what it means when the only language you have is the language of the slave-owners, because your own African language has been prohibited on penalty of having your tongue cut out.

Edict 1
Every owner of slaves shall, wherever possible, ensure that his slaves belong to as many ethno-linguistic groups as possible. If they cannot speak to each other, they cannot then foment rebellion and revolution.

Edict 2
Every slave caught speaking his native language shall be severely
punished. Where necessary, removal of the tongue is recommended.
The offending organ, when removed, should be hung on high in a
central place, so that all may see and remember.

when the smallest cell remembers –
how do you
how can you
when the smallest cell
                    remembers
lose a language

And:

absencelosstears laughter grief
in any language
                    the same
only larger
                    for the silence
                              monstrosity
obscenity
tongueless wonder
blackened stump of a tongue
                              torn
out
            withered
            petrified
                              burnt
on the pyres of silence
a mother's child foreign
                              made
by a tongue that cursed
                    the absence
in loss
tears laughtergrief
                    in the word[8]

But it is not only in campaigning that writing is a powerful force for
change and transformation. It is perhaps above all so in celebration,
spirituality and the expression of desire. These things communicated in

poetry, hymn, song are an unambigious refusal to allow the diminishment or reduction of our humanity. This is why I write and sing.

A peaceful land

*What is being a nation? A talent springing in the heart. And love
of country? Keeping house among a cloud of witnesses. (Waldo
Williams)*[9]

When one hundred thousand people
met to march from Glasgow Green,
there were millions more walked with them,
a cloud of witnesses unseen,
from the past and from the future,
and the cry on every hand,
'not in our name do you go to war,
this must be a peaceful land'.

And how shall we teach our children
love of country, pride of place?
Shall we say, we once were heroes,
of a fiery, fighting race;
and forget the stains of violence –
people beaten, enslaved and banned?
Or shall we now be peacemakers
in a hospitable land?

From the Pentland to the Solway,
from the Forth down to the Clyde,
city streets and quiet places
and the turning of the tide;
shall we rise on wings of eagles
soaring over wave and sand,
never seeing beneath the surface
to the scars upon the land?

We are armoured and defended
like an empire dressed for war.
But we face no threat or peril
and we don't know what it's for.
'Take the missiles from the waters',

it's our dream and our demand.
Turn the weapons into ploughshares,
Give us back a peaceful land.

There's a choice that lies before us.
How shall Scotland best be known?
For the glories of its history
and its loveliness alone?
Or shall care for all earth's people
be the song for which we stand,
and the flowering of our nation
as a just and peaceful land?[10]

Notes

1 Kathy Galloway, 'Heredity', in Nancy E. M. Bailey (ed.), *A Scottish Childhood*, vol. 2, Glasgow: HarperCollins, 1998, pp. 152–3.

2 Kathy Galloway completed her term as Leader in 2009 and joined Christian Aid.

3 *Coracle*, the quarterly magazine of the Iona Community, Glasgow: The Iona Community.

4 Kathy Galloway, 'Child's heaven', in Bailey (ed.), *A Scottish Childhood*, vol. 2, p. 154.

5 Tom Leonard, 'Proem', *Outside the Narrative*, Exbourne: Etruscan Books & Word Power Books, 2009.

6 Kathy Galloway, 'Real', *The Dream of Learning Our True Name*, Glasgow: Wild Goose Publications, 2004, p. 14.

7 Kathy Galloway, 'Rejoicing in heaven', *The Dream of Learning Our True Name*, p. 98.

8 Marlene Nourbese Philip, 'Edicts'; 'When the smallest cell remembers', p. 67; 'absencelosstears', p. 92, in *She Tries Her Tongue; her silence softly breaks*, Charlottetown PEI, Canada: Ragweed Press 1989.

9 Waldo Williams, 'What Is Man?' (Pa beth yw dyn?)', in *Dail Pren* (*The Leaves of the Tree*), Aberystwyth: Gwasg Aberystwyth, 1956.

10 Kathy Galloway, 'A peaceful land', in Neil Paynter (ed.), *Gathered and Scattered*, Glasgow: Wild Goose Publications, 2007; Tune: 'Beach Spring' (American traditional).

Sue Gilmurray

This is my song

I have never thought of myself primarily as a hymn-writer, yet I have undoubtedly written hymns. When, for the first time, I joined others on a hymn-writing weekend in the autumn of 2008, I felt quite at home: the territory was familiar. Much of my creative output, however, refuses to fit neatly into the 'hymn' category.

That I have a facility for writing melodies and verses is undeniable, and it has always been a part of me. In early childhood, as soon as I started learning the piano, I also started making up my own tunes on it. Early efforts, unsurprisingly, were quite derivative. By the age of 12 or 13 I was tentatively trying to write both (cringe-makingly trite) pop songs and religious verses. I went to church with my parents, and *The English Hymnal* was familiar ground, so I knew the sort of thing that was expected.

My school had a good music department, and I took O level and A level music there, and learned to sing in the choir. My own songs would arrive now and again, not so derivative now, as an idea surfaced in my mind and I tried to give it expression in words and music. I wrote because I felt the need, not for any particular audience, though I was excited and pleased when a song had an airing in a school assembly or service. I also sang in local folk clubs, in a folk trio with my brother and a friend, typical 1960s fare copied from records: Bob Dylan, Donovan, Ralph McTell, Joan Baez.

At university, where I read classics, I grew up a lot as a Christian, and began to write songs based on a personal faith. We used them sometimes at Christian Union events, but I enjoyed a varied musical diet, also singing in chapel choirs and Gilbert and Sullivan operas.

After graduating I worked for a couple of years for Scripture Union, a clerical job at their distribution centre in Bristol, and would go and sing solos at the churches of various colleagues – Anglican, Methodist, Pentecostal, Baptist, Brethren. I heard the Fisherfolk and sang songs from *Sound of Living Waters*.[1] I loved to sing, and was thrilled if I found that one of my own songs really reached people, though most were not written for congregational singing.

In the early years of my marriage, before the children were born, I worked in the Church House Bookshop in Westminster, and would sing at church events in a quartet with my husband and a couple of friends. During this time I wrote a cycle of songs based on *The Lion, the Witch and the Wardrobe*.[2] It was performed in the chapel at Church House and very well received. I did wonder about trying to get it published, but the whole copyright question was too thorny.

About this time, helping to lead a small choir in my local church, I started writing pieces for the choir and congregation to sing, and have continued to this day. For more than twenty years now I have been combining a full-time job as an academic librarian with singing and writing music in a variety of styles for a lively Anglican parish church. This song was written for Passiontide, and the chorus works as a counter-melody to the hymn 'Glory be to Jesus', while the verses have their own tune:

Gather up your burden of shame and loss,
take it up without delay,
bring it all to the man on the cross,
for he died just to take it away

Bring out the pain, bring out the fear,
all you have borne alone,
pain of your life, fear of your death,
familiar or unknown.
Chorus

Bring out the sin, bring out the guilt,
yesterday's or today's,
dark in your soul, dragging you down,
spoiling your words and ways.
Chorus

Take in his life, take in his gift,
knowing how much it cost,
healing and help, pardon and peace,
never alone or lost.
Chorus[3]

I still think of myself as first and foremost a folk musician. Although my instrument is keyboard, not the more typical guitar, my songs generally have regular metres and tempi, with harmonies based on chords a guitar can strum or pick. Often there is a symmetrical pattern, a repeated line, or a chorus. I am reaching out with an idea or a story, and an invitation to join in and sing with me. I write to express myself, to worship God, to sing *to* other people, and often I am also trying to elucidate something true, and make a song (or hymn) for us *all* to sing.

He said we must forgive to be forgiven,
and life is in his words.

He said we should do good to those who hate us,
and life is in his words.

He said when we make peace we are God's children,
and life is in his words.

We leave behind our lies to follow Jesus,
we leave behind our wars to follow Jesus,
we leave behind our selves to follow Jesus,
for life is in his words.[4]

So far, though, I have not mentioned what has truly spurred on my song- and hymn-writing for about fifteen years now: peace and the peace movement.

I had taken part in some CND activities in the 1980s when my children were small and the threat posed by nuclear weapons suddenly loomed larger. I wrote one or two songs about the issue, but then became preoccupied with work and family, and found little time for activism. Meeting members of the Anglican Pacifist Fellowship (APF) in the mid-1990s awoke the activist in me again, as it brought into sharp focus the question of war and the Christian faith. Despite the life, teaching and example of Jesus, most of us Christians calmly accept our country's maintenance of a nuclear deterrent, its leading part in the international arms trade, its enormous expenditure on ever more sophisticated and destructive weapons, and its recourse to the killing of the people of other countries and the sacrifice of its own troops in war.

Once I had joined the APF I wanted fresh songs and hymns expressing the gospel of peace and encouraging Christians to explore what it meant to try to follow Christ, instead of the spurious doctrine of the just war, and started producing my own. I wrote both Christian and secular songs as I learnt more about the issues and tried to apply new insights to the old debates about Christianity and the use of violence. This one, 'People of Jesus', was written, and recorded for APF, as a song, but has since been used as a hymn:

> After all the bitter lessons of our age,
> after all the wars that should have ended war,
> in so many lands the same old battles rage,
> people killing as their fathers killed before.
> Who can hope that this will cease?
> Who can work for justice and for peace?
> Who, if not the people of Jesus,
> who if not the children of the cross?
> Look to him, our shining example,
> gaining the victory where the world sees loss.[5]

Most of my work has not been aimed at publication, but has been written for my church or its choir to sing, or for use at a peace event. Suitable items have then been taken up and used by friends and friends of friends. One anti-arms-trade song called 'The war machine rolls round' has found its way into the repertoire of several political choirs, and on to song-sheets used at demonstrations, a sort of publication by grapevine:

> We've an industry that lives and thrives
> making tools to shatter human lives,
> and our honest workers ply their skill
> helping distant tyrants maim and kill
> as the war machine rolls round.
> And the war machine rolls round and round
> and the poor and the weak get trampled on the ground,
> and from where we stand their cries are drowned
> by the clink of the franc and the dollar and the pound
> as the war machine rolls round.[6]

Inspiration can come in a variety of ways. I am thinking, reading, discussing, listening to sermons, mulling matters over on a day-to-day basis, and something will trigger the impulse to set an idea down in verse. Often the tune will evolve while I am working on the words; occasionally it will come later. If it is in a regular metre, the text may well fit existing hymn tunes.

Sometimes a specific event or situation will be the trigger. I wrote 'Carol for the world' in 2001, trying to approach that year's Christmas in the wake of the enormity of 9/11, and it was published in *Worship Live* some years later. It is in the same metre as 'O little town of Bethlehem' and 'It came upon the midnight clear', not to mention 'I heard the voice of Jesus say', and can be sung to any of these tunes, though I did write it its own eventually. These are verses two and three of five:

The eastern world grows dark with hate,
the western world with rage,
and battle-fires and funeral pyres
illuminate the stage
where leaders stalk in pride and power
while people shrink in fear.
What is it worth, a saviour's birth
about this time of year?

We know it was for peace he came
when angels filled the skies:
can we sing still about goodwill
with wars before our eyes?
we need forgiveness, mercy, grace,
and love so strong and clear
as he would show, so long ago,
about this time of year.[7]

In 2001 I wrote a song for a children's charity concert, a lullaby for parents or grandparents, expressing the hope and desire that their child would be spared conflict and suffering in later life:

I wish that I could make you free
of all the troubles yet to be,
the hurt, the hate, the cruelty
the world can visit on us.[8]

Logic then compelled me to face up to the diet of violence and ruthlessness so often fed to children in their upbringing:

There's a cowboy hero in a comic strip,
he's got a straight six-shooter firing from the hip,
he's gonna shoot the enemy down![9]

Then the appalling way in which children have been used in war and conflict in some parts of the world:

> The kid from Sierra Leone
> has a gun in his small, bony hands,
> and he shakes when he's left on his own . . .[10]

These songs had no place in the original concert, but they grew into *The Way of Peace*, a cycle of seven songs, which starts from the lullaby, faces squarely the evil done to children, then pivots on the fourth song towards hope, draws encouragement from past progress such as the abolition of the slave trade, exhorts us to teach one another peace, and ends with the hope that a child will be the one to lead us out of darkness and into light.

Some of the songs have appeared in *Worship Live*,[11] and the cycle has been performed several times. It can be sung with Bible readings and prayers between the songs, or with non-religious poems – I have used ones by Rudyard Kipling, e. e. cummings and others – because the whole work, though inspired by Christian faith, contains no religious language. Even the prayer that is the sixth song, 'Teach me the way of peace', might be addressed by a child to an adult, or any human being to another, just as well as by a person to God:

> Teach me the way of peace,
> not a peace that is frail and feeble
> but a peace that is strong and firm and brave,
> a healing of wounds, a facing of truth,
> a building of new understanding,
> and generous, generous always.[12]

My own church used *The Way of Peace* on a Good Friday, as an evening meditation. I was thrilled to have it used, but felt that the final song, 'And a child will lead us', was so upbeat as to jar on some people's sensibilities on such a solemn day of the Church's year. I looked around for a suitable hymn to come after the cycle and sum up the event, something which brought together Jesus the victim and Jesus the victor, Jesus the weak and Jesus the strong. In the end I wrote a new one, and we have used it several times thereafter:

> He is a child, takes away my pride by his very weakness,
> he is a man, meets me on the road, proves himself my friend,

CONTEMPORARY WOMEN HYMN-WRITERS

he is the Lamb, reaches to my soul, purging it of poison,
he is the Lord, leads me into life, worship's truest end.

Thus does one thing lead to another.

Many of the traditional hymns I grew up with have beautiful, sing-able tunes, but some don't. It is possible to be distracted from a good hymn text by the prospect of labouring through five or six verses of a tune that is boring, awkward to sing, too high, or otherwise unattract-ive. And some just plod, so our worship plods too. I have occasionally written new tunes for existing hymns since my youth, and they are usu-ally livelier and 'dance' more than the originals. Even if the words are in common metre, there is no need for the tune to be a totally predict-able series of notes with all the stresses in the usual places. I love to let the words suggest something more distinctive, which I hope will be a pleasure to sing.

Particularly interesting is the chance to write the first original tune for someone else's new hymn, an opportunity given by *Worship Live*. I have also written tunes for some texts by Christopher Idle, one of the best recent hymn-writers. It is very satisfying to write a melody for a text in an unusual metre, and to be aware that it fits and, in some way, illuminates the words.

In my youth, I wouldn't have said no to fame and fortune, though I'd have preferred to be known as a folk singer rather than a hymn-writer. These days I still want, as I always have, to use words and music to convey something that matters, with as much beauty and cogency as possible. I don't mind whether it's in church or outside it; but Christ's teaching, the mutual benefit of Christian fellowship, and the wonder-ful potential for inspiration and action that worship can release, mean that I shall always hope to share words, music and ideas in a Christian context. I welcome the chance to have material published as a way of sharing it more widely, but it is not a burning ambition. Maybe it should be!

The only time in my Christian life that I have felt handicapped by my gender was in childhood, when I was unable to join my boys-only parish choir. I have never felt slighted as a singer or musician because I am a woman. Nonetheless, I can't help but be aware that my gender is under-represented in church music, on the composing side even more than in the writing of hymn texts. I attended an enjoyable evening recently when the Royal School of Church Music (RSCM) launched a new musical resource for church choirs,[13] and it included not a single contribution from a female writer or composer. This was not deliberate, neither did anyone there (the majority were women) remark on it: it is normal. I find much the same in the secular world when I am looking for peace songs to sing, and also when I look at the sphere of classical music. There are some notable exceptions, but the majority of composers are male.

The reasons for this are probably complex. After so many generations in which the vast majority of women in Western culture were confined to the domestic sphere, it takes more than legislation to make our opportunities equal to those of men. Some women become militants and pioneers but, for most of us, our own perceptions and expectations need to develop over time. What matters is that we should all be able to develop the gifts we have been given by our creator. I am increasingly convinced that the exercise of our creativity is one of the most important and life-enhancing things we can do for ourselves; and, praise God, it is in its nature that we can also share it with one another.

Notes

1 See above, p. 190.

2 C. S. Lewis, *The Lion, the Witch and the Wardrobe*, Harmondsworth: Puffin, 1959, repr. 1972.

3 Unpublished.

4 Martin John Nicholls (ed.), *Hunger for Justice*, London: Kevin Mayhew, 2004; recorded by Sue Gilmurray and Celebration, *Finest hour*, Milton Keynes: Anglican Pacifist Fellowship, 1999.

5 Christopher Idle and Sue Gilmurray, *Songs for the Road to Peace*, Milton Keynes: Anglican Pacifist Fellowship, 2008; recorded on *Finest Hour*, 1999.

6 *Finest hour*, 1999.

7 *Worship Live* 30, Autumn 2004, p. 12.

8 Sue Gilmurray, *The Way of Peace*, CD and score, Ely: Mightier Pen Music, 2001.

9 *The Way of Peace*.

10 *The Way of Peace*; *Worship Live* 33, Autumn 2005, p. 8.

11 Lullaby in *Worship Live* 33, October 2005, p. 3; 'The tide turns' in no. 38, June 2007, p. 3; 'Candlelight' in no. 39, October 2007, p. 15.

12 *The Way of Peace*.

13 John Barnard and David Iliff, *Season by Season*, London: RSCM, 2008.

Shirley Erena Murray

Of women, and of women's hopes we sing,
of sharing in creation's nurturing,
of bearing and of birthing new belief,
of passion for the promises of life.[1]

When I wrote this in 1988, during the Ecumenical Decade of the Churches in Solidarity with Women, I was joining my sisters in an idea of 'This is *our* song'.

'Rise up, O men of God'[2] had had its day, and it was felt that 'have done with lesser things' had probably referred to women, in the guise of Eve, along with Mary. It was a time of excited ferment in New Zealand, where the Women's Movement had had a significant impact, and Christian feminism was demanding changes in church power structures, language and opportunity.

It did not occur to me then, having already nailed my colours to the mast of inclusiveness, and tailoring language to suit an ideology of gender balance, that this could be a contradiction in itself. Since the theme of the Decade was 'Who will roll the stone away?' it seemed self-evident that we women would and could challenge and gain a share in the patriarchal church on our own. It took one quiet male to point out that he could not participate in any congregational singing of this, were it ever suggested, especially as it went on to say:

We praise the God whose image is our own,
the mystery within our flesh and bone,
the womanspirit moving through all time
in prophecy, Magnificat and dream.

In this way, early on in my hymn-writing, I learned that the politics of inclusiveness are subtle, language is an inherently dangerous tool and it is wise to heed the needs of the *whole* congregation, when new and possibly jolting ideas are involved.

I had been working in the Research Unit of the Labour Party in Parliament Buildings, and was witnessing the attempts of the women MPs to

achieve social justice in many areas affecting equal pay, equal opportunity and more help for families and childcare. The next verse seemed
apt for the Church of the time:

> We labour for the commonwealth of God,
> and equal as disciples, walk the road,
> in work and status, asking what is just
> for sisters of the family of Christ.

The final verse had to address both men and women:

> Forgiving what is past, we seek the new:
> a finer justice, and a peace more true,
> the promise of empowering for our day
> when men and women roll the stone away.

How I started

But to go back a little: in the late 1970s, I was part of an adventurous
Presbyterian congregation at St Andrew's on the Terrace, Wellington.
They had put up with my first attempts at writing new texts to familiar
tunes and they took them on board with equanimity. Besides, I was the
minister's wife.

The reason why I began to write hymns is connected to this fact. It is
also connected to the ethos of being a New Zealander.

We have an attitude of 'do it yourself' – a kind of pioneer spirit which
is not intimidated by too much tradition and actually welcomes inven-
tiveness. (It will also rapidly cut down any tall poppies who think they
are 'above themselves'.) It seemed to me that the hymns we sang had no
resonance with the world I lived in, other than to join us with the traditional European 'three-tier' theology, even if disturbed by such thinkers
as J. A. T. Robinson, or our own victim of a heresy trial, Professor
Lloyd Geering, Principal of Knox Presbyterian Theological College.[3]

There was no imagery that evoked our particular environment, no
landscape of thought to accommodate the southern hemisphere seasons
(think of 'In the bleak midwinter' in high summer, for example), no
connection with the Maori culture of our society, which is officially
bicultural, nothing to sing to articulate our own hopes and visions.

There was also a language issue for me, apart from the obvious difficulty of God-language and inclusive language. Many of the hymns we

sang from my childhood onwards may have been theologically obso-
lescent, but into the bargain were often embarrassingly sentimental and
poorly crafted 'poetry' or incomprehensible biblical jargon (See 'Praise
to the Holiest in the Height',vv. 2–5[4]).

I appreciate and relate to precise and clean language, as opposed to
flowery and fudgy. I am, in knitting parlance, a plain rather than purl
sort of writer. I like language with crunch and bite that gives a jolt of reality. I like using short syllables (see 'God was in Christ'[5]), but also words
mellifluous enough to be poetic and singable – above all, singable.

So I have used such tough words as drugs, dollars, laser, raped, bullet,
soup-kitchen, stock markets, stigma/enigma, along with the gentler
vocabulary of compassion: enfold, hugs, playful, intuition, nurse, knit,
cherish, for example.

Living in a Presbyterian manse and hearing the desperation of my
husband John Murray as he tried to find hymns that would connect
with his preaching thrust, I began, very hesitantly, to write words to
familiar tunes. Two of my first public attempts were for Amnesty International events – one a 'Song for human rights' and the other 'God of
freedom, God of justice'.[6]

Samuel Butler is quoted as saying, 'Life is like playing a violin solo
in public and learning the instrument as one goes on.'[7] I feel that way
about the public aspect of hymn-writing. It is like laying out one's soul
on the church carpet and hoping one has learned enough of the craft
to be picked up.

Once considered, at the time I began, it seemed there were so many
urgent themes that needed addressing: peacemaking, racism, refugees,
care of the earth (I first wrote a 'green' hymn, 'Honour the earth'[8] in
1980, but it has taken decades for this to become a serious and sung
part of theology), healing, the city, AIDS. And along with these, new
interpretations of the sacraments and seasons of the church year. 'Now
to your table spread'[9] was written for World Communion Sunday, then
celebrated more widely. I might now think differently, in a multifaith
world, about the implications of the line:

as though all humankind around one table stood.

'O God, we bear the imprint of your face'[10] came out during the racist
upheaval of the anti-apartheid movement which split our country in
1981, and along the way, I was addressing the ordinary needs of people
in a congregation: baptismal, wedding and funeral hymns for community occasions.

While keeping consciously and carefully to inclusive language and concepts, I was also becoming bolder about using non-pious or overly 'devotional' vocabulary from everyday usage.

Who gave encouragement?

A strong imperative to keep writing was the project, headed by my husband John and a small group of friends, to create a New Zealand hymnbook that would be

- indigenous – reflecting our own country's history and culture,
- ecumenical – for all churches, and
- contemporary – to find new songs in the imagery and words of our own day.[11]

It is relevant to say that of the active musicians and writers on this editorial board, there were three women, four men and a male chair-person. The women represented were a Catholic Dominican nun, a Gospel Chapel composer and a Presbyterian laywoman. A Baptist woman teacher/composer joined the team for the next book.[12]

By 1993, *Alleluia Aotearoa* was born, and a new era of conscious-ness raised. I felt a wave of encouragement emanating from people, Australians as well as New Zealanders, who first adopted and sang these hymns.

One aspect of creating this hymnbook was to realize that there are far fewer text writers than composers, women or men. Very few people do both well – one counter example being Professor Colin Gibson, an editor with this group. I eventually began to avoid familiar traditional tunes in favour of the freshness and vitality of newly minted ones, and Colin set many of my first texts, as did Jillian Bray and Douglas Mews, other music editors. There was a surge of talent released, but more musical than textual.

During this process, in 1987 the Presbyterian Church of Aotearoa/New Zealand gave me a grant to publish a small book of 28 texts for the use of New Zealand churches, *In Every Corner Sing: New Hymns to Familiar Tunes in Inclusive Language*. All the tunes chosen were from the widely accepted Australian hymn book *With One Voice*, which had a New Zealand Supplement.

My collection travelled, via an American friend, to the desk of the editors of the 1990 hymnal of the Presbyterian Church USA.[13] This book was the entrée to acceptance by a major publisher, Hope Publishing Company, and the prelude to a larger collection of the same name, with 84 texts. The person who believed in my work and became a very good friend was George H. Shorney, President of Hope Publishing and a Presbyterian. His encouragement and introductions to composers and writers of hymns in the USA blessed me with many long-lasting friendships.

One of these was Brian Wren. His visit to New Zealand in 1988, and his stimulating teaching, led me to try different imagery, metres and themes. His 'Seven Hints for Hymn-writers' from his early collection *Faith Looking Forward*[14] is still a memorable and valuable reference point for me.

What Language Shall I Borrow was a breakthrough revelation in terms of understanding language bias. *Praying Twice*[15] has become an invaluable resource for me, as for many others. Most of all, he gave me confidence, and has never ceased to be a wonderfully generous and supportive influence.

Through Hope Publishing, I visited and spoke to the Hymn Society of the USA and Canada, and subsequently have travelled to give workshops for the Christian Conference of Asia and the World Council of Churches. I have also written theme songs for World Council of Churches (WCC) Assemblies and Christian Conference of Asia (CCA) gatherings.

This is a particular discipline, which I found demanding, since it was usually tied to biblical themes, as in 'God, in Your Grace Transform the World' (Ninth Assembly, Brazil, WCC Worship Book, 2006) and 'Fresh as the Morning', (CCA Tenth Assembly, Sri Lanka, 1995) which had to follow six Bible studies, one for each day.

Parallel to all this was a friendship with Dr I-to Loh, the eminent Taiwanese ethnomusicologist who was in the process of completing *Sound the Bamboo*, the ground-breaking Asian hymnal of 2000.[16] Many of the hymn texts needed an English-language version of the words fitted to an Asian tune, and he enlisted me to help with this. It was a fascinating and highly demanding exercise, since the myriad varieties of Asian music require a different ear, and a respect for different note values and instruments. The precise meanings of the original words were often too difficult to discern, since they sometimes arrived on poorly reproduced copies in unfamiliar notation. Nevertheless, I struggled along with this, and, when I finally visited Taiwan for a WCC workshop, was overwhelmed by the appreciation there of what it meant to sing hymns in one's own idiom and culture, a tribute to I-to Loh's vision.

Publication was also a test of deciding (if I was allowed – often I have *not* been) which tunes would interpret my words and would work as singable items in hymnals. A case in point was 'Loving Spirit',[17] which was written to fit the stresses of the tune 'Omni Die'. Though the metre 8787 looked obvious, its stresses were not, and a rash of tunes instantly appeared, some of which were ridiculously disjointed or inappropriate. This was an important learning curve for me.

Working with composers, however, did create many warm friendships with people, in New Zealand, the USA, and in WCC circles with such as Per Harling. Carlton Young is an exceptional one of these. Others I have never met in person but have felt an instant empathy with, such as Jane Marshall and Jim Strathdee. Another wild goose of a friend whose work has influenced me is the astonishing John Bell and the Iona Community songs. There are many to whom I owe 'lift-off' for my texts.

Development and changing perceptions

Over time, I think the craft of my writing has developed by becoming more adventurous in the use of imagery, and themes with contemporary connection. I have never wanted to stay with 'credal Christianity' and possibly repeat traditional givens.

I have, though, in 2004 interwoven old and new by using Psalm 23 as antiphon to a hymn of invitation to communion:

The bread is blessed, the wine is poured,
the joyful feast of Christ our Lord!
    You prepare a table before me,
    my cup overflows to the brim.

This bread be shared till all have food,
this wine run red for human good.
    You restore the spirit within me,
    you lead me in pathways to peace.

Not one be left, not one be lost,
the stone be rolled, the Cross uncrossed.
    Your unfailing goodness and mercy
    prepare me a room in your house . . .[18]

I have wanted to move on to where Christ consciousness as well as Christian conscience meshes with the world I experience in my own life and time. Almost everything I have written revolves, ultimately, round the concept of 'peace' in all its many manifestations. One of the most used of my texts (to my great astonishment) was written for a women's conference on the theme of 'Making Space':

> Come and find the quiet centre
> in the crowded life we lead,
> find the room for hope to enter,
> find the frame where we are freed:
>> clear the chaos and the clutter,
>> clear our eyes, that we can see
>> all the things that really matter,
>> be at peace, and simply be.[19]

My boldest attempt to 'speak peace' in my own context, has been to write a national hymn for Anzac Day 2005 – the most solemnly 'religious' day of our nation and Australia's, commemorating the First World War battle of Gallipoli and its aftermath battles:

> Honour the dead, our country's fighting brave,
> honour our children, left in foreign grave,
> where poppies blow, and sorrow seeds her flowers,
> weep for the crosses marked forever ours.

> Weep for the places ravaged with our blood,
> weep for the young bones buried in the mud,
> weep for the powers of violence and greed,
> weep for the deals done in the name of need.

> Honour the brave whose conscience was their call,
> answered no bugle, went against the wall,
> suffered in prisons of contempt and shame,
> branded as cowards on our country's name.

> Weep for the waste of all that might have been,
> weep for the cost that war has made obscene,
> weep for the homes that ache with human pain,
> weep that we ever sanction war again.

Honour the dream for which our nation bled,
held now in trust to justify the dead,
honour their vision on this solemn day:
peace known in freedom, peace the only way.[20]

Perhaps because this speaks at a time when war commemoration and
tourist travel to gravesites has intensified, or because it has a magnificent
tune by Colin Gibson and was recorded by the prestigious NZ Army
Band (all factors to be counted in), this has been adopted all over our
country. I have continued to try writing hymns/songs that truly reflect
the now more multicultural nature of our country, and have used common Maori words that give the feeling of communal acceptance.

Back in 1987 I was struggling with the unreality of singing an incarnational Christmas without its shadow side, and the endless greed of
consumer societies set against the much more needy ones. Hence 'Hunger Carol' ('Child of joy and peace' v. 4):

Son of poverty,
shame us till we see
        self-concerned how we deny you,
        by our greed we crucify you
        on a Christmas tree,
Son of poverty.[21]

Also in 1987, when I was involved in the effort to make New Zealand
nuclear-free, I was aware of the many people of goodwill, but not necessarily Christian, who have always worked tirelessly to bring about
peace in all its forms. So it was that, without any direct reference to
God, Jesus or the Holy Spirit, I wrote a small piece which has become
more widely accepted than I would have guessed. I have continued to
be aware of the value of this for the wider circle of 'believers':

This thread I weave,
this step I dance,
        this stone I carve,
        this ball I bounce,
                this nail I drive,
                this pearl I string,
                        this flag I wave,
                        this note I sing,

this pot I shape,
this fire I light,
 this fence I leap,
 this bone I knit,
  this seed I nurse,
  this rift I mend,
   this child I raise,
   this earth I tend,

this cheque I write,
this march I join,
 this faith I state,
 this truth I sign,
  this is small part
  in one small place
   of one heart's beat
   for one great Peace.[22]

In 1993, I wrote a 'breakthrough' carol which has travelled farthest of all my carols:

Star-Child, earth-Child,
go between of God,
love Child, Christ Child,
heaven's lightning rod,
 This year, this year let the day arrive
 when Christmas comes for everyone, everyone alive!

Street child, beat child,
no place left to go,
hurt child, used child
no one wants to know,
 This year, this year . . .[23]

By 1994 I was writing:

God weeps
 at love withheld,
 at strength misused,
 at children's innocence abused,
and till we change the way we love,
     God weeps.

God bleeds
  at anger's fist
  at trust betrayed
  at women battered and afraid,
and till we change the way we win,
        God bleeds.[24]

In 1998, 'For everyone born, a place at the table':

For woman and man, a place at the table,
revising the roles, dividing the share,
with wisdom and grace, dividing the power,
for woman and man, a system that's fair . . .

for just and unjust, a place at the table,
abuser, abused, with need to forgive,
in anger, in hurt, a mindset of mercy
for just and unjust, a new way to live,

   and God will delight when we are creators
   of justice and joy, compassion and peace,
   yes, God will delight when we are creators
   of justice, justice and joy![25]

In 2002, a carol in reaction to the war in Iraq:

Summer sun or winter skies

Shadows track the hawk in flight
   Christmas now –
children born in fire and fight
silent night a violent night.
   Hawks are in control
   of a nation's soul

There where terror plies its trade
   Christmas now –
children learn to be afraid,
minefields of distrust are laid,
   evil is in force
   on a winning course.

Child of peace, God's human face,
    Christmas now –
come to plead war's counter-case,
bring the dove a nesting-place,
    though her wings are torn,
    though her blood is drawn . . .[26]

And by 2009, after struggling with the churches to sing 'green' hymns:

Silent spring song

Now is the time for a reckoning,
now all is flowering and flourishing,
    God, help your children
    mindfully listen:
soon there may be just a silent spring.

Silent the voices in bush and tree,
silent the creatures of land and sea,
    God, help your children
    mindfully listen:
ours are the hands that took earth for free.

We are the root of the earth's unease,
we are the pirates who dredge the seas,
    God, help your children
    mindfully listen:
ours is the creed doing as we please . . .[27]

Irregular metres, for me, give more flexibility for both words and music to speak in a contemporary idiom. While it may be regrettable for some that we no longer sing so often in four-part harmony (and there are other ways of enjoying congregational music!), it is obvious from what is sung on the popular media that *any* song can be sung – however breakaway from traditional forms – if the tune line is compelling enough and the words say what we want to say. Listen to how we still hum along to Beatles and Abba hits, or songs with transition passages such as 'Bridge over troubled water'.

Difficulties in publishing

I have never, from the very beginning, had anything but acceptance for my work. But I have had issues with editors of publications who have *changed* my work. The most recent example of this is the hymnal *Church Hymnary* (fourth edition), where my words have several times been altered without any consultation or permission.

My first experience of this began with the Presbyterian Church Hymnal, *Hymns, Psalms and Spiritual Songs* (1990), which changed the first line of 'Loving Spirit' by substituting 'Holy Spirit' (in case?) and omitted an 'offending' verse, presumably because it had the word 'lover' therein!

Summing up – gender influence

Apart from texts that take women overtly as their theme ('Make Plain the Vision' or 'Woman's Song' and 'Roll the Stone Away',[28] along with some other 'occasional' hymns such as the one quoted first in this article), I do not see my gender as influencing what I write or as any bar to being published.

I began writing both to fill a need in our congregation's life and to write myself into faith. Subsequently, I have tried to address southern-hemisphere theology and the faith identity of being a New Zealander, along with the challenges of eco-theology and the continuing exploration of what it means to be Christian now.

My local New Zealand environment, church and friends gave immediate encouragement, and this was followed by swift acceptance and publication in the USA, UK and Australia.

I have had no setbacks and have been commissioned to write hymns for world events (WCC Assemblies) and national events, such as the General Assembly of the Presbyterian Church of Aotearoa/New Zealand, as well as on occasions such as the 2010 American Guild of Organists' National Convention.

This, so far, is the story of my song.

Notes

1 Shirley Erena Murray, *In Every Corner Sing*, Carol Stream IL: Hope Publishing Company, 1992, no 56.

2 William Pierson Merrill (1867–1954).

3 The three tiers are earth, heaven and hell: J. A. T. Robinson, *Honest to God*, London: SCM Press, 1963. The trial was in 1967 on the charge of 'grave impropriety of conduct in teaching doctrines contrary to the Bible and Westminster Confession of Faith . . . and gravely disturbing the peace and unity of the Church'.

4 John Henry Newman (1801–90).

5 *In Every Corner Sing*, no. 34.

6 'Song for human rights', no. 59, and 'God of freedom, God of justice' no. 29, *In Every Corner Sing*.

7 Cited in Mardy Grothem, *i never met a metaphor I didn't like*, London: Collins, 2008, p. 125.

8 *In Every Corner Sing*, no. 31.

9 *In Every Corner Sing*, no. 52.

10 *In Every Corner Sing*, no. 54.

11 Cf. John Murray, Introduction, *Alleluia Aotearoa*, Palmerston North: New Zealand Hymnbook Trust, 1993.

12 *Carol Our Christmas*, Palmerston North: New Zealand Hymnbook Trust, 1996.

13 *Hymns, Psalms and Spiritual Songs: Presbyterian Hymnal*, Louisville KY: Westminster/John Knox Press, 1990.

14 Brian Wren, *Faith Looking Forward*, Oxford: Oxford University Press, 1983.

15 Brian Wren, *Praying Twice: The Music and Words of Congregational Song*, Louisville KY: Westminster John Knox Press, 2000.

16 *Sound the Bamboo*, Muang, Thailand: Christian Conference of Asia, 1990, revised 2000.

17 *In Every Corner Sing*, no. 48.

18 Shirley Erena Murray, *Touch the Earth Lightly*, Carol Stream IL: Hope Publishing Company, 2008, no. 46.

19 *In Every Corner Sing*, no. 10.

20 *Touch the Earth Lightly*, no. 20.

21 *In Every Corner Sing*, no. 5.

22 *In Every Corner Sing*, no. 70.

23 Shirley Erena Murray, *Every Day in your Spirit*, Carol Stream IL: Hope Publishing Company, 1996, no. 23.

24 *Every Day in your Spirit*, no. 12.

25 *Faith Forever Singing*, Palmerston North: New Zealand Hymnbook Trust, 2000, no. 17.

26 *Touch the Earth Lightly*, no. 44.

27 *Touch the Earth Lightly*, no. 36.

28 'God of our foremothers' ('Make Plain the Vision'), Shirley Erena Murray, *Faith Makes the Song*, Carol Stream IL: Hope Publishing Company, 2002, no. 16; 'With my whole heart' ('Woman's song'), *Every Day in your Spirit*, no. 36; 'Roll the Stone Away' ('Where God enlightens, bless the light'), *Every Day in your Spirit*, no. 30.

Interview with Betty Carr Pulkingham

Tell me a bit about your early Christian journey – what were the major influences on you? How did you come to Christ?

I was raised in a very faithful Christian family. My parents were both Christian – but not at the same church, so I was opened in my early years to the fact that there were various blooms on the plant that is Christianity. Denominationalism never frightened me. I grew up with an organic ecumenical feel.

My mother was a lifelong Baptist. My father had Scottish Presbyterian roots, but joined the Methodist Episcopal Church – this was before the two branches of the Methodist Church united to form the United Methodist Church. As my father travelled a lot, she agreed that I should go to the Methodist Sunday school, so that I could spend time with him.

I didn't have a Damascus Road conversion experience, but absorbed a lot from my parents. Who was it that said Christianity is not so much taught as caught? I caught it from my family.

My father was a judge, so taught me about fairness and justice and compassion. He was a very fair-minded man. My mother had had a more dramatic conversion as a teenager. When I wanted to be baptized at the Methodist church, at the age of 11, she made sure I knew what I was doing – that this was no light thing, but that I was giving my life to Jesus Christ. So I took it to heart, and took responsibility in my baptism.

There were good teachers, and a couple of youth leaders in particular, at the church, who influenced me. The Methodist church was a good, nurturing place, where I spent my teenage years.

Were you always involved in Christian music?

I was just talking to someone the other day, who asked me about early musical influences and two things came to mind.

The first was in kindergarten when I was five years old. The teacher used to put out Indian rugs for the children to lie down and rest on. While we were resting, she used to play classical music. Lying there, reposing, I thought I had died and gone to heaven! All that beauty just washed over me.

The other was on visits to my paternal grandparents. My father had four brothers. It was a humble little house, and I used to be put to bed in a small bedroom off the sitting room. I could hear the muffled sound of the men in conversation, and occasionally they would sing a hymn. One uncle had a beautiful bass voice, and the wonderful sound of male harmonies wrapped me in a blanket of love. It drew me into a sense of the goodness of God – this was a safe place; God was a safe place.

I started to study the piano at the age of eight, and was asked, when I was about ten, to play hymns for the Sunday school. Later, at about twelve or thirteen, I sang solos in the evening services, and I was one of the worship leaders for the youth fellowship. The Methodist church was excellent at encouraging young people to use their gifts.

I had a voice teacher who was choir director at the Episcopal church, and invited me to join them. This was during the worst period of the Second World War, and we would kneel at the end of communion, and sing a prayer hymn for peace. The power of that corporate prayer for peace flooded my soul. I felt really in touch with God. I began to appreciate the Anglican ethos of worship – not abandoning my roots, but going into other rooms in the house of Christianity.

There was an excellent choral director at my school, and I used to sing in Glee Clubs and operettas. When I went to university – in fact, to what was then called the Women's College of the University of North Carolina – I wanted to major in music. My father thought this very impractical, but my mother was my advocate! Even then, they wrote to the Dean of the Music School expressing their doubt that I was up to doing the course. At the end of the first term, my results were straight A's, so I guess they were convinced!

So for four years I majored in piano, and spent a lot of time in the practice room.

I first came across your name when a group of young American Christians came to Britain – they were called 'The Fisherfolk' and they introduced us to the songs that we later found in Sound of Living Waters *and* Fresh Sounds – *which you compiled. How did that come about?*

The Fisherfolk were actually named by an English clergyman! My husband Graham was invited by Cuthbert Bardsley, the then Bishop of Coventry, to bring his household to live and work in the diocese. He had seen a documentary based on the work being done by our church, the Church of the Redeemer, in Houston. He felt that our church was living a life close enough to the middle class way of life that his flock could identify, yet sacrificial enough to challenge them.

The Church of the Redeemer had an outreach called 'Fishermen Incorporated'. When the aforementioned clergyman was introducing us to the congregation, he could see that people were not engaged by that title, so he just came out with, 'Please welcome these young Fisher-folk' – and that was the name from then on. It just happened. God named us!

We came over in 1972, my husband and I and five of our six children – the eldest son being in New Zealand at the time. My daughter went right through the British educational system, including a PhD at Edin-burgh. The doors just kept opening for her.

The books, *Sound of Living Waters* and *Fresh Sounds*, came out of the worshipping life of the Church of the Redeemer and our work in the UK. At the Church of the Redeemer, we learnt to incorporate our new music with traditional hymns. We never abandoned the traditional hymns.

We had some very good advice along the way. An older man, who was teaching Bible classes, held up the Episcopal Church hymnal and said, 'You know, you have everything in there that you need for good doctrine and biblical grounding. Don't do what the Pentecostals did earlier in the century. They threw away the hymn books and sang nothing but choruses.'

Also, we learnt that good liturgy has to build on and be an expres-sion of the people. We had a variety of people at the church, and this led to a variety of music in worship. Hence the books have a mixture of traditional hymns and songs.

We settled into Coventry and, while we were there, made important contacts with publishers, contacts that would later bear much fruit. However, after a while, we outgrew the accommodation at Coventry and needed somewhere bigger.

We knew a community of Anglican Benedictines at Nashdom Abbey. Through them, we heard about a community of Anglican nuns, the Order of the Good Shepherd, living in Yeldall Manor in Berkshire. At that time, there were only three sisters left, and they needed to find somewhere different.

That meant that, through the Anglican Benedictines, we were able to get a very good lease arrangement on the Manor, which was a won-derful place. Our bishop now was the Bishop of Oxford, who was also the chaplain to all the Anglican religious orders, and he helped us to define ourselves more clearly as an experimental religious community. We chose the name 'Community of Reconciliation'.

More people from the United States joined us, and English families would come and live with us for a while and share in this community life. Several people stayed at the Manor, and others went to another community in Dorset. We had teams of young people going out by invitations into churches. I was anchored to a typewriter and piano, working on the arrangements for the songs for them to sing.

In 1975, the Primate of the Scottish Episcopal Church invited my husband Graham to move to become Provost of the Cathedral of the Isles. So we, including a substantial number of Celebration Community members, moved there to the Isle of Cumbrae.

There are many more women writers in those books and in the charismatic, Pentecostal traditions generally than in the so-called 'hymn explosion' of the same time. Why do you think that is?

Well, the Spirit brings freedom!

The Pentecostal, charismatic movement, at least in the States, was a liberating thing. There are still very strong reactionary forces in the Church against women assuming too much of a leadership role; the tension has not been entirely resolved. But the charismatic/Pentecostal influence is freeing for women.

First, it frees women to experience their own personal renewal. As long as they are sitting under a cloud of male authority, there is no opportunity to experience this for themselves. And it gives courage to express this. Growing up in a male-dominated culture, women have to break out of it somehow, to grow into their full stature in Christ.

But personal renewal doesn't automatically lead to freedom. Others need to encourage along the way. I had some wonderful people encouraging me. Graham was a great encourager of women.

Do you think that women's writing is distinctive at all?

It is more empathetic in tone, just because of the gift God gives to women. However, that does not exclude male writers – we are not 100 per cent male or 100 per cent female. There is a wide spectrum. My friend Carl Daw writes very empathetically. Think of his 'Like the murmur of the dove's song, like the challenge of her flight'.[1] He uses female imagery all the time.

Have you faced any particular difficulties or opportunities because you are a woman?

I'm sure I have. The obstacles are as much an internal battle as external. That is why I say that it is not automatic for women to step into new freedom. We have to fight with some of the awful baggage that we carry round inside of us, which makes us timorous about being heard.

Some women manage it, and shout aloud. But a lot have to work at it more.

Let me tell you a funny story. When Lionel Dakers was Director of the Royal School of Church Music, he invited me, with my young co-worker Kevin Hackett, to lunch at his London Club. We were early, as we didn't want to keep such a distinguished man waiting!

He arrived, and greeted us warmly, and said, 'I hope you don't mind, but we will have to dine downstairs, because women are not allowed on the main floor.' I will never forget the experience of walking down that flight of stairs. It was like descending into hell. It was a visceral experience, which I felt very deeply.

I guess other obstacles have been things I will never know about – things that didn't happen, maybe publications or ministry appearances. But I don't feel put down in any way, or overlooked. I have had wonderful opportunities.

I do try to encourage other women, as God gives me the opportunities. I was always with younger women in the Fisherfolk. My ministry contacts were all with younger women, and I am still in touch with a number that have gone on to do remarkable things.

One is living outside Jerusalem, attached to a Roman Catholic convent, and living a life of intercessory prayer. Another is a woman priest in Connecticut – quite a number have gone into ordained ministry. Ordained or not, all of the women I have known and loved and worked with have 'gone into ministry' and *are* ministers of the gospel.

Notes

1 Carl Daw, 'Like the murmur of the dove's song', in Carl Daw, *A Year of Grace*, Carol Stream IL: Hope Publishing Company, 1990, no. 85. This text has appeared in many collections since.

Cecily Taylor

'I can't say I didn't like it, but it's not what we're *used* to!' So remarked a member of the congregation after one of our new worship sessions (evening service of course, to be on the safe side!). It was the beginning of the 1970s; I think I might have heard one or two of Geoffrey Beaumont's brave new tunes for old words on the radio, and later Fred Kaan's new words for old tunes, but in our small corner, John Maynard and I were spontaneously co-writing mostly new words for new tunes. This was a bigger leap for people, but some of the old tunes must have been new once, even if we didn't count the ones that were originally country dances or belonged to popular songs and adapted later – some at a slower more formal pace.

Church services were not very venturesome; 'God-language' was still the norm, so it felt daring and maybe a little presumptive to address the Almighty in any mode other than the traditional 'Thee' and 'Thou', but it seemed important and relevant to write new lyrics in a more everyday idiom. Also, as a member of a worship committee, subject gaps in available hymnody became more obvious to me. For instance, when planning a Christian Aid service, John and I combined on 'The hungry ones',[1] since there was nothing available encapsulating the various needs the organization was meeting.

Anyway, in the very beginning, my involvement had all started with a poem triggered off by the desire to step back from violent news coverage and the growing pre-Christmas commercials that had been creeping up on us since the end of summer. The poem began:

I can't hear the angels,
the bombs roar and slay;
somewhere a baby is wounded and crying,
somewhere a baby is crying . . .[2]

It hadn't got off to a very promising start because shortly after sending the poem to the *Congregational Monthly*,[3] a gremlin had fun with the typesetting, and in the first line, where there should have been an 'h', it had a 'b'. I asked the editor to apologize to the angels for me, and he replied, 'I will, if I get there before you!' I thought my minister would enjoy the tale and gave him a (correct) copy of the poem. Unknown to me, he handed it on to John Maynard who'd asked him for some words to set for the Collingwood Boys' Choir he conducted.

Within a week a manuscript arrived out of the blue, and later when I heard the choristers singing it in harmony it was a most moving experience. From then on, until his stroke and subsequent death over a decade later, John and I collaborated on various items, and opportunities arose for the boys to sing within services at local churches (besides their own school concerts) both new items by various authors as well as traditional works.

On several occasions, I chose readings on the particular theme to intersperse between the choir's musical items, and we were fortunate in having soloists and an actor friend who were willing to help. The choir was known from their various participation in radio and television programmes, and invitations arrived for us to arrange a couple of sessions to be given in the crypt of St Paul's Cathedral.

Although we didn't realize it at the time, we were part of the much larger movement happening within segments of many churches feeling their way into a more contemporary approach to worship. It was one that was to resonate with the various musical developments in society generally. The Twentieth Century Church Light Music Group was gradually having an influence, and Southern Television's series *Hymn for Britain* and *Songs of Celebration* – featured on ITV in 1973 – were contributing a great deal to the 'hymn explosion', as it was called later. The *New English Bible*'s translation of 1961, 'made in the language of the present day', could have been having a subtle embryonic effect of originally triggering this 'explosion' by the early 1970s. I submitted a recent paraphrase of Psalm 23 to the *Songs of Celebration* with a tune that had evolved while I was writing it (as happens occasionally). It was a surprise when the item reached the finals of the festival.[4]

In 1973, the Collingwood Boys' Choir was invited to contribute to London's *Festival of the Spirit*, organized by Derek Wensley, when we produced a modern type of service at St Martin-in-the-Fields on the theme of 'The Fruits of the Spirit' including our new item 'The bright wind is blowing'. The whole week-long festival of varying types of worship took place in churches and halls all over the city, and at the grand finale in Trafalgar Square on Whit Sunday we all joined hands and pranced about joyfully as we sang Sydney Carter's 'Lord of the Dance'.[5]

During this period I was assisting John in compiling several collections of contributors' new song material including *So Much to Sing* and *In Tune* (co-editing the latter), both published by Vanguard Music.[6] After Derek had introduced me to Stainer & Bell, the Managing Director Bernard Braley was an enormous encourager, and published my poetry collection *Contact* in 1972. One of the firm's projects was *Blueprint*,[7] four volumes of new resource material, suitable for church services, school assemblies and for use elsewhere, and I was glad to be one of the contributors of songs as well as poems. Over the years I have enjoyed the firm's challenges to contribute new material to song collections such as *New Horizons, New Orbit, Story Song* and *Sound Bytes*.[8]

I've found it so interesting working with various composers; items vary in style from those suitable for congregations and/or choirs, to soloists (sometimes in folk style with guitar accompaniment), and some, like 'The Blessing of Light', set by June Boyce-Tillman,[9] contain the opportunity for liturgical dance. A different approach to dance is contained in the celebration for the return of the Prodigal – 'Dog-gone Son'[10] (first written as a ballad) – where an American-style 'caller' would be the soloist while those who chose could dance the Virginia Reel to Lyn Howe's arrangement of 'Turkey in the straw'. Just the thing for a harvest supper! Lyn also set 'On nights like this',[11] which takes the form of a soliloquy as an older shepherd tells a youngster of his strange experience that first Christmas, the congregation joining with the choir in the angels' refrain.

It was fun writing 'Slow down Moses',[12] which Juliet Krouwel set in the style of a barber's shop quartet. For the multiracial 'Kingdom come',[13] Richard Graves composed a catchy calypso beat. I shall always be grateful that through the years I've been fortunate in working with colleagues who have the gift of composing melodious, easy-to-pick-up tunes. However, the song-writing has only formed a thin strand of my life as in the early 1970s I had become involved in community relations and minority rights, and as time passed this priority gradually occupied more of my time.

Within the churches a growing number of women were becoming aware of the greater contribution they could make within the life and worship of their religious communities, a feeling that evolved into the Women in Theology movement. This was part of the broader concept of equality and respect enshrined within the human rights agenda.

By the 1980s, inclusive language was becoming important and influencing religious terminology in liturgy. Unfortunately there isn't an appropriate pronoun for a unisex God or for a being considered to be above human gender altogether, so this presented a new challenge for hymn-writers especially, and also compilers of new collections who felt obliged to edit non-inclusive language.

With new texts, subject matter was naturally widening to include contemporary concerns about the condition and desperate needs of the modern world. My own lyrics and poems evolved in between the community liaising, family demands and spiritual exploration. Many of the poems have been able to be included in poetry magazines, various journals, and anthologies across the inter-denominational spectrum like those edited by Donald Hilton and Geoffrey Duncan.[14]

It's always encouraging to feel compositions are being shared even not knowing where and when. Poems and songs are like children – they go out into the world and you just hope they do well. With the songs earlier on it seemed that it could be a case of the 'Lesser Spotted Lyricist', but it comes to light nowadays that they're appearing in hardback hymn books as far apart as Australia, Canada and Britain, and it looks as though 'Emmaus Road', 'The bright wind is blowing' and 'Our world is one world' to the tune 'Chernobyl',[15] especially, are all becoming favourites, so this is a warm thought.

It must be inevitable that the content of any writer's work is influenced by experience and built on evolving concepts. My spiritual adventure, like that of many other people, is like a pebble thrown into a pool where the ripples of discovery have never ceased to expand ever wider as time has passed. So where has hymnody fitted in? In retrospect I think one of my earliest junior school memories is of perplexity as I sang, 'Bright the vision that delighted/Once the sight of Judah's seer . . .'.[16] What Judas' ear had to do with it I never could fathom!

The Anglican Sunday school I attended was a great pleasure, not only because beautiful pictures were given out for us to collect in our slotted albums, but also there was a blue-carpeted alcove, with a little lattice window used for the 'children's corner'. I loved the diminutive furniture, the bright wall pictures and books. It was a great shock and grief when I attended a service there over fifty years later to find that the space had a door fitted for the broom cupboard it had by then become. Turning out the other day, I found my album of Sunday pictures and remembered that the illustration for the hymn 'My God how wonderful Thou art',[17] of a young girl looking out at the star-filled night sky, was my favourite, as was the tune, though I didn't fully understand all the words at the time.

With 1939, and wartime evacuation as a family, came the experience of village life and the small Church of England village school where I learnt about Moses, and when we forgot who he was had to write

out, fifty times or more, 'Moses the law-giver'. We chanted some of
the catechism in case the rector tested us when he next visited, but it
was all confusing at the time; nevertheless, I did grow fond of some of
the hymns, like 'Breathe on me breath of God',[18] which seemed to hold
some intangible meaning. As a family it wasn't long before the rector
encouraged us into the choir, and then of course *Hymns Ancient &
Modern* became staple diet.

My school life was considerably varied but, by the age of 12, I landed
up at my sixth school, small and privately run, which attempted to
fill in some of the yawning gaps, and where Scripture was taken as an
exam subject, and Confirmation seemed to be a natural progression.
However, as time went on, and I came to know the usual services in a
mechanical way, the helpfulness wore off.

By the time the war ended, I was a teenager back in our own sub-
urban home and enjoying a Congregational youth group introduced
to me by a friend. Once a month after Sunday evening service we met
in one or other member's home for what were called Coffee Crushes,
though I had a sneaky feeling that there were other 'crushes' going on
at the same time! Here we enjoyed choosing our favourite hymns from
Congregational Praise, which we sang with great gusto, such as 'Lord
of all hopefulness', 'God of grace and God of glory', 'Sometimes a light
surprises',[19] to their beautiful tunes. These were rendered by a press-
ganged pianist member and only interrupted at half-time by loads of
homemade cakes and sandwiches, washed down of course by the previously mentioned beverage.

Feeling very much at home in the church influenced me greatly; both
the youth group leader and minister were an inspiration in their nurturing and loving ways – my spiritual journey was becoming more
meaningful and linked to life. At 17, I joined the church, and altogether
my membership spanned 40 years, covering the early period while I
was at teacher training college specializing in early years education.
Subsequently I met my husband at the church after he was demobbed,
and at different times helped in the children's department and became
a 'contact group' person visiting members and attenders in my immediate home area. It was later that I served on the worship committee
and joined another concerned with prayer and healing, creating artistic
displays for its church noticeboard.

In the early 1960s, my poetry connections had led to the discovery of a local group where the host and hostess, who happened to be
wardens of a Quaker meeting house, gave me a warm welcome. The
whole experience of enjoying the poetry, getting to know the members,

and making lasting friendships had a profound effect upon me, as also did a long pen friendship with an elderly Quaker poet, a friend of the hostess.

Meanwhile, a majority of Congregational churches had linked up with the Presbyterians to become the United Reformed Church. I was still involved, but despite having close friendships with the various ministers and members over the years, I was beginning to suffer from spiritual claustrophobia. There was church dogma I could no longer accept, the set structure of the main services met my needs no longer, and the ambivalent attitude to war concerned me.

I remained a church member until about 1987, perhaps for longer than I might have done, supporting my husband, who was one of the church secretaries, but eventually I had to leave, and he understood my position as did Ray Adams, the minister at the time, who has set some of my lyrics. Leaving was a very big decision for me, but it hasn't meant an end to the friendships.

On my continuing explorations, I attended a couple of most inspiring Wrekin Trust conferences[20] and joined a meditation group. Then after attending Croydon Meeting House for a number of years I joined the Religious Society of Friends with its unprogrammed worship and wider approach to spirituality; it felt like my natural home. The various courses at Woodbrooke, the Quaker study centre at Selly Oak, and over recent years the Quaker Universalist Group with its meetings and conferences, provide extra spiritual nourishment.

Writers at the forefront of biblical scholarship and others also extend my spiritual understanding, and it is exciting that the rippling circles in the pool continue to expand. Following earlier archaeological discoveries, over the last sixty years there have been further valuable finds of ancient manuscripts like the Dead Sea Scrolls of the Essene community, dating from before and just after the beginning of the Christian era, and the hoard of Christian gospels and treatises, some previously unknown, at Nag Hammadi in Egypt. Finds such as these have opened up our understanding of New Testament times.

There are many illuminating authors to whom I owe gratitude,[21] who cover the fascination of such subjects as the history of mythology, the Gnostic gospels, views held in common between a growing number of mystics and scientists, the battles for Scripture and the faiths we never knew, why Christianity needs to change, a study of spiritual intelligence, our quest for the historical Jesus, and our changing perception of God from the wrathful Yahweh to the loving Father/Mother concept and the indwelling Spirit of Love working through human lives.

As St Teresa of Avila pointed out long ago, 'Christ has no body on earth but ours . . .'.[22] The world is our responsibility, and my prayer is:

> Give us the eyes of love's perception,
> listening ears for your inner voice;
> yours be the prompting in all decisions –
> Spirit that guides our choice.[23]

I have come to realize increasingly that the Gospels themselves, as well as the parables and other biblical stories, are able to be understood at many levels; we can take them at face value or seek inner symbolic meanings to the outer teachings. I hinted at this in the more recent lyric 'The story of a birth so long ago', in which verse 3 runs:

> And to the stable of our lives love comes,
> among the earthy things of every day,
> it nestles in the manger of our hearts;
> love comes to nourish us, and like the star
> will guide us on our way.[24]

However, on a less serious note I would like to end with a word of warning to any new women hymn-writers who, like me, may be a little sensitive on a certain point, as I explain in the following ditty, entitled 'From whom no secrets are hid':

> With the year of my birth at the foot of the page
> there's no point in a hair tint concealing my age;
> with such hymn-writerism I can't even bluff it –
> and they'll fill in that gap just as soon as I snuff it.[25]

Notes

1 Revised version: *Worship Live* 38, June 2007, p. 6; originally published as 'The hungry man', in *New Orbit*, and in Morris D. Pike (ed.), *Your Need for Bread is Mine*, New York: Friendship Press, 1977.

2 *Worship Live* 24, October 2002, p. 18.

3 *Congregational Monthly*, published by the Congregational Union of England and Wales.

4 *Songs of Celebration: A Collection of New Hymns featured in Southern Television's Hymn Competition 1973*, London: Weinberger, 1973.

5 Sydney Carter (1915–2004).

6 John Maynard (comp.), *So Much to Sing*, London: Vanguard Music, 1971, for younger children; John Maynard and Cecily Taylor (comps), *In Tune: Over 60 Hymns and Songs for Churches Schools and Groups*, London: Vanguard Music, 1973, for teens and adults.

7 John Bailey (ed.), *Blueprint: A series of reference books for use in secondary school assemblies, religious education and liberal studies classes, project work, church worship and Sunday school, adult education*, 4 vols, London: Galliard, 1976.

8 *New Horizons*, London: Galliard, Stainer & Bell, 1974; *Story Song*, London: Stainer & Bell Ltd/Trustees for Methodist Church Purposes, 1993; *Sound Bytes*, London: Stainer & Bell, 1999.

9 June Boyce-Tillman, *A Rainbow to Heaven*, London: Stainer & Bell, 2006, no. 103.

10 Musical arrangement: *Hymns and Congregational Songs*, vol. 1, no.1, London: Stainer & Bell, 1988, no. 14; steps for Virginia Reel, *Worship Live* 12, October 1998, p. 12.

11 Stainer & Bell sheet music, ref. W164 [1987].

12 Stainer & Bell, sheet music ref. W214. Also in *Sing in the Spirit: A Book of Quaker Songs*, Birmingham: Leaveners Press, 2005, book and CD, http://www. leaveners.org/qmm/songbook.html. There are various music groups within the Society; the Leaveners form the *Quaker Performing Arts Project*, http://www. leaveners.org/.

13 *Hymns and Congregational Songs*, vol. 3, no.1, London: Stainer & Bell, 1992, no. 99.

14 For example, Donald Hilton (comp.), *Liturgy of Life*, Redhill: National Christian Education Council, 1991; *No Empty Phrases: An Anthology of Poetry and Prose for Christian Education and Worship Based on the Lord's Prayer*, Redhill: National Christian Education Council, 1999; Geoffrey Duncan (comp.), *What a World*, London: Granary Press, 2002; *A Place for Us*, London: Granary Press, 2004.

15 'Alleluia Christ is risen!', no. 30, 'The bright wind is blowing', no. 36, in Janet Wootton and June Boyce-Tillman (eds), *Reflecting Praise*, London: Stainer & Bell/Women in Theology, 1993; 'Our world is one world', Andrew Pratt (ed.), *Sound Bytes*, London: Stainer & Bell Ltd., 1999, no. 82.

16 Richard Mant (1776–1848).

17 Frederick William Faber (1814–63).

18 Edwin Hatch (1835–89).

19 William Cowper (1731–1800).

20 An educational charity concerned with the spiritual nature of humanity and the universe, founded by Sir George Trevelyan.

21 For example, Karen Armstrong, David Boulton, Gregg Braden, Bart D. Ehrman, Satish Kumar, Maurice Nicoll, Elaine Pagels, John Selby Spong, Geza Vermes, Dana Zohar and Ian Marshall.

22 Teresa of Avila (1515–82).

23 *Worship Live* 22, January 2002, p. 5.

24 © Stainer & Bell. Published in *Sing in the Spirit*.

25 *News of Hymnody*, London: Grove Press, 1989.

June Boyce-Tillman

Background

As a somewhat lonely only child I developed an elaborate and vivid imagination that expressed itself in a variety of ways, which varied from creating 'stories' for piano to story and poetry writing. I was also a deeply religious child with a carefully tended altar in my bedroom and a well-developed prayer life based on my relationship with the natural world (I was brought up in the New Forest) and on the adult services that my mother insisted I attended rather than the Sunday school.

My theology was drawn largely from hymns that I learned from memory. Some of these I understood better than others. I remember struggling with the second verse of 'Hark the herald'[1] in particular. After three years studying music at Oxford University, where I encountered the work of Sydney Carter (then published by a back-street press in Soho), I lived and worked in London, in Notting Hill, just after the race riots. It was the era of folk in worship, and, clutching my guitar, I sang the songs published by Bernard Braley at Stainer & Bell. I transcribed the songs submitted for the Songs from the Square festivals led by Brian Frost and learned how to write contemporary material and draw the theology of hymns from social issues and circumstances. As a primary school teacher, my initial creativity was in the form of songs for assemblies and concerts and cantatas for festivals, and in editing several collections for Stainer & Bell for which I often arranged songs and hymns.

In general, this early work was arranging and helping others with their songs and hymns rather than writing my own. It was after several experiences of severe depression (when the medication was removed), that I started to write my own hymns and songs, the first being a song celebrating darkness for a local evangelical hymn competition. It was not surprising that it did not attract a prize. It was refined later into 'The harvest of darkness', which was set to Millicent D. Kingham's tune 'Benson',[2] and begins:

It was dark in the dawn of time
when the waters of chaos seethed,

darkness was brooding across the abyss
as the Spirit she gently breathed,
slowly she hovered across swelling waves
till the world from the chaos emerged
then the rest in the dark was transfigured with light
as the Spirit worked out her plan.[3]

Development

A lecture tour of Australia gave me time to undertake my first tranche
of hymns, which were versifications of Celtic texts so that they could
be used in contemporary worship. One of the most popular of these has
been used for healing services in various places. It was written in July
1986 and based on a text by Ann MacDonald in *Carmina Gadelica*.[4] It
was revised, and the tune 'The Anointing' written, for a Eucharist for
the healing of the wounds of child abuse, held at St Michael's Convent,
Ham Common, in 1992, where it was beautifully sung by Sister Aileen
CSC while Pat Macey mixed the oils for the anointing that was part of
the liturgy.

Give thou to me, O God,
the healing power of oil.
Give thou to me, O God,
a place beside the healer of my soul;
give thou to me, O God,
a death with joy and of peace.[5]

I was creating tunes and words together and experimenting with new
metres. The hymns started to come easily when I least expected it.
On Doncaster station in 1985 I was contemplating the story of Mary
Magdalene. I used the timeless phrase 'a woman and man' as in the folk
tradition in which I had been brought up, making the story an archetypal story:

A woman in her grief
within a garden cried,
lost in sense of deep bereavement
for the man she loved had died.

She wandered through the paths
to search out where he lay,
in devotion, bringing spices
her great debt to him to pay.

A man in working clothes
was also in that place,
but her loss was overwhelming
and she did not know his face.

He gently said one word:
he called her by her name.
It was just the sound she longed for
and her heart was set aflame.

She recognised her love
who told her not to stay;
so she left her contemplation
for the world of everyday.

At times, God, You seem close
but help us not to cling.
May such ecstasy be harnessed
for the world's transfiguring.[6]

A challenge at a Hymn Society conference to write hymns about the city led to the hymn 'Holy Spirit listening loving', which begins:

Holy Spirit, list'ning, loving,
breathe within our city stress;
fill the hearts of all the lonely
with a sense of loveliness;
and enable all who listen
to respond within Your breath.[7]

Some of my hymns used rhyme but others did not. I set it to a plain-song-like tune, 'Ad perennis vitae fontem'.[8]

Support

God was very good to me at this time in placing me in situations and with people who were supportive and offered me occasions to write material. Ianthe Pratt and the Association for Inclusive Language were behind all my work and for her I wrote an early hymn in 1990 entitled 'Count me in':

On a day when all were counted,
Mary found no place to rest,
pressing forward with her burden,
sharing in our homelessness.

Jesus, born of exiled mother,
healer, friend of all the oppressed,
be with all who feel excluded
from the circles of the blessed.

You were also once at variance
with the custom of Your day,
breaking bonds of race and gender
in Your friends along the way.

Sister, brother, wife and mother –
could these all be names for You?
Counsellor of ancient Wisdom,
we would to ourselves be true.[9]

It was Ianthe who helped me publish my early hymns in two collections that were photocopied in the local secondary school and that I sold privately for a long time – *In Praise of All-encircling Love I and II*.[10] They also included Hildegard transcriptions with translations and organ pieces that I wrote for services with the Sisters of the Church at Ham Common, where I am an associate.

Holy Rood House – Centre for Theology, Healing and the Arts – in Thirsk in Yorkshire, led by Elizabeth and Stanley Baxter,[11] has been a context for which I wrote much new material. I go there at least once a year and sometimes two and three times. Many of my new ideas have been piloted there and over 10 hymns produced for special occasions, such as this one for the New Year in 1998, to the tune 'Noel' (usually used for 'It came upon a midnight clear'):[12]

Hymn for times of change

Sing high, sing low, swing free, let go,
God of the turning round,
in times of change may we discern
the true angelic sound.
For there are songs of gentler power,
that warfare needs to hear.
These nurturing sounds will bring us strength,
and make the peace song clear.[13]

Another two contexts were Catholic Women's Network, with their regular Friday liturgies, and the Sisters of the Glorious Ascension in Montauroux, France. My holidays were occasions for writing new material in gratitude for the sisters' support:

Transfiguration

In the moment when truth is revealed in its clarity
the Being of God is made plain;
and we see the divinity in our humanity
as on the mountain the Voice said to Jesus:

'You are my beloved;
in You I am well pleased.'[14]

The recording of some of the hymns and songs was financed by Carol Boulter, convenor of WomenChurch Reading. *Voice of Experience*[15] was issued for her husband's sixtieth birthday and was an immensely important staging point in getting the hymns and songs better known. I owe Carol so much and finally wrote her a present that was used for her installation as the High Sheriff of Berkshire in 2008:

The magistrates' hymn

Within th' encircling planets God's Spirit gently flows,
restoring right connection through which creation grows;
with subtle understanding God takes each tiny part
and makes them fit together within a wounded heart.
We pray You, vibrant Spirit, infuse our hearts today
that we may act within You and understand Your Way.

The joy of right relationship the cosmos can inbreathe,
as You encircle all things and lovingly re-weave
the strands of human living. The joy, disputes and pain
are taken and re-woven to make life flow again;
and we are called to do Your work and make the weaving fair,
reflect Your deep transforming love infusing all our care.

Our human institutions, our politics, our wealth
bear fruit in justice-making to serve a nation's health;
the difficult decisions – to nurture and control –
the maintenance of order and all that is involved
take place within Your Wisdom still making all things new;
we ask that Your amazing grace will fill all we pursue.[16]

To write a hymn for a formal public service is not easy. While such gatherings are comfortable with singing texts in archaic language, the danger with contemporary language is that one might be asking people to sing what they do not believe in a language that they do understand. Here I had to address this problem. For such a service I needed to find a well-known tune to write for and preferably (from my own point of view) one that I had not written words for before. In the end I decided on 'Thaxted' by Gustav Holst.[17] This is well known for the words 'I vow to thee my country'. These words are loved by many and viewed as problematic by many others. When using a hymn tune, the well-known words will always shine through the new text in people's minds; so often I try to make the new words a commentary or dialogue with the old ones.

The service itself was concerned with justice and justice-making. Dr Carolyn Boulter – the High Sheriff – had worked in research in science education for much of her professional life and so I wanted to include that aspect in the text. I decided on the image of God the Weaver. This is an image found widely in contemporary theology associated with the continual action of God in the making and remaking of the cosmos, and draws on a strand of theology called Wisdom theology. It also draws on my research into the twelfth-century theologian Hildegard of Bingen,[18] who saw God as having created everything in right relationship and creation growing and flourishing when it is in right relation. The first verse then sets out this image of God weaving and reweaving the tapestry and paying particular attention to where it is torn or cut – the woundedness of creation. It also contains reference to the original source of the tune – Jupiter, from *The Planets Suite*.

As I considered the role of the structures that control justice in our society I felt that the weaving image was extremely useful. The police and the courts in general deal with those areas where relationship has broken down and the fabric of creation is wounded. In that sense they are called to be co-weavers with God in the areas of the woundedness of creation. The line in the middle of verse two with a full stop in the middle shows how the lines here are rewoven as they do not coincide with the musical phrases.

The last verse deals with the difficulty of making the right decisions in this process of restoring right relationship – in particular whether the people need nurturing or controlling and how far these two functions interact with one another. But it ends with the essential nature of this work if a nation is to remain healthy and flourishing and a prayer that we use discernment in our decisions to be partners in this action which is at the heart of the universe.

The exciting thing about being in the service and meeting people after they had sung the hymn was to be able to engage in dialogue about Wisdom theology with them. Although these ideas are regularly discussed in theological circles it is unlikely that many of the people present would be familiar with such debates. When I started writing hymns 25 years ago, I saw part of my role as to make contemporary developments in theology available to a wider audience.

Many of my hymns have been written as presents, such as this one for Ianthe's eightieth birthday in gratitude for a rich, longstanding friendship. It was sung to the tune 'Diademata', usually used for 'Crown him with many crowns':[19]

All in a garden green
there stands the Wisdom tree;
the leaves exude the golden sheen
of creativity.
Her curling roots reach down;
her branches fan the air;
her trunk is gnarled and as a crown
she wears a blessing prayer.

Under her shady boughs
a scrumptious feast is laid;
her garden forms a welcoming home
where liturgy is prayed.
We gather in a ring,

find courage in her pow'r
and, fed by Wisdom's ancient spring,
our lives come into flow'r.

Many and diverse friends
find hope within her rooms;
we grasp the strength her Spirit sends
and touch each other's wounds.
Our struggling reaches birth
and, learning Wisdom's song,
we find the pearl of greatest worth –
a place where all belong.[20]

Some of the presents include references to incidents particular to the person for whom it was written. This hymn was written as a thank you to the Revd Andrew Todd, who was then a chaplain at King Alfred's College. He and I shared a valuing of the Eucharist, which begins:

Deep inside creation's mystery
stands a table set with bread,
and a cup of grapes' rejoicing,
love full-bodied, sparkling red.

Verse 4 of the hymn,

Human voices join the chorus;
chant and jazz and mystic prose,
hymns of Fellowship all make the
counterpoint of One who knows[21]

refers to ongoing debates about the use of traditional hymnody and worship songs in the college chapel. The chant, however, refers to the fact that in his audition for the King Alfred Singers, he sang the Easter plainchant 'Exultet'.

Through Women in Theology, I met the Revd Dr Janet Wootton. With her I edited *Reflecting Praise*, a collection of material by women. Women in Theology and Stainer & Bell undertook the project together. The Introduction summarized the editorial policy:

There exists a great wealth of women's creativity as composers and poets from every generation. Much of this is only now being rediscovered, as women reclaim their own history . . . Preference has been given to pieces that have women as author, translator, composer, or arranger, or which tell the stories of women . . . All hymns use inclusive language for humans. A number use female or inclusive images when referring to God, many exploring new or newly reclaimed images . . . Most exciting of all, new writers continue to spring up in the field of inclusive language, broadening its scope, and introducing the idea to wider audiences.[22]

It was the first collection of its kind, and brought me in touch with many new women hymn-writers.

My experience was that the theology certainly of the Protestant churches was spread largely by hymnody. As I went deeper into feminist theology circles, I realized that the only way it would get into the wider world would be by means of hymns. This has proved true on several occasions. One of these was the use of 'We sing a love' for the opening of the 2008 Lambeth Conference:

We sing a love that sets all people free,
that blows like wind, that burns like scorching flame,
enfolds like earth, springs up like water clear.
Come, living love, live in our hearts today.

We sing a love that seeks another's good,
that longs to serve and not to count the cost,
a love that, yielding, finds itself made new.
Come, caring love, live in our hearts today.

We sing a love, unflinching, unafraid
to be itself, despite another's wrath,
a love that stands alone and undismayed.
Come, strength'ning love, live in our hearts today.

We sing a love that, wand'ring, will not rest
until it finds its way, its home, its source,
through joy and sadness pressing on refreshed.
Come, pilgrim love, live in our hearts today.

We sing a burning, fiery, Holy Ghost
that seeks out shades of ancient bitterness,
transfig'ring these, as Christ in ev'ry heart.
Come joyful love, live in our hearts today.[23]

The hymn had been written as a commission for a wedding but includes within it my own experience of marriage. Verse 3 includes the love that is often not suggested in wedding services. In the final verse, Holy Ghost is used deliberately to counteract the 'shades of ancient bitterness'. Though the use of this archaism has been questioned, sometimes an older word can be reclaimed now with a power lacking in more familiar words.

I was slower to address the feminine in God than inclusive images. At first I desired to be acceptable and did not want to rock the boat. I started with songs like 'Tambourine woman'. This song was written in May 1988, after a course on discovering your clown, run by Sandra Pollerman, who helped me to find my clowns. It was also an attempt to find a feminine version of the popular song of the 1960s, 'Mr Tambourine Man'.[24]

> One day as I went out a-walking,
> a stranger appeared unto me.
> Her skirt was made up of weird patches
> a rainbow in bold tapestry.
> Silk ribbons beguiling in colour
> flowed out from her strange tambourine.
> Behind her a vast crowd of people
> came leaping and singing this theme:
>
> *We'll follow the tambourine woman*
> *and join in her tambourine song.*
> *We're riding a rainbow to heaven*
> *and dancing our journey along.*[25]

Inclusive language is a contentious issue and opinion has in general become more conservative in this area in the last ten years, as 'political correctness' has been increasingly ridiculed. As I have got older, I have become more radical and less concerned about other people's opinion. This greater sense of security was partly encouraged by work on the life and work of Hildegard of Bingen (1098–1179),[26] who found her voice in her early forties and was excommunicated at 80 for her speaking out against authorities. It was from her that I found the best description of the perfect hymn:

> The words of a hymn represent the body, while the melody represents the soul. Words represent humanity, and melody represents divinity.

Thus in a beautiful hymn, in which words and melody are perfectly matched, body and soul, humanity and divinity, are brought into unity.[27]

I often use traditional metres and write to a particular known tune. I love making the highs and lows of the words fit the tune perfectly. This was particularly true of

We shall go out with hope of resurrection.
We shall go out, from strength to strength go on.
We shall go out and tell our stories boldly,
tales of a love that will not let us go.
We'll sing our songs of wrongs that can be righted.
We'll dream our dreams of hurts that can be healed.
We'll weave a cloth of all the world united
within the vision of a Christ who sets us free.

We'll give a voice to those who have not spoken.
We'll find the words for those whose lips are sealed.
We'll make the tunes for those who sing no longer,
vibrating love alive in every heart.
We'll share our joy with those who are still weeping.
Chant hymns of strength for hearts that break in grief.
We'll leap and dance the resurrection story
including all within the circles of our love.[28]

This was originally written for a liturgy designed by Nicola Slee for the Southwark Ordination Course in 1990, entitled *Broken Silence*; but it has been used for a wide variety of situations including weddings and funerals and John Sentamu's consecration in York Minster. It is set to the traditional Irish tune often called 'Danny Boy',[29] so that words like 'dance' fall at the high point of the tune.

I enjoy the crafting of the traditional hymn but also like the freedom of the song with its particular tune. The chants often come in a very different way and have more direct inspiration rather than crafting. I was walking in southern France and using the time for meditation with a mantra. Gradually the mantra formed itself into a chant with a tune, and I stopped to write it down:

I will hold you in the hollow of my hand, my hand my hand
I will hold you in the hollow of my hand,

I will hold you in the hollow of my hand, my hand my hand
I will hold you in the hollow of my hand.

I will hold you with the ripples of the sea . . .[30]

Under pressure, I can produce hymns very quickly. The Vice-Chancellor
of Winchester University, Professor Paul Light, and his wife Vivienne,
were leaving in 2006, and I had intended to write a hymn for them. It
was the day of the concert and nothing had been done. I decided at the
beginning of the drive from London to Winchester that I would write
a 'Hymn to Wisdom', starting with Hildegard's antiphon to Wisdom.
As I turned on Classic FM they were playing Schubert's Entr'acte from
Rosamunde. I decided it would make an excellent tune. By the time I
had passed Basingstoke, I had completed the verses in my head, including reference to Paul in the phrase 'manager's judgement' and Viv, who
is an artist, in 'artist's creation'. I stopped in a lay-by and wrote them
down. I got Diana Owen, a piano lecturer at the university, to play the
Schubert to me, and I wrote it down and added a descant for the choir.
They learned it in the hour before the concert and there it was – composed in a day:

Circling encircling Wisdom deep within,
gently embracing life-giving care,
circling encircling Wisdom deep within,
we bring You reverence and prayer today.
One wing flies heav'nward, one wing flies earthward,
one wing flies everywhere,
You will enfold us, You will empower us.
We bring You reverence and prayer today.

Circling encircling Wisdom deep within,
gently embracing life-giving care,
circling encircling Wisdom deep within,
we bring You reverence and prayer today.
Questions of doctrine, moral dilemmas,
we lay them in Your wings.
Strengthen our weakness, soften our power,
we bring You reverence and prayer today.

Circling encircling Wisdom deep within,
gently embracing life-giving care,

circling, encircling Wisdom deep within
we bring You reverence and prayer today.
Artist's creation, manager's judgement,
These can reveal Your love.
May all our knowing draw on Your values,
we bring You reverence and prayer today.

Circling, encircling Wisdom deep within
gently embracing life-giving care,
circling encircling Wisdom deep within
we bring You reverence and prayer today.
You are incarnate in our creation;
in all Your glory shines,
work with our doubting, challenge our smugness.
We bring You reverence and prayer today.[31]

Particular hymns

Ecumenical and interfaith dialogue have generated hymns and chants
like 'We gather here together',[32] written for my good friend the Revd
Robert Kaggwa at Digby Stuart College, Roehampton University,
where I am a Council member. The tune is usually used for 'Thy hand,
O God, has guided' with its powerful chorus, 'one Church, one faith,
one Lord'.[33] The words of an old tune will always shine through the
new words and I have played with this phenomenon, replacing 'one
Church, one faith, one Lord' with the concept of drawing nearer 'In
love and with respect'.[34]

Also written for Roehampton University was my latest chant for an
interfaith celebration:

At the heart of the cosmos,
There lies deepest mystery
We can know and not know. [35]

Some of my hymns have been commissions and several of these, like the
one for the Queen's Jubilee,[36] have been from the Revd Jean Mayland. I
wrote 'Tides come flowing claiming freedom' for the Lambeth Conference 2008 in response to a commission from WATCH (Women and the
Church), concerned with the place of women in Anglican structures.[37]

Sir John Taverner asked for a hymn text for his piece 'Hymn for the Sovereign'. It was used at a ceremony celebrating the centenary of the Knights Bachelor at St Paul's Cathedral in November 2008 in the presence of the Queen. Sir John set various invocations for a variety of faiths and the verses of the hymn are interspersed between these. He sent me a tune in 2006, and asked me to make a metrical version in inclusive language of the passage from Ecclesiasticus that is often translated 'Let us now praise famous men'. The text begins:

Let us honour all our forebears
whose being gave us life,
the illustrious and unknown,
the weak and those with might.
Those who seek out Wisdom's insight
Will abide in God.

Some were rulers of the nations;
some found their truth in books;
some told stories in their homes;
some cleaned and swept and cooked.
Chorus[38]

Sir John used a melisma in the descant on the word 'cooked', a word seldom found in liturgical music. Some expressed surprise at the inclusion of sweepers and cleaners in celebrations of this kind but acknowledged that they probably should be included!

Summary

My journey as a hymn-writer has been long and complex. It was wonderful to see its products in the form of *A Rainbow to Heaven*, published by Stainer & Bell in 2007. It has been informed by my musical training and my experience of church from my earliest childhood, as well as a variety of contexts for liturgical experiment by radical groups of various kinds. Through it I have been able to turn some of the most difficult experiences of my life into objects of beauty. It has enabled me to theologize my life. I hope it will help others find an experience of God in even the most difficult times of their lives and find a God intimately bound up in the warp and weft of living, constantly weaving and reweaving.

Notes

1 'Hark the herald angels sing', Charles Wesley (1707–88)

2 Millicent Kingham, (b. *c.* 1866), tune 'Benson', in the *English Hymnal*, London: Henry Frowde, 1906, no. 548.

3 June Boyce-Tillman, *A Rainbow to Heaven*, London: Stainer & Bell, 2007, p. 31. See above, p. 203.

4 Ann MacDonald, in Alexander Carmichael, *Carmina Gadelica: Hymns and incantations with illustrative notes on words, rites, and customs, dying and obsolete: orally collected in the Highlands and Islands of Scotland and translated into English*, Edinburgh: Norman McLeod, 1900.

5 *Rainbow to Heaven*, p. 85.

6 *Rainbow to Heaven*, p. 8.

7 *Rainbow to Heaven*, p. 38.

8 Tours Breviary, 1781, in *The English Hymnal*, no. 350.

9 *Rainbow to Heaven*, p. 57.

10 June Boyce-Tillman, *In Praise of All-Encircling Love: Hymns and Songs in Inclusive Language*, London: Hildegard Press/Association for Inclusive Language, 1992; *In Praise of All-Encircling Love 2: Hymns, Songs and Liturgical Pieces in Inclusive Language*, London: Hildegard Press/Association for Inclusive Language, 1994.

11 www.holyroodhouse.freeuk.com.

12 Arthur Sullivan (1842–1900), in *The English Hymnal* no. 26.

13 *Rainbow to Heaven*, p. 61.

14 *Rainbow to Heaven*, p. 125.

15 June Boyce-Tillman, *Voice of Experience*, CD of 22 songs, London: Hildegard Press, 1999.

16 Unpublished, © Stainer & Bell Ltd.

17 Gustav Holst (1874–1934).

18 June Boyce-Tillman, *The Creative Spirit: Harmonious Living with Hildegard of Bingen*, London: Canterbury Press, 2000.

19 George Job Elvey (1816–93).

20 Unpublished.

21 *Rainbow to Heaven*, p. 21

22 Janet Wootton and June Boyce-Tillman (eds), *Reflecting Praise*, London: Stainer & Bell/Women in Theology, 1993.

23 *Rainbow to Heaven*, p. 65.

24 Bob Dylan, 'Mr Tambourine Man'.

25 *Rainbow to Heaven*, p. 145.

26 See above, p. 205.

27 Robert Van der Weyer (ed.), *Hildegard in a Nutshell*, London: Hodder & Stoughton, 1997, p. 79.

28 *Rainbow to Heaven*, p. 81.

29 Anon. Irish, 'Londonderry air'.

30 Unpublished.

31 *Rainbow to Heaven*, p. 38.

32 *Rainbow to Heaven*, p. 102

33 'Aurelia' by S. S. Wesley (1810–76).

34 *Rainbow to Heaven*, p. 76.

35 Unpublished.

36 'Wisdom will set us free', *Rainbow to Heaven*, p. 90.

37 Unpublished.

38 John Taverner, *Hymn for the Sovereign*, London: Chester, 2008. Hymn text unpublished.

Bibliography

Early and medieval

Benedict, Kimberley M., 2004, *Empowering Collaborations: Writing Partnerships between Women and Scribes in the Middle Ages*, London: Routledge.

Boyce-Tillman, June, 2000, *The Creative Spirit: Harmonious Living with Hildegard of Bingen*, London: Canterbury Press.

Dronke, P., 1984, *Women Writers of the Middle Ages: A Critical Study of Texts from Perpetua († 203) to Marguerite Porete († 1310)*, Cambridge: Cambridge University Press.

Dronke, Peter, 1986, *Poetic Individuality in the Middle Ages: New Departures in Poetry, 1000–1150*, 2nd edn, London: Westfield College, University of London Committee for Medieval Studies.

Kienzle, Beverly Mayne and Pamela J. Walker (eds), 1998, *Women Preachers and Prophets through Two Millennia of Christianity*, Berkeley: University of California Press.

Lees, Clare and Gillian Overing, 2001, *Double Agents: Women and Clerical Culture in Anglo-Saxon England*, Pennsylvania: University of Pennsylvania Press.

McNamara, Jo Ann, 1987, 'Muffled Voices: The Lives of Consecrated Women in the Fourth Century', in Thomas Shank (ed.), *Of Medieval Religious Women*, vol. 1, Cistercian Study Series no. 71, *Distant Echoes*, Kalamazoo MI: Cistercian Publications, pp. 11–29.

Mews, Constant J., 2003, 'Liturgy and Identity at the Paraclete: Heloise, Abelard and the Evolution of Cistercian Reform', in Marc Stewart and David Wulstan (eds), *The Poetic and Musical Legacy of Heloise and Abelard: An Anthology of Essays by Various Authors*, Ottawa, Canada: The Institute of Mediaeval Music, Westhumble, Surrey: The Plainsong and Mediaeval Music Society, pp. 19–33.

Muessig, Carolyn, 1998, 'Prophecy and Song: Teaching and Preaching by Medieval Women', in Beverly Mayne Kienzle and Pamela J. Walker (eds), *Women Preachers and Prophets through Two Millennia of Christianity*, Berkeley: University of California Press.

Newman, Barbara, 1987, *Sister of Wisdom: St Hildegard's Theology of the Feminine*, Berkeley: University of California Press.

Perpetua, 1984, 'Diary', in P. Dronke, *Women Writers of the Middle Ages: A Critical Study of Texts from Perpetua († 203) to Marguerite Porete († 1310)*, Cambridge: Cambridge University Press, pp. 2–4.

Petroff, Elizabeth, 1979, *Consolation of the Blessed*, New York: Alta Gaia Society.

Radice, Betty, revised M. T. Clanchy, 2003, *The Letters of Abelard and Heloise*, London: Penguin Books.

Shank, Thomas (ed.), 1987, *Of Medieval Religious Women*, vol. 1, Cistercian Study Series no. 71, *Distant Echoes*, Kalamazoo MI: Cistercian Publications.

Silvas, Anna M., 2008, *Macrina the Younger, Philosopher of God*, Turnhout, Belgium: Brepols Publishers n.v.

Stewart, Marc and David Wulstan (ed.), 2003, *The Poetic and Musical Legacy of Heloise and Abelard: An Anthology of Essays by Various Authors*, Ottawa, Canada: The Institute of Mediaeval Music, Westhumble, Surrey: The Plainsong and Mediaeval Music Society.

Vitry, Jacques de, *Sermo de virginibus*, Douai, Bibliothéque municipale 503, ff. 217v–220r.

Vitry, Jacques de, *Sermo s. Cecilie*, Douai, Bibliothéque municipale 503, ff. 158v–160v.

Wulstan, David, 2003, 'Heloise at Argenteuil and the Paraclete', in Marc Stewart and David Wulstan (eds), *The Poetic and Musical Legacy of Heloise and Abelard: An Anthology of Essays by Various Authors*, Ottawa, Canada: The Institute of Mediaeval Music, Westhumble, Surrey: The Plainsong and Mediaeval Music Society, pp. 67–90.

Early modern to eighteenth century

Ash, John, 1777, *Sentiments on Education, collected from the best writers; properly methodized, and interspersed with occasional observations*, Dublin: W. Whitestone.

Ashley Smith, J. W., 1954, *The Birth of Modern Education: The Contribution of the Dissenting Academies, 1660–1800*, London: Independent Press.

Broome, J. R., 2007, *A Bruised Reed: The Life and Times of Anne Steele*, Harpenden: Gospel Standard Trust Publications.

David Hempston, 2005, 'John Wesley (1703–1791)', in Carter Lindberg (ed.), *The Pietist Theologians*, Oxford: Blackwell, pp. 256–71.

Davie, Donald, 1993, *The Eighteenth-Century Hymn in England*, Cambridge: Cambridge University Press.

de Baar, Mirjam, 2004, '*Ik moet spreken: Het spiritueel leiderschap van Antoinette Bourignon (1616–1680)*, Utrecht: Walburg, English summary, p. 181.

Dutton, Ann, 1742, 'A Letter to the Rev. Mr. J. Wesley. In vindication of the Doctrines of Absolute Election, Particular Redemption, Special Vocation, and Final Perseverance. Occasioned chiefly by some things in his Dialogue between a Predestinarian and his friend; and in his Hymns on God's Everlasting Love', London: S. Mason.

Dutton, Ann, 1743, *A Brief Account of the Gracious Dealings of God, with a Poor, Sinful, Unworthy Creature* (London), and in three volumes, with an appendix and letter (prefixed) on the lawfulness of a woman's appearing in print, London, 1750.

Erdmann, Axel, 1999, *My Gracious Silence: Women in the Mirror of Sixteenth-*

Century Printing, Lucerne, Switzerland: Gilhofer & Ranschburg GmbH.

Hindmarsh, D. Bruce, 2005, *The Evangelical Conversion Narrative, Spiritual Autobiography in Early Modern England*, Oxford: Oxford University Press.

Johansen, John, 1980, *Moravian Hymnody*, Moravian Music Foundation Publications, no. 9, Winston-Salem: The Moravian Music Foundation.

Kidd, Thomas, 2007, *The Great Awakening: The Roots of Evangelical Christianity in Colonial America*, New Haven CT: Yale University Press.

Kienzle, Beverly Mayne, and Pamela J. Walker (eds), 1998, *Women Preachers and Prophets through Two Millennia of Christianity*, Berkeley: University of California Press.

Kinkel, Gary Steven, 1990, *Our Dear Mother the Spirit: An Investigation of Count Zinzendorf's Theology and Praxis*, Lanham MD: University Press of America.

Kübler, Theodore, 1865, *Historical Notes to the Lyra Germanica*, London: Longman, Green, Longman, Roberts and Green.

Leaver, Robin, 1995, *Elisabeth Creutziger: The Magdeburg Enchiridion 1536 and Reformation theology*, The Kessler Reformation Lecture, 18 October 1994, Occasional Publications of the Pitts Theological Library.

Leopold, Ulrich S. (ed.), 1965, 'Liturgy and Hymns', in *Luther's Works*, vol. 53, Philadelphia: Fortress Press.

Lindberg, Carter (ed.), 2005, *The Pietist Theologians*, Oxford: Blackwell.

Marshall, Madeleine Forell and Janet Todd, 1982, *English Congregational Hymns in the Eighteenth Century*, Kentucky: University Press of Kentucky.

McKee, Elsie Anne, 1999, *Katharina Schütz Zell*, vol. 1, *The Life and Thought of a Sixteenth-Century Reformer*, Leiden: Brill.

Robin, Diana Maury, 2007, *Publishing Women: Salons, the Presses, and the Counter-Reformation in Sixteenth-Century Italy*, Chicago: University of Chicago Press.

Stjerna, Kirsi, 2008, *Women and the Reformation*, Oxford: Blackwell Publishing

Vogt, Peter, 1998, 'A Voice for Themselves: Women as Participants in Congregational Discourse in the Eighteenth-century Moravian Movement', in Beverly Mayne Kienzle and Pamela J. Walker (eds), *Women Preachers and Prophets through Two Millennia of Christianity*, Berkeley: University of California Press, pp. 227–47.

Ward, Patricia A., 2005, 'Madame Guyon (1648–1717)', in Carter Lindberg (ed.), *The Pietist Theologians*, Oxford: Blackwell, pp. 161–73.

Nineteenth century

Allchin, A. M., 1986, *Ann Griffiths: The Furnace and the Fountain*, Cardiff: University of Wales Press.

Allchin, A. M., 1991, *Praise Above All: Discovering the Welsh Tradition*, Cardiff: University of Wales Press.

Armstrong, Isobel, Joseph Bristow and Cath Sharrock (eds), 1996, *Nineteenth-Century Women Poets: An Oxford Anthology*, Oxford: Clarendon Press.

Babington, E. B., 1875, *Memoir of Charlotte Elliott, author of 'Just as I am,' etc.*

By her sister E. B. [i.e. E. Babington], London.

Balfour, Clara, 1854, *A Sketch of Mrs Barbauld*, London: W. & F. G. Cash.

Barbauld, A. L., 1778, *Lessons for Children*, London: J. Johnson.

Barbauld, A. L., 1792, *Civic Sermons to the People*, London.

Barbauld, A. L. 1793, *Sins of Government, Sins of the Nation Etc., A Discourse for the Fast Appointed on April 19th 1793: by A Volunteer*, London: J. Johnson.

Barbauld, A. L. 1823, 'Thoughts on Public Worship: Thoughts on the devotional taste, on sects, and on establishments', in Jared Sparks, *A Collection of Essays and Tracts in Theology from Various Authors*, Boston, vol. IV, pp. 310–11.

Baxter, Richard, 1650, *The saints' everlasting rest; or, a treatise of the blessed state of the saints, in their enjoyment of God in heaven.*

Brown, Kenneth O., 1992, *Holy Ground: The Study of the American Camp Meeting*, New York: Garland.

Cliff, Philip B., 1986, *The Rise and Development of the Sunday School Movement in England 1780–1980*, Redhill: National Christian Education Council.

Clifford, Deborah Pickman, 1979, *Mine Eyes Have Seen the Glory: A Biography of Julia Ward Howe* Boston: Little, Brown.

Cobb Jr., Buell E., 1989, *The Sacred Harp: A Tradition and its Music*, Athens GA: University of Georgia Press.

Crosby, Fanny, 1906, *Memories of Eighty Years*, Boston MA: J. H. Earle & Co.

de Jong, Mary, 1986, 'I want to be like Jesus: The self-defining power of evangelical hymnody', *Journal of the American Academy of Religion* 54, Fall, pp. 461–93.

Douglas, Ann, 1977, *The Feminization of American Culture*, New York: Alfred A. Knopf.

Ferguson, Moira, 1992, *Subject to Others: British Women Writers and Colonial Slavery, 1670–1834*, London, Routledge.

Fliedner, Theodor, 1867, *Life of Pastor Fliedner*, trans. Catherine Winkworth, London.

Gottfried of Disibodenberg and Theodoric of Echternach, 1996, *The Life of the Saintly Hildegard*, trans. Hugh Feiss, Toronto: Peregrina Publishing.

Grant, Mary, 1994 [1900], *Private Woman, Public Person: An Account of the Life of Julia Ward Howe from 1819–1868*, Brooklyn NY: Carson.

Greenwell, Dora 1866, 'Our Single Women', in Dora Greenwell, *Essays*, London and New York, pp. 1–68.

Greenwell, Dora, 1866, *Essays*, London and New York.

Greenwell, Dora, 1926, *Two Friends*, ed. with an Introduction and Summary by Constance L. Maynard, London: R. Allenson Ltd.

Gregory, Gill, 1998, *The Life and Work of Adelaide Procter*, Aldershot: Ashgate.

Grierson, Janet, 1979, *Frances Ridley Havergal: Worcestershire Hymn-writer*, Bromsgrove: Havergal Society.

Grosvernor, Roxalana (ed.), 1845, *Sayings of Mother Ann and the First Elders* (Sabbathday Lake manuscript, before 1845).

Hall, Florence Howe, 1913, *Julia Ward Howe and the Woman Suffrage Movement*, Boston: Dana Estes & Co.

Hobbs, June Hadden, 1997, *'I sing for I cannot be silent': The Feminization of*

American Hymnody, 1870–1920, Pittsburgh PA: University of Pittsburgh Press.

Hoggart, R., 1995, *The Way We Live Now*, London: Chatto & Windus.

Hotz-Davies, Ingrid, 2001, *The Creation of Religious Identities by English Women Poets from the Seventeenth to the Early Twentieth Century: Soulscapes*, Studies in Women and Religion, vol. 42, Lampeter: The Edwin Mellen Press.

Howe, Julia Ward, 1900, *Reminiscences 1818–1899*, Boston: Houghton Mifflin & Co.

Hull, John, 2005, 'Isaac Watts and the Origins of British Imperial Theology', *International Congregational Journal*, vol. 4, no. 2, February, pp. 59–79.

Hustad, Donald, 1981, *Jubilate! Church Music in the Evangelical Tradition*, Carol Stream IL: Hope Publishing Co.

Hyde, Derek, 1998, *New-Found Voices: Women in Nineteenth-Century English Music*, 3rd edn, Aldershot: Ashgate.

Jackson, George Pullen, 1943, *White and Negro Spirituals: Their Life Span and Kinship*, Locust Valley NY: J. J. Augustin.

Jerome, *Epistola*, in Migne, *Patrologiae Cursus Completus, Latina* 22:1091.

Kelynack, William, 1950, *Companion to the School Hymn Book of the Methodist Church* London: Epworth Press.

King, James, 1885, *Anglican Hymnology, being an account of the 325 standard hymns of the highest merit according to the verdict of the whole Anglican Church*, London: Hatchards.

Leaver, Robin A., 1978, *Catherine Winkworth: The Influence of her Translations on English Hymnody*, St Louis MO: Concordia Publishing House.

MacNemar, Richard, 1807, *The Kentucky Revival: or a Short History of the outpouring of the Spirit of God in the Western States of America, with a brief account of Shakerism*, Cincinnati: J. W. Browne.

Marsh, Jan, 1994, *Christina Rossetti: A Literary Biography*, London: Jonathan Cape.

Martineau, Harriet, 1832–33, *Illustrations of Political Economy*, vols 1–9, London.

Martineau, Harriet, 1877, *Autobiography with Memorials by M. W. Chapmen*, Windermere.

Maynard, Constance L., 1926, *Dora Greenwell: A Prophet for our own Times on the Battleground of our Faith*, London: H. R. Allenson Ltd.

Mills, Arthur E., 1950, *Children's Hymns and Hymn Writers*, comp. Arthur E. Mills, London: Epworth Press.

Monthly Repository, 1806–38, London.

Ninde, Edward S., 1921, *The Story of the American Hymn*, New York: Abingdon Press.

Orchard, Stephen and John H. Y. Briggs (eds), 2007, *The Sunday School Movement: Studies in the Growth and Decline of Sunday Schools*, Bletchley: Paternoster Press.

Orchard, Stephen, 2007, 'From Catechism Class to Sunday School', in Stephen Orchard and John H. Y. Briggs (eds), *The Sunday School Movement: Studies in the Growth and Decline of Sunday Schools*, Bletchley: Paternoster Press, pp. 1–16.

Packer, Lona Mosk, 1963, *Christina Rossetti*, Cambridge: Cambridge University Press.

Palazzo, Lynda, 2002, *Christina Rossetti's Feminist Theology*, Hampshire: Palgrave.

Palmer, Phoebe, 1859, *Promise of the Father; or, A neglected speciality of the last days. Addressed to the clergy and laity of all Christian communities*, Boston: H. V. Degen.

Proceedings of a Peace Meeting held at Union League Hall, New York, December 23d, 1870, For the purpose of Free Consultation on the subject of a Woman's Peace Congress for the World as Proposed by Mrs Julia Ward Howe of Boston, Philadelphia, Boston PA: John Gillam & Co., Printers.

Rosman, Doreen, 2007, 'Sunday Schools and Social Change in the Twentieth Century', in Stephen Orchard and John H. Y. Briggs (eds), *The Sunday School Movement: Studies in the Growth and Decline of Sunday Schools*, Bletchley: Paternoster Press, pp. 149–60.

Rossetti, Christina, 'In the bleak midwinter', http://news.bbc.co.uk/1/hi/entertainment/arts_and_culture/7752029.stm.

Sanville, George W., 1943, *Forty Gospel Hymn Stories*, Winona Lake IN: The Rodeheaver Hall-Mack Co.

Sieveking, Amalie Wilhemine, 1863, *Life of A. W. Sieveking*, trans. Catherine Winkworth, London.

Sizer, Sandra A., 1978, *Gospel Hymns and Social Religion: The Rhetoric of Nineteenth-Century Revivalism*, Philadelphia: Temple University Press.

Skrine, Peter, 1992, *Susanna and Catherine Winkworth: Clifton, Manchester and the German Connection*, Occasional Paper Second Series, no. 2, Croydon: The Hymn Society of Great Britain and Ireland.

Stephenson, Harold W., 1922, *The Author of Nearer my God to Thee – Sarah Flower Adams*, London: Lindsey Press.

Stowe, Harriet Beecher, 1852, *Uncle Tom's Cabin, or Negro Life in America*, Leipzig: Bernhard Tauchnitz.

Stowe, Harriet Beecher, 1994, *Uncle Tom's Cabin*, ed. E. Ammons. Norton Critical Edn, New York: W.W. Norton.

Tamke, Susan, 1978, *Make a Joyful Noise unto the Lord: Hymns as a Reflection of Victorian Social Attitudes*, Athens OH: Ohio University Press.

The Song Service Reporter: A Journal chiefly devoted to Sunday School music, etc., 1890, Leeds: Phlox Publishing Office.

Wallace, Valerie, 1995, *A Life of the Hymn-writer Mrs Alexander, 1818–1895*, Dublin: Lilliput Press.

Whitson, Robley, 1983, *The Shakers: Two Centuries of Spiritual Reflection*, London: SPCK.

Williams, Gary, 1999, *Hungry Heart: The Literary Emergence of Julia Ward Howe*, Amherst: University of Massachusetts Press.

Winkworth, Susanna and M. J. Shaen, 1883–86, *Letters and Memorials of Catherine Winkworth*, Clifton: privately printed.

Winslow, Octavius, 1871, *The King in his Beauty: A Tribute to the Memory of Miss Charlotte Elliott, Authoress of 'Just as I am' etc. etc.*, London: John F. Shaw.

Wootton, Janet, 2008, 'Hymns and Slavery', *Hymn Society Bulletin* 254, vol. 18, no. 9, January, pp. 306–18; 255, vol. 18, no. 10, pp. 305–15.

http://www.harriettubman.com/itsharriet.html.

Twentieth and twenty-first century

Barkley, John M., 1927, 'The Revision, 1963–1973', in James Moffatt (ed.), *Handbook to the Church Hymnary*, 3rd edn, London: Oxford University Press, pp. 55–67.

Cosnett, Elizabeth, 1990, 'Language in Hymns: One Woman's Experience', *Bulletin of the Hymn Society* 182, January, pp. 158–63.

Davies, H., 1962, *Worship and Theology in England 1900–1965*, Princeton NJ: Princeton University Press.

Duck, Ruth, 1992, 'First Church Sings,' *The Hymn*, vol. 43, no. 3, July, pp. 20–7.

Farjeon, Annabel, 1986, *Morning has Broken: A Biography of Eleanor Farjeon*, London: Julian MacRae.

Farjeon, Eleanor, 1941, *Magic Casements*, London: Allen & Unwin.

Farjeon, Eleanor, 1958, *Edward Thomas, the Last Four Years: Book One of the Memoirs of Eleanor Farjeon*, London: Oxford University Press.

Fraser, Ian, 1985, 'Beginnings at Dunblane', in Robin Leaver and James H. Litton (eds), *Duty and Delight: A Memorial Tribute to Eric Routley (1917–1982), Ministry, Church Music, Hymnody*, Norwich: Canterbury Press, pp. 171–90.

Furlong, Monica, 1991, Introduction: A 'Non-Sexist Community', in St Hilda Community, *Women Included: A Book of Services and Prayers*, London: SPCK, pp. 5–15.

Graham, Ysenda Maxtone, 2001, *The Real Mrs Miniver: Jan Struther's Story*, London: John Murray.

Gray, Donald, 2005, 'The Birth and Background of the English Hymnal', in Alan Luff (ed.), *Strengthen for Service: 100 years of the English Hymnal 1906–2006*, Norwich: Canterbury Press pp. 1–30.

Harvey, Anne, 1999, *A Life Kept Always Young: An Introduction to Eleanor Farjeon*, Occasional Papers Series, no. 7, Cheltenham: Dymock Poets Archive & Study Centre.

Hewlett, Michael, 1969, 'Thoughts about words', *Hymn Society of Great Britain and Northern Ireland Bulletin* 115, Spring, pp. 11–14.

Holbrook, Arthur S., 1968, 'Annual Conference 1968', *Hymn Society of Great Britain and Northern Ireland Bulletin* 114, Winter, pp. 235–9.

Jones, Hugh Cunliffe, 1965, 'Wanted! New Hymn-Writers', in *The English Hymnal Service Book*, in *Hymn Society of Great Britain and Northern Ireland Bulletin* 105, December, pp. 56–8.

Leask, Margaret Anne, 2000, 'The Development of English-Language Hymnody and its use in Worship 1960–1995', University of Durham, DX214549.

Leaver, Robin and James H. Litton (eds), 1985, *Duty and Delight: A Memorial Tribute to Eric Routley (1917–1982), Ministry, Church Music, Hymnody*, Norwich: Canterbury Press.

Leaver, Robin, 1980, *A Hymn Book Survey 1962–80*, Grove Worship Series, no. 71, Bramcote, Nottinghamshire: Grove Books.

Luff, Alan (ed.), 2005, *Strengthen for Service: 100 years of the English Hymnal 1906–2006*, Norwich: Canterbury Press.

Micklem, Caryl, 1962, Review of *Baptist Hymn Book*, in *The English Hymnal Service Book*, in *Hymn Society of Great Britain and Northern Ireland Bulletin* 96, Summer, pp. 118–20.

Moffatt, James (ed.), 1927, *Handbook to the Church Hymnary*, 3rd edn, London: Oxford University Press.

Rauschenbusch, Walther, 1907, *Christianity and the Social Crisis*, New York: Macmillan & Co.

Routley, Eric, 1962, 'Comment', *The English Hymnal Service Book*, in *Hymn Society of Great Britain and Northern Ireland Bulletin* 96, Summer, pp. 120-4.

Routley, Eric, 1974, 'Hymns: Stop the Plane, I want to get off,' in Lionel Dakers (ed.), *English Church Music*, Croydon: Royal School of Church Music.

Routley, Eric, 1982, 'Scriptural Resonances in Hymnody', *Reformed Liturgy and Music*, vol. 16, no. 3, Summer, pp. 120-5.

Saliers, Don E., 1994, *Worship as Theology*, Nashville TN: Abingdon Press.

Taylor, Cyril, 1962, Review, *The English Hymnal Service Book*, in *Hymn Society of Great Britain and Northern Ireland Bulletin* 96, Summer, pp. 111-18.

Wakefield, Gordon S., 1968, 'The Hymnody of the Past Fifty Years', *Hymn Society Bulletin*, no 114, Winter, pp. 239-51.

Webster, Donald, 1992, *The Hymn Explosion and its aftermath*, Croydon: Royal School of Church Music.

Wilson, John, 1960, 'The Public School Hymn Book 1949 and 1959, *Bulletin of the Hymn Society* 89, Summer, pp. 1-10.

Wootton, Janet, 2000, 'Interview with Estelle White', *Feminist Theology*, vol. 8, January, pp. 85-9.

Wootton, Janet, 2009, 'Hymn-writing: the Lost Generation', *Hymn Society Bulletin* 257, vol. 19, no. 1, January, pp. 9-16.

Wootton, Janet, (2010), 'Singing the land strange with the Lord's song', given to the joint meetings of the Hymn Societies in Opole, Poland, July 2009, to be published in the *Bulletin of Internationale Arbeitsgemeinschaft für Hymnologie*, Spring.

Wren, Brian, 1983, *Faith Looking Forward*, Oxford: Oxford University Press.

Wren, Brian, 1989, *What Language Shall I Borrow? God-talk in Worship: A Male Response to Feminist Theology*, London: SCM Press.

Wren, Brian, Fred Kaan and Fred Pratt Green, 1985, 'New Hymnody: Some Problems and Prospects', in Robin Leaver and James H. Litton (eds), *Duty and Delight: A Memorial Tribute to Eric Routley (1917-1982), Ministry, Church Music, Hymnody*, Norwich: Canterbury Press, pp. 217-88.

Wren, Brian, 2009, *Hymns for Today*, Westminster: John Knox Press.

http://www.childrensbookcircle.org.uk/farjeon.asp.

General

Benson, Louis Fiztgerald, 1915, *The English Hymn: Its Development and Use in Worship*, London: Hodder & Stoughton.

Benson, Louis Fiztgerald, 1927, *The Hymnody of the Christian Church*, Philadelphia: Westminster Press.

Brauninger, Dee, 'Birth of a Hymn', http://www.ucc.org/assets/pdfs/duck.pdf, pp. 5-6.

Dearmer, Percy (comp.), 1933, *Songs of Praise Discussed: A Handbook to the*

Best-known Hymns and to Others Recently Introduced, London: Oxford University Press.

Julian, John, 1925, *A Dictionary of Hymnology: Setting Forth the Origin and History of Christian Hymns of all Ages and Nations*, rev. edn, with new Supplement, London: John Murray.

Long, Kenneth, 1971, *The Music of the English Church*, London: Hodder & Stoughton.

Milgate, Wesley, 1982, *Songs of the People of God: A Companion to the Australian Hymn Book/With One Voice*, London: Collins.

Ogasapian, John, 2007, *Church Music in America 1620–2000*, Macon GA: Mercer University Press.

Parry, Kenneth Lloyd (ed.), 1953, *Companion to Congregational Praise*, London: Independent Press.

Philip, Marlene Nourbese, 1989, *She Tries Her Tongue; Her Silence Softly Breaks*, Charlottetown, PEI, Canada: Ragweed Press.

Routley, Eric, 1952, *Hymns and Human Life*, London: John Murray.

Routley, Eric, 1958, *The English Carol*, London: Herbert Jenkins.

Routley, Eric, 2005, *A Panorama of Christian Hymnody*, Collegeville MN: The Liturgical Press, 1979; also 2nd edn, ed. and expanded by Paul Richardson, Chicago IL: GIA Publications.

Ruether, Rosemary Radford, 1983, *Sexism and God-talk: Towards a Feminist Theology* London: SCM Press.

Ruether, Rosemary Radford, 1985, *Women-Church: Theology and Practice of Feminist Liturgical Communities* London, Harper & Row.

St Thomas More Group, http://www.ocp.org/artists/840.

Schneider-Böklen, Elisabeth, 1995, *Der Herr hat Grosses mir getan: Frauen im Gesangbuch*, Stuttgart: Quell Verlag.

Temperley, Nicholas, 1979, *The Music of the English Parish Church*, Cambridge: Cambridge University Press.

Watson, J. R., 1997, *The English Hymn: A Critical and Historical Study*, Oxford: Clarendon Press.

Watson, Richard and Kenneth Trickett (ed.), 1988, *Companion to Hymns & Psalms*, London: Methodist Publishing House.

Wren, Brian, 2000, *Praying Twice: The Music and Words of Congregational Song*, Louisville KY: Westminster John Knox Press.

Sources of hymns, poems and translations

100 Hymns for Today: A Supplement to Hymns Ancient and Modern, 1969, London: William Clowes & Sons.

Abelard, Peter, *Hymnarius Paraclitensis*, in Joseph Szövérffy, 1975. *Peter Abelard's Hymnarius Paraclitensis: An Annotated Edition with Introduction: Part II The Hymnarius Paraclitensis Text and Notes*, Albany NY: Classical Folia Editions.

Abelard, Peter, 1975, Feasts of Holy Women, Matins, first and second nocturns, in Joseph Szövérffy, *Peter Abelard's Hymnarius Paraclitensis: An Annotated Edition with Introduction: Part II The Hymnarius Paraclitensis Text and*

Notes, Albany NY: Classical Folia Editions, pp. 256–7.

Aikin, John, 1772, *Hymns for Public Worship: selected from various authors, and intended as a supplement to Dr. Watts's Psalms*, Warrington.

Ainslie, John, Stephen Dean and Paul Inwood (eds), 1972, *Praise the Lord, revised and enlarged*, London: Geoffrey Chapman.

Alleluia Aotearoa, 1993, Palmerston North: New Zealand Hymnbook Trust Inc.

Andersen, Elizabeth A., 2003, *Mechthild of Magdeburg: Selections, The Flowing Light of the Godhead*, Cambridge: D. S. Brewer.

Bailey, John (ed.), 1976, *Blueprint: A series of reference books for use in secondary school assemblies, religious education and liberal studies classes, project work, church worship and Sunday school, adult education*, 4 vols, London: Galliard.

Bailey, John (ed.), 1981, *Theme Work: Assembly Material for Junior, Middle and Lower Secondary Schools*, London: Stainer & Bell.

Bailey, Nancy E. M. (ed.), 1998, *A Scottish Childhood*, vol. II, Glasgow: HarperCollins.

Baptist Hymn Book, The, 1962, London: Psalms and Hymns Trust.

Barbauld, A. L., 1781, *Hymns in Prose for Children*, London: J. Johnson.

Barnard, John and David Iliff, 2008, *Season by Season*, London: Royal School of Church Music.

Barth, Pudentia, M. Immacula Ritscher and Joseph Schmidt-Görg (eds), 1969, *Hildegard von Bingen: Lieder, nach den Handschriften herausgegeben*, Salzburg: Otto Müller Verlag.

Beard, John R., 1837, *A Collection of Hymns for Public and Private Worship*, London: John Green.

Because We Are One People, 1974, Chicago: Ecumenical Women's Center.

Beecher, Henry Ward (ed.), 1856, *The Plymouth Collection of Hymns and Tunes for the use of Christian Congregations*, New York: A. S. Barnes & Co.

Belknap, J., 1797, *Sacred Poetry, consisting of Psalms and Hymns, adapted to Christian Devotion, in public and private, selected from the best authors*, Boston: Thomas & Andrews.

Bell, John and Graham Maule, 1987, 1988, 1989, *Wild Goose Songs*, vols 1–3, Glasgow: Wild Goose Publications.

Bell, John and Graham Maule, 1997, *Love and Anger: Songs of Lively Faith and Social Justice*, Glasgow: Wild Goose Publications.

Bliss, Philip and I. D. Sankey (comp.), 1875–91, *Gospel Hymns and Sacred Songs* Cincinnati: John Church & Co., New York: Biglow & Main, nos. 1–6.

Booth, Evangeline Cory, 1937, *Songs of the Evangel*, new and enlarged edn, London: Salvation Army Publishing and Supplies.

Booth-Clibborn, Catherine (comp.), 1930, *Wings of Praise. A Collection of Gospel Songs. Compiled and Edited by The Maréchale [i. e. Catherine Booth-Clibborn]. Containing many original compositions by A. S. Booth-Clibborn and other members of the Booth-Clibborn family*, London: Marshall, Morgan and Scott.

Borthwick, Jane and Sarah Findlater, 1854, *Hymns from the Land of Luther*, Edinburgh.

Borthwick, Jane, 1875, *Alpine Lyrics: A Selection from the Poems of Meta*

Heusser-Schweizer, Translated by H.L.L., London: T. Nelson & Sons.

Bourignon, Antoinette, 1686, *Toutes les Oeuvres de Mlle Bourignon*, Amsterdam.

Boyce-Tillman, June, 1992, *In Praise of All-Encircling Love: Hymns and Songs in Inclusive Language*, London: Hildegard Press and the Association for Inclusive Language.

Boyce-Tillman, June, 1994, *In Praise of All-Encircling Love 2: Hymns, Songs and Liturgical Pieces in Inclusive Language*, London: Hildegard Press and the Association for Inclusive Language.

Boyce-Tillman, June, 1999, *Voice of Experience*, CD of 22 songs, London: Hildegard Press.

Boyce-Tillman, June, 2006, *A Rainbow to Heaven*, London: Stainer & Bell.

Boys' Brigade Hymnbook, 1958, Hemel Hempstead: Boys' Brigade.

Bull, William (ed.), 1801, *Poems Translated from the French of Madame de la Mothe Guion by the late William Cowper to which are added some original poems not inserted in his works*, Newport Pagnell.

Cantate Domino, 1980, 4th edn, Oxford: Oxford University Press.

Carmichael, Alexander, 1900, *Carmina Gadelica. Hymns and incantations with illustrative notes on words, rites, and customs, dying and obsolete: orally collected in the Highlands and Islands of Scotland and translated into English*, Edinburgh: Norman McLeod.

Carol Our Christmas, 1996, Palmerston North: New Zealand Hymnbook Trust.

Carol Praise, 1987, London: Jubilate Hymns.

Celebration Hymnal, 1976, Great Wakering: Mayhew-McCrimmon.

Christian Hymns, 1977, Bridgend: Evangelical Movement of Wales.

Christian Life Hymnal, 2006, Peabody MA: Hendrickson Publishers Ltd.

Church Hymnary, 1898, Glasgow and Belfast: Henry Frowde.

Church Hymnary, 1927, rev. edn, 1927, London: Oxford University Press.

Church Hymnary, 1973, 3rd edn, Oxford: Oxford University Press.

Church Hymnary, 2005, 4th edn, Norwich: Canterbury Press.

Church Missionary Hymn Book, 1899, London: Church Missionary Society.

Clairvaux, Bernard of (attr.), *Jubilus Rhythmicus, De Nomine Jesu* in Migne, *Patrologiae Cursus Completus, Latina*, 184, 1517, 898.

Colonna, Vittoria, 1551, *Libro Quarto delle rime di diversi eccellentiss. autori nella lingua volgare. Nuovamente raccolte*, Bologna: Anselmo Giaccarello.

Colonna, Vittoria, 2008, *Sonnets for Michelangelo*, p. 333, cited in Abigail Brundin (2008), *Vittoria Colonna and the spiritual poetics of the Italian Reformation*, Aldershot: Ashgate.

Common Ground: A Song Book for All the Churches, 1998, Edinburgh: Saint Andrew Press.

Complete Anglican Hymns Old and New, 2000 and 2002, Buxhill: Kevin Mayhew.

Congregational Church Hymnal, 1887, London: Hodder & Stoughton.

Congregational Praise, 1951, London: Congregational Union of England and Wales.

Cosnett, Elizabeth, 2001, *Hymns for Everyday Saints: 36 Hymns with Commentaries*, London: Stainer & Bell.

Cox, Frances E., 1890, *Hymns from the German, Translated by F. E. Cox*, London: SPCK.

Cox, Frances Elizabeth, 1841, *Sacred Hymns from the German*, London: William Pickering.

Daw, Carl, 1990, *A Year of Grace*, Carol Stream IL: Hope Publishing Co.

Dean, Stephen (ed.), 1984, *Celebration Hymnal*, vol. 2, Great Wakering: Mayhew McCrimmon Ltd.

Dean, Stephen (ed.), 1989, *New Songs of Celebration*, Great Wakering: Mayhew McCrimmon Ltd.

Dearmer, Percy, 1928, *The Oxford Book of Carols*, Oxford: Oxford University Press.

Dobson, Marjorie, 2004, *Multi-coloured Maze*, London: Stainer & Bell.

Dorling, William, 1889, *Poems by Dora Greenwell (Selected) with a Biographical Introduction by William Dorling*, London: Walter Scott.

Dream of Learning Our True Name, The, 2004, Glasgow: Wild Goose Publications.

Duck, Ruth, 1992, *Dancing in the Universe*, Chicago: GIA Publications.

Duck, Ruth C., 1981, *Bread for the Journey*, New York: The Pilgrim Press.

Duck, Ruth C., 1998, *Circles of Care*, Cleveland, Ohio: The Pilgrim Press.

Duck, Ruth C., 2005, *Welcome God's Tomorrow*, Chicago: GIA Publications.

Duck, Ruth C. and Michael G. Bausch, 1981, *Everflowing Streams: Songs for Worship*, New York: The Pilgrim Press.

Dunblane Praises for Schools: I Juniors, 1970, Dunblane.

Duncan, Geoffrey (comp.), 2002, *What a World*, London: Granary Press.

Duncan, Geoffrey (comp.), 2004, *A Place for Us*, London: Granary Press.

Dutton, Ann, 1734, *A Narration of the Wonders of Grace in Verse*, London.

Eaklor, Vicki L., 1988, *American Antislavery Songs: A Collection and Analysis* New York: Greenwood.

Elliott, Charlotte, 1836, *Hours of Sorrow; or Thoughts in Verse, Chiefly adapted to Seasons of Sickness, Depression and Bereavement*, London: James Nisbett and Co.

English Hymnal, The, 1906, London: Henry Frowde.

English Hymnal Service Book, The, 1962, London: Oxford University Press.

Faith Forever Singing, 2000, Palmerston North: New Zealand Hymnbook Trust.

Festival Hymns and Tunes: Otley Sunday School Union at the 96th Anniversary Whitsuntide, 1922, Manchester: Manchester Sunday Schools Union.

Festival Hymns and Tunes: Union Street Congregational Sunday School Hyde, Hymns for Whitsuntide, 1922, Manchester: Manchester Sunday Schools Union.

Finest hour, 1999, CD, Milton Keynes: Anglican Pacifist Fellowship.

Folk Praise, 1977, Leigh on Sea: Kevin Mayhew.

Fox, William J., 1841, *Hymns & Anthems*, London.

Fudge, Roland, Peter Horrobin and Greg Leavers (eds), 1983, *Mission England Praise*, Basingstoke: Marshall, Morgan & Scott.

Gaunt, Alan and Alan Luff, 1997, *Hymns and Letters: Ann Griffiths*, London: Stainer & Bell.

Gilmurray, Sue, 2001, *The Way of Peace*, CD and score, Ely: Mightier Pen Music.

God is Good, God is Truth, God is Beauty, Praise Him, 2005, Stowmarket: Kevin Mayhew.

Goodwillie, Christian with Joel Cohen (ed.), 2002, *Shaker Songs: A Celebration of Peace, Harmony & Simplicity*, New York: Black Dog & Leventhal.

Greenwell, Dora, 1869, *Carmina Crucis*, London: Bell & Daldy.

Guion, J. M. B. de la Mothe, 1722, *Poesies & Cantiques Spirituels sure divers Sujets qui regardent la Vie Interieure ou l'Esprit du Vrai Christianisme*, Cologne.

Hastings, Selina, Countess of Huntingdon, 1770, *The collection of hymns, sung in the Countess of Huntingdon's Chapel*, Bath: T. Mills.

Havergal, Frances Ridley, 1874, *The Ministry of Song*, 5th edn, London: J. Nisbet & Co.

Havergal's Psalmody and Century of Chants, from "Old Church Psalmody," "Hundred Tunes," and unpublished manuscripts of W. H. Havergal Edited by Frances Ridley Havergal, 1871, London: Robert Cocks & Co.

Heaven Shall Not Wait, 1987, Glasgow: Wild Goose Publications/The Iona Community.

Hickman, Hoyt L. (ed.), 2000, *The Faith We Sing*, Nashville TN: Abingdon Press.

Hildegard of Bingen, 1998, *Symphonia* with introduction, translation and commentary by Barbara Newman 2nd edn, Ithaca: Cornell University Press.

Hildegard of Bingen, *Patrologiae Cursus Completus, Latina*, 197, 91–130.

Hildegard of Bingen, Wiesbaden, Landesbibliothek Hs. 2, 'Riesenkodex', Rupertsberg, 1180–90, 405 Rª.

Hilton, Donald, (comp.), 1991, *Liturgy of Life*, Redhill: National Christian Education Council.

Hilton, Donald (comp.), 1999, *No Empty Phrases: An Anthology of Poetry and Prose for Christian Education and Worship Based on the Lord's Prayer*, Redhill: National Christian Education Council.

Holbrook, D. and E. Poston (ed.), 1967, *Cambridge Hymnal*, Cambridge: Cambridge University Press.

Horrobin, Peter and Greg Leavers (eds), 1986, *Junior Praise*, Basingstoke: Marshall Pickering.

Horrobin, Peter and Greg Leavers (eds), 1996, *New Mission Praise*, London: Marshall Pickering.

Horrobin, Peter and Greg Leavers (eds), 1999, *Complete Mission Praise*, London: Marshall Pickering.

Horrobin, Peter and Greg Leavers (eds), 2005, *Complete Mission Praise*, London: Collins.

Horrobin, Peter and Greg Leavers (eds), 2008, *Complete Junior Praise*, London: Collins.

Howe, Julia Ward, 1854, *Passion Flowers*, Boston: Ticknor, Reed, and Fields.

Humphreys, Cecil Frances. 1846, *Verses for Holy Seasons with questions for examination by C.F.H.*, ed. Walter Farquhar Hook, London: Francis and John Rivington.

Hymns & Psalms, 1983, London: Methodist Publishing House.

Hymns & Songs: A Supplement to the Methodist Hymn Book, 1969, London: Methodist Publishing House.

Hymns Ancient and Modern for use in the Services of the Church, 1861, London: Novellow.

Hymns Ancient and Modern for use in the Services of the Church, 1904, London: William Clowes and Sons.

Hymns and Congregational Songs, 1989–, London: Stainer & Bell, vol. 1–.

Hymns for a Pilgrim People: A Congregational Hymnal, 2007, Chicago IL: GIA Publications Inc. and National Association of Congregational and Christian Churches.

Hymns for Public and Social Worship, selected chiefly for the use of the Stockport Sunday School, 1848, Manchester: J. Ambery.

Hymns Old and New, 1989, Roman Catholic edn, Stowmarket: Kevin Mayhew.

Hymns selected and original, principally intended to aid the devotional exercises of children and teachers in the Leeds Sunday School Union, 1833, Leeds: Heaton.

Hymns, Psalms and Spiritual Songs: Presbyterian Hymnal, 1990, Louisville KY: Westminster/John Knox Press.

Idle, Christopher and Sue Gilmurray, 2008, *Songs for the Road to Peace*, Milton Keynes: Anglican Pacifist Fellowship.

Kaan, Fred, 1982, *The Hymn Texts of Fred Kaan*, London: Hope Publishing Co. and Stainer & Bell.

Kendrick, Graham (ed.), 1998, *The Source*, Stowmarket: Kevin Mayhew.

Kendrick, Graham (ed.), 2001, *The Source 2*, Stowmarket: Kevin Mayhew.

Kendrick, Graham (ed.), 2005, *The Source 3*, Stowmarket: Kevin Mayhew.

Kendrick, Graham (ed.), 2005, *The Source, Combined Words Edition*, Stowmarket: Kevin Mayhew.

Knapp, Albert, 1858, *Lieder einer Verborgenen*, Leipzig.

Laudate, 1999, Brandon: Decani Music.

Leifchild, Rev J., 1842, *Original Hymns Adapted to General Worship and Special Occasions by Various Authors*, London.

Leo, F (ed.), 1881, *Venanti Honori Clementiani Fortunati Presbyteri Italici Opera Poetica*, Monumenta Germaniae Historica, Auctorum Antiquissimorum, IV.I.

Leonard, Tom, 2009, *Outside the Narrative*, Exbourne: Etruscan Books & Word Power Books.

Let's Praise, 1988, London: Jubilate Hymns.

Making Melody, 1983, Nottingham: Assemblies of God Publishing House/ Reflections Distribution.

Martineau, Harriet, 1826, *Addresses with Prayers and Original Hymns For the Use of Families and Schools*, London.

Mary Louise Bringle, 2002, *Joy and Wonder, Love and Longing*, Chicago: GIA Publications.

Maynard, John and Cecily Taylor (comps), 1973, *In Tune: Over 60 Hymns and Songs for Churches Schools and Groups*, London: Vanguard Music.

Maynard, John (comp.), 1971, *So Much to Sing*, London: Vanguard Music.

McKinney, B.B. (ed.), 1940, *The Broadman Hymnal*, Nashville TN: The Broadman Press.

Merrick, Daniel B. (ed.), 1995, *Chalice Hymnal*, St Louis MO: Chalice Press.

Millennial Praises: Containing a collection of gospel hymns in four parts adapted to the day of Christ's second appearing, 1913, Hancock. http://passtheword. org/SHAKER-MANUSCRIPTS/Millennial-Praises/mpraisesndex.htm.

Missionary hymns: composed and selected for the services at the annual missionary meetings of the Society in London and for the Monthly Meetings for Prayer in Town and Country, 1801, London: London Missionary Society.

Missionary hymns: composed and selected for the public services at the annual meetings of the London Missionary Society and for the Prayer Meetings of Auxiliary Societies in Town and Country, 1840, London: London Missionary Society.

More Hymns for Today: A Second Supplement to Hymns Ancient and Modern, 1980, Canterbury: Hymns Ancient and Modern Ltd./Canterbury Press.

Morley, Janet and Hannah Ward (eds), 1986, *Celebrating Women*, London: Women in Theology and Movement for the Ordination of Women.

Morley, Janet, 1988, *All Desires Known*, London: Movement for the Ordination of Women and Women in Theology.

Morris, William, 1955, *Cofio Ann Griffiths 1805*, Caernarfon: Llyfrfa'r Cyfundeb.

Murray, Shirley Erena, 1992, *In Every Corner Sing*, Carol Stream IL: Hope Publishing Co.

Murray, Shirley, 1996, *Every Day in your Spirit*, Carol Stream IL: Hope Publishing Co.

Murray, Shirley, 2002, *Faith Makes the Song*, Carol Stream IL: Hope Publishing Co.

Murray, Shirley, 2008, *Touch the Earth Lightly*, Carol Stream IL: Hope Publishing Co.

New Catholic Hymnal, 1971, London: Faber Music Ltd.

New Horizons, 1974, London: Galliard/Stainer & Bell.

New Redemption Hymnal, 1986, Bletchley: Word (UK) Ltd.

Newton, John and William Cowper, 1779, *Olney Hymns*, 3 vols, London.

Nicholls, Martin John (ed.), 2004, *Hunger for Justice*, London: Kevin Mayhew.

One is the Body, 2002, Glasgow: Wild Goose Publications.

One World Songs, 1978, London: Methodist Church Division of Social Responsibility/Methodist Publishing House.

Paynter, Neil (ed.), 2007, *Gathered and Scattered*, Glasgow: Wild Goose Publications.

Peacock, David and Geoff Weaver (eds), 1993, *World Praise*, London: Jubilate Hymns/Marshall Pickering.

Perpetua et Felicitatis, 'Passio', Migne, *Patrologiae Cursus Completus, Latina*, 3, 13D–58A.

Perpetua, *Passio SS Perpetuae et Felicitas*. Migne, *Patrologiae Cursus Completus, Latina*, 3, 17A–45A.

Perry, M. and D. Peacock (eds), 1987, *Carol Praise*, London: Jubilate Hymns/Marshall Pickering/HarperCollins Religious.

Perry, M. and D. Peacock (eds), 2006, *Carol Praise 2006*, London: HarperCollins,

Pike, Morris D. (ed.), 1977, *Your Need for Bread is Mine*, New York: Friendship Press.

Porete, Marguerite, 1965, *Miroir des simples ames* 103v; R. Guarnieri (ed.), 'Il "Miroir des simples ames" di Margherita Porete', *Archivo italiano per la storia della pieta* IV, pp. 501–635.

Porete, Marguerite, 1984, *Miroir des simples ames*, in P. Dronke, *Women Writers of the Middle Ages: A Critical Study of Texts from Perpetua († 203) to Marguerite Porete († 1310)*, Cambridge: Cambridge University Press, p. 227.

Pratt, Andrew and Marjorie Dobson, 2006, *Poppies and Snowdrops*, Peterborough: Inspire.

Pratt, Andrew and Marjorie Dobson, 2008, *Nothing Too Religious*, Peterborough: Inspire.

Primitive Methodist Sunday School Union Hymn Book, 1879, London: Ralph Fenwick.

Procter, Adelaide Anne, 1858, *Legends and Lyrics: A Book of Verses*, London.

Procter, Adelaide Anne, 1862, *A Chaplet of Verses*, London.

Procter, Adelaide Anne (ed.), 1861, *The Victoria Regia: a volume of original contributions in poetry and prose*, London.

Public School Hymn Book, The, 1949, 1959, edited by a committee of the Headmasters' Conference, London: Novello & Co.

Pulkingham, Betty and Jeanne Harper (comps), 1974, *Sound of Living Waters: Songs of Renewal*, London: Hodder & Stoughton.

Pulkingham, Betty and Jeanne Harper (comps), 1976, *Fresh Sounds*, London: Hodder & Stoughton.

Raby, F. J. E., 1953, *Christian Latin Poetry from the Beginnings to the Close of the Middle Ages*, 2nd edn, Oxford: Clarendon Press.

Redemption Hymnal, 1951, Wendover: Rickfords Publishing.

Rejoice and Sing, 1991, London: Oxford University Press.

Rogers, Rev. Stanley (comp.), 1894, *Centenary Mission Hymnal*, London: London Missionary Society.

Rossetti, Christina Georgina, 1904, *Poetical Works of Christina Georgina Rossetti, with a Brief Memoir and Notes &c. by W. M. Rossetti*, London: MacMillan & Co.

Rossetti, Christina, 1865, *Goblin Market and other Poems*, London and Cambridge: MacMillan & Co.

Routley, Erik, 1985, *Rejoice in the Lord: A Hymn Companion to the Scriptures*, Grand Rapids MI: Eerdmans.

Russell, Arthur T., 1851, *Psalms and Hymns partly original, partly selected, for the use of the Church of England*, Cambridge: John Deighton.

St Hilda Community, 1991, *Women Included: A Book of Services and Prayers*, London: SPCK.

Sankey, Ira D. (comp.), 1897, *Sacred Songs and Solos: New Hymns and Solos and the Christian Choir*, London: Morgan & Scott.

School Hymn Book of the Methodist Church, 1950, London: Methodist Youth Department.

Select Hymns, for the use of the Union Sunday School, George Leigh-Street 1819, Manchester: The Observer Office.

Selection of Psalms and Hymns for the use of Disley Church and Sunday School, 1839, Manchester: H. Whitmore.

Sidney, Sr Philip and Mary Herbert, Countess of Pembroke, 1823, *The Psalmes of David, Translated into Divers and Sundry Kindes of Verse, more rare and excellent for the Method and Variety than ever yet hath beeng done in English*.

Begun by the noble and learned Gent, Sir Philip Sidney, Knt., and finished by the Right Honorable The Countess of Pembroke, his sister, Hereford: John Davies.

Sing Alleluia, 1987, London: HarperCollins.

Sing in the Spirit: A Book of Quaker Songs, 2005, book and CD, Birmingham: Leaveners Press; http://www.leaveners.org/qmm/songbook.html.

Sister Jane Patricia, 1986, *The Hymns of Abelard in English Verse*, New York: University Press of America.

Smith Peter D. (ed.), 1967, *Faith, Folk and Clarity*, London: Galliard.

Smith, Peter D. (ed.), 1967, *Faith, Folk and Festivity*, London: Galliard.

Smith, Peter D., 1968, *Faith, Folk and Nativity: A New Collection of Songs*, London: Galliard.

Smith, Peter (ed.), 1972, *New Orbit: Songs and Hymns for Under Elevens*, Great Yarmouth: Galliard.

Smith, Peter D. (ed.), 1974, *Jesus Folk*, London: Stainer & Bell.

Snepp, Charles Busbridge, 1872, *Songs of Grace and Glory, for Private, Family and Public Worship*, London: W. Hunt & Co.

Song Book of the Salvation Army, 1953, London: Salvationist Publishing and Supplies.

Song Book of the Salvation Army, 1986, London: Salvationist Publishing and Supplies.

Songs for the Seventies: a Collection of Contemporary Hymns, 1972, Great Yarmouth: Galliard, Edinburgh: Saint Andrew Press.

Songs of Celebration: A Collection of New Hymns featured in Southern Television's Hymn Competition, 1973, London: Weinberger.

Songs of Fellowship, 1991, Eastbourne: Kingsway Music.

Songs of Fellowship 2, 1998, Eastbourne: Kingsway Music.

Songs of Fellowship 3, 2003, Eastbourne: Kingsway Music.

Songs of Fellowship 4, 2007, Eastbourne: Kingsway Music.

Songs of God's People, 1988, Oxford: Church of Scotland and Oxford University Press.

Songs of Praise, 1925, Oxford: Oxford University Press.

Songs of Praise: Enlarged Edition, 1931, London: Oxford University Press.

Sound Bytes, 1991, London: Stainer & Bell.

Sound the Bamboo, 1990, rev. edn 2000, Muang: Thailand, Christian Conference of Asia.

Source3, The, 2005, Stowmarket: Kevin Mayhew.

Steele, Anne, 1808, *The Works of Anne Steele*, Boston: Munroe, Francis and Parker.

Steele, Anne, 1863, *Hymns, Psalms and Poems*, with Memoir by John Sheppard, London: Daniel Sedgwick.

Story Song, 1993, London: Stainer & Bell and the Trustees for Methodist Church Purposes.

Sydney Carter, 1968, *Songs of Sydney Carter in the Present Tense*, Book 1, London: Galliard/Stainer & Bell.

Szövérffy, Joseph, 1975, *Peter Abelard's Hymnarius Paraclitensis: An Annotated Edition with Introduction: Part II The Hymnarius Paraclitensis Text and Notes*, Albany NY: Classical Folia Editions.

Tate, N. and N. Brady, 1696, *A New Version of the Psalms of David: fitted to the tunes used in churches*, London.

Taylor, Ann and Jane, 1810, *Hymns for Infant Minds*, London.

Taylor, Helen M., 1959, *Tunes from Nyasaland*, London: Overton Institute of the Livingstonia Mission.

Tillman, June (ed.), 1989, *The Oxford Assembly Book: Songs, Readings and Discussion for Primary and Middle School Assemblies*, Oxford: Oxford University Press.

Trotman, Wilfrid (ed.), 1966, *Praise the Lord: Hymns, Psalms and Canticles for Community Use*, London: Geoffrey Chapman.

Umiltà, AASS (Acta Sanctorum) 22 Maii, *Humilitas, Analecta de virtutibus, scriptus, translationibus & miraculis*.

United Church of Christ, 1995, *New Century Hymnal*, Cleveland OH: The Pilgrim Press.

van Hilten, Wil, Marijke de Bruijne and Eileen Silcocks (eds), 1984, *Eva's Lied: 42 nieuwe liederen, onstaan binnen de feministische theologie*, Kampen: J. H. Kok.

Voices Found: Women in the Church's Song, 2003, New York: Church Publishing Inc.

Voices United: The Hymn and Worship Book of the United Church of Canada, 1996, Ontario: The United Church Publishing House.

Watts, Isaac, 1715, *Divine and Moral Songs Attempted in Easy Language for the Use of Children*.

Watts, Isaac, 1731, *Horae Lyricae: Poems, Chiefly of the Lyric Kind*, corrected edn, London.

Watts, Isaac, 1776, *The Psalms of David Imitated in the Language of the New Testament and applied to the Christian State and Worship*, London.

Wedding Book, The, 1989, London: Jubilate/HarperCollins.

Wesley, John and Charles, 1739, *Hymns and Sacred Poems*, London.

White, Kenneth, 2003, *Open World: The Collected Poems 1960–2000*, Edinburgh: Polygon Books.

Who are you looking for? Easter Liturgies for the WCC Ecumenical Decade, Churches in Solidarity with Women, 1988–1998, 1988, London: British Region of the Ecumenical Forum of European Christian Women and the Women's Interchurch Consultative Committee.

Wilmart, André, 1943, *Le "Jubilus" sur le nom de Jésus dit de Saint Bernard* (the text of the poem, with a commentary by A. Wilmart), *Ephemerides liturgicae*, anno. 57, p. 285.

Winkworth, Catherine, 1855, *Lyra Germanica: Hymns for the Sundays and Chief Festivals of the Christian Year*, London: Longman, Brown, Green and Longmans.

Winkworth, Catherine, 1858, *Lyra Germanica: Second Series, The Christian Life*, London: Longman, Brown, Green, Longmans and Roberts.

Winkworth, Catherine, 1863, *The Chorale Book for England*, London: Longman, Green, Longman, Roberts and Green.

Winkworth, Catherine, 1869, *Christian Singers of Germany*, London: MacMillan & Co.

With One Voice: A Hymn Book for all the Churches, 1979, London: Collins; first published as *The Australian Hymn Book*, 1978.

Wootton, Janet and June Boyce-Tillman (eds), 1993, *Reflecting Praise*, London: Stainer & Bell and Women in Theology.

Wootton, Janet (ed.), *Worship Live*, 1994–, London: Stainer & Bell, issue 1–.

Wootton, Janet, *Eagles' Wings and Lesser Things*, 2007, London: Stainer & Bell.

Zinzendorf, Nicolaus Ludwig Graf von, 1981, *Nicolaus Ludwig Graf von Zinzendorf Herrnhuter Gesangbuch: christliches Gesang-Buch der Evangelischen Brüder-Gemeinen von 1735, mit einem Vorwort von Erich Beyreuther und Gerhard Meyer un einer Einleitung, 'Zinzendorf und seine Gesangbücher als Ausdruck barocken Lebensgefühls' von Gerhard Meyer*, Hildesheim: Ols.

http://www.ccli.co.uk/songselect/
http://www.hymntime.com/tch/
http://www.stainer.co.uk/hymnquest/

Acknowledgements and Sources

The author and publisher have sought permission to reproduce text under copyright, and acknowledge with thanks consent to use the following material. Any omissions would be gratefully received for acknowledgement in future editions.

June Boyce-Tillman, 'A woman in her grief', 'One day when all were counted', 'We sing a love that sets all people free', 'We shall go out with hope of resurrection', 'Circling encircling Wisdom deep within', in *Rainbow to Heaven*, London: Stainer & Bell Ltd, www.stainer.co.uk; 'Within th' encircling planets', unpublished, © London: Stainer & Bell Ltd, www.stainer.co.uk

Elizabeth Cosnett, 'Can man by searching find out God', 'For God's sake let us dare', 'For nine months Mary held', in *Hymns for Everyday Saints*, London: Stainer & Bell Ltd, www.stainer.co.uk

Marjorie Dobson, 'Light from the darkness came', 'Birth brings a promise of new life awaking', 'When we see the pattern changing' and 'Lord, you call us to your service', in Marjorie Dobson, *Multi-coloured Maze*, London: Stainer & Bell Ltd, www.stainer.co.uk; 'Sun beats down on travelling strangers', *Worship Live* 36, October 2006; 'God, hold us, enfold us, through desolate loss', in Andrew Pratt and Marjorie Dobson, *Poppies and Snowdrops*, Peterborough: Inspire, 2006.

Ruth Duck, 'Womb of life and source of being' and 'Doxology' © 1992 by GIA Publications, Inc., 7404 S. Mason Ave., Chicago, IL 60638, www.giamusic.com 800.442.1358. All rights reserved. Used by permission.

Ann Griffiths, 'Dyma babell y cyfarfod', 'Nag Edryched neb I gloffi', and Alan Gaunt, 'Here we find the tent of meaning', 'Do not stare with hesitation', in Alan Gaunt and Alan Luff, *Hymns and Letters: Ann Griffiths*, London: Stainer & Bell Ltd, 1997, www.stainer.co.uk.

Tom Leonard, 'Proem', ©Tom Leonard from *outside the narrative*, Etruscan Books / WordPower 2009.

Shirley Murray, 'Honour the dead' in *Touch the Earth Lightly*, Carol Stream, IL.:Hope Publishing Co. 1996; 'This thread I weave' in *In Every Corner Sing*, Carol Stream, IL.:Hope Publishing Co. 1992. Shirley Erena Murray's hymns are copyrighted and used by permission of Hope Publishing Company, Carol Stream, IL 60188.

Marlene Nourbese, 'Edits', 'When the smallest cell remembers' and 'absencelosstears', in Marlene Nourbese, *She Tries Her Tongue: Her Silence Softly Breaks*, Charlottetown PEI, Canada: Ragwood Press, 1989.

Jan Struther (1901–53), 'When a knight won his spurs', in *Enlarged Songs of Praise*, 1931. Reproduced by permission of Oxford University Press. All rights reserved.

Cecily Taylor, 'Alleluia Christ is risen', 'Some days the fog comes creeping' in Janet Wootton and June Boyce-Tillman (eds), *Reflecting Praise*, London: Stainer & Bell Ltd, www.stainer.co.uk; 'I can't hear the angels', in *Worship Live* 24; 'Jesus was gone but his Spirit guided', in *Worship Live* 22; 'The story of a birth so long ago', *Sing in the Spirit*, London: Stainer & Bell Ltd, www.stainer.co.uk

VV 2–3 of #125 in *The Hymns of Abelard in English Verse*, trans. Sister Jane Patricia, p. 132 © 1986 the University Press of America, Inc.

Betty Wendelborn, 'In the shaking of God's mantle', no. 71, *Alleluia Aotearoa*, Palmerston North: New Zealand Hymnbook Trust Inc., 1993; and 'O Mother Jesus', London: Stainer & Bell Ltd, www.stainer.co.uk.

Janet Wootton,'Dear Mother God, your wings are warm about me', in Janet Wootton and June Boyce Tillman (eds), Reflecting Praise, London: Stainer & Bell,1993.

Index of Names and Subjects

Index of First Lines of Hymns

Lightning Source UK Ltd.
Milton Keynes UK
21 April 2010

153079UK00001B/1/P